STAR WARS™

YEAR BY YEAR
A VISUAL HISTORY

UPDATED AND EXPANDED EDITION

Project Editor Shari Last
Senior Designer Anna Formanek
Designers Owen Bennett, Anna Pond
Pre-production Producer Rebecca Fallowfield
Senior Producer Alex Bell
Managing Editor Sadie Smith
Design Manager Ron Stobbart
Art Director Lisa Lanzarini
Publisher Julie Ferris
Publishing Director Simon Beecroft

DK would like to thank Emma Grange for editorial assistance,
Sarah Smithies for picture research and Helen Peters for the index.

Lucasfilm
Senior Editor Frank Parisi
Image Unit Tim Mapp
Story Group Pablo Hidalgo, Leland Chee, Matt Martin
Creative Director of Publishing Michael Siglain

For previous editions of this book, DK would like to thank J.W. Rinzler, Troy
Alders, Stacey Leong, Tina Mills, Pamela Afram, Dan Bunyan, Jo Casey, Lucy
Dowling, Elizabeth Dowsett, Laura Gilbert, Jon Hall, Guy Harvey, Julia March,
Nathan Martin, Lynne Moulding, Jennifer Murray, Mark Richards, Catherine
Saunders, Victoria Taylor, Rhys Thomas, Toby Truphet and Kara Wallace.

First published in Great Britain in 2010; revised in 2012.
This updated edition published in 2016 by Dorling Kindersley Limited
80 Strand, London WC2R 0RL
A Penguin Random House Company

10 9 8 7 6 5 4 3 2 1
001—280845—09/16

Page design copyright © 2010, 2012, 2016 Dorling Kindersley Limited

A catalogue record for this book is available from the British Library.

ISBN: 978-0-24123-241-5

Printed in China

A WORLD OF IDEAS:
SEE ALL THERE IS TO KNOW

www.dk.com
www.starwars.com

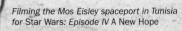

*Filming the Mos Eisley spaceport in Tunisia
for Star Wars: Episode IV A New Hope*

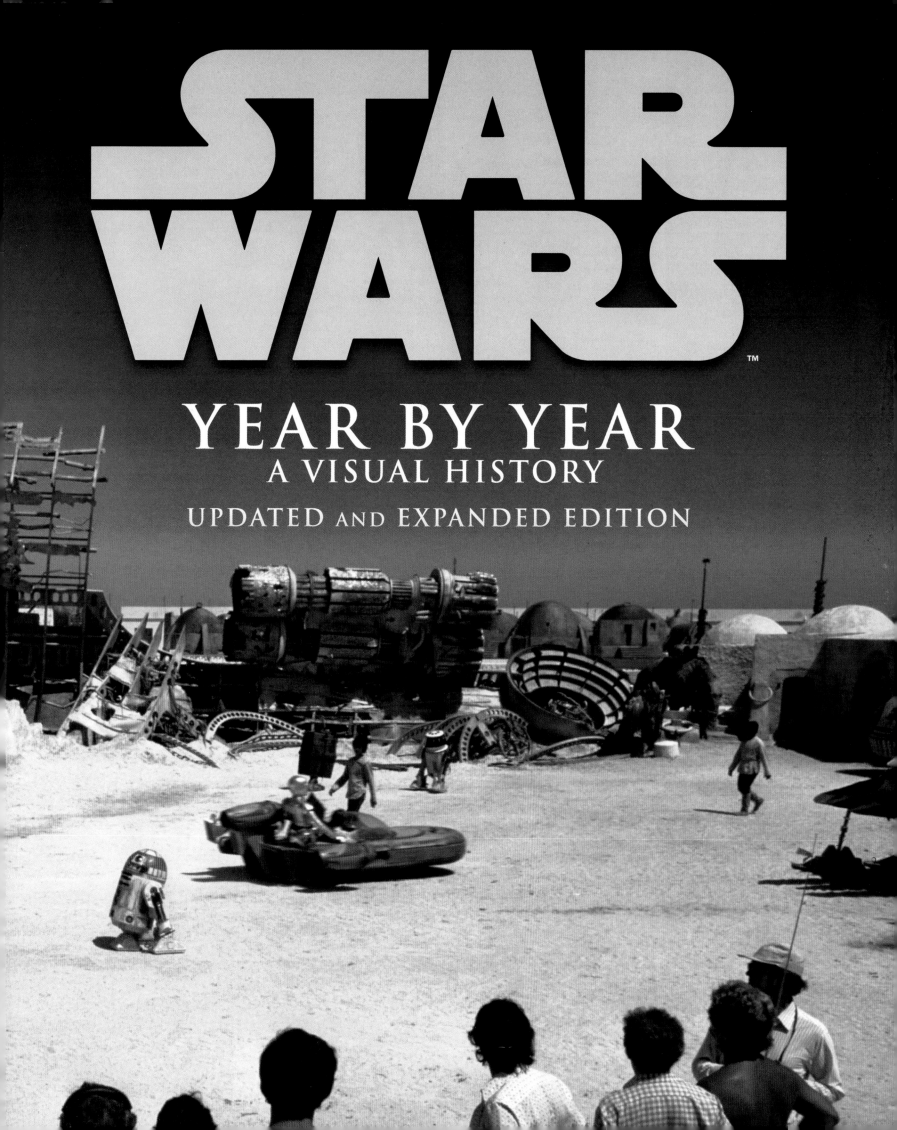

STAR WARS™

YEAR BY YEAR
A VISUAL HISTORY

UPDATED AND EXPANDED EDITION

CONTENTS

LIFE BEFORE *STAR WARS*

Written by Ryder Windham

10

THE ORIGINAL TRILOGY (1973–1983)

Written by Ryder Windham

26

BETWEEN THE TRILOGIES (1984–1996)

Written by Daniel Wallace

114

THE PREQUEL TRILOGY (1997-2005)

Written by Pablo Hidalgo

180

CLONE WARS & BEYOND (2006-2012)

Written by Pablo Hidalgo

264

STAR WARS: A NEW ERA (2013-2016)

Written by Pablo Hidalgo

324

INTRODUCTION

"I wanted to make a film for kids that would strengthen contemporary mythology"

George Lucas

IN 1977, GEORGE LUCAS released his epic "space opera" *Star Wars*, a spectacular reworking of the science-fiction, space-fantasy, and World War II battle movies that had so captivated him as a child. *Star Wars* proceeded to take the world by storm, generating mass appreciation and an enduring fan following. As the two sequels were released over the next six years, the franchise became a major influence in its own right, spawning an entire industry of spin-off literature, comic books, computer and video games, merchandise, and collectibles.

Star Wars has become so ingrained in the cultural psyche that world leaders have defined themselves with reference to it and Jedism has even been proposed as a new religion. By 2005, when the final installment of the Prequel Trilogy was released into a world now inundated with *Star Wars*, there was hardly a soul on Earth who had not heard of it.

Today, *Star Wars* has become so fully a part of the cultural and social framework that real-world events have been shaped by the Saga, almost as much as they have shaped it. *Star Wars Year By Year: A Visual Chronicle* places the Saga in this

fascinating context, as world events and the *Star Wars* timeline play out side by side.

In addition to its place in popular culture, the technology developed for the *Star Wars* movies has consistently made a big impression on the film industry. Everything from its sound design to its digital advances has influenced the way movies are made, with Lucas's visual effects house, Industrial Light & Magic (ILM), working on many of the most pioneering and visually exciting films of the last three decades.

In this book, you will discover how George Lucas brought his dream to life—six times—and share the trials and tribulations of movie making. You will also trace the career paths of key *Star Wars* cast and crew while keeping track of global politics, technological advancements, and other box office successes—and the effects of *Star Wars* upon many of them. A month-by-month snapshot view of the *Star Wars* timeline against a real-world backdrop enables startling and insightful connections to be made, providing a deeper understanding of the genesis and growth of one of the most important movie Sagas of all time.

AUTHOR'S NOTE

I WAS STILL WORKING on *Star Wars: The Ultimate Visual Guide* (DK Publishing, 2005) when Lucasfilm executive editor J. W. Rinzler first mentioned the idea of a nonfiction pictorial history of *Star Wars*. Laura Gilbert, a DK editor, subsequently asked if I'd be interested in the pending project—a chronology of "movie-making events, comic book and novel releases, TV-related spin-offs, *Clone Wars* animation, key merchandise releases, fan events, and more." Yes, I was interested. I especially liked the potential for "more." I began working on a detailed synopsis and selecting images.

Then I learned about the deadline and nearly choked. Recovering fast, I encouraged the hiring of additional writers and contributors. I really can't express how glad and relieved I was when Dan Wallace, Pablo Hidalgo, and Gus Lopez signed on.

All involved agreed that the new book should contain numerous non-*Star Wars* news items and photos to help present *Star Wars* in an overall historic context. We would also include occasional inconsistencies between the movies, novels, comics, and merchandise. Our intention was not to highlight errors, but to account for idiosyncratic items that sometimes shaped our memories of *Star Wars*.

Attentive readers will notice that Marvel Comics' *Star Wars* comic books have dates on the covers that differ from their entry dates. In case you didn't know, cover dates on old comics were not publication or ship dates, but served to inform newsstand vendors when to remove unsold copies from points of purchase. Pete Vilmur, a fellow *Star Wars* author, editor at Lucas Online, and great pal, dug deep to find Lucasfilm's records for the ship dates, which helped us pinpoint when the comics introduced various details to the "Expanded Universe" of *Star Wars* stories.

The research wasn't all familiar territory. I discovered many surprises, including odd links between *Star Wars* and apparently unrelated moments in history. I'd never before pondered any connection between Ian Fleming's James Bond novel *From Russia, With Love* (1957) and *Star Wars: The Clone Wars* (2008). But consider… In 1961, President John F. Kennedy ignited international interest in Fleming's novels when he listed *From Russia* among his favorite books. The following year, the movie *Dr. No* made a star of Sean Connery. Subsequently, Connery reportedly served as the unofficial model for the supermarionation puppet Scott Tracy in Gerry Anderson's *Thunderbirds* (1965). And in a 2008 interview, George Lucas cites *Thunderbirds* as an inspiration for the stylized characters in *The Clone Wars*.

Coincidences? Evidence of the Force? Beats me, but I had lots of fun connecting all the dots.

This very collaborative book came together under the editorial supervision of Lucy Dowling and Elizabeth Dowsett, and art direction of Ron Stobbart. The other writers and I shudder to tell DK that *Star Wars Year by Year* is largely unfinished. After all, it's a safe bet that we can look forward to more *Star Wars* for years to come.

Ryder Windham

Inspiration & Influences

Gertie the Dinosaur
February 8, 1914: Gertie the Dinosaur, an animated film by Winsor McCay, premieres in Chicago. A great animator and the creator of the comic strip Little Nemo, McCay pioneers new animation techniques like using colored images.

Flash Gordon Comic Strip
January 8, 1934: The science-fiction comic strip Flash Gordon debuts. Written by Don Moore and drawn by Alex Raymond, it is conceived to compete with the futuristic strip, Buck Rogers. The comic strip will later provide the inspiration for two Flash Gordon movies.

Flash Gordon Film Serial
April 6, 1936: Flash Gordon, a film serial based on the comic strip and starring Olympic gold medalist for swimming, Larry "Buster" Crabbe, premieres. In the 1950s, Flash Gordon serials air on Adventure Theater, one of George Lucas's favorite television shows.

GROWING UP IN THE 1940s and 1950s, George Lucas's literary taste tends toward Jules Verne's novel *Twenty Thousand Leagues Under the Sea,* the *Flash Gordon* comic strip, and comic books ranging from *Tommy Tomorrow* to *Donald Duck.* He also enjoys the *Flash Gordon* movie serials, even though he recognizes their technical limitations. Walt Disney's films and the Warner Bros. cartoons also have their appeal. These boyhood passions will both inspire and influence Lucas's later work.

Snow White
December 21, 1937: Walt Disney's Snow White and the Seven Dwarfs, the first full-length animated feature film from a US filmmaker, premieres. George Lucas sees the re-release in 1952.

Orson Welles
October 30, 1938: Orson Welles's radio adaptation of H.G. Wells's The War of the Worlds airs in the US. The next day, newspapers report the realistic-sounding drama inspired "panic" among many listeners who believed aliens from Mars were invading Earth.

Carol Hughes and Buster Crabbe in the TV series Flash Gordon Conquers the Universe (1940)

From Flash to Buck
February 6, 1939: Buck Rogers, a 12-part movie serial based on the same-titled comic strip, premieres in the US. The serial stars former Flash Gordon actor Buster Crabbe.

GEORGE LUCAS

GEORGE WALTON LUCAS JR. *is born in Modesto, California, on May 14, 1944. George and his three sisters spend their earliest years in the suburbs of Modesto, where his parents, George Sr. and Dorothy, own a stationery store. In the late 1950s, the Lucas family moves just outside the city to a ranch-style house set among 13 acres of walnut trees. Here, Lucas's interests expand from comics, radio dramas, Saturday matinee serials, and television Westerns to motorcycles, cars, and rock-and-roll.*

Lucas as passenger in a race car driven by Allen Grant, 1963

George Lucas, 8th grade

Car Crazy

At 15, Lucas begins to take an interest in cars. "Once I was 16, I got my license and I could really drive around, out on the streets, and I kind of got lost in cruising from that point on—cars were all-consuming to me," Lucas recalls. He goes on to modify his yellow Fiat Bianchina by adding a roll bar and a heavy-duty racer's seat belt. He later becomes head of the pit crew for driver Allen Grant at the Pacific Grand Prix.

Modesto Timeline

1944
George Walton Lucas Jr. is born in Modesto, California.

1954
George Sr. buys the family its first television set.

1955
The Lucas family makes the first of many visits to Disneyland.

1957
The Lucas family moves to an outlying ranch on Sylvan Road in Modesto.

Age 6

1962
Lucas crashes his Fiat Bianchina and requires hospitalization.

1962
Lucas enrolls in Modesto Junior College.

Age 14

1964
Lucas graduates from Modesto Junior College and enrolls in film school at the University of Southern California.

Age 17

Modesto, California
Modesto, which is Spanish for "modesty," is a thriving farming and fruit-growing community in California. Modesto's Burge's Drive In eventually inspires Mel's Drive In, a heavily featured location in Lucas's film American Graffiti (1973).

First Supercomputer
December 1943: Colossus I, an electronic computing device used by British codebreakers to decipher encrypted German messages during World War II, begins operating. It ushers in a new era and the rise of modern computers.

Chesley Bonestell
May 1944: LIFE magazine publishes paintings of views of Saturn by artist Chesley Bonestell. Readers are astonished by Bonestell's thoughtfully researched, photorealistic visions of other worlds. A book featuring Bonestell's art, Conquest of Space (1949), becomes a bestseller.

13

Howdy Doody
December 27, 1947: The first regularly scheduled, nationally broadcast television program, Puppet Playhouse, premieres on NBC. The program is later renamed The Howdy Doody Show, and airs until 1960. Buffalo Bob Smith hosts the show, which stars the freckle-faced marionette puppet Howdy Doody.

Hopalong Cassidy
June 24, 1949: The first Western series on television, Hopalong Cassidy, starring William Boyd, premieres on NBC. Boyd had played the titular cowboy in 66 films between 1935 and 1948, and anticipating the popularity of television, he obtained the rights to all of his "Hoppy" films, which are later reformatted for television.

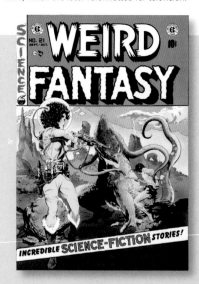

EC Comics
1949–1954: William M. Gaines, owner of Entertaining Comics (popularly known as EC Comics), publishes titles for horror, crime, and science fiction to compete with superhero comics. Gaines's comics feature cover art and stories by many artists, including Jack Davis, Will Elder, Frank Frazetta, Jack Kamen, Bernard Krigstein, John Severin, Al Williamson, and Wally Wood.

Destination Moon
June 27, 1950: Destination Moon, directed by Irving Pichel, premieres in New York. Based on Robert Heinlein's novel Rocketship Galileo, the science-fiction film depicts a manned lunar voyage. Heinlein and artist Chesley Bonestell serve as technical advisors for the George Pal production.

MAD #1
August, 1952: MAD #1 (cover date October–November), a satire anthology comic book, is released. In 1954, MAD thumbs its nose at the newly created Comics Code Authority (see p.15) by switching to a magazine format.

Shane
April 23, 1953: Shane, directed by George Stevens and starring Alan Ladd, premieres in New York. Based on Jack Schaefer's Western novel, Shane tells the story of the friendship between a young boy (Brandon DeWilde) and a former gunfighter who can't escape his past (Alan Ladd).

Ivy Mike
November 1, 1952: The US detonates a fusion device, codenamed Ivy Mike, on Enewetak, an atoll in the Pacific Ocean. Considered the first successful test of a hydrogen bomb, Ivy Mike vaporizes the island Elugelab.

Ray Harryhausen
June 13, 1953: The Beast from 20,000 Fathoms, directed by Eugène Lourié and based on a story by Ray Bradbury, is released. Beast features visual effects by Ray Harryhausen, who becomes renowned for his work in stop-motion model animation. Greatly inspired by King Kong (1933), Harryhausen previously worked on Mighty Joe Young (1949).

Comic Book Hearings
1954: The United States Senate Subcommittee on Juvenile Delinquency holds a series of public hearings regarding the potential impact of crime and horror comics on juvenile delinquency. Several comic book publishers create the Comics Code Authority (the CCA), their own regulatory censor, which essentially prohibits all crime and horror comics.

Disneyland Opens
July 17, 1955: Walt Disney's theme park, Disneyland, opens in Anaheim, California. The 160-acre site is divided into Main Street USA, Adventureland, Fantasyland, Frontierland, and Tomorrowland.

Rock and Roll
January 27, 1956: Elvis Presley's "Heartbreak Hotel" is released, and becomes the year's bestselling single. The following year, on May 27, "That'll Be the Day," is released and becomes a number-one hit. It is written and performed by Buddy Holly (below) and Jerry Allison as members of The Crickets.

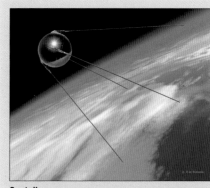

Sputnik
October 4, 1957: The Soviet Union launches the first man-made satellite, Sputnik, into orbit. The launch begins the 30-year Space Race, a competition between the Soviet Union and the US to outdo each other in achievements in space exploration.

Darby O'Gill and the Little People
June 26, 1959: Walt Disney's Darby O'Gill and the Little People, directed by Robert Stevenson, is released. The film stars Albert Sharpe, Janet Munro, and Sean Connery, and features matte paintings by Peter Ellenshaw.

From *Flash Gordon* to *Star Wars*

As his interest in films deepens, Lucas reconsiders the Flash Gordon movie serials. He begins to wonder what would happen if they were done really well, and believes that children would love them even more. In the years to come, Lucas will come to realize that fantasy films and Westerns are largely a thing of the past, leaving children without any modern mythology to fuel their imaginations. The combination of his personal fondness for escapist adventure movies and his desire to relive and share that excitement with a younger generation will lead him to develop his own "space opera."

The decade of change
1960s

THE 1960s ARE A TIME of great turbulence. Following a campaign which included the first televised debate between US presidential candidates in 1960, John F. Kennedy defeats Richard M. Nixon to win the election. The "conflict" in Vietnam becomes a war that leads to an unprecedented anti-war movement. In music, The Beatles lead the "British Invasion." At the movies and on television, traditional heroes give way to anti-heroes. It is during this remarkable period that George Lucas becomes a filmmaker.

> "The sixties were amazing.
> I was in college and was just the right age."

George Lucas
1979 interview with Alan Arnold

LIVING THROUGH THE 1960s, Lucas, like everyone else at the time, feels something special is happening. In a 1979 interview, he recalls, "Everybody hoped it would continue, but it passed. Everything changes." By the end of the 1960s, Kennedy is dead, The Beatles have broken up, Nixon is President, and the Vietnam War is raging.

1960

Family Entertainment
Although some family-friendly movies and television shows in 1960 employ subversive humor, most of them present wholesome stories about kind, loving families, in which even the most precocious children usually realize they should have listened to their parents or guardians in the first place. The expense and debatable quality of color televisions, as well as initially limited availability of shows broadcast in color, prompts most Americans to stick with their black-and-white sets.

October 3: The Andy Griffith Show premieres on CBS TV. The series stars Andy Griffith (above left) and introduces young actor Ronny Howard (above right).

By 1960, 52 million American households have a television set.

December 10: Walt Disney's Swiss Family Robinson, directed by Ken Annakin, is released.

1961

Yojimbo
April 25: *Yojimbo*, directed by Akira Kurosawa and starring Toshirô Mifune, premieres in Japan, and is released five months later in the US. Kurosawa draws from Western films and Dashiell Hammett's books, *Red Harvest* and *The Glass Key*, to tell the story of a masterless samurai who manipulates rival gangs in a lawless town.

Yojimbo is nominated for the Best Costume Design Award at the 1962 Academy Awards®.

1962

Doctor Doom
Created by writer Stan Lee and artist Jack Kirby, supervillain Doctor Doom makes his debut in Marvel Comics' *The Fantastic Four* #5 (cover date July). Victor Von Doom is fascinated by the occult and dons a mask after his face is badly disfigured when he tries to "contact the nether world."

No more mad scientist: Doctor Doom possesses supernatural powers and becomes the archetype for armor-encased villains.

🌐 SOVIET UNION PUTS FIRST MAN INTO SPACE

🌐 US JOINS VIETNAM WAR

Kennedy's Apollo Program

May 25: After inheriting the Apollo Program from the presidency of Dwight D. Eisenhower, President John F. Kennedy presents a bold challenge to Congress and government space agencies: send a man to the Moon and return him safely to Earth by the end of the decade.

Shifting Gears

June 12: Three days before his high school graduation, Lucas is in his Fiat Bianchina heading home from the city library, when his classmate Frank Ferreira tries to pass him at high speed in a Chevy Impala. "I never saw him," Lucas recalls. "He hit me broadside just as I was turning into our drive." Lucas is rushed to Modesto City Hospital and spends the next two weeks in intensive care. The experience transforms many of his ideas about life and ends his ambition to race cars. After recovering, he enrolls in Modesto Junior college to study psychology, anthropology, and philosophy.

THE MODESTO BEE

Youth Survives Crash

Lucas's Fiat (below) rolls several times before wrapping around a tree. The crash makes the front page of The Modesto Bee (above).

Dr. No is the first of Fleming's James Bond books to be adapted into a movie.

James Bond

October 5: *Dr. No*, an adaptation of Ian Fleming's spy novel, premieres in London. It is directed by Terence Young and stars Sean Connery as a British secret agent with a license to kill. A year before the release of *Dr. No*, Fleming's novel *From Russia, With Love*, became a bestseller in the US after *LIFE* magazine listed it among President Kennedy's 10 favorite books.

In the horror movie Dementia 13, a family is terrorized by an ax murderer.

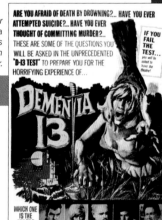

ARE YOU AFRAID OF DEATH BY DROWNING?... HAVE YOU EVER ATTEMPTED SUICIDE?... HAVE YOU EVER THOUGHT OF COMMITTING MURDER?... THESE ARE SOME OF THE QUESTIONS YOU WILL BE ASKED IN THE UNPRECEDENTED "D-13 TEST" TO PREPARE YOU FOR THE HORRIFYING EXPERIENCE OF...

IF YOU FAIL THE TEST...

DEMENTIA 13

WHICH ONE IS THE KILLER?

Sir Alec Guinness (above right) as Prince Feisal in Lawrence of Arabia. Guinness won a Best Actor Academy Award® for Bridge on the River Kwai in 1957.

Alec Guinness

December 10: *Lawrence of Arabia* premieres in London. Directed by David Lean, the film stars Peter O'Toole as T.E Lawrence and Sir Alec Guinness as Prince Feisal. Guinness (b. 1914) had played numerous Shakespearean roles opposite John Gielgud and Laurence Olivier before appearing in several film comedies for Ealing Studios, including *Kind Hearts and Coronets* (1949), in which he plays eight different characters. He would go on to play Obi-Wan Kenobi in *Star Wars*.

1963

Kennedy Shot

November 22: President Kennedy is fatally shot in Dallas, Texas. Lee Harvey Oswald is arrested on charges of murder, but is shot dead by nightclub operator Jack Ruby two days later. The following year, an official investigation concludes that Oswald acted alone in killing Kennedy, although conspiracy theories persist to this day.

Kennedy is on a presidential motorcade with his wife Jacqueline when he is shot. He is taken to Parkland Memorial Hospital where he is later pronounced dead.

The Wunderkind

September 25: *Dementia 13* is released. Produced by the prolific and legendarily thrifty Roger Corman, the film is co-written and directed by Corman's 24-year-old protégé, Francis Ford Coppola, who had left the University of California at Los Angeles (UCLA) that same year.

1964

Film School

Lucas's father buys his son a 35mm camera to encourage his interest in photography. Lucas enrolls at the University of Southern California (USC) School of Cinema-Television. While attending car races as a photographer, he becomes friends with cinematographer Haskell Wexler. Friends and fellow students at USC will include Hal Barwood, Robert Dalva, Caleb Deschanel, Bob Gale, Howard Kazanjian, Randal Kleiser, Willard Huyck, John Milius, Walter Murch, Matthew Robbins, Richard Walter, and Robert Zemeckis.

Aerial view of the University of Southern California campus

The Beatles and *Strangelove*

Two of George Lucas's favorite films from 1964 are Stanley Kubrick's anti-war comedy, *Dr. Strangelove*, and Richard Lester's The Beatles musical, *A Hard Day's Night*. Both films have the same director of cinematography, Gilbert Taylor. The future voice of Darth Vader, James Earl Jones, makes his movie debut in *Dr. Strangelove*, with makeup by Stuart Freeborn. Both films make use of handheld cameras to create a documentary-style feel.

January 29, 1964: Dr. Strangelove is released in the US. The film stars Peter Sellers (seated) and George C. Scott.

August 11, 1964: A Hard Day's Night is released. The film stars (from left to right) Paul McCartney, George Harrison, Ringo Starr, and John Lennon.

Bob Hope in Vietnam

In his first USO (United Service Organizations) tour in Vietnam, comedian Bob Hope entertains US troops at Vinh Long in the Mekong Delta. His troupe includes singer Anita Bryant and actress Jill St. John.

1965

Italian Westerns

November 18: *For a Few Dollars More* is released in Italy. Directed by Sergio Leone and starring Clint Eastwood, the Italian/German/Spanish co-production is the second film in what becomes known as *The Man With No Name* series, which began with *A Fistful of Dollars* (1964) and concludes with *The Good, The Bad, and The Ugly* (1966). Filmed in Spain, these low-budget "Spaghetti Westerns" transform Eastwood from a relatively unknown TV actor into an international star.

For a Few Dollar's More movie poster. Clint Eastwood's (left) poncho will inspire the costume for Boba Fett.

Vietnam War Escalates

February 7: The US Air Force executes Operation Flaming Dart, which sends 49 F-105 Thunderchiefs to attack targets located in North Vietnam. The following month, 3,500 US Marines are dispatched to protect US Air Force bases in South Vietnam, and Operation Rolling Thunder begins a sustained aerial bombardment of North Vietnam that lasts over three years. The media reports on the conflict in unprecedented detail, allowing the public to see much of its horror.

F-105 Thunderchiefs radar-bombing over North Vietnam

1966

Star Trek

September 8: *Star Trek* premieres on NBC TV. Created by Gene Roddenberry, the science-fiction series depicts the adventures of the multiethnic, mixed-gender crew of the USS *Enterprise* in the 23rd century. A young Richard Edlund (later employed by ILM) works for one of the outside special-effects houses used on *Star Trek*. Despite the promise of a "five-year mission," *Star Trek* is canceled at the end of its third season, but later becomes an immensely popular franchise.

Look Fast for Ford

October 12: *Dead Heat on a Merry-Go-Round* premieres in New York. Directed by Bernard Girard and starring James Coburn, the film features the theatrical debut of an uncredited Harrison Ford (b. 1942), who plays a hotel bellboy. Ford goes on to play minor roles in various television series including *Gunsmoke* and *Love, American Style*, but supplements his acting career by becoming a professional carpenter.

Camilla Sparv and Harrison Ford on the set of Dead Heat on a Merry-Go-Round.

December 15: Walt Disney dies of lung cancer at the age of 65. He never gets to see his planned second theme park—Walt Disney World—open in Florida.

1967

THX (Dan Natchsheim) runs for his freedom in George Lucas's short film, Electronic Labyrinth: THX 1138 4EB. Lucas utilizes locations at Los Angeles International Airport to depict a subterranean city.

Student Films

Lucas's futuristic "breakout" student film, *Electronic Labyrinth: THX 1138 4EB*, is released, depicting a bleak, monotonous future where emotions are outlawed. Lucas has shown promise with several of his earlier films, including *Five, Four, Three* (1965), a satire about the making of a teen beach movie, done in collaboration with fellow USC students Randal Kleiser and Christopher Lewis, and *Look at Life* (1965), a fast-paced montage of images from *LIFE* magazine, which won Lucas a number of awards at various film festivals. USC awards Lucas the Samuel Warner Memorial Scholarship for the short *Electronic Labyrinth: THX 1138 4EB*, allowing him access to Warner Bros. Studios. There, he meets Francis Ford Coppola, who is in the process of directing *Finian's Rainbow*.

Lucas meets Spielberg

February: Aspiring filmmaker Steven Spielberg sees *Electronic Labyrinth: THX 1138 4EB* at the USC student film festival at the Fairfax Theater in Los Angeles. Spielberg is so impressed by the film that he takes the opportunity to introduce himself to Lucas. Spielberg recalls, "There was so much virtuosity in the craft, the vision, and the emotion of that story that I couldn't believe it was a student film."

Alec Guinness and James Earl Jones

October 31: *The Comedians* is released. Directed by Peter Glenville, the film stars Elizabeth Taylor, Richard Burton, Alec Guinness, and James Earl Jones. Based on the novel by Graham Greene, the film features Guinness as Major H.O. Jones, a mercenary soldier and arms dealer. James Earl Jones plays Dr. Magiot, a revolutionary Haitian doctor.

Alec Guinness in The Comedians

1968

Prize Winner

January: Lucas submits *Electronic Labyrinth: THX 1138 4EB* to the 1967-1968 National Student Film Festival. One of the Festival's judges is director Irvin Kershner, who is "greatly impressed" by *THX*. Lucas wins the drama prize.

Things to Come?

April: Released within three days of each other, Stanley Kubrick's *2001: A Space Odyssey* and Franklin J. Schaffner's *Planet of the Apes* are two very different science-fiction films that show the dangers of placing too much faith in technology. Kubrick's film, inspired by Arthur C. Clarke's short story *The Sentinel*, spans the dawn of mankind to the next evolution, and features special effects by Douglas Trumbull and the makeup of ape-men by Stuart Freeborn. Schaffner's film shows a world where apes are superior to humans.

Film poster for 2001: A Space Odyssey, created by Robert McCall

The American astronaut Taylor (Charlton Heston) realizes he's not in alien territory at the climax of Planet of the Apes.

Chariots of the Gods?

Swiss writer Erich von Däniken publishes *Chariots of the Gods?*, which popularizes his hypothesis that numerous ancient structures are "evidence" of alien visitations. Two years later, von Däniken scripts a same-titled documentary film that is nominated for an Academy Award®.

filmmaker

September: While Francis Ford Coppola directs *The Rain People* for Warner Bros., Lucas makes a documentary about it titled *filmmaker*. *The Rain People* stars Shirley Knight, James Caan, and Robert Duvall. Although Lucas—who also works on the film as a production assistant—enjoys making documentaries, Coppola encourages him to develop his own stories for movies.

1969

President Nixon

January 20: Richard M. Nixon is sworn in as the 37th President of the United States. He had previously served as the 36th Vice President of the United States during Dwight D. Eisenhower's presidency (1953–1961).

Having previously lost the election to John F. Kennedy in 1960, Nixon beats Hubert Humphrey in the race for the presidency.

March 10: *The Godfather*, a novel by Mario Puzo, is published. The film rights for Puzo's story of a fictional Sicilian Mafia family ruled by Don Vito Corleone, are purchased even before the novel's publication.

Zoetrope

Walter Murch and George Lucas

May: Francis Ford Coppola founds his own film production company American Zoetrope, with Lucas as executive vice president. Their goal is to re-create the atmosphere and creativity they enjoyed at college. Coppola plans a feature-length remake of Lucas's *THX 1138* as Zoetrope's first production. Warner Bros. agrees to back *THX*, and loans Zoetrope $300,000 to establish its premises, buy equipment, and fund scripts. Lucas hires Walter Murch to run Zoetrope's nascent mixing studio.

July 14: *Easy Rider* is released. Directed by Dennis Hopper, the film is a box office hit and major studios begin to realize that there is money to be made from low-budget, independent films.

Dennis Hopper (left) and Peter Fonda in Easy Rider

One Small Step

July 20: While US astronaut Michael Collins orbits the Moon in the command module *Columbia*, the lunar module *Eagle* carries Neil Armstrong and Buzz Aldrin down to the Moon's Sea of Tranquility. On Earth, more than half a billion television viewers watch Armstrong climb down the module's ladder and onto the lunar surface.

Buzz Aldrin, photographed by Neil Armstrong

August 15–18: The Woodstock Music & Art Fair, a three-day musical festival that runs over to include a fourth day, is held in Bethel, New York. Over 500,000 people show up. A documentary movie, edited in part by Martin Scorsese, commemorates the event.

August 18: Jimi Hendrix performs at Woodstock

Medium Cool

August 27: *Medium Cool*, written and directed by Haskell Wexler, premieres in New York. Wexler blends feature film and documentary footage to place fictional characters in genuine historic events.

Haskell Wexler during filming of Medium Cool

Also in 1969...

Apollo Animated

CBS News presents animated sequences to show viewers how Apollo mission astronauts will travel to and from the moon. The animations are by Ralph McQuarrie, a former artist for the Boeing Company in Seattle, and presently one of the three artists who make up the studio named Reel Three.

Ralph McQuarrie's artwork for CBS News

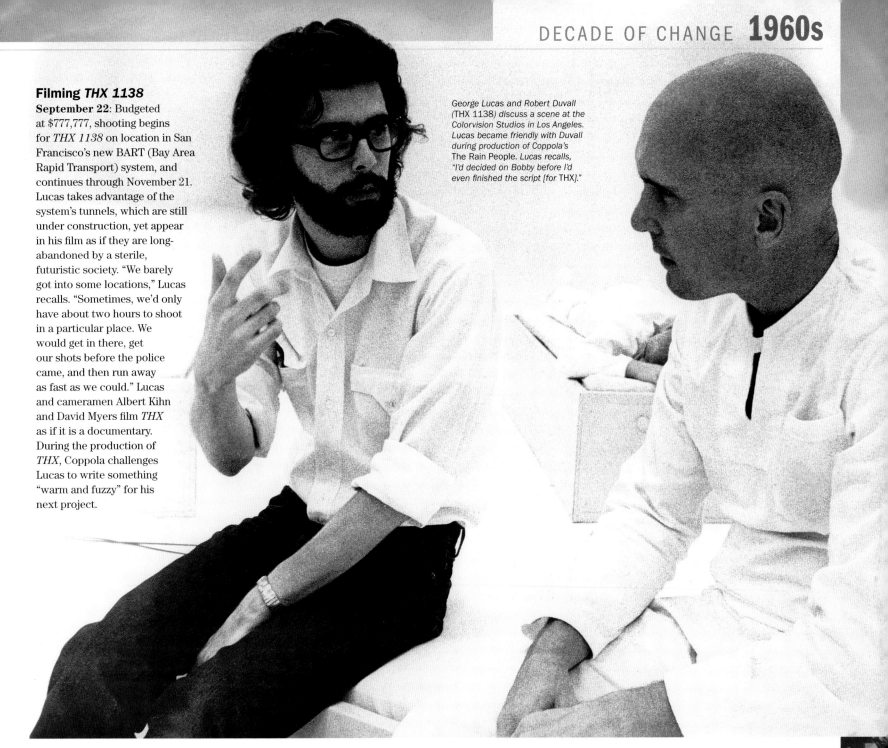

Filming *THX 1138*

September 22: Budgeted at $777,777, shooting begins for *THX 1138* on location in San Francisco's new BART (Bay Area Rapid Transport) system, and continues through November 21. Lucas takes advantage of the system's tunnels, which are still under construction, yet appear in his film as if they are long-abandoned by a sterile, futuristic society. "We barely got into some locations," Lucas recalls. "Sometimes, we'd only have about two hours to shoot in a particular place. We would get in there, get our shots before the police came, and then run away as fast as we could." Lucas and cameramen Albert Kihn and David Myers film *THX* as if it is a documentary. During the production of *THX*, Coppola challenges Lucas to write something "warm and fuzzy" for his next project.

George Lucas and Robert Duvall (THX 1138) discuss a scene at the Colorvision Studios in Los Angeles. Lucas became friendly with Duvall during production of Coppola's The Rain People. Lucas recalls, "I'd decided on Bobby before I'd even finished the script [for THX]."

Jim Henson with Ernie and Kermit the Frog

Sesame Street

November 10: *Sesame Street* premieres on National Educational Television. The educational children's series features the Muppets: puppet characters created and performed by Jim Henson and Frank Oz. The Muppets are already well known to audiences, having appeared in television shows and commercials. The following year, *TIME* magazine proclaims that *Sesame Street* "is not only the best children's show in TV history, it is one of the best parents' shows."

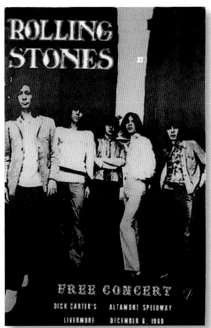

Altamont

December 6: George Lucas works as a camera operator for directors David Maysles, Albert Maysles, and Charlotte Zwerin. They film a free concert featuring the Rolling Stones, Jefferson Airplane, and other performers at Altamont Speedway, a racetrack six miles from San Francisco. The Hell's Angels motorcycle club act as security. Many spectators are injured and four die. The documentary film of the concert, *Gimme Shelter*, is released exactly one year later. For many, the Altamont concert signals the end of the carefree spirit of the 1960s.

Poster for the notorious Altamont concert

JOHN LENNON'S "BED-IN" FOR PEACE ⊙ STONEWALL RIOTS IN NYC ⊙ WOODSTOCK FESTIVAL ⊙

An uncertain future

1970s

"The professional world was much more unpleasant than I thought."

Francis Ford Coppola
on the film business in Hollywood

LUCAS SPENDS THE early part of 1970 editing *THX 1138*. While the film shows a bleak vision of the future, it also portrays a counter-culture movement, an absence of hippies (no one has long hair), and a place where citizens are punished for *not* taking drugs. Warner Bros. executives finally view *THX 1138* in November of 1970, and their negative reaction crushes Zoetrope and Lucas's reputation. Coppola continues to encourage Lucas to develop a "warm" movie. He responds with *American Graffiti*.

1970

M*A*S*H

January 25: The film *M*A*S*H* premieres in New York. Directed by Robert Altman, and produced and distributed by Twentieth Century-Fox, it stars Donald Sutherland and Elliott Gould and features Robert Duvall. Set during the Korean War, the film's blend of comedy with drama is immensely popular with audiences and critics.

*Donald Sutherland as Hawkeye Pierce and Elliott Gould as Trapper John McIntyre in M*A*S*H.*

February 3: Warwick Davis (Wicket the Ewok) is born in Epsom, England. He has congential spondyloepiphyseal dysplasia, a rare disorder of bone growth that results in dwarfism.

Patton

April 2: *Patton* is released. Directed by Franklin J. Schaffner and starring George C. Scott, the film's screenplay is co-written by Edmund H. North and Francis Ford Coppola.

George C. Scott as General George S. Patton

Black Thursday

November 19: Coppola meets with Warner Bros. executives, who watch *THX 1138* for the first time. The executives become upset because Lucas's film is different from the one Coppola had proposed. Moreover, they do not know how to promote or sell it, given the film's esoteric character. Warner Bros. demands that Coppola repay the $300,000 loan for the development of six other films that they no longer want, which include *The Conversation*, *The Black Stallion*, and Lucas's ideas for *Apocalypse Now*. This disastrous meeting becomes known at Zoetrope as "Black Thursday." The consequences of Black Thursday leave Coppola heavily in debt. Coppola soon agrees—at Lucas's urging—to direct *The Godfather* for Paramount. Dismayed by business with Warner Bros., Lucas founds his own company, Lucasfilm Ltd. With *Apocalypse Now* in limbo, Lucas asks producer Gary Kurtz, who was to line-produce that film, to budget Lucas's next movie, *American Graffiti*. Lucas also recruits Jim Bloom as a production associate.

PRODUCTION CONTROL
DIR 11
MECHANIZED

George Lucas's security badge, worn during filming of THX 1138.

American Zoetrope's San Francisco headquarters, which open in 1969.

October 15–16: Lalo Schifrin's score for *THX 1138* is recorded. The Argentine composer is well known for his theme music for the popular television series *The Man From U.N.C.L.E.* and *Mission: Impossible*.

1971

THX 1138 Released

March 11: *THX 1138* is released, but not in the form Lucas intended. Warner Bros. had taken the film away from him and assigned Warner Bros. staffer Rudi Fehr to edit it. Fehr removed five minutes from *THX 1138* without any apparent reason. "It didn't make any sense," Lucas says. "Whether it's five minutes shorter or longer, it didn't change the movie one bit… That's about the level of intelligence that was going on." Although *THX 1138* gathers some positive reviews, the experience with Warner Bros. alienates Lucas from Hollywood and fuels his desire to have complete control over his films.

Robert Duvall as the eponymous THX 1138

The Future is here.
THX II38

Warner Bros. presents THX 1138 · An American Zoetrope Production · Starring Robert Duvall and Donald Pleasence · with Don Pedro Colley, Maggie McOmie and Ian Wolfe · Technicolor® · Techniscope® · Executive Producer, Francis Ford Coppola · Screenplay by George Lucas and Walter Murch · Story by George Lucas Produced by Lawrence Sturhahn · Directed by George Lucas · Music by Lalo Schifrin

Unsure how to market THX 1138, Warner Bros. releases a one-sheet poster that focuses on an android security guard.

March 31: Ewan McGregor (the young Obi-Wan Kenobi) is born in Perth, Scotland. His uncle is actor Denis Lawson, who will play Wedge Antilles in the original *Star Wars* trilogy.

April: Francis Ford Coppola wins a Best Original Screenplay Academy Award® for *Patton*. The film wins a total of seven Academy Awards®, including Best Actor, Best Director, and Best Picture.

May: *THX 1138* is screened at the Cannes Film Festival. Lacking a festival pass, Lucas sneaks into the screening. In Cannes, he meets with David Picker, president of United Artists, who expresses interest in *American Graffiti* and a "space-opera fantasy film."

Summertime Blues

After enlisting Willard Huyck and his wife Gloria Katz to draft a 15-page treatment for *American Graffiti*, Lucas spends most of the summer working on the *Graffiti* screenplay, first with USC friend Richard Walter, then by himself.

Mark Hamill

October 30: Mark Hamill (b. 1951), a veteran actor of numerous television commercials, makes his dramatic debut on network television in the seventh episode of *The Headmaster*. The series stars Andy Griffith as the character in charge of a California private school. The following year Hamill returns to television screens as a guest star in an episode of the popular series *The Partridge Family*.

December 28: Lucasfilm and United Artists make a financing agreement for Lucas to write the script for *American Graffiti* and to develop eventually a "second picture." Although the second picture's title is not indicated in the agreement, Lucas is already referring to it as *The Star Wars*.

1972

Space Shuttle 🌐🌐🌐

January 5: President Nixon announces "the development of an entirely new type of space transportation system" that is centered on "a space vehicle that can shuttle repeatedly from Earth to orbit and back."

NASA Administrator James C. Fletcher and President Nixon announce the space shuttle program.

Pocket Calculator 🌐🌐🌐

February 1: Hewlett-Packard introduces the HP-35, the first scientific hand-held "pocket" calculator, which is priced at $395. HP sells 300,000 units in just three-and-a-half years.

The HP-35 is the first ever pocket scientific calculator to go on sale.

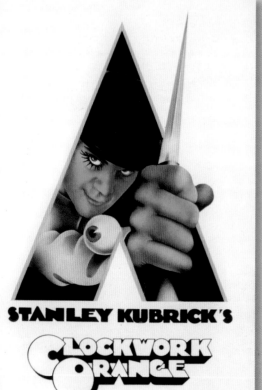

STANLEY KUBRICK'S
CLOCKWORK ORANGE

David Prowse plays a bodyguard in A Clockwork Orange.

Malcolm McDowell, who plays the psychotic Alex, appears on the poster for A Clockwork Orange.

A Clockwork Orange

February 2: *A Clockwork Orange* is released. Directed by Stanley Kubrick and based on the 1962 dystopian novel by Anthony Burgess, the movie stars Malcolm McDowell. The controversial film also features bodybuilder David Prowse and production design by John Barry.

"Ronny" Howard Revisited

February 25: "Love and the Happy Days" appears as an episode of the TV series *Love, American Style*, broadcast on ABC. It features former child star Ron Howard as Richie Cunningham and eventually leads to the genesis of the *Happy Days* TV show. During the casting of *American Graffiti*, George Lucas requests a screening of the episode, and offers a role to Howard.

Pioneer 10 🌐🌐🌐

March 3: NASA launches *Pioneer 10*, a deep space probe designed to carry a plaque to serve as a message for extra-terrestrial life. Four months later, the probe becomes the first spacecraft to travel through the asteroid belt.

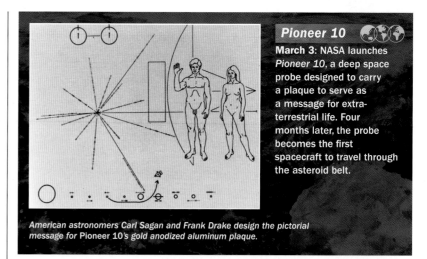

American astronomers Carl Sagan and Frank Drake design the pictorial message for Pioneer 10's gold anodized aluminum plaque.

Amazing companions on an incredible adventure...that journeys beyond imagination!

"silent running"

starring **Bruce Dern** with Cliff Potts · Ron Rifkin · Jesse Vint

Silent Running

March 10: *Silent Running* is released. Directed by Douglas Trumbull and starring Bruce Dern, the film depicts a future in which the last specimens of Earth's plant life are preserved in greenhouse domes on space freighters. It features ambulatory service robots as "drones," who walk on two legs.

🌐 *LUNA 20* LANDS ON THE MOON 🌐 ATARI IS FOUNDED 🌐 JANE FONDA TOURS NORTH VIETNAM 🌐

The Godfather

March 24: *The Godfather* is released. Directed by Francis Ford Coppola and based on the novel by Mario Puzo, the movie stars Marlon Brando and features Robert Duvall. An uncredited Lucas creates a montage sequence of crime-scene photos. Coppola's film proceeds to break box office records and gets him out of the debt he accrued from *THX 1138* and the Black Thursday debacle (see p.22).

Marlon Brando as Don Vito Corleone in The Godfather

Christopher Lee as Count Dracula in Dracula A.D. 1972.

Peter Cushing as Dracula's nemesis, Professor Van Helsing

Watergate Scandal

June 17: The Watergate scandal comes to light when five CIA operatives retained by President Nixon's Committee to re-elect the President are arrested for burglarizing the offices of the Democratic National Committee at the Watergate office complex in Washington, DC.

Hammer Horror

June 30: *Dracula A.D. 1972* premieres in West Germany. Directed by Alan Gibson, the Hammer Film Production stars Christopher Lee (b. 1922) and Peter Cushing (b. 1913). Hammer is a UK production company founded in 1934, known for its horror films. Cushing made his film debut in James Whale's *The Man in the Iron Mask* (1939), and Lee made his in Laurence Olivier's *Hamlet* (1948), which also featured Cushing. Respected actors, close friends, and frequent co-stars, Lee and Cushing appear together in many Hammer films as well as the *Star Wars* Saga.

Filming *American Graffiti*

June 26: Lucas wants *American Graffiti* to be filmed as if it were a documentary about different characters interacting over the course of a single night. The production's grueling 29-day shoot requires most scenes to be filmed at night. Lucas asks cinematographer Haskell Wexler to make the movie "look like a jukebox." For the outdoor cruising scenes, Wexler obliges by adding brighter lights to the existing street lamps and asking shop owners to leave their storefront lights on overnight.

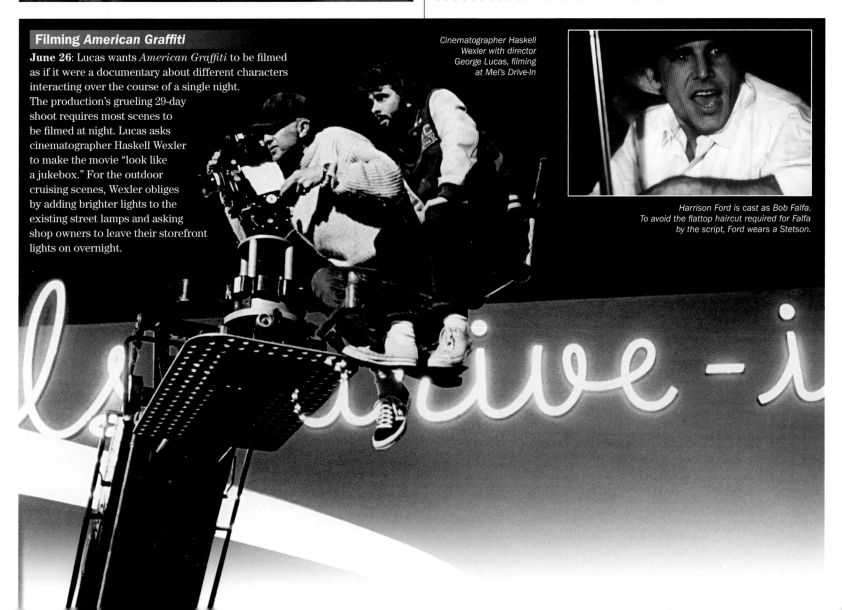

Cinematographer Haskell Wexler with director George Lucas, filming at Mel's Drive-In

Harrison Ford is cast as Bob Falfa. To avoid the flattop haircut required for Falfa by the script, Ford wears a Stetson.

AS SOMEONE WHO questions authority and enjoys popular entertainment, George Lucas is a product of his generation. He has little interest in working on a project that he doesn't believe in. He wants to be a filmmaker, not an executive. He refuses lucrative offers to direct movies that are scripted by others, and strives for nothing less than total control of his own movies. Despite his remarkable imagination, he has no idea that his failure to obtain the film rights for *Flash Gordon* might lead to any great success...

1973-1983

THE ORIGINAL TRILOGY

1973

ALTHOUGH COLUMBIA PICTURES has shown renewed interest in *Apocalypse Now*, they drop it in early 1973. George Lucas shops *Apocalypse Now* to several other studios, but no one wants it because the Vietnam War is too controversial. Desperate and heavily in debt, Lucas decides to develop his space fantasy project—*The Star Wars*.

American troops in Vietnam waiting for air support

> "I figured what the heck, I've got to do something. I'll start developing *Star Wars*." **George Lucas**

LUCAS ORIGINALLY CONSIDERS making a new *Flash Gordon* movie, and even approaches the comic strip's owner, King Features Syndicate. But because King Features wants 80 percent of the gross income and Federico Fellini to direct the project, Lucas becomes determined to make his own story instead. He also sees the value in being able to create his own film from scratch.

JANUARY

Paris Peace Accords

January 27: The signing of the Paris Peace Accords ends direct US military involvement in the Vietnam War and temporarily stops the fighting between north and south.

Mel's Drive-In was modeled on a real diner in Modesto, CA (see pp.12–13).

A scene outside Mel's Drive-In, taken from American Graffiti

American Graffiti's First Public Screening

January 28: *American Graffiti*'s first public screening takes place at San Francisco's Northpoint Theater. Despite an overwhelming positive response from the audience, Universal executives decide to cut nearly five minutes from Lucas's film so it can be released as a TV movie.

Organizing Ideas

January–April: While working on his science-fiction story, Lucas reviews Akira Kurosawa's *The Hidden Fortress* and draws inspiration from the characters and situations. He also creates and revises lists of names for characters and planets. With the Vietnam War and *Apocalypse Now* still on his mind, he converts concepts from *Apocalypse* into a space fantasy. As with *THX 1138* and *American Graffiti*, he uses the idea of an action sequence with high-speed vehicles for the film's ending.

Toshirô Mifune plays the hero in The Hidden Fortress

Poster for The Hidden Fortress

The bickering peasants in The Hidden Fortress, Tahei and Matakishi, provide inspiration for Lucas as he develops a pair of robot characters for The Star Wars.

Journal of the Whills
I

this is the story of Mace Windy, a revered Jedi-bendu of Opuchi, as related to us by C.J. Thorpe, padawaan learner to the famed Jedi.

I am Chuiee two-thorpe of Kissel. My father is Han Dardell Thorpe, chief pilot of the renown galatic cruiser Tarnack. As a family we were not rich, except in honor, and valuing this above all mundane possessions, I chose the profession of my father, rather than a more profitable career. I was 16 I believe, and pilot of the trawler Balmung, when my ambitions demanded that I enter the exalted Intersystems Academy to train as a potential Jedi-templer. It is here that I became padawaan learner to the great Mace Windy, highest of all the Jedi-bendu masters, and at that time, Warlord to the Chairman of the Alliance of Independent systems.

Never shall I forget the occasion upon which I first set eyes upon Mace Windy. It was at the great feast of the Pleabs. There were gathered under one roof, the most powerful warriors in the galaxy, and although I realized my adoration of the Master might easily influence my memory, when he entered the hall, these great and noble Warlords fell silent. It was said he was the most gifted and powerful man in the Independent Systems. Some felt he was even more powerful than the Imperial leader of the Galactic Empire.

Handwritten first page of Lucas's Journal of the Whills

Jedi Journal
Lucas uses his lists and notes to sketch out a two-page handwritten idea fragment titled *Journal of the Whills (Part I)*. This fragment refers to a "Jedi-bendu" named "Mace Windy" and to "C.J. Thorpe, padawan learner to the famed Jedi."

Alan Ladd Jr. at Fox
Alan Ladd Jr., the son of iconic actor Alan Ladd, is hired as vice president for creative affairs at Twentieth Century-Fox in January 1973. Ladd had previously worked as a motion picture talent agent at Creative Management Associates and as an independent producer in London, where he produced nine films in four years. Ladd's first project for Fox is the science-fiction film *Zardoz* (1974), directed by John Boorman and starring Sean Connery.

Alan Ladd Jr.

APRIL

April 4: The World Trade Center officially opens in New York City. The complex's twin 110-story towers briefly hold the record for the tallest buildings on Earth.

MAY

First Treatments
Lucas completes a 10-page handwritten treatment titled *The Star Wars*. Making 14 pages when typed up, this treatment summary features a general named Luke Skywalker. Lucas submits his finished treatment to United Artists and Universal, but both studios pass on it.

First page of Lucas's handwritten treatment for The Star Wars

JUNE

M*A*S*H and Apes
According to Twentieth Century-Fox executive Warren Hellman, Fox's sole source of viable income in June 1973 is the television series *M*A*S*H*, a spin-off of Robert Altman's film. On June 15, Fox releases *Battle for the Planet of the Apes*, the fifth and final film in its *Planet of the Apes* series. *Battle* is a box-office success, and Fox is interested in developing another profitable science-fiction franchise.

Theatrical poster for Battle for the Planet of the Apes

The original cast of M*A*S*H: (L–R) Alan Alda, Loretta Swit, Mike Farrell, Harry Morgan, and Larry Linville

Lucas Meets Ladd
Hearing friends praise the still-unreleased *American Graffiti*, Alan Ladd Jr. arranges a screening. Ladd is so impressed by the film that he organizes a meeting with Lucas, who tells him about his ideas for a space fantasy. After having *The Star Wars* rejected by both Universal and United Artists, Lucas secures a deal with Ladd at Twentieth Century-Fox.

JULY

Is It a Deal?

July 13: Lucasfilm's legal representative, Tom Pollock, writes to Twentieth Century-Fox's vice president of business affairs William Immerman to negotiate a deal for Fox to finance the development of the screenplay and production of *The Star Wars*. If Fox doesn't like the screenplay or any revised draft, they can bow out of the deal.

Bruce Lee Dies

July 20: Actor and highly influential martial artist Bruce Lee dies in Hong Kong, six days before the release of his film *Enter the Dragon*. Doctors attribute the 32-year-old actor's death to an acute cerebral edema caused by a reaction to a prescription painkilling drug.

After playing Kato in the 1960s TV series The Green Hornet, Bruce Lee achieves legendary fame for his roles in Hong Kong action films.

SEPTEMBER

September 2: J.R.R. Tolkien dies in Bournemouth, England, at the age of 81. The university professor and author is best known for his fantasy novels *The Hobbit* (1937), and *The Lord of the Rings* trilogy: *The Fellowship of the Ring* (1954), *The Two Towers* (1954), and *The Return of the King* (1955).

NOVEMBER

Westworld

November 21: *Westworld* is released. Written and directed by Michael Crichton, *Westworld* stars Yul Brynner as the Gunslinger, an android at a fictional amusement park for adults. It is yet another cautionary tale of technology-gone-wrong and is the first major feature film to employ 2-D computer generated images, used to present the android's point of view.

Yul Brynner's android character is modeled on his role as Chris in The Magnificent Seven *(1960).*

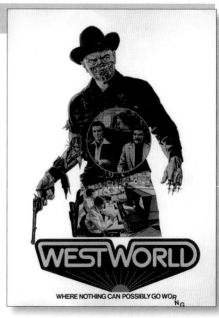

AUGUST

American Graffiti a Smash

August 11: Released with little fanfare by Universal, *American Graffiti* exceeds all expectations and helps launch the careers of actors Richard Dreyfuss, Ron Howard, Paul Le Mat, Charles Martin Smith, Cindy Williams, Candy Clark, Mackenzie Phillips, Harrison Ford, and Suzanne Somers. The movie also brings fame to disc jockey Wolfman Jack, who plays himself and generates a wave of nostalgia for 1950s and early 1960s music. A critical success, *American Graffiti* becomes one of the greatest money-makers in motion picture history, in terms of its profit-to-cost ratio.

August 19: Ahmed Best (the voice of Jar Jar Binks) is born in New York City.

It's a Deal

August 20: Nineteen days after the release of *American Graffiti*, Lucas signs a deal memo with Fox to write and direct *The Star Wars* for $150,000, plus a

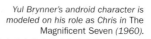

Lucasfilm's legal representative Thomas Pollock signs the deal memo with Fox for The Star Wars.

degree of profit participation. But the production contract will continue to be negotiated for several years, as Fox executives drag their feet: Except for Ladd, no one has any confidence in *The Star Wars*.

Fred Roos

August 24: Fred Roos, who had served as casting director for *American Graffiti*, agrees to help Lucas cast *The Star Wars*. Roos had cast Harrison Ford as a political activist in *Zabriskie Point* (1970), but his performance was cut. Roos will also cast Ford in Coppola's *The Conversation* (1974).

While in college, Lucas realizes that cruising in cars is a uniquely American mating ritual. As society changes, Lucas conceives American Graffiti as a paean to his youth.

Also in 1973...

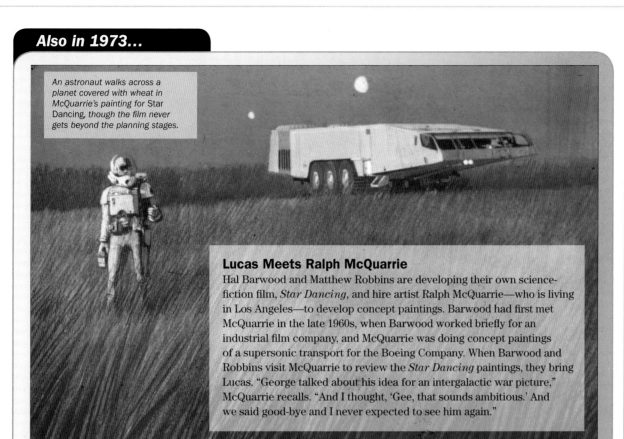

An astronaut walks across a planet covered with wheat in McQuarrie's painting for Star Dancing, though the film never gets beyond the planning stages.

Lucas Meets Ralph McQuarrie

Hal Barwood and Matthew Robbins are developing their own science-fiction film, *Star Dancing*, and hire artist Ralph McQuarrie—who is living in Los Angeles—to develop concept paintings. Barwood had first met McQuarrie in the late 1960s, when Barwood worked briefly for an industrial film company, and McQuarrie was doing concept paintings of a supersonic transport for the Boeing Company. When Barwood and Robbins visit McQuarrie to review the *Star Dancing* paintings, they bring Lucas. "George talked about his idea for an intergalactic war picture," McQuarrie recalls. "And I thought, 'Gee, that sounds ambitious.' And we said good-bye and I never expected to see him again."

DECEMBER

Artist's impression of Pioneer 10 above the surface of Jupiter

Pioneer 10

December 3: *Pioneer 10* is the first spacecraft to transmit close-up images of Jupiter back to Earth. *Pioneer 10* survives Jupiter's intense radiation and continues on its mission beyond the solar system.

The deuce coupe's license plate, THX 138, is an abbreviated tribute to Lucas's first feature film.

American Graffiti *theatrical release poster by cartoonist Mort Drucker, who is famous for his satires of movies in MAD magazine.*

1974

LUCAS WORKS ON THE rough draft for *The Star Wars* through the winter of 1973 and 1974. In a 1979 interview, he recalls, "In *Star Wars*, I was striving to make a strong positive statement. My first film [*THX 1138*] was a parable about the way we are living out our lives today. I realize it was a rather depressing statement. People really weren't interested in a depressing statement. Being a pessimist doesn't seem to accomplish anything." However, Lucas finds that writing his "space opera" is not easy.

"I hate writing—I've always hated it." George Lucas
in a 1979 interview

THROUGH HIS STUDY of anthropology, Lucas developed an interest in folklore and mythology, and their roles in society. "I came to realize that America has no modern fairy tales. You could say that the Western movie is the last of our myths. I feel that young people need some kind of fantasy life. Essentially, folklore is a very simple form of teaching."

Cover art for John Carter of Mars (1940), a juvenile story co-authored by Edgar Rice Burroughs and his son, John Coleman Burroughs, who also illustrated the story.

Lucas also watches Howard Hawks's *Air Force* (1943), Michael Curtiz's *The Adventures of Robin Hood* (1938), and Fritz Lang's *Metropolis* (1927), and videotapes aerial battle sequences from *Tora! Tora! Tora!* (1970), *The Dam Busters* (1955), and other World War II films to create a 16mm short to establish his vision for spaceship dogfights.

The robot Maria in Fritz Lang's Metropolis

JANUARY

Drawing Inspiration
Lucas reviews many comics, books, and movies, gleaning concepts that he will incorporate into *The Star Wars*. In spring of 1974, he reads *John Carter of Mars* by Edgar Rice Burroughs, *The Golden Bough: A Study in Magic and Religion* by Scottish anthropologist Sir James George Frazer, and many other fantasy books. Lucas says, "I'm trying to make a classic genre picture, a classic space opera—and there are certain concepts that have been developed by writers, primarily Edgar Rice Burroughs, that are traditional, and you keep those traditional aspects about the project."

Clockwise from bottom right: Ron Howard, Anson Williams, Donny Most, and Henry Winkler in Happy Days

Happy Days Are Here
January 15: *Happy Days* premieres on ABC television. Ron Howard resumes the role of Richie Cunningham in the situation comedy set in the 1950s in Milwaukee, Wisconsin.

⊕ OIL EMBARGO CRISIS ENDS ⊕ FIRST BARCODE USED ON PACKAGING ⊕ INDIA TESTS ITS FIRST

FEBRUARY

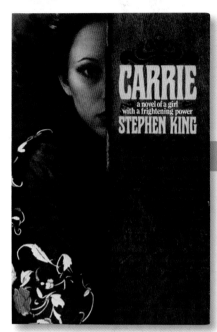

APRIL

Carrie

Stephen King's first published novel, *Carrie*, is the story of a bullied high-school girl with telekinetic powers. The hardcover edition sells 13,000 copies, but the subsequent paperback sells over 1 million copies in its first year.

First edition book cover of Carrie

Dark Star

Dark Star premieres at the Los Angeles International Film Exposition. Directed by John Carpenter, the quirky science-fiction film's spaceship, *Dark Star*, is designed by artist Ron Cobb. A drifting piece of debris from the spaceship is marked "Toilet Tank THX 1138."

The Conversation

April 7: *The Conversation* is released. Written and directed by Francis Ford Coppola, the film stars Gene Hackman and features Cindy Williams, Harrison Ford, Terri Garr, and an uncredited Robert Duvall. Although the filming was originally completed before the Watergate scandal, *The Conversation*'s plot is widely interpreted by Americans as Coppola's artistic response to the event. The sound for the film is designed by Walter Murch.

Release poster for The Conversation

MAY

Rough Draft

Lucas completes the rough draft for *The Star Wars*. The story features the Jedi versus the Sith, two bickering robots, Princess Leia, and Han Solo, but is still far from the final draft.

Lucas decorates the title page of his rough draft with a prominent government stamp.

Frankenstein Finale

May 2: *Frankenstein and the Monster from Hell* is released in the UK. Directed by Terence Fisher, and starring Peter Cushing as Victor Frankenstein and David Prowse as the Monster, it is the final chapter in Hammer Film's *Frankenstein* series.

David Prowse is unrecognizable as the Monster, thanks to makeup artist Eddie Knight.

JULY

First Draft Summary

Lucas finishes the first draft of his script for *The Star Wars*. Although the rough draft and first draft are the same in terms of the story, the names of numerous characters are changed in the latter version. The first draft changes the Knights of the Sith to the Legion of Letow, Wookees to Jawas (described as huge gray and furry beasts), Annikin Starkiller to Justin Valor, Princess Leia to Princess Zara, and the robots R2D2 and C3PO into A-2 and C-3. Lucas reverts or revises various names in subsequent drafts.

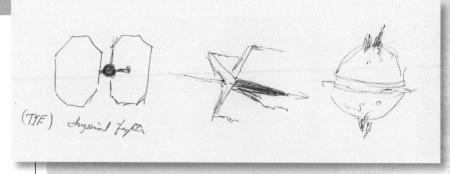

To convey his spacecraft ideas to Cantwell and McQuarrie, Lucas provides sketches of the TIE fighter, X-wing, and Death Star.

AUGUST

Nixon Exits

August 8: After audio tapes reveal President Nixon's discussion with his chief of staff about using the CIA to block the FBI from further investigation of the Watergate scandal, Nixon announces his resignation, effective the following day.

President Ford

August 9: Following Nixon's sudden resignation, his vice president, Gerald R. Ford (b. 1914) becomes the 38th president of the United States. Ford has the odd distinction of being the only president who was not elected for president or vice president. He became vice president after Spiro Agnew resigned amid scandal in 1973.

August 23: Ray Park (the Sith Lord Darth Maul) is born in the Southern General Hospital in Glasgow, Scotland. His father is a fan of Bruce Lee.

NOVEMBER

Ed Catmull

Ed Catmull becomes director of the Computer Graphics Lab at the New York Institute of Technology, after writing his doctoral thesis on bicubic patches, the Z-buffer, and texture mapping.

Colin Cantwell and Ralph McQuarrie

Lucas hires model maker Colin Cantwell and concept artist Ralph McQuarrie to begin working on *The Star Wars*. Cantwell's experience includes work on Kubrick's *2001: A Space Odyssey* (1968) and Douglas Trumbull's *The Andromeda Strain* (1971). Lucas provides reference material, verbal descriptions, and his own sketches to communicate his ideas for spacecraft. Cantwell's concept model for the Y-wing starfighter is among the first models that Lucas approves. McQuarrie subsequently incorporates Cantwell's Y-wing and other vehicle designs into his own environment and character paintings.

Cantwell's prototype model for a "pirate ship"

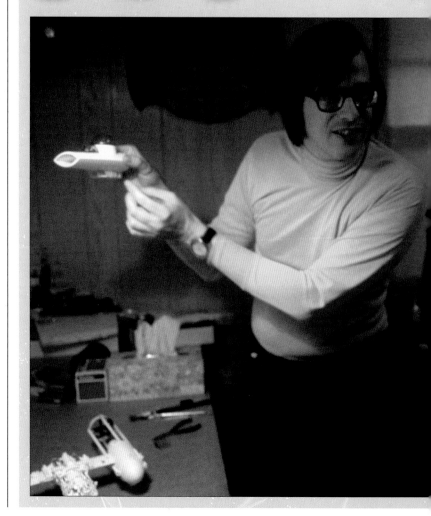

Lucas and Ralph McQuarrie examine concept sketches.

DECEMBER

The Godfather: Part II

December 12: *The Godfather: Part II* premieres in New York. Directed by Francis Ford Coppola, who co-wrote the screenplay with Mario Puzo, the film stars Al Pacino, Robert Duvall, and Robert De Niro. The following year, the film wins six Academy Awards®, including Best Screenplay, Best Director, and Best Picture.

Al Pacino (above, center) as Michael Corleone, and Robert De Niro (right) as Michael's father, Vito Corleone, who appears in flashback sequences in The Godfather: Part II.

Concept Art

McQuarrie's work begins with sketches of the robots now known as C-3PO and R2-D2. Inspiration comes from several sources, including *Metropolis* (1927) for "a kind of human robot… a public relations guy," and *Silent Running* (1972) for "a stubby little robot." Lucas tells McQuarrie that the villain, now named Darth Vader, should wear "some sort of mask." Because Lucas's script describes Vader leaping across the vacuum of space, McQuarrie suggests a head-concealing helmet with breathing apparatus.

Colin Cantwell shows a section of the Y-wing model to Lucas.

Also in 1974...

Radioland Murders Rough Draft

Willard Huyck and Gloria Katz prepare a rough draft based on Lucas's story treatment for *Radioland Murders*, a comedy mystery set in the 1930s. Lucas is obligated to produce *Radioland* because it was part of his multi-picture deal—which also included *American Graffiti*—with Universal.

The Man with the Golden Gun

December 20: *The Man with the Golden Gun* is released. Directed by Guy Hamilton, the ninth film in the James Bond series stars Roger Moore as agent 007, and Christopher Lee (pictured) as the eponymous assassin Francisco Scaramanga.

MUHAMMAD ALI REGAINS HIS WORLD TITLE ⊕ *PIONEER 11* PHOTOGRAPHS JUPITER'S RED SPOT ⊕

1975

RALPH MCQUARRIE already has an extensive career as a technical illustrator and several film posters to his credit when he first meets Lucas. McQuarrie admits he finds satisfaction in watching machinery and studying "how bits of things relate to each other." Working on *The Star Wars*, he finds his collaboration with Lucas stimulating because the movie's story is "not set in time. This gives me quite a sense of liberation. With this sort of freedom, an illustrator's work is enormous fun."

"I felt, oh yes—this is what I was meant to do." Ralph McQuarrie

MCQUARRIE RECALLS, "George wanted the illustrations to look really nice and finished, and the way he wanted them to look on-screen—he wanted the ideal look. In other words, don't worry about how things are going to get done or how difficult it might be to produce them—just paint them as he would like them to be." Of their collaboration, McQuarrie maintains, "As much as I designed this, George really designed it, too."

First Concept Paintings
After Lucas approves initial concept sketches, McQuarrie creates five key illustrations between January and March. The artist works mostly in gouache, opaque or semi-opaque watercolor, or a combination of gouache and acrylic, and spends about two days on each painting. His painting of Darth Vader engaged in a lightsaber duel in a spaceship's curved-wall corridor influences set design as well as costumes. Although Lucas's second draft describes Vader as "a seven-foot-tall Sith Knight," McQuarrie envisions the black-armored villain as a "short, rat-like" character, and the painting emphasizes his fighting prowess rather than height.

JANUARY

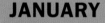

Adventures
Of
The Starkiller

An embossed gold cover is one of several mock-ups for Lucas's second draft.

Second Draft
January 28: Lucas completes his second draft, titled *Adventures of the Starkiller*, a radical reworking of the first draft. According to Lucas, only a few scenes remain unchanged. The new opening sequence focuses on R2-D2 and C-3PO, now referred to as "droids." The changes startle Alan Ladd Jr. and Coppola, who thought the first draft was fine.

🌐 **ALTAIR 8800 RELEASED**

Droids in the Desert

In his first painting for Lucas, McQuarrie depicts the droids R2-D2 and C-3PO—aka Artoo Detoo and See Threepio—on a sand planet. "I gave Artoo three legs, figuring he'd throw himself forward like a person on crutches. I picked up some landscape from a photograph [of the Oregon coast] because I liked the cliff, and I just put the sand dunes in." At Lucas's instruction, McQuarrie revises C-3PO, making him appear less human and more mechanical.

January 5: Artoo and Threepio leave the pod in the desert

February 14–15: "Laser duel." McQuarrie illustrates Jedi Deak Starkiller's fight with Darth Vader on a Rebel ship.

February 20: The Imperial city of Alderaan floats in gray clouds.

City in the Clouds

In Lucas's second draft of the script, Luke Starkiller and Han Solo—"a young Corellian pirate"—travel across space to rescue Luke's brother Deak, who has been imprisoned by Darth Vader on the Imperial "island city" of Alderaan, which is suspended in the atmosphere of a same-named "gray gaseous planet." Due to budgetary concerns, subsequent script revisions eliminate the floating city from the story.

February 22: "Battle for the Death Star (fighters dive on sphere)." McQuarrie envisions the Death Star's laser cannon with a deep power core, in which energy is charged before being fired at the opening on the battle station's surface.

March: "Cantina." McQuarrie presents Han Solo's showdown with an alien while the droids watch.

🌐 *WHEEL OF FORTUNE* PREMIERES

Concept artist Ralph McQuarrie is responsible for much of the look of the Original Trilogy, including Tatooine—Luke Skywalker's home planet—with its desert-style landscape and twin suns. For a few weeks during preproduction, the character of "Luke" became a young woman, as evidenced in this particular painting, which also shows McQuarrie's design for a landspeeder with "gull wing" doors inspired by Mercedez-Benz. McQuarrie's production paintings depict key scenes from the scripts, setting the mood for the movie and inspiring some of the models, sets, and costumes. John Barry and Joe Johnston provide additional key art direction and concepts.

Imperial TIE fighters speed through Alderaan's cloudy atmosphere in Alex Tavoularis's storyboards for The Star Wars.

FEBRUARY

Alex Tavoularis

Alex Tavoularis, the brother of production designer Dean Tavoularis, who had worked on *The Godfather*, is hired to draw storyboards for the opening sequence of *The Star Wars*. As with McQuarrie's concept paintings, the purpose of Tavoularis's storyboards is not only to communicate visual information to other members of the production but to calculate the expense of special effects shots for the sequence. His other credits include *The Conversation* (1974) and *Hard Times* (1975).

Drawn before character designs were finalized, Tavoularis's storyboards illustrate C-3PO (above) escaping from Darth Vader (left) and armored Imperial stormtroopers (below).

MARCH

Carrie Fisher

March 13: *Shampoo* is released. Directed by Hal Ashby, the movie stars Warren Beatty and features Carrie Fisher (b. 1956) in her theatrical debut. The daughter of legendary entertainers Debbie Reynolds and Eddie Fisher, Carrie left high school in 1973 to appear with her mother on Broadway in the musical *Irene*.

Carrie Fisher plays Lorna Karp in Shampoo, a satire of late-1960s sexual politics.

Lucas Meets John Williams

After Lucas tells Steven Spielberg that he's considering a classical, romantic soundtrack for *The Star Wars*, Spielberg introduces him to composer John Williams, who scored Spielberg's first two theatrical releases, *The Sugarland Express* (1974) and *Jaws* (1975).

APRIL

Richard Edlund, Rose Duignan, John Dykstra, Lucas, and Joe Johnston consult about effects.

Lucas Meets Dykstra

Lucas decides to start his own special effects house to save time and money. At the effects company Future General he meets with Douglas Trumbull's colleague John Dykstra, who assisted Trumbull on *2001* and *Silent Running*. Lucas explains his ambition to see spaceships in dogfights, and shows Dykstra his own collection of aerial battles culled from various war movies. Dykstra says the effects can be achieved if Lucas finances the building of a motion-control camera.

MAY

Betamax

May 10: Betamax, a home video cassette recorder system developed by Sony, is released. Sony's SL-6200 video tape recorder (VTR) ships as a console with a 48 centimeter (19 inch) Sony Trinitron TV. The price is $2,495.

Industrial Light & Magic

John Dykstra finds an empty warehouse in Van Nuys for Lucas's special effects house. The location inspires Lucas to name the company Industrial Light & Magic (ILM). Lucas recalls, "We were sitting in an industrial park and using light to create magic." Dykstra's former colleague Richard Alexander, Alexander's colleague Richard Edlund, and model shop supervisor Grant McCune are among ILM's first hires.

JUNE

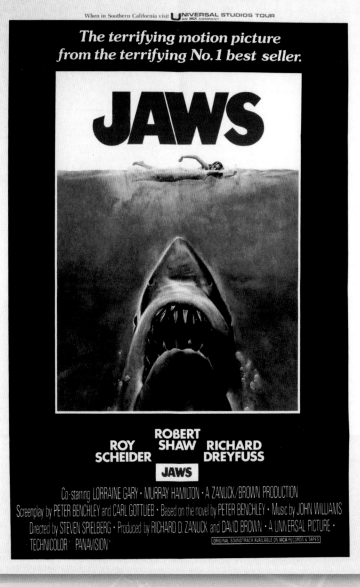

Jaws

June 20: *Jaws* opens. Directed by Steven Spielberg and based on Peter Benchley's novel, the film stars Roy Scheider, Robert Shaw, and Richard Dreyfuss. *Jaws* breaks the box office record previously set by *The Godfather*, and becomes the first movie to earn $100 million in theatrical rentals.

JULY

Joseph Campbell

While working on the third draft summary for *The Star Wars*, Lucas reads Joseph Campbell's *The Hero With A Thousand Faces*, a book he'd already read while studying anthropology. Lucas is influenced and inspired by Campbell's observations on the cross-cultural and historical similarities of mythical heroes and their journeys.

Ben Burtt

Because Walter Murch is not available for the sound effects and sound design for *The Star Wars*, Lucas contacts his friend, professor Ken Miura,

To create Wookiee sounds, Ben Burtt records a bear called Pooh.

at the USC film department, who highly recommends Ben Burtt. Gary Kurtz meets with Burtt to discuss Lucas's movie, and hires Burtt to create sound effects for spaceships, weapons, and a Wookiee. Burtt begins recording the sounds of animals and vehicles at various locations.

AUGUST

Third Draft

August 1: Lucas completes his third draft, now titled *The Star Wars: From the Adventures of Luke Starkiller*. Significant changes include Deak Starkiller being replaced by Princess Leia, and a previously unnamed old male Jedi becomes General Ben Kenobi. Possibly in keeping with Joseph Campbell's analysis of mythology, Luke Starkiller becomes a loner whose deceased father was a Jedi.

Casting Begins

Lucas's friend, producer Fred Roos, enlists casting director Dianne Crittenden to begin casting for *The Star Wars* at the Zoetrope offices at Goldwyn Studios. The early casting process tests about 250 actors a day for three weeks. Brian De Palma joins Lucas and looks for actors for his upcoming film of Stephen King's *Carrie*. De Palma considers a young Carrie Fisher for the title role.

Lucas Meets Joe Johnston

Needing someone to help with the re-design of concept models and to create storyboards for front-projection sequences, ILM's production manager Bob Shepherd hires Joe Johnston to start the art department. After meeting with Lucas and John Dykstra, Johnston re-designs the models so they will work better with the bluescreen process. Shepherd praises Johnston as "the only one" at ILM who "could really make images that you understood."

Johnston works on a Y-wing model

Storyboard art featuring a TIE fighter in battle above the Death Star

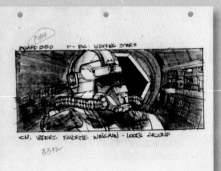

Storyboard art featuring Vader's wingman

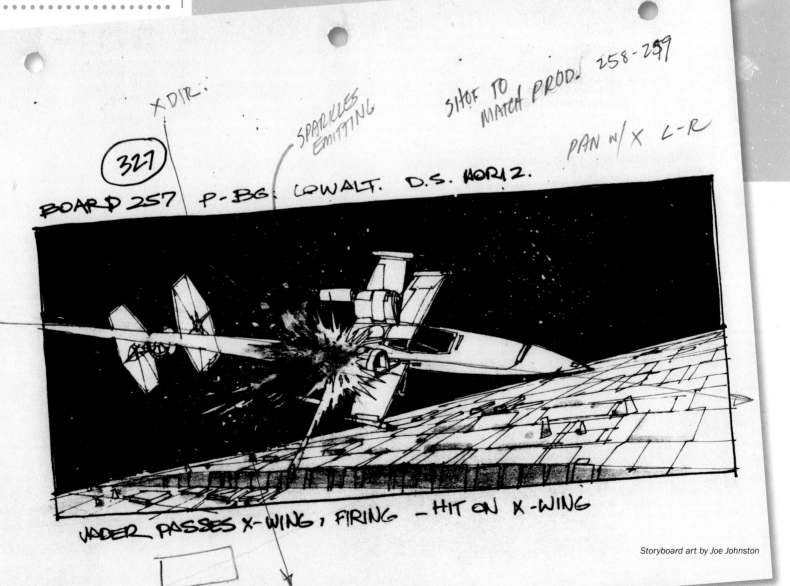

Storyboard art by Joe Johnston

42

SEPTEMBER

Anthony Daniels

Kenny Baker

David Prowse

Peter Mayhew

UK Casting

Because Lucas decides to film much of the movie in England, English actors are cast for the supporting roles, including prominent costumed characters. Anthony Daniels (b. 1946), an actor whose experience ranges from stage work to radio dramas and mime, is cast as C-3PO. Although a remote-controlled, motorized R2-D2 is planned for some scenes, an empty R2-D2 costume with a rotatable dome that requires a small actor leads to the casting of Kenny Baker (b. 1934), a cabaret performer. Offered the roles of either Darth Vader or Chewbacca, David Prowse (b. 1935) chooses the villain. Peter Mayhew (b. 1944), a porter at London's King's College Hospital, is cast as Chewbacca.

Mifune or Guinness?

Lucas, influenced by his admiration for Kurosawa, toys with the idea of casting a Japanese actor—possibly Toshirô Mifune from *The Hidden Fortress*—in the role of Ben Kenobi. However, famed English actor Alec Guinness receives a copy of the script and finds himself excited despite the sci-fi genre being a new direction for him. He is "impressed [by the] new breed of filmmaker."

Alec Guinness realizes the commercial potential in Star Wars and signs a contract that includes two percent of the net profits.

Space: 1999

September 4: The television series *Space: 1999* premieres in the UK. Created by Gerry and Sylvia Anderson, the science-fiction series stars Martin Landau and Barbara Bain, and features special effects by Brian Johnson. Guest actors include Peter Cushing, Christopher Lee, and David Prowse.

Lucas orders a redesign of Han Solo's "pirate ship" when he realizes it closely resembles Space: 1999's Eagle Transporter ship. Both were based on 2001's lunar shuttle.

Christopher Lee as Captain Zantor, an alien from a dying planet whose spacecraft crash lands on the Moon in the episode "Earthbound."

OCTOBER

Saturday Night Live

October 11: *Saturday Night Live,* a late-night variety show, premieres on NBC. The show's cast includes (from left) Laraine Newman, John Belushi, Jane Curtin, Gilda Radner, Garrett Morris, Dan Aykroyd, and Chevy Chase.

NOVEMBER

Happy Days

November 11: On *Happy Days,* Ron Howard and Cindy Williams reunite when Fonzie (Henry Winkler) introduces Richie (Howard) to Laverne DeFazio and Shirley Feeney (Penny Marshall and Williams) in the episode "A Date with Fonzie."

DECEMBER

Mark Hamill

Harrison Ford

Star Screentests

Although Lucas wants "unknown" actors for *The Star Wars,* Fred Roos thinks Harrison Ford would be ideal for Han Solo. Roos hires Ford—currently a professional carpenter—to install a door at the American Zoetrope offices. Roos also suggests to Lucas that Ford should read with "everybody." Lucas agrees. Video-taped actors include Amy Irving, William Katt, Kurt Russell, Perry King, Mark Hamill, Carrie Fisher, and *Graffiti* actors Cindy Williams and Charles Martin Smith. Ultimately, Hamill is cast as Luke Starkiller, Ford as Han Solo, and Fisher as Leia in January 1976.

Carrie Fisher

Metric Act Passed

December 23: Congress passes the Metric Conversion Act "to coordinate and plan the increasing use of the metric system in the United States." Defiant Americans stand by their yardsticks.

🌍 GENERAL FRANCO DIES & SPAIN STARTS ON ROAD TO DEMOCRACY 🌍

1976

BECAUSE TWENTIETH Century-Fox had almost no faith in *Star Wars*, it dragged on contract discussions. Nevertheless, Lucas negotiates to secure certain rights to sequels, licensing, and merchandising for *The Star Wars*. During the year, Lucas changes his movie's title to *Star Wars*, and Luke Starkiller becomes Luke Skywalker. Lucas also endures the most difficult shoot of his career thus far.

> "I was compromising right and left just to get things semi-done. I was desperately unhappy." **George Lucas**
> *after filming on location in Tunisia*

JANUARY

Fourth Draft
January 1: Lucas completes the fourth draft, titled *The Adventures of Luke Starkiller as taken from the "Journal of the Whills."* The draft begins with a fade in and the intro, "A long time ago, in a galaxy far, far away an incredible adventure took place…" Also, the desert planet previously known as "Utapau" is now "Tatooine," and Ben Kenobi does not die when he confronts Darth Vader on the Death Star. Lucas continues working on his script after filming commences.

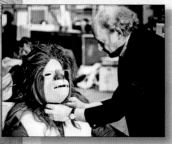

Costume and Makeup
Costume designer John Mollo and makeup artist Stuart Freeborn begin work on *The Star Wars*. Mollo had served as a historical advisor on Stanley Kubrick's *Barry Lyndon* (1975). Freeborn's career already spans four decades, and his credits include *Oliver Twist* (1948) and Kubrick's *Dr. Strangelove* (1964) and *2001: A Space Odyssey* (1968).

Concorde
January 21: The first commercial Concorde flights take place in the UK and France. Only two airlines have purchased the supersonic aircraft: British Airways and Air France. Their scheduled routes run from London to Bahrain, and from Paris to Rio (via Dakar).

New Sitcom
January 27: *Laverne & Shirley*, a spin-off from *Happy Days*, premieres on ABC. The sitcom stars Penny Marshall and Cindy Williams as employees at a brewery in Wisconsin.

The sale of the droids is the first scene to be shot.

MARCH

Actors Phil Brown (Uncle Owen) and Mark Hamill (Luke)

Filming Begins

March 22: Principal filming for *The Star Wars* begins in Tunisia. The bottom portion of a Jawa sandcrawler has already been constructed on the salt flats at Nefta, and awaits the cast and crew. Despite malfunctions with the remote-controlled R2-D2, an incredibly uncomfortable C-3PO costume for Anthony Daniels, and improvised pyrotechnics to blow up a red droid's head, the first scene is shot.

March 26: During the height of filming *The Star Wars*, Tunisia is hit with its first winter rainstorm in 50 years.

Change of Plan

Lucas decides that the story will be more dramatic if Ben Kenobi dies, sacrificing himself on the Death Star so that his allies can escape from Darth Vader. Lucas tells Alec Guinness of this decision, and also explains how Kenobi will disappear and survive as a spirit who can communicate with Luke. According to Lucas, Guinness is initially shocked, and responds, "You mean I get killed but I don't have a death scene?" Guinness soon admits to a journalist that he is "pretty much lost" by his requirements for the picture, but adds, "I simply trust the director."

Apocalypse Now

Apocalypse Now, directed by Francis Ford Coppola, begins filming. Shooting is scheduled for five months but takes over a year because of numerous problems. In the movie, Harrison Ford plays the small part of an officer.

APRIL

Mark Hamill, Alec Guinness, Gary Kurtz, and George Lucas

Alec Guinness's Birthday

April 2: Cast and crew celebrate Sir Alec Guinness's 62nd birthday while on location in Djerba, which doubles for the Mos Eisley spaceport.

③ BEN KENOBI.

8-1-76

go back to
FL Kimono +
Sash

Costume sketch for Ben Kenobi by John Mollo, January 8, 1976.
Before actor Alec Guinness is filmed for his first scene as Kenobi, he
puts on his brand new costume and lies down on the desert floor to
make his robe look used and dirty, which is consistent with George
Lucas's vision of Tatooine.

REBEL RANGERS
β3.

12-1-76

Costume sketches for "Rebel rangers" by John Mollo, January 12, 1976.
With his brother, Mollo has co-authored several books on military fashion, and
also worked as the historical and military advisor for *The Charge of the Light
Brigade* (1968) and *Nicolas and Alexander* (1971) before he is hired to design
costumes for *Star Wars*.

APRIL

Mark Hamill (Luke), Anthony Forrest (Fixer), Koo Stark (Camie), and Garrick Hagon (Biggs)

Above: Garrick Hagon and Mark Hamill in Djerba. Below: Harrison Ford (Han Solo) and Declan Mulholland (Jabba) at EMI Studios.

Tatooine Scenes

Following the suggestions of his friends Matt Robbins and Hal Barwood, who believe Luke should be introduced before the sale of the droids, Lucas films scenes of Luke observing a space battle. Luke then travels to Anchorhead so he can report his sighting to the local mechanic Fixer and his girlfriend Camie. Luke also meets his best friend, Biggs Darklighter, a cadet from the space academy. The Anchorhead scenes are filmed in Djerba on April 4, but are cut from the final film. By April 12, production has moved to EMI Studios (aka Elstree Studios) in England, where Lucas films Han Solo meeting Jabba the Hut [sic] at the Mos Eisley spaceport.

JULY

First Apple Computer

Founded three months earlier by Steve Jobs, Steve Wozniak, and Ronald Wayne, Apple Computer sells its first product, the Apple I Computer Kit, a hand-built circuit board. The Apple I costs $666.66, and does not include a keyboard, monitor, or case.

The Apple I Computer

Charles Lippincott Slide Show

July 2–5: *Star Wars* is still filming in England as Lucas's *Star Wars* publicist Charles Lippincott presents a promotional slide show for the movie at the Hyatt House Hotel at Los Angeles's Westercon.

Charles Lippincott reveals a slide image of Carrie Fisher as Princess Leia to an audience at the Westercon comic convention.

Entebbe Rescue

July 4: The Israel Defense Forces rescues 103 hostages held by Palestinian hijackers of an Air France passenger plane at Entebbe Airport in Uganda. The hostage-rescue mission is codenamed Operation Thunderball.

Bicentennial

July 4: The United States Bicentennial celebrates the 200th anniversary of the Declaration of Independence with a fireworks extravaganza in New York City.

All-Stars and Motor Kings

July 16: *The Bingo Long Traveling All-Stars & Motor Kings* is released. It is directed by John Badham and co-written by Lucas's friend Hal Barwood.

The Bingo Long Traveling All-Stars & Motor Kings stars future Star Wars actors Billy Dee Williams (left) and James Earl Jones (middle), as well as Richard Pryor (right) as 1930s baseball players fighting racial segregation.

🌐 SYRIAN TROOPS ENTER LEBANON

Poster 1   1st Edition Artist: Howard Chaykin **Luke Skywalker** © The Star Wars Corporation 1976

Comic-Con

July 21–25: Having negotiated a deal with Marvel Comics to adapt *Star Wars* as a comic book series, Charles Lippincott and the creative team attend the San Diego Comic Book Convention at the El Cortez Hotel. Lucas has personally selected editor/writer Roy Thomas and artist Howard Chaykin for the adaptation. Lucas is a fan of Thomas's work on *Conan the Barbarian*, and Chaykin's *Cody Starbuck* in the fantasy comic anthology *Star Reach*.

Howard Chaykin's promotional poster sells for $1.75 at the 1976 Comic-Con.

Last Day Shooting

July 23: Second-unit shooting for *Star Wars* is completed at EMI Studios, but some additional scenes still remain to be shot in the US.

Lucas visits Spielberg

After leaving England, Lucas stops in Mobile, Alabama, to visit Spielberg on the set of *Close Encounters of the Third Kind*, and shows him stills from *Star Wars*. Spielberg is amazed by the stills, but Lucas seems disappointed with everything about the movie.

AUGUST

Beyond Stressful

August 1: Lucas returns to ILM to discover that "they'd spent half their budget, and had only one shot in the can." 360 effects shots remain, and they have only eight months left. Flying back from ILM, Lucas experiences severe chest pains, and he proceeds to a hospital after landing in the Bay Area, where he stays overnight. He is discharged the next day after doctors determine he had not been having a heart attack.

OWETO RIOTS IN SOUTH AFRICA ✪ CN TOWER OPENS IN TORONTO ✪ *VIKING 1* LANDS ON MARS ✪

SEPTEMBER

Worldcon

September 2–6: Advance promotion continues with the display of *Star Wars* art, costumes, and props at the World Science Fiction Convention, aka Worldcon, in Kansas City.

Lippincott, Kurtz, and Hamill at Worldcon

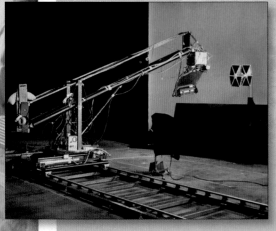

The Dykstraflex (above) is just one of the innovative technologies developed by ILM. Separate contraptions for filming the starships (below, seen with first cameraman Richard Edlund and model builder Paul Huston) have to be constructed from scratch.

Breaking New Ground

ILM is under increasing pressure to create the special effects to schedule. After a slow, disorganized, and difficult start, the team gains experience and puts its newly acquired technical knowledge to effective use, even developing pioneering techniques of its own, such as mastering motion control photography with the Dykstraflex. Helped out by several external effects houses, not to mention the number of employees working 16-hour shifts and sleeping on site, ILM manages to complete most of the movie's effects in time.

Dr. James D. Fletcher (far left), NASA Administrator, with Star Trek cast members and Gene Roddenberry (third from right), series creator.

Space Shuttle *Enterprise*

September 17: The first space shuttle orbiter prototype is named *Enterprise* at a dedication ceremony in Palmdale, California. Originally intended as *Constitution*, the Approach and Landing Test craft's new name is the result of a write-in campaign that favored the USS *Enterprise* from the television series *Star Trek*. Gene Roddenberry and most of the cast of *Star Trek* attend the ceremony.

OCTOBER

VHS to Rival Betamax

October 9: A new video cassette system, manufactured by JVC, is released. "VHS" originally stands for Vertical Helical Scan, but becomes Video Home System. The JVC HR-3300 is priced at $1,400.

NOVEMBER

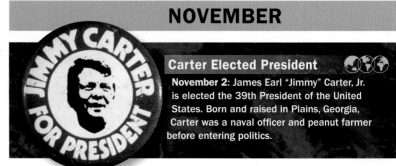

Carter Elected President

November 2: James Earl "Jimmy" Carter, Jr. is elected the 39th President of the United States. Born and raised in Plains, Georgia, Carter was a naval officer and peanut farmer before entering politics.

VIKING 2 LANDS ON MARS ❂ THE CHIMPANZEE BECOMES A THREATENED SPECIES ❂ CHAIRMA

GEORGE LUCAS, THE MAN WHO BROUGHT YOU <u>AMERICAN GRAFFITI</u>, NOW BRINGS YOU AN ADVENTURE AS BIG AS THE COSMOS ITSELF: <u>STAR WARS</u>, THE STORY OF A BOY, A GIRL, AND A UNIVERSE. IT'S A SPECTACLE LIGHT YEARS AHEAD OF ITS TIME. FROM 20TH CENTURY-FOX.

First "Teaser" Theatrical Advance Poster

The original *Star Wars* logo features a "W" with vertical ascenders. ILM concept artist Joe Johnston subsequently redesigns the logo to make it work better for the planned shot of the film's opening credits.

Carrie

November 3: *Carrie* is released. Directed by Brian De Palma and based on the novel by Stephen King, the horror film stars Sissy Spacek and John Travolta.

Amy Irving (left) and William Katt (above) tested for the roles of Princess Leia and Luke Skywalker but were hired by De Palma instead.

Also in 1976...

Crew Patch
One of Ralph McQuarrie's designs for a *Star Wars* logo is utilized on this patch for crew members.

Star Wars Novelization

November 12: Del Rey publishes the *Star Wars* novelization. The book's cover reveals that Ralph McQuarrie continues to modify Vader's appearance. In a 2004 interview for *Star Wars Insider* #76, McQuarrie recalls, "George looked at the helmet and said it never looked better!" Although the book is credited to George Lucas, it is in fact ghostwritten by Alan Dean Foster, who works from various drafts of Lucas's screenplay. Foster has previously written the novelization for John Carpenter's and Dan O'Bannon's *Dark Star* and several *Star Trek* novels. The novel identifies the Emperor as Palpatine, Darth Vader as a Sith Lord, and includes Luke witnessing the opening sequence's space battle and his meeting with Biggs on Tatooine (scenes cut from the film), and Han Solo's meeting with Jabba the Hut [sic]. Foster's contract is a two-book deal.

Star Wars novelization cover art by Ralph McQuarrie

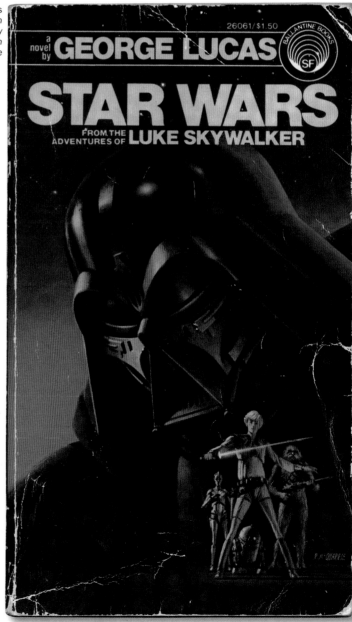

ILM's Richard Edlund adjusts the *Millennium Falcon* model used for motion control photography during production of *Star Wars*. Designed by Joe Johnston after conversations with George Lucas, the *Falcon*'s shape—a flying disc with a starboard outrigger cockpit—was inspired by the shape of a hamburger.

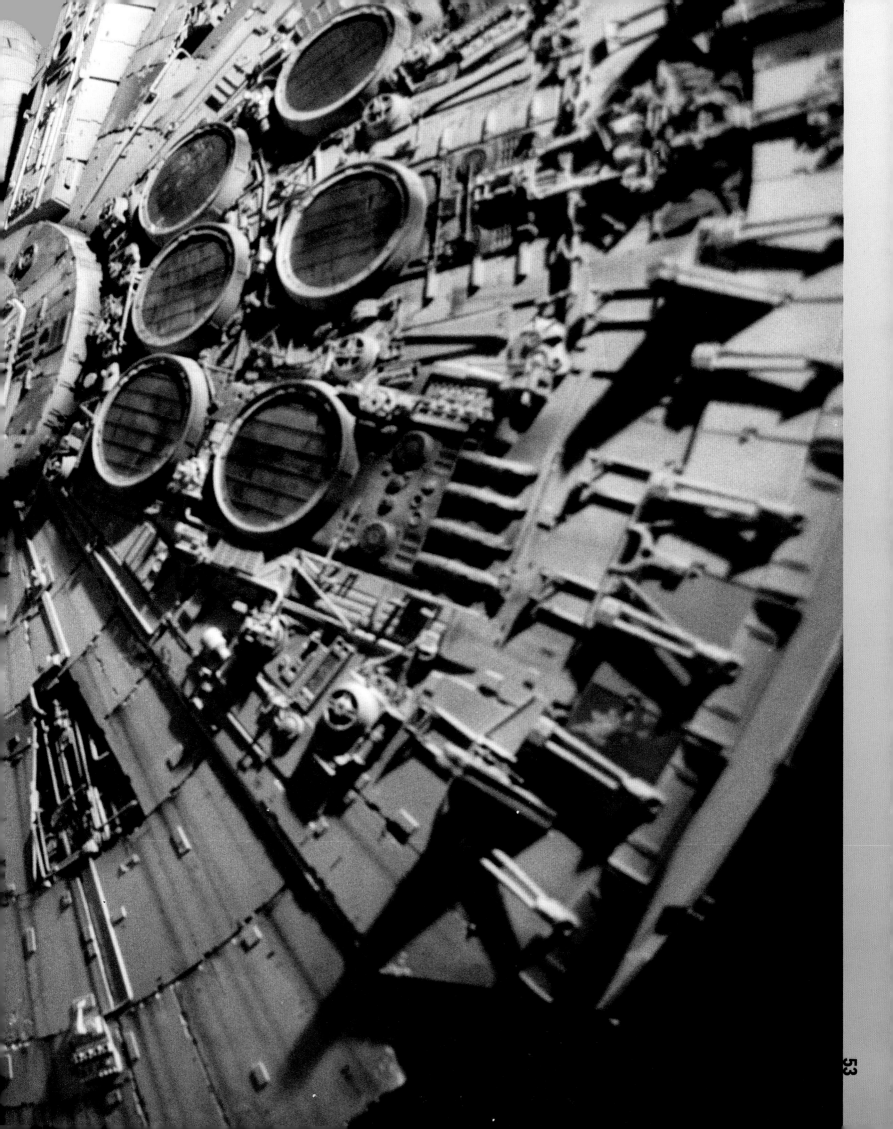

1977

IN THE EARLY MONTHS of 1977, George Lucas's ILM team is still working frantically to complete visual effects shots for *Star Wars*, and three editors are working long hours to assemble the footage into a cohesive story. Last-minute additions of a monocular monster for the trash compactor scene and a matte painting of the Mos Eisley Cantina's exterior are among the film's final shots. Lucas's highest expectation for *Star Wars* is that it will break even at the box office.

> "It was a darn good story dashingly told, and beyond that I can't explain it."
>
> **Alec Guinness**
> *asked about the success of*
> Star Wars *in a 1979 interview*

JANUARY

Hostage Drama

January 9: *Raid on Entebbe* airs on NBC television. Directed by Irvin Kershner, and starring Peter Finch, Charles Bronson, and Yaphet Kotto, the film is a dramatization of how the Israel Defense Forces rescued Israeli hostages from Palestinian terrorists at Entebbe Airport in Uganda in 1976.

Hamill Injured

January 11: Mark Hamill crashes his new BMW on the Antelope Valley Freeway in California, and requires reconstructive surgery to his face. A body double replaces Hamill for the final shooting of additional scenes with the landspeeder, filmed at China Lake Acres, north of Los Angeles.

MARCH

Star Wars Soundtrack

March 5–16: John Williams conducts the London Symphony Orchestra to record the *Star Wars* soundtrack. It is recorded over the course of 14 sessions at Anvil Studios in Denham, England.

The First *Star Wars* Comic

March 8: The first issue of Marvel Comics' six-issue adaptation of *Star Wars* hits the stands with a cover date of July. Writer Roy Thomas and artist Howard Chaykin work from Lucas's screenplay and limited visual reference to create the comic, which includes the scene where Luke witnesses the space battle over Tatooine before he meets Biggs Darklighter at Anchorhead—a scene that Lucas has already decided to cut from the film. Chaykin and Tom Palmer collaborate on the cover art, which echoes the layout of the poster Chaykin had created for the previous year's San Diego Comic-Con. On the cover, both Luke and Ben Kenobi wield red lightsabers, and Darth Vader's helmet is green. Twentieth Century-Fox executives doubt the promotional value of the comic adaptation, but *Star Wars* #1 quickly sells out.

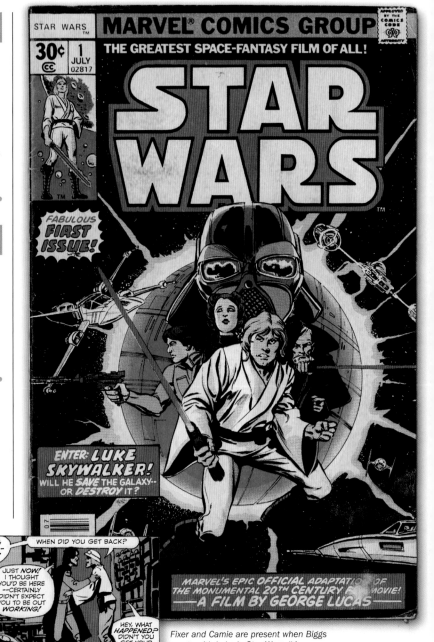

Fixer and Camie are present when Biggs meets with Luke in Star Wars #1.

APRIL

Star Wars Comic #2

April 12: Marvel's *Star Wars* #2 ships (cover date August). The issue features Han Solo's meeting with Jabba. Lucasfilm had informed the comic's creative team that Jabba would not appear in the film, but allows penciller Chaykin to base Jabba's likeness on a photograph of an alien that the film's production department called variously "Walrus," "Ming," or "Mingo."

Jabba and his goons confront Han Solo in Mos Eisley

Style "A" theatrical one-sheet (above) by Tom Jung. Fox hires comic artist Nick Cardy to add the droids and adjust details on Luke and Leia's clothing.

Posters by Tom Jung

Commissioned to create a poster for *Star Wars*, artist Tom Jung loosely bases Luke and Leia's pose on the heroic-action style of famed fantasy artist Frank Frazetta, and adds a white streak across the top of the lightsaber beam to form a cross.

Below: Tom Jung designs this half-sheet before creating the Style "A" poster.

Star Wars Comic #3

May 10: Marvel's *Star Wars* #3 ships (cover date September). In this issue, the *Millennium Falcon* enters the Death Star. Because of limited visual reference for the comic's creative team, the *Falcon* lacks laser cannon turrets, and the Death Star does not appear nearly as immense as it will in the film.

Cover art for Star Wars #3 by Howard Chaykin and Tom Palmer

MAY

Sneak Preview

May 1: The first public screening of *Star Wars* takes place in San Francisco's Northpoint Theater. To maintain secrecy, the invitation-only preview screening is advertised on the marquee as the world premiere of "Alaska." Although the sound mix is not complete, the preview is a huge success with the audience.

Interior art for Star Wars #3 by Howard Chaykin and Steve Leialoha

The audience gathers for the preview. They received their invites as flyers handed out at movie theaters.

Also in 1977...

Vader Promotion

Charles Lippincott enlists Kermit Eller, an employee at Don Post Studios, to wear the Darth Vader costume at the American Booksellers Association Convention in San Francisco in May. Eller will continue to personify Darth Vader at future public events.

Eller's Darth Vader costume is an actual prop from the movie.

In November, readers are invited to meet Darth Vader in person.

The Release

STAR WARS OPENS in 32 theaters in Los Angeles, San Francisco, and New York on May 25. Lucas is sitting in a Hamburger Hamlet across the street from Mann's Chinese Theatre (previously Grauman's Chinese Theatre) when he sees a huge crowd, and then limousines pull up. Mann's Chinese Theatre has the biggest opening day in its 50-year history, taking in $19,358 at approximately $4 a ticket. The limousines belong to *Playboy* founder Hugh Hefner and his entourage, who watch the movie twice in a row.

SPECIAL PRIVATE SCREENING

STAR WARS

MONDAY, MAY 2, 1977 - 7:30 P.M.

MGM SCREENING ROOM, MGM STUDIOS

10202 W. WASHINGTON BLVD., CULVER CITY

ADMIT ONE

Private Screening
A ticket to the exclusive private screening of Star Wars, held at MGM Studios on May 2.

Worldwide Release Dates

USA
25 May 1977

France
19 October 1977

Italy
21 October 1977

Australia
27 October 1977

Brazil
18 November 1977

UK
27 December 1977

Hong Kong
26 January 1978

Japan
30 June 1978

Book Now
A Star Wars handbill urges the public to book tickets and see "The Year's Best Movie."

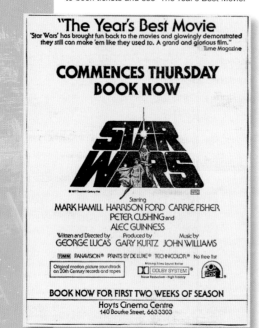

"The Year's Best Movie
'Star Wars' has brought fun back to the movies and glowingly demonstrated they still can make 'em like they used to. A grand and glorious film."
Time Magazine

**COMMENCES THURSDAY
BOOK NOW**

STAR WARS

Starring
MARK HAMILL HARRISON FORD CARRIE FISHER
PETER CUSHING and
ALEC GUINNESS
Written and Directed by   Produced by   Music by
GEORGE LUCAS GARY KURTZ JOHN WILLIAMS
70MM PANAVISION® PRINTS BY DE LUXE® TECHNICOLOR® No free list
Original motion picture soundtrack on 20th Century records and tapes DOLBY SYSTEM

BOOK NOW FOR FIRST TWO WEEKS OF SEASON
Hoyts Cinema Centre
140 Bourke Street, 6633303

A long time ago in a galaxy far, far away...

STAR WARS

TWENTIETH CENTURY-FOX Presents
A LUCASFILM LTD. PRODUCTION
STAR WARS
Starring MARK HAMILL HARRISON FORD CARRIE FISHER
PETER CUSHING
and
ALEC GUINNESS
Written and Directed by GEORGE LUCAS Produced by GARY KURTZ Music by JOHN WILLIAMS
PANAVISION® PRINTS BY DE LUXE® TECHNICOLOR®
PG PARENTAL GUIDANCE SUGGESTED Original Motion Picture Soundtrack on 20th Century Records and Tapes DOLBY SYSTEM

Speedy Poster
Because of their recent work on a Lord of the Rings calendar, twin brothers Greg and Tim Hildebrandt are popular fan-favorites among fantasy art aficionados. Commissioned to do a Star Wars poster based on Tom Jung's composition, the Hildebrandts collaborate to complete their work in about 36 hours.

Surprise Screening
Lucas is surprised to see Star Wars premiering at Mann's because it had not been scheduled to screen there. But when William Friedkin's Sorcerer (1977) is delayed, Star Wars fills the vacancy.

STAR WARS

Cast and Crew Screening

Before Star Wars *is released to the general public, Lucas holds a private screening for cast and crew on May 21, 1977. The screening is held at the Academy Award Theater in Beverly Hills.*

Photo Display

Star Wars *photographs are displayed outside Mann's Chinese Theatre.*

Teaser Poster

Printed for small billboards, the Star Wars *teaser "B" seven-sheet is displayed only in cities that are screening* Star Wars *in 70mm. It is the only* Star Wars *poster that has the May 25 release date.*

Souvenir Program

Published by Lucasfilm licensee George Fenmore Associates and sold in theater lobbies, the Star Wars *souvenir program has cover art (above) featuring one of Tom Jung's posters and 18 pages of information about the production, cast, and characters (detail at right).*

Lines at Loews

Long lines form outside Loews at Astor Plaza in Manhattan (pictured), and also at the Orpheum. Six days after opening, the total box office for Star Wars *is a very healthy $2.5 million.*

MAY

Lucas and Spielberg

An exhausted Lucas arrives in Hawaii for a short vacation. Steven Spielberg joins him, and they build a sandcastle on the Mauna Kea hotel beach. After Spielberg expresses his interest in directing a James Bond movie, Lucas discusses his own idea for *Raiders of the Lost Ark*, the adventures of Indiana Smith. Because the hero's name reminds Spielberg of the film title *Nevada Smith* (1966), Lucas later changes it to Indiana Jones.

JUNE

Grand Theft Auto

June 16: *Grand Theft Auto* is released. Executive produced by Roger Corman, and filmed in just 15 days, the comedy chase movie is the first feature film directed by Ron Howard, who is also the co-writer and star.

Darth Vadar

Factors, Etc. releases a licensed series of *Star Wars* pin-back badges, including one on which Darth Vader's name is misspelled. Meanwhile, tons of bootleg buttons and badges are also in circulation.

JULY

Disco Album

Star Wars and Other Galactic Funk by Meco (real name Domenico Monardo) is released by Millennium Records. The instrumental music album includes the *Star Wars* theme reworked as a disco tune.

C-3PO on *People*

July 18: C-3PO is on the cover of *People* magazine, which features short interviews with *Star Wars*'s director and cast. Lucas maintains he is through with directing "because I don't enjoy being the boss. If I do a sequel, I'll be an executive producer."

Also in 1977...

California Originals releases a series of *Star Wars* tankards sculpted by Jim Rumph. Lucas first imagined *Star Wars* merchandise while working on the screenplay; he found himself wishing he had a Wookiee mug.

AUGUST

Cards and Masks

Topps, Inc. releases its first series of *Star Wars* cards, consisting of 66 cards and 11 stickers. The backs of the cards contain either facts about the movie, story summaries, or photo fragments that can be assembled into a puzzle. Don Post Studios releases a series of *Star Wars* character masks.

Star Wars masks are advertised in a variety of magazines.

A Luke Skywalker card and Tusken Raider sticker

Footprints at Mann's

August 3: C-3PO (Anthony Daniels), Darth Vader (Kermit Eller), and R2-D2 (remote-controlled by Mick Garris) set their hand and footprints in the concrete forecourt at Mann's Chinese Theatre. Gary Kurtz supplies the signature for the handprint-challenged R2-D2 while John Williams's *Star Wars* score blares from loudspeakers.

A crowd of 8,000 turns out to see some of their favorite Star Wars characters at Mann's Chinese Theatre.

Gary Kurtz watches Darth Vader (Kermit Eller) leave his mark in wet concrete.

APPLE II COMPUTER GOES ON SALE ⊕ A 25-HOUR BLACKOUT IN NEW YORK CITY ⊕ "SON OF SAM"

Also in 1977...

Star Wars Digest

Given the success of the film, the *Star Wars* story is released in digest form in August, 1977. The story is adapted from *The Adventures of Luke Skywalker*, written by George Lucas.

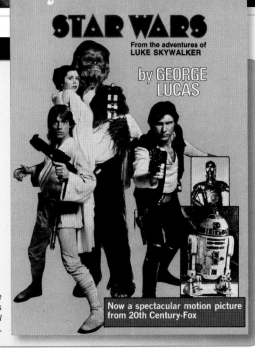

This digest form of the Star Wars novel does not use the traditional Star Wars logo.

Re-Release of *THX 1138*

THX 1138 is re-issued by Warner Bros., as the studio hopes to exploit Lucas's success with *Star Wars*. Despite Warner's marketing and the reinstatement of the five minutes of film that had been deleted from the original release, *THX 1138* does not become a commercial success, but it later gains cult appreciation.

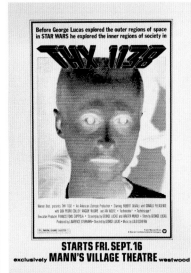

Also in 1977...

"Star Jaws!"

Spider-Man meets *Star Wars* in Marvel's *Spidey* comic #31 (cover date February), written by Kolfax Mingo. The web-spinning superhero stars as Luke Skywalker while Dr. Doom takes on the part of Vader.

Donny and Marie

September 23: The sibling team of Donny and Marie Osmond perform an elaborate *Star Wars*–themed musical sequence on *The Donny & Marie Show* on ABC. The sequence also features Kris Kristofferson, Paul Lynde, Redd Foxx, Anthony Daniels, Peter Mayhew, and a remote-controlled R2-D2. Darth Vader is voiced by Thurl Ravenscroft, best known as the voice of Tony the Tiger.

The King

August 16: Elvis Presley, the entertainer who revolutionized popular music and was known as "The King of Rock and Roll," dies in his mansion home, Graceland, in Memphis, Tennessee.

Rolling Stone

August 25: The cast of *Star Wars* is on the cover of *Rolling Stone*. Interviewed by Paul Scanlon, Lucas reiterates his intention to retire from directing, and reveals that one of his ideas for a *Star Wars* sequel is "the young days of Ben Kenobi." Asked for details, he replies, "It's about Ben and Luke's father and Vader when they are young Jedi Knights. But Vader kills Luke's father, then Ben and Vader have a confrontation, just like they have in *Star Wars*, and Ben almost kills Vader. As a matter of fact, he falls into a volcanic pit and gets fried and is one destroyed being."

The Making of Star Wars

September 16: *The Making of Star Wars* is broadcast on ABC television. Executive produced by Gary Kurtz, directed by Robert Guenette, written by Richard Schickel, narrated by William Conrad, and hosted by C-3PO (Anthony Daniels) and R2-D2 (Kenny Baker), the documentary features interviews with the cast and crew of *Star Wars*.

Escape from the Death Star

Kenner releases the first *Star Wars* board game, *Escape From the Death Star*. The game is extremely popular and is reproduced all over the world, in countries that include Japan, Germany, Italy, and France.

SEPTEMBER

September 5: NASA launches *Voyager 1*, a robotic space probe. It is designed to take advantage of the relatively new technique of gravity-assisted speed boosts, which use the gravity of planetary bodies for a "slingshot effect" to economize fuel, time, and money. *Voyager 1*'s mission is to study the planets and boundaries of the solar system.

The Italian movie, Star Pilot (left), is also known as 2+5: Missione Hydra, and the German 2069 (right), as Ach Jodel Mir Noch Einen.

Star Wars Bandwagon

September 26: Two space–themed movies are released, cashing in on *Star Wars* mania. But *Star Pilot* (originally released 1966) and *2069: A Sex Odyssey* (1974) fail to make a cinematic impact.

Star Wars Sketchbook

September: *The Star Wars Sketchbook* is published. Featuring concept and production sketches by Joe Johnston, the book's entry for TIE fighters indicates that TIE is an acronym for Twin Ion Engine, and also includes a design for a "TIE Boarding Craft."

Sketch of TIE fighters traveling alongside a TIE boarding craft

Cover art for The Star Wars Sketchbook

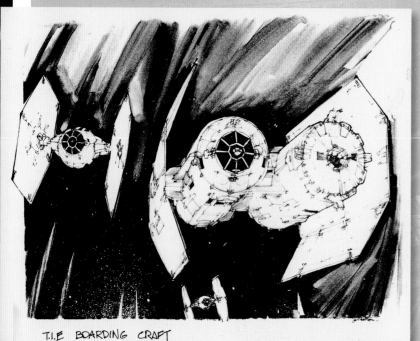

T.I.E BOARDING CRAFT

OCTOBER

Pizzazz

Marvel Comics publishes *Pizzazz* #1, a popular culture monthly magazine, with C-3PO and R2-D2 on the cover. The first issue features the beginning of an exclusive, serialized *Star Wars* comic story.

Galactic Funk #1

October 1: Meco's *Star Wars And Other Galactic Funk* album is #1 on the *Billboard* chart, where it stays for two weeks.

Also in 1977...

Lunchboxes

Metal and plastic *Star Wars* lunchboxes are produced in the US by King Seeley Thermos. The metal lunchbox comes in two versions, with either a star field or character art around the sides, and a plastic thermos jug.

NOVEMBER

Also in 1977...

LED Watch

This Microelectronic Digital *Star Wars* watch, from Texas Instruments, is one of a few licensed merchandise items that are released following the success of *Star Wars*.

Box art for the Early Bird Certificate Package

Early Bird Package

Unable to release *Star Wars* action figures in time for Christmas because of the lead time required for production, Kenner releases the Early Bird Certificate Package, which quickly becomes known as the "empty box." The box does in fact contain a mail-in voucher for the first four *Star Wars* action figures, and a promise that the toys will ship in early 1978.

The package includes a mail-in certificate, a colorful display stand (left), and stickers.

VOYAGER I LAUNCHES ☀ PELÉ PLAYS FINAL SOCCER GAME ☀ ATARI 2600 RELEASED ☀ OUTER

Heroes Released

November 4: *Heroes* is released. Directed by Jeremy Kagan, the drama about traumatized Vietnam veterans stars Henry Winkler, Sally Field, and Harrison Ford.

The Godfather Revised

November 12: NBC broadcasts the first of four episodes of *The Godfather: A Novel for Television*, a re-edited version of Coppola's first two *Godfather* movies. Coppola adds previously cut footage and presents the tale of Don Corleone—played by Robert De Niro in flashback sequences in *The Godfather: Part II*, and by Marlon Brando in *The Godfather*—in chronological order.

Close Encounters of the Third Kind

November 16: *Close Encounters of the Third Kind* is released. Written and directed by Steven Spielberg, the adventure drama about aliens visiting Earth stars Richard Dreyfuss, Melinda Dillon, and Teri Garr. The movie features special effects by Douglas Trumbull, an alien "mother ship" designed by Ralph McQuarrie, and a story-integral musical score by John Williams. *Star Wars* model kits were cannibalized as parts of the alien mother ship, and an inverted R2-D2 is briefly visible on the ship's rim in one scene.

Hollywood Bowl

November 20: Zubin Mehta conducts the Los Angeles Philharmonic in the first public *Star Wars* concert, which is staged at the sold-out Hollywood Bowl. Composer John Williams had written the "Suite from *Star Wars*" exclusively for the event, which also includes a poetry reading by *Star Trek*'s William Shatner and a laser show.

Laser Media produces the laser show while Zubin Mehta conducts the Star Wars concert.

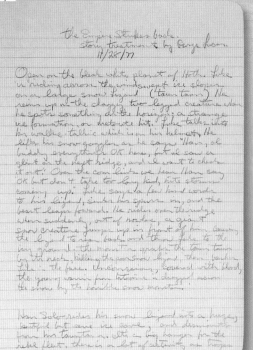

First page of Lucas's story treatment for Empire

Early *Empire*

November 28: Lucas completes the story treatment for the first *Star Wars* sequel, *The Empire Strikes Back*. The treatment opens with Luke Skywalker being attacked and bashed in the face by a "giant snow creature," a story point that addresses Mark Hamill's facial wounds from his car accident in January 1977. Lucas hires Leigh Brackett to write the *Empire* screenplay.

DECEMBER

Saturday Night Fever

December 16: *Saturday Night Fever* is released. Directed by John Badham and featuring music by the Bee Gees, the movie stars John Travolta as Tony Manero, who rules the disco dance floor at a Brooklyn Club named 2001 Odyssey.

Bob Hope Christmas Special

December 19: *The Bob Hope All Star Christmas Comedy Special* is broadcast on NBC television. Mark Hamill guest stars as Luke Skywalker in a skit titled *Scar Wars*, which features Bob Hope as Bar Vader. The *Special* also features Kermit the Frog and Miss Piggy, performed respectively by Jim Henson and Frank Oz.

Also in 1977...

Theological View

The Force of Star Wars by Frank Allnutt is published by Spire Books. The author makes numerous associations between *Star Wars* and Biblical scripture, and likens Governor Tarkin and Darth Vader to Satan and the Antichrist. Allnut also predicts an "invasion from outer space" by "Jesus Christ and his believers returning in triumph."

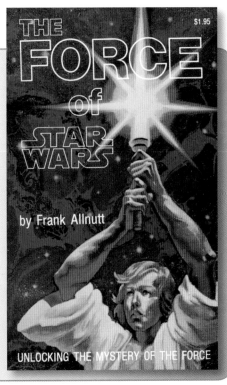

Cover art for The Force of Star Wars. Later editions were retitled Unlocking the Mystery of the Force.

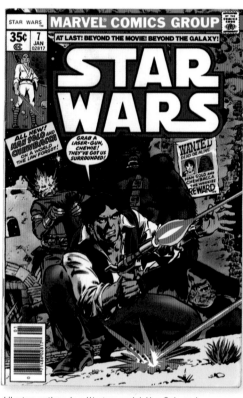

Like two outlaws in a Western serial, Han Solo and Chewbacca find themselves near a "WANTED" poster bearing their likenesses. Star Wars #7 (cover date January) ships on September 13, 1977, and features the story "New Planets, New Perils," co-written by Roy Thomas and Howard Chaykin, with art by Chaykin and Frank Springer, and cover art by Gil Kane and Tony Di Zuniga.

Beginning with issue #7, the Marvel *Star Wars* series tells the first stories of what would become the Expanded Universe. Han Solo and Chewbacca, hoping to pay off their debt to Jabba the Hutt, instead run into the familiar triangular outline of an Imperial Star Destroyer. This time, however, the warship belongs to notorious space pirate Crimson Jack.

1978

AFTER CONSIDERING a number of potential directors for the next *Star Wars* movie, Lucas enlists Irvin Kershner in early 1978. Kershner is 54 years old and has never directed a big visual effects movie, but Lucas admires his work, especially *Raid on Entebbe* (1977), which was produced in a short time frame.

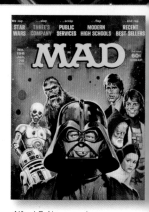

Alfred E. Neuman dons Darth Vader's helmet in MAD magazine's parody of Star Wars.

> "I told George the only way I'd do the film is if I felt I could top the first one. He laughed and said that's why he wanted me to do it."
>
> **Irvin Kershner**

JANUARY

Hardware Wars

Hardware Wars is released. Written, produced, and directed by Ernie Fosselius, the 13-minute *Star Wars* parody features "spaceships" that are obviously household appliances dangling from strings. Filmed in four days at a production cost of about $8,000, and promoted with the tagline, "You'll laugh, you'll cry, you'll kiss three bucks goodbye," *Hardware Wars* proceeds to gross $500,000.

A cassette player doubles as a spaceship.

Fluke Starbucker (Scott Matthews), Augie "Ben" Doggie (Jeff Hale), Ham Salad (Bob Knickerbocker), and Chewchilla the Wookiee Monster

Early Bird Delivers

Toy-buyers who took advantage of Kenner's Early Bird mail-in offer receive the first four action figures—Luke Skywalker with a double-telescoping lightsaber, Princess Leia, Chewbacca with a greenish-colored bowcaster, and R2-D2—along with plastic "foot pegs" that allow the figures to stand on the cardboard stage that came with the Early Bird package.

The first four figures to arrive as part of Kenner's Early Bird offer

Cosmos 954

January 24: Cosmos 954, a Soviet reconnaissance satellite with a decaying orbit and an onboard nuclear reactor, re-enters Earth's atmosphere. The USSR claims the satellite is destroyed during re-entry, but a joint American-Canadian team finds radioactive debris over a wide area of Canadian territory.

FEBRUARY

Brackett's First Draft

February 17: Leigh Brackett completes her first draft of a script titled *Star Wars Sequel, from The Adventures of Luke Skywalker*. Although her script is superficially faithful to Lucas's story treatment, Lucas finds the dialogue and actions of the characters inconsistent with his vision of *Star Wars*.

Grammy Awards

February 23: Composer John Williams wins three Grammy Awards for the *Star Wars* soundtrack: Best Instrumental Composition (for "Main Title from *Star Wars*"), Best Original Score Written for a Motion Picture or a Television Special, and Best Pop Instrumental Performance.

At Shrine Auditorium in Los Angeles, John Williams leaves the National Academy of Recording Arts & Sciences' 20th Annual Grammy Awards with three gilded gramophone statuettes (aka "Grammys").

February 27: Lucasfilm incorporates a new division, Black Falcon Ltd., to handle the company's new licensing endeavors during the period that certain merchandising rights revert to Lucasfilm from Fox.

🌐 **BOMB EXPLODES AT SYDNEY HILTON, AUSTRALIA** 🌐 **FIRST COMPUTER BULLETIN BOARD SYSTE**

MARCH

First Retail Figures

The first 12 *Star Wars* figures go on sale in stores. Except for the shorter characters like R2-D2, the poseable figures are 9.5 centimeters (3¾ inches) tall—substantially smaller than G.I. Joe and Mego figures. By year's end, Kenner sells more than 42 million *Star Wars* toys.

The Luke Skywalker action figure has five points of articulation.

Cee-Threepio *Artoo-Detoo* *Jawa*

Luke Skywalker *Princess Leia* *Han Solo* *Ben Kenobi*

Sand People *Chewbacca* *Darth Vader* *Death Squad Commander* *Stormtrooper*

A Second Mail Away

Kenner offers a plastic Action Collector's Stand that is more substantial than the cardboard stand that was included in their Early Bird package. The stand has miniature turntables for the first 12 *Star Wars* figures.

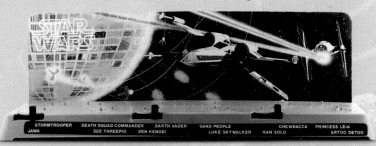

The plastic Action Collector's Stand from Kenner's second Star Wars mail away offer

Splinter of the Mind's Eye

March 1: Del Rey publishes *Splinter of the Mind's Eye*, a novel by Alan Dean Foster based on story discussions with Lucas. Written while *Star Wars* was still in production, *Splinter* features Luke, Leia, C-3PO, and R2-D2 in an adventure that leads to a devastating encounter with Darth Vader on a jungle world. The story also reveals that Luke can swim, but Leia cannot. *Starlog* magazine notes that Foster's *Star Wars* contract "allows *Splinter* to be filmed in the future, perhaps as one of the nine planned sequels to the original film." Notably absent from the story is Han Solo because Harrison Ford—unlike Mark Hamill and Carrie Fisher—is not already contracted for sequels.

Cover art by Ralph McQuarrie

Laserblast

March 1: *Laserblast* is released. Directed by Michael Rae and starring Kim Milford, the science-fiction movie features the destruction of a *Star Wars* billboard.

March 18: Scriptwriter Leigh Brackett dies of cancer.

APRIL

Vinyl Cape Jawa

Kenner releases a Jawa action figure with a vinyl cape, but later decides that the diminutive Jawa will have more sales appeal with a cloth cape.

The discontinued "vinyl cape" Jawa becomes a hard-to-find collectible, especially in carded mint condition.

The popular culture magazine *Pizzazz*, published by Marvel Comics from 1977 to 1979, features *Star Trek*'s Mr. Spock, a *Close Encounters* alien, and Darth Vader on the cover of issue #7.

50th Academy Awards®

April 3: *Star Wars* wins six Oscars at the 50th Academy Awards®, which is hosted by Bob Hope. Ben Burtt receives a Special Achievement Award for his sound effects for alien, creature, and droid voices.

Star Wars Academy Award® Nominations: Best Picture: Gary Kurtz and George Lucas; Best Director: George Lucas; Best Supporting Actor: Alec Guinness; Best Original Screenplay: George Lucas; Best Music Original Score: **John Williams**; Best Editing: **Marcia Lucas, Paul Hirsch, and Richard Chew**; Best Visual Effects: **John Stears, John Dykstra, Richard Edlund, Grant McCune and, Robert Blalack**; Best Costume Design: **John Mollo**; Best Art Direction: **John Barry**; Best Sound: **Don MacDougall, Ray West, Bob Minkler, and Derek Ball**.

(Bold indicates winners)

Mark Hamill presents Ben Burtt with the Special Achievement Award alongside C-3PO and R2-D2.

The snowy landscape of Finse in Norway

Location, Location

April 4: Director Irvin Kershner, producer Gary Kurtz, associate producer Robert Watts, production designer Norman Reynolds, executive producer George Lucas, and John Barry, who remains a consultant, have a general meeting in Los Angeles. They review photographs of possible locations for the worlds of the sequel, and agree that the treeless expanses of Finse in Norway are ideal for the ice planet Hoth.

April 26: *Ringo* is broadcast on NBC. Directed by Jeff Margolis and starring Ringo Starr, the television special features Carrie Fisher, Art Carney, and George Harrison.

Carrie Fisher, Ringo Starr, and TV actor John Ritter in Los Angeles

MAY

Continuity Gaffe

May 23: Marvel's *Star Wars* #15 (cover date October) reveals that Luke Skywalker can't swim, but Princess Leia can, which contradicts the novel *Splinter of the Mind's Eye*. In subsequent *Star Wars* comics letter columns, fans note the discrepancy, possibly the first true gaffe in the embryonic Expanded Universe.

Luke can't swim in "Star Duel." The story is by Archie Goodwin with pencils by Carmine Infantino and inks by Terry Austin.

American Graffiti is re-released, this time reinstated with the three scenes that had been cut by Universal. Audiences finally get to hear Harrison Ford sing "Some Enchanted Evening." The re-release earns $63 million at the box office.

CARTER POSTPONES WORK ON NEUTRON BOMB "ONE LOVE" PEACE CONCERT IN JAMAICA

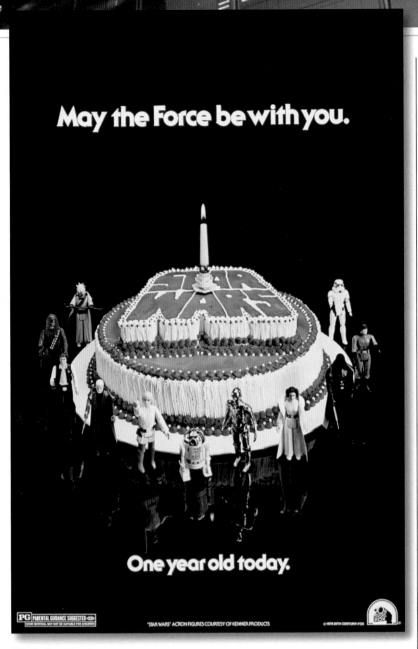

May the Force be with you.

One year old today.

Birthday Poster

Star Wars is not only one year old, but is still showing in many theaters. To commemorate the occasion, a special poster receives very limited distribution to selected theaters and media. West Hollywood's Cake & Art bakery makes the custom cake that is photographed by Weldon Anderson. The poster includes all but one of the first 12 action figures to be released—the Jawa is missing.

JUNE

June 2: *Corvette Summer* is released. Co-written by Hal Barwood and Matthew Robbins and directed by the latter, the movie stars Mark Hamill and Annie Potts and features Kim Milford (previously seen in *Laserblast*) and Danny Bonaduce (The *Partridge Family*).

Promotional still of Mark Hamill and Annie Potts astride a Chevrolet Corvette Stingray

Lawrence Kasdan

June 15: Screenwriter Lawrence Kasdan, who had met Lucas through Steven Spielberg, delivers his first draft script of *Raiders of the Lost Ark* to Lucas. During a lunch meeting, Lucas hires Kasdan to polish Lucas's second draft screenplay for *The Empire Strikes Back*. Brackett's script is discarded, but her name stays on the credits "because I liked her a lot," Lucas says. "She was sick at the time she wrote it and she really tried her best."

June 16: *Grease*, the movie adaptation of the hit Broadway musical, is released. Directed by Randal Kleiser (Lucas's roommate at USC), *Grease* stars John Travolta and Olivia Newton-John.

The Grease poster, designed by Diener-Hauser.

Valance the Hunter

June 27: *Star Wars* #16 (cover date October) introduces Valance, a former "Imperial stormtrooper officer of ruthless promise" who is now a mercenary and bounty hunter with an intense hatred of droids. Written by Archie Goodwin, "The Hunter" is the first *Star Wars* comic story in which the movie's principal characters are not prominently featured, appearing only in a one-page summary sequence.

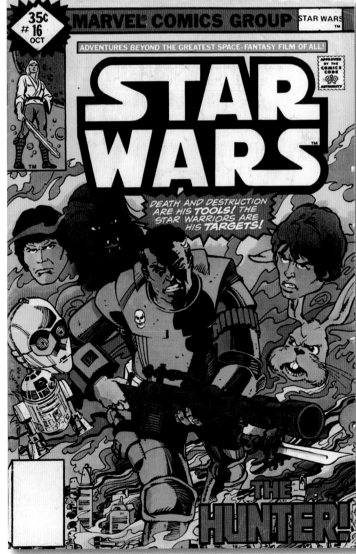

Cover art for Star Wars #16 by Walt Simonson

THE *GARFIELD* COMIC STRIP DEBUTS 🌎 GAY AND LESBIAN SOLIDARITY MARCH HELD IN SYDNEY 🌎

JULY

First Re-Release

July 21: *Star Wars* is re-released and includes an additional line of dialogue that had been in the script but was omitted from the first release. C-3PO says: "The tractor beam is coupled to the main reactor in seven locations. A power loss at one of the terminals will allow the ship to leave."

The Star Wars theatrical re-release poster. The artists, Charles White III and Drew Struzan, are inspired to expand the composition and create the trompe l'oeil wood surface when they realize the original design cannot accommodate the required text in the credit block.

Also in 1978...

Death Star

Palitoy releases a build-your-own cardboard Death Star. The playset is available in the UK, Australia, France, New Zealand, and Canada.

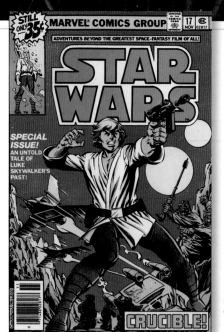

Flashback to Tatooine

July 25: Marvel Comics ships *Star Wars* #17 (cover date November). Written by Archie Goodwin and Chris Claremont and drawn by Herb Trimpe and Allen Milgrom, "Crucible" is the very first *Star Wars* story to depict events—by way of an expansive flashback sequence—that transpire before the movie. Luke reminisces about shooting womp rats and fighting Tusken Raiders on Tatooine. Dialogue between Luke's Uncle Owen and Aunt Beru reinforces that Luke's deceased father was Owen's brother.

Star Wars #17 cover art by Dave Cockrum and Bob McLeod

A younger Luke targets womp rats on Tatooine.

AUGUST

Star Wars Fan Club

The Official *Star Wars* Fan Club distributes a membership kit that includes a charter membership card, a pin back metal badge, a cloth patch, the first issue of a bi-monthly newsletter, and two items—a triangular decal and poster—featuring art by Ralph McQuarrie.

The Fan Club kit's decal was originally designed by Ralph McQuarrie to go on film cans and other items related to the production of Star Wars.

The first newsletter includes a profile on Lucas and Star Wars trivia. After a contest in issue #2, the newsletter is re-titled Bantha Tracks, a name proposed by Fan Club member Preston Postle.

SEPTEMBER

Buying the Ranch

Lucas buys the 1,700-acre Bulltail Ranch in Nicasio's Lucas Valley, California, between Petaluma to the north and San Rafael to the south. He plans to use the land to develop a place that filmmakers can use as a creative retreat.

Lucas Valley had been named for John Lucas, who had inherited the land from his uncle in the 1880s, and was not a relative of George Lucas.

Battlestar Galactica

September 17: *Battlestar Galactica* premieres on ABC. The Universal production boasts spacecraft designed by Ralph McQuarrie and special effects by John Dykstra. In later episodes, footage from *Silent Running* is recycled to add vegetation-carrying "Agro Ships" to *Galactica*'s rag-tag fleet.

Outer-space dogfights feature heavily in Battlestar Galactica. Here, two Cylons flank Richard Hatch, Lorne Greene, and Dirk Benedict.

Also in 1978...

12-inch Action Figures

Kenner releases larger *Star Wars* action figures. However, most buyers prefer the smaller ones.

Pencil Sharpener

UK toy company Helix releases a colorful Death Star pencil sharpener.

Han Solo 30-cm (12-inch) action figure

Letraset Premiums

Shreddies includes Letraset "action transfer sheets" to paste onto the illustrated cereal box.

Fans collect four different Star Wars Letraset sets from Shreddies packages.

Boba Fett's Debut

September 24: Boba Fett makes his first public appearance at the San Anselmo Country Fair parade in San Anselmo, California. Walking alongside Darth Vader (Kermit Eller), the mysterious bounty hunter's battle-worn attire is substantially different from his original conception as a white-armored "supertrooper."

Darth Vader, Grand Marshal for the annual Country Fair parade in San Anselmo, marches with the unidentified Boba Fett. The temperature is 34 degrees Celsius (94 degrees Fahrenheit).

Independent-Journal

$3.25 A month by carrier   15c Per copy   San Rafael, California, Monday, September 25, 1978   Telephone 454-3020

NOVEMBER

November 7: *Star Wars* ends its record-setting run at the Westgate Theater in Portland, Oregon, where it has played for 76 continuous weeks.

The Star Wars Holiday Special

November 17: *The Star Wars Holiday Special* airs on CBS television. Directed by Steve Binder (and an uncredited David Acomba), and based in part on a story attributed to an uncredited Lucas, the show is described by Fox's production notes as a "two-hour visual and audio delight" starring "the cast from the hit motion picture, *Star Wars*, along with special guest stars in a live-animated-musical-potpourri of pure entertainment complete with astonishing electronic special effects." Highlights include McQuarrie's matte paintings of the Wookiee homeworld Kashyyyk and an animated cartoon sequence that introduces Boba Fett. In the *Special*, Kashyyyk is pronounced "Kazzookk" and is spelled that way in the script, reflecting Lucas's earliest notes on the Wookiee homeworld. The *Special* is never rebroadcast or officially released on video.

THE STAR WARS HOLIDAY SPECIAL

Cover of the original press kit folder for The Holiday Special

Above: Concept painting of Kashyyyk by Ralph McQuarrie. Inset: Chewbacca's son, Lumpy (Patty Maloney), and father, Itchy (Paul Gale), in the Wookiee treehouse.

TV Guide would rank *The Holiday Special* #59 in their Top 100 Unexpected TV Moments.

Boba Fett appears in The Faithful Wookiee, *an animated short produced by Nelvana Limited.*

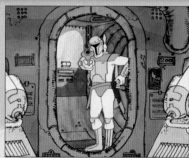

In a cantina on Tatooine, Ackmena (Bea Arthur) tends the bar while an Ithorian customer sits nearby.

At a hidden Rebel outpost, Princess Leia (Carrie Fisher) communicates with Wookiees on Kashyyyk while C-3PO (Anthony Daniels) watches and listens politely.

Fisher on *Saturday Night Live*

November 18: Carrie Fisher is the guest host on NBC's *Saturday Night Live*. Fisher appears as Princess Leia in the sketch "Beach Blanket Bimbo from Outer Space," a parody of 1950s teenager movies, in which Fisher strips to a gold bikini and sings "New Kid on Earth."

Carrie Fisher as Princess Leia and Bill Murray as Frankie Avalon on Saturday Night Live

DECEMBER

The usual gang of idiots, ever eager to make more money, produce a musical version of *Star Wars* in *MAD* #203. "The Force and I" features parodies of popular songs from *Cabaret, The Sound of Music, West Side Story*, and other musicals.

MAD cover art by Jack Rickard

Force 10

December 8: *Force 10 From Navarone* is released. Directed by Guy Hamilton, and based on the novel by Alistair MacLean, the movie stars Robert Shaw and Harrison Ford. *Force 10* also features *Star Wars* actors Leslie Schofield (Chief Bast) and Angus McInnes (Gold Leader); actors Michael Sheard (Admiral Ozzel) and Christopher Malcolm (Zev, aka Rogue 2) from the upcoming movie *The Empire Strikes Back* (1980); and Wolf Kahler (Dietrich) from the upcoming *Raiders of the Lost Ark* (1981).

Laser player 🌐🌐🌐

December 15: The first LaserDisc player, manufactured by Philips Magnavox, is released in Atlanta, Georgia, where it sells for $749. The manufacturers are immediately besieged by customer complaints of technical problems. The first LaserDisc title marketed in North America is *Jaws*.

The movie Slap Shot (1977), directed by George Roy Hill and starring Paul Newman, appears in this advertisement for the Magnavox VH-8000 player.

Superman

December 15: *Superman: The Movie* is released. Directed by Richard Donner, and based on the comic book hero created by Jerry Siegel and Joe Shuster, *Superman* stars Marlon Brando, Gene Hackman, and Christopher Reeve (whose personal trainer for the role was David Prowse). *Superman* also features Phil Brown (Uncle Owen from *Star Wars*), *Empire* actors John Hollis (Lobot) and John Ratzenberger (Major Derlin), and music by John Williams. Several members of *Superman*'s production crew subsequently work on *Empire*, including John Barry, Norman Reynolds, Stuart Freeborn, and David Tomblin.

Christopher Reeve stars as the title character in Superman: The Movie.

Also in 1978...

Action Figure Vehicles

Kenner releases the X-wing, TIE fighter, and Luke's landspeeder in scale with their increasingly popular action figures.

Takara Toys

Star Wars is released in Japan on June 30. Lucasfilm licensee Takara releases many unique toys, including a 20-centimeter (8-inch) tall C-3PO action figure.

Boba Fett Offer

Kenner's first mail-away offer for a *Star Wars* action figure is Boba Fett, which is initially promoted with a "Rocket Firing Back Pack."

FREE BOBA FETT™ WITH PURCHASE OF ANY FOUR STAR WARS ACTION FIGURES (See details on back)

These early prototypes of the missile-firing Boba Fett figure undergo several safety changes before being released in 1979.

Once a year the artists at Lucasfilm are able to release their creativity in a new way—the company holiday card. For over three decades, *Star Wars* iconography has been used to spread a little holiday cheer in new and unexpected ways.

1978 Lucasfilm

1983 Lucasfilm

1979 Lucasfilm

1981 Lucasfilm

1985 Lucasfilm

1984 Lucasfilm

1995 LucasArts

1980 Lucasfilm

1997 Lucasfilm

1999 Lucas Learning

1999 Lucasfilm

1998 Lucasfilm

2005 JAK (Lucasfilm's production arm)

2000 LucasArts

2002 Lucas Digital

2000 Lucasfilm

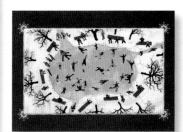

2000 Lucas Learning

2007 Lucasfilm

2008 Lucasfilm

1979

ONE OF THE NEW main characters in *Empire*, the small Jedi Master named Yoda, poses a challenge to production because he's less than 91 centimeters (three feet) tall. Briefly considered options include using a monkey, a little person, a child wearing prosthetic makeup, or a stop-motion puppet. Joe Johnston and Ralph McQuarrie produce numerous designs for Yoda before Lucas asks makeup artist Stuart Freeborn to "have a go" at designing the character. Freeborn draws inspiration from a photo of Albert Einstein and also his own face to sculpt a head for a hand puppet.

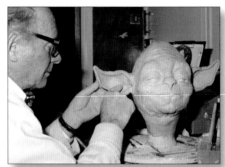

Stuart Freeborn creates a clay sculpture of Yoda's head.

"If that puppet didn't work, the whole film was going to fail."

George Lucas
on Yoda

R. M°QUARRIE

LUCAS ENTHUSIASTICALLY approves Freeborn's design for Yoda, and engineering begins on the complicated mechanisms needed to operate the puppet's facial "muscles" and eyes. Seeking a puppeteer for Yoda, and advice on how to build an animatronic puppet, Lucas consults Muppets-creator, Jim Henson, who recommends Frank Oz. Oz is already famous for his performances as Cookie Monster, Miss Piggy, and Fozzie Bear. Ultimately, operating Yoda will require not only Oz, but three assistants.

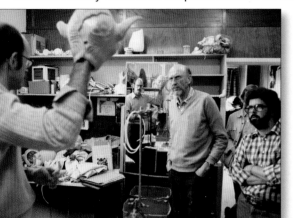

Frank Oz tests the Yoda puppet's head for Irvin Kershner and George Lucas.

In Ralph McQuarrie's production painting (dated August 1979) for Empire, Yoda is initially envisioned as a spindly-limbed, 61 centimeter (two foot) tall humanoid as he meets with Luke inside his dwelling on Dagobah.

JANUARY

Innocent Kiss
January 23: *Star Wars* #23 (cover date May) presents the first kiss between Luke and Leia since the Battle of Yavin. Although the comic's creators and readers can only imagine what the future holds for the characters and their relationship, the kiss is nevertheless "awkward."

Interior art from "Flight into Fury" in Star Wars #23 by writer Archie Goodwin and artists Carmine Infantino and Bob Wiacek.

FEBRUARY

Obi-Wan Flashback
February 27: *Star Wars* #24 (cover date June) features a flashback story about Obi-Wan Kenobi when he was a Jedi Knight serving the Republic. During a "peacetime" mission "before the Empire," Kenobi meets Bail Organa's droid 68-RKO, who addresses the Jedi as "General Obi-Wan Kenobi."

"Silent Drifting" is the first Star Wars comic written by Mary Jo Duffy. Cover art for Star Wars #24 by Carmine Infantino and Bob Wiacek.

MARCH

Chilly Reception
March 5: Principal photography on *Empire* begins with a 10-day shoot in Finse, Norway, which is only accessible by railroad in the winter. A very unexpected blizzard buries pre-dug trenches and production equipment under 10 feet of snow, and also cuts off Finse from the rest of the world. Despite sub-freezing temperatures and blinding snow that make operating a camera almost impossible, Kershner decides the first scenes to be shot will be Luke escaping from the wampa ice monster's lair. The crew films from the hotel's back doorway so the camera won't freeze while Mark Hamill runs outside in the snow.

Mark Hamill in costume, on set in Norway

Filming Luke (Mark Hamill) on his tauntaun during the Finse shoot for Empire.

Harrison Ford stands on a smoke-filled set during filming of *The Empire Strikes Back.* In this never-before-seen production photograph, Ford holds the breathing apparatus that Han Solo, Princess Leia, and Chewbacca wear when exploring their alien environment. Having mistaken the insides of a space slug for an asteroid cave, the Rebels soon realise that "this is no cave." Although Ford appears relaxed, *Empire's* troubled production takes its toll. Noxious fumes from the man-made steam (heated mineral oil) for smoky interiors make everyone ill, and tempers sometimes flare.

Voyager 1 Update

March 5: At a distance of 206,700 kilometers (128,400 miles), *Voyager 1* makes its closest approach to Jupiter. The spacecraft discovers at least eight volcanoes on Jupiter's moon Io and also two new moons before proceeding toward Saturn in early April.

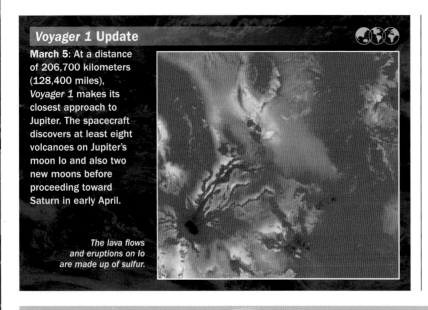

The lava flows and eruptions on Io are made up of sulfur.

March 12: *The Maverick Moon* is published. Written by Eleanor Ehrhardt (uncredited) and illustrated by Walter Wright, the story features Luke and Leia, with Luke as a member of a student group, the Planetary Pioneers, training to be a pilot at The New Academy of Space Pilots on an unnamed world. There is no mention of the Rebellion or the Empire.

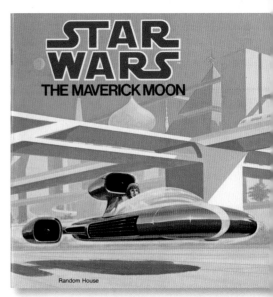

Random House

A student at the Academy, Luke races his landspeeder "at breakneck speed" to meet Princess Leia in The Maverick Moon.

Comic Strip Debut

March 11: The *Star Wars* newspaper comic strip begins publication by the *Los Angeles Times* Syndicate. At launch, the strip appears in 214 newspapers. The strip is written and drawn by veteran artist Russ Manning, whose previous credits include *Magnus, Robot Fighter* for Gold Key Comics, and a long run on the *Tarzan* comic strip. Manning works with freelance assistants to produce separate continuities for the *Star Wars* daily black-and-white strip and the Sunday colored strip.

The first Star Wars comic strip is announced in the Los Angeles Times.

Stage Fire

March 13: After leaving Finse, the *Empire* cast and crew resume work at Elstree Studios. Production is hampered because one of Elstree's sound stages burns down just before shooting is scheduled to begin.

APRIL

First Han Solo Novel

April 1: *Han Solo at Stars' End*, a novel by Brian Daley, is published by Del Rey. Because editorial constraints require the Han Solo and Chewbacca adventure to be set before the events of the first *Star Wars* movie, but without any other principal characters or interaction with the Empire, Daley sends the smuggling duo to a new region of space, the Corporate Sector.

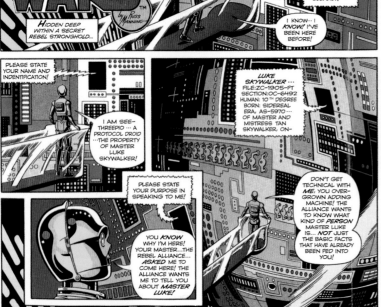

In the Star Wars comic strip by Russ Manning, C-3PO converses with Mistress Mnemos, a supercomputer who asserts Luke Skywalker has an affiliation with "Tan Skywalker."

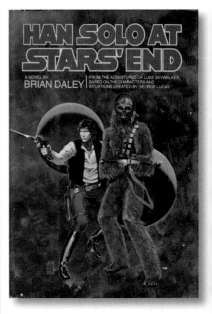

Dust jacket illustration by Dean Ellis

MAY

May 18: *Hanover Street* is released. Directed by Peter Hyams and starring Harrison Ford and Leslie-Anne Down, the film also features William Hootkins (Porkins from *Star Wars*) and actor John Ratzenberger, who plays Major Derlin in *Empire*.

In Hanover Street, Harrison Ford plays David Halloran, an American pilot sent on a secret mission during World War II.

Also in 1979...

Boba Fett Arrives Disarmed

Summer: Kenner's mail-away Boba Fett action figure ships with a non-firing rocket that is glued into his backpack. Earlier in 1979, Mattel, Inc. recalls missile-firing *Battlestar Galactica* toys—which had met all safety standards—after the reported death of a child who had swallowed a red plastic missile.

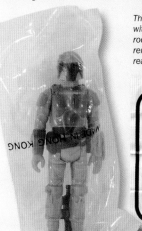

The Boba Fett figure arrives with a note explaining the rocket launcher has been removed "for safety reasons."

STAR WARS

NOTE TO CONSUMERS

Originally our STAR WARS Boba Fett action figure was designed to have a spring-launched rocket. The launcher has been removed from the product for safety reasons. If you are dissatisfied with the product, please return it to us and we will replace it with any STAR WARS mini-action figure of your choice.

Thank you for your support.

Boba Fett action figures arrive nearly a year before the theatrical release of Empire.

Snaggletooth

Kenner's Cantina Adventure Set ships in 1978, and includes the action figure Snaggletooth, whose appearance—a tall alien in a blue suit—is fashioned from limited photo reference. In 1979, a better photo reference results in a shorter "red Snaggletooth," but confusion ensues when this figure ships in the Cantina box that still pictures "blue Snaggletooth."

STAR WARS
CANTINA ADVENTURE SET

The original blue Snaggletooth and the revised red Snaggletooth

The Cantina Adventure Set is available only through the Sears Christmas Catalog in 1978 and 1979.

Alien

May 25: *Alien* is released. Directed by Ridley Scott and written by Dan O'Bannon and Ronald Shusett, the movie stars Sigourney Weaver and Tom Skerritt as members of a crew on a starship terrorized by an alien life form. *Alien* features costume design by John Mollo and special effects supervised by Brian Johnson, whose next job would be *Empire*. *Alien*'s art department includes concept artist Ron Cobb, who previously designed creatures for the Cantina sequence in *Star Wars*.

Warrant Officer Ripley (Sigourney Weaver) searches for a murderous alien onboard a starship in Alien.

JUNE

John Barry Dies

June 1: Production designer John Barry, just 43 years old, dies from a rare form of infectious meningitis after collapsing on the set of *Empire*. His death stuns everyone.

June 26: *Han Solo's Revenge* by Brian Daley is published. Han, Chewie, and their new allies, the droids Blue Max and Bollux (Zollux in the novel's UK edition), are swept into a scheme involving the Corporate Sector Authority.

HAN SOLO'S REVENGE
A NOVEL BY
BRIAN DALEY

Dust jacket illustration by Dean Ellis

AND WHAT'S THAT CRAZY *CORELLIAN* UP TO...? THERE'S *NO WAY* HIS SHIP CAN BLAST OUT OF THAT MOUNTAIN --

--NOT THROUGH *SOLID ROCK* THICK ENOUGH TO WITHSTAND AN *IMPERIAL BOMBARDMENT!*

ORDER OUT EVERY *HAND*... I MEAN TO SETTLE *ACCOUNTS* WITH SOLO ONCE AND FOREVER!

Jabba Returns

June 26: Marvel Comics' *Star Wars* #28 (cover date October) ships. In "Whatever Happened to Jabba the Hut?" [sic], Han and Chewie once again confront the biped alien gangster named Jabba, who has placed a bounty on Han for failure to pay a debt. Han winds up rescuing Jabba, who agrees to call off the bounty.

Star Wars #28, written by Archie Goodwin, art by Carmine Infantino and Gene Day

June 26: *Moonraker*, directed by Lewis Gilbert, premieres in London. The 11th film in the James Bond series and the fourth to star Roger Moore, *Moonraker* sends secret agent 007 into outer space, in a premise seemingly inspired by *Star Wars*.

Detail of Moonraker theatrical poster by artist Bob Peak

JULY

Skylab's Return

July 11: Skylab re-enters Earth's atmosphere after six years in orbit. NASA had intended to use a space shuttle to boost Skylab to a higher orbit. Skylab plunges to Earth, scattering debris across the southern Indian Ocean and Western Australia.

AUGUST

More American Graffiti

August 3: *More American Graffiti* is released. Written and directed by Bill L. Norton, the movie reunites most of the cast from *American Graffiti*, and includes a cameo by Harrison Ford. For the Vietnam sequences, George Lucas films handheld aerial shots over forests near Stockton, California, offering a glimpse of how Lucas might have filmed his version of *Apocalypse Now*.

The sights and sounds of the '60's. There were bittersweet times... There were crazy times... and it was all unforgettable.

PAUL LE MAT · CINDY WILLIAMS · CANDY CLARK
CHARLES MARTIN SMITH · MACKENZIE PHILLIPS · BO HOPKINS
and RON HOWARD
A LUCASFILM LTD. PRODUCTION
"MORE AMERICAN GRAFFITI"
AND WOLFMAN JACK'S GONNA BE THERE TOO!
Based on characters created by GEORGE LUCAS and GLORIA KATZ and WILLARD HUYCK
Written and Directed by B. W. L. NORTON
Produced by HOWARD KAZANJIAN · Executive Producer GEORGE LUCAS
Original Sound track available exclusively on MCA Records & Tapes
Read the BERKLEY book

COMING SOON TO THEATRES EVERYWHERE!

More American Graffiti theatrical poster by Stanley Moore and Alton Kelley

Audiences for the re-release receive this coupon book for Kenner Star Wars toys.

Second Re-Release for *Star Wars*

August 15: *Star Wars* is re-released for the second time and includes a live-action trailer for *The Empire Strikes Back*. Narrated by Harrison Ford, the trailer includes a brief glimpse of C-3PO ripping a "warning" sign from a door. This is part of a sequence involving caged wampas that is ultimately cut from the film.

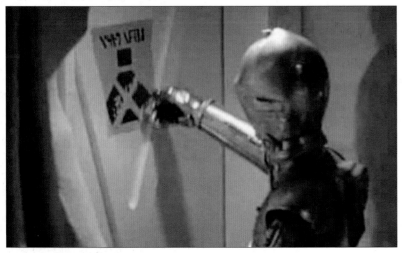

C-3PO (Anthony Daniels) removes a warning sign to trick Imperial snowtroopers into entering a chamber filled with wampa ice monsters.

Also in 1979...

Moving Card

Ralph McQuarrie illustrates Lucasfilm's announcement of its move from several trailers across the street from Universal Studios' lot to the Egg Company building, which has been renovated by George and Marcia Lucas.

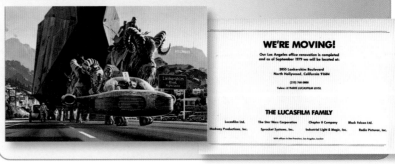

Apocalypse Now

August 15: *Apocalypse Now* is released after winning the coveted Palme d'Or at the 1979 Cannes Film Festival. Directed by Francis Ford Coppola—who co-wrote the screenplay with John Milius—the picture was plagued by production problems and went wildly over budget. The cast includes Marlon Brando, Martin Sheen, Robert Duvall, and Harrison Ford (as "Lucas"), whose performance was filmed in 1976, after his work on *Star Wars*.

As a nod to George Lucas, Harrison Ford names his Apocalypse Now character "Col. Lucas."

August 28: A wrap party is held on the "bog planet" set, even though filming is not yet finished. "It was a great party," Irvin Kershner recalls. "It was like Armistice Day: 'The War is over! We have triumphed!'"

Many members of cast and crew didn't know that the name of the "bog planet" was Dagobah until it was printed on the party invitation.

SEPTEMBER

September 5: Alec Guinness arrives on set and completes his shots within six hours. Having told the producers that "wretched eye trouble" might prevent him from working under bright lights, his participation in *Empire* had been uncertain. Guinness will receive one quarter of one percent of *Empire*'s gross receipts.

Irvin Kershner directs Alec Guinness

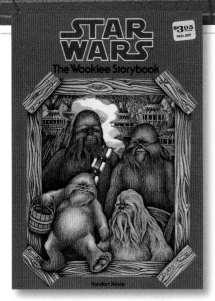

September 12: *The Wookiee Storybook* is published. Written by Eleanor Ehrhardt and illustrated by Patricia Wynne, the children's book features Wookiee characters introduced in *The Star Wars Holiday Special* and includes allusions to recent American history. Anticipating Chewbacca's 200th birthday party, his father Itchy says, "It will be a bicentennial celebration just like the ones they have on planets far, far away!"

After a three-year absence from Kashyyyk, Chewbacca reunites with his family in The Wookiee Storybook.

Tatooine Sojourn

September 19: In the syndicated *Star Wars* comic strip, Luke, C-3PO, and R2-D2 return to Tatooine for the first time since they left with Ben Kenobi. Luke revisits the Mos Eisley Cantina and Ben's home, and destroys an Imperial facility before he leaves Tatooine at the end of the serial titled "Tatooine Sojourn."

Star Wars comic strip written by Steve Gerber and illustrated by Russ Manning

September 24: *Empire* photography is completed with an insert of Luke on Hoth and coverage in the haunted cave on Dagobah. Because Hamill has already completed his role and left the production, Luke is performed by Hamill's stand-in, Joe Gibson.

Preparations for the dream-like sequence on Dagobah, in which a vision of Darth Vader is beheaded by Luke.

Also in 1979...

Sonic Controlled Landspeeder
Available only through J.C. Penney's Christmas catalogs, Kenner's sonic-controlled landspeeder changes direction by using a remote-control shaped like R2-D2.

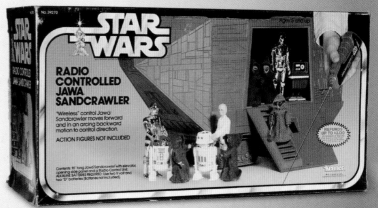

Sandcrawler
Kenner's two-channel radio-controlled sandcrawler weighs 1.12 kg (2.5 lbs), operates from up to 6 meters (20 feet) away, and retails for about $30.00.

Buck Rogers Redux

September 27: Buster Crabbe, the actor who originated the roles of Flash Gordon and Buck Rogers, guest stars as Brigadier Gordon on the third episode of the TV series *Buck Rogers in the 25th Century* on NBC. Developed and produced by Glen A. Larson, the new Buck Rogers show recycles props, costumes, and effects shots from Larson's *Battlestar Galactica.*

Also in 1979...

Public Service Announcement
A *Star Wars*–themed anti-drunk driving public service announcement (PSA) is broadcast on television stations in association with the US Department of Transportation and the National Highway Traffic Safety Administration. John Williams's Cantina music plays while one *Star Wars* alien helps another move away from a bar, and the PSA's narrator intones, "When friends drink too much, even in galaxies far, far away, friends don't let friends drive drunk."

OCTOBER

Return to Tatooine

October 2: Luke and the droids return again to Tatooine in Marvel Comics' *Star Wars* #31 (cover date January). Luke revisits the Lars Homestead, reunites with Fixer and Camie, and also revisits the Mos Eisley Cantina, apparently for the first time since his departure with Ben Kenobi. The approval processes between Lucasfilm and its licensees are still being worked out, as situations in the Marvel story do not mesh with the contemporaneous storyline in the *Star Wars* comic strip.

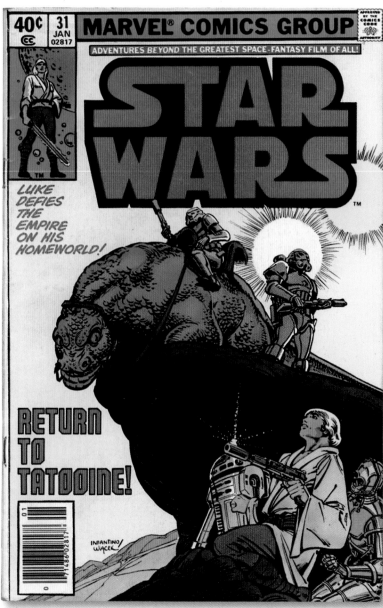

Cover art for Star Wars #31 by Carmine Infantino and Bob Wiacek

Pictured in Star Wars #31, the Imperial Troop Transporter is based on the Kenner toy of the same name that is also released in 1979.

THIS IS *TAGGE COMMAND,* UNIT THREE. ANY *SUCCESS* YET?

Also in 1979...

Imperial Troop Transporter

Kenner releases the Imperial Troop Transporter, which is modeled on a vehicle that appears in the Rebel base sequence in *Star Wars*. The toy includes an illustrated booklet that shows stormtroopers using the transporter as they search for the droids on Tatooine during the events of *Star Wars*.

The Transporter's booklet illustrates the Imperial assault on the Jawa sandcrawler.

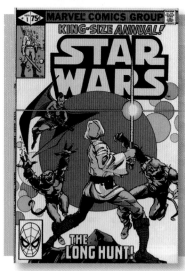

Star Wars Annual #1

Marvel Comics releases the first *Star Wars Annual*. Written by Chris Claremont, the story features Luke Skywalker and Princess Leia traveling to the planet Tirahnn and meeting winged humanoid natives, the S'kytri. According to the S'kytri, Obi-Wan Kenobi and two of his Jedi students visited Tirahnn during the Clone Wars; one student was Darth Vader, and the other carried the lightsaber that Luke now possesses.

Cover art by Walt Simonson

NOVEMBER

The Empire Strikes Back theatrical advance one-sheet is distributed to US theaters. The poster is designed by Tony Seiniger and David Reneric, who also developed the tilting *Empire* logo.

The Empire advance poster's image is used in Japan, Italy, and Australia.

John Williams begins composing the 108-minute musical score for *Empire*. Darth Vader's more significant role inspires Williams to write a "Grand Imperial March" for the villain's theme. The score is recorded with the London Symphony Orchestra, in England, over the course of two weeks.

Also in 1979...

US Lieutenant Colonel Jim Channon writes a confidential paper for top Pentagon brass called *Evolutionary Tactics*, a field manual for the "First Earth Battalion." Throughout its hand-illustrated pages are unorthodox field tactics designed to transform a soldier into a spiritually guided "Warrior Monk." The manual resonates well enough in post-Vietnam military command to warrant further exploration into paranormal abilities, including something identified as Project Jedi.

Art Indeed

The Art of Star Wars is published. Written by Carol Titelman, the book features concept and production art by McQuarrie, Johnston, Mollo, and others. It also includes "the complete script of the film," a modified version of Lucas's fourth draft that incorporates revisions to the screenplay during production. The book will be reprinted many times and inspires a generation of artists, many of whom will later join the film industry.

November 15: *The Lord of the Rings* is released. Directed by Ralph Bakshi, the animated movie features John Hurt and Anthony Daniels performing respectively the voices of Aragorn and Legolas.

DECEMBER

Alan Ladd Jr. leaves his position at Fox after Fox executives criticize him for the deal—which they had approved—granting *Star Wars* sequel and licensing rights to Lucasfilm. Ladd subsequently founds a new production house, The Ladd Company.

New Enterprise

December 7: *Star Trek: The Motion Picture* is released. Directed by Robert Wise, story by Alan Dean Foster, and screenplay by Harold Livingston and an uncredited Gene Roddenberry, the movie reunites the cast of the *Star Trek* TV series, and foretells the fate of a *Voyager* space probe. John Dykstra is the special photographic effects supervisor (at his own effects company, Apogee, Inc., which had created the effects for *Battlestar Galactica* as well).

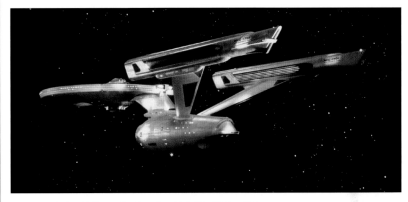

A film still of the USS Enterprise *from* Star Trek: The Motion Picture

December 21: *The Black Hole*, a Walt Disney production, is released. Directed by Gary Nelson, Disney's first PG-rated movie features the longest computer graphics sequence thus far, and many matte paintings by Harrison Ellenshaw. A *Star Wars* veteran, Ellenshaw would join *Empire*'s production immediately after completing his work on *The Black Hole*.

The Black Hole *movie poster*

Also in 1979...

Millennium Falcon Toy

Kenner releases its highly anticipated *Millennium Falcon* Spaceship, which is designed to accommodate *Star Wars* 9.5-centimeter (3¾-inch) action figures. Two key Kenner employees who work on the toy are Jack Farrah, who does the product development, and Mark Boudreaux, who figures out the *Falcon*'s scale, chooses the play features, and handcrafts a rough model for Kenner management. The 58-centimeter (23-inch) long *Falcon* features "battle alert sound," an opening cockpit, folding entrance ramp, swiveling radar dish, "laser gun" with swiveling seat, game table, secret floor panel to cover a smuggling compartment, and a "remote force ball for Light Saber practice."

Kenner's Millennium Falcon has a shipping weight of 1.7 kg (3 lbs 12 oz), and retails for $24.77 in the 1979 Sears Wish Book.

Plush Jawa

Manufactured by Regal, this plush Jawa is sold only in Canada. Squeeze his left hand and he squeaks.

1980

IN THE FIRST THREE MONTHS of 1980, ILM is still working on additional effects shots. Secrecy surrounds the production, with few knowing what James Earl Jones's dialogue as Darth Vader will reveal. Despite the critical success of *The Godfather: Part II* (1974), the reputation of sequels is that they are never as good or profitable as the earlier films.

Filming on the set of Empire *in 1980*

"I think it's a better film than the first one... but I have no idea what the rest of the world will think."

George Lucas
on Empire, *March 13, 1980*

JANUARY

Mark Hamill on the set of The Muppet Show.

The Muppet Show

January 16: Mark Hamill guest stars on *The Muppet Show*. Directed by Peter Harris, the episode also features Anthony Daniels as C-3PO, Peter Mayhew as Chewbacca, and Kenny Baker as R2-D2. The dual storyline alternates between sketches with Hamill and his "cousin" Luke Skywalker, who hopes to rescue Chewbacca from "a bunch of weird turkeys." Luke appears in the "Pigs in Space" segment with Miss Piggy (performed by Frank Oz) and Gonzo as "Derth Nader."

FEBRUARY

Droids on *Sesame Street*

Anthony Daniels appears as C-3PO with a radio-controlled R2-D2 on *Sesame Street*. After arriving by flying saucer, the droids deliver a holographic message for Oscar the Grouch, and play a game of Blind Man's Bluff with Big Bird, who mistakes a mailbox for R2-D2.

Skywalker Identified

February 5: Marvel's *Star Wars* #35 (cover date May) ships. In "Dark Lord's Gambit," written by Archie Goodwin, Luke Skywalker and Darth Vader meet in person for the first time in the Marvel series, on the planet Monestery. Without any mention of their encounter in the novel *Splinter of the Mind's Eye*, readers continue to question the continuity in *Star Wars* publishing.

Star Wars #35 cover art by Carmine Infantino and Bob Wiacek portrays Darth Vader in gigantic proportions.

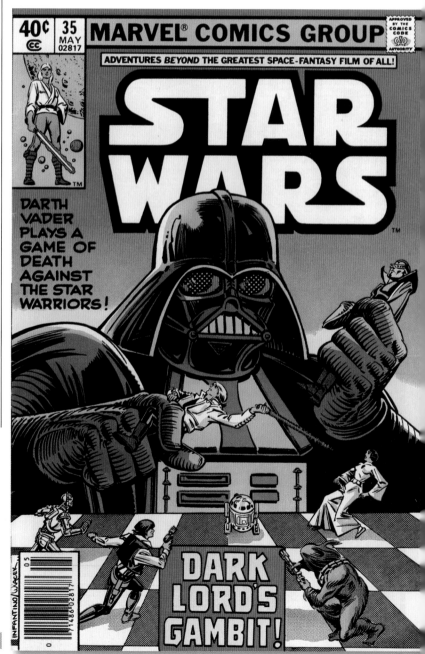

40¢ 35 MAY 02817 CC

MARVEL® COMICS GROUP

ADVENTURES *BEYOND* THE GREATEST SPACE-FANTASY FILM OF ALL!

STAR WARS

DARTH VADER PLAYS A GAME OF DEATH AGAINST THE STAR WARRIORS!

DARK LORD'S GAMBIT!

VOYAGER I FINDS JANUS, A MOON OF SATURN

APRIL

Luke Duels Vader

April 1: Marvel Comics' *Star Wars* #37 (cover date July) ships. "Mortal Combat!," written by Archie Goodwin, continues the confrontation between Luke and Vader on Monestery. Luke realizes he's "not ready" for "a final fight" with Vader, and escapes into space with his allies. In the epilogue, Jabba the Hut (sic) discovers that Han Solo destroyed his investment in a pirate ship, and reinstates the bounty on Solo. Han learns of the bounty after defending himself against a would-be assassin.

Cover art by Carmine Infantino and Bob Wiacek

Empire Novelization

April 12: The *Empire* novelization is published by Del Rey. Written by Donald F. Glut, an amateur filmmaker and one of Lucas's former classmates from USC, the novelization is largely faithful to the screenplay, but also contains various idiosyncratic details, most of which are attributed to production changes. For example, Yoda is described as being "blue-skinned," and Zuckuss is a "human type" bounty hunter. By the end of the week of *Empire*'s theatrical release, the novelization sells 2 million copies.

The novelization's cover features Roger Kastel's unmodified painting for Empire, *including details omitted from the poster.*

52nd Academy Awards®

April 14: The 52nd Academy Awards® are presided over by Johnny Carson. *Kramer vs. Kramer* is nominated for nine awards and wins for Best Picture, Best Director, Best Writing, Best Actor in a Leading Role, and Best Actress in a Supporting Role. *Apocalypse Now* is nominated for eight awards and wins two, for Best Cinematography and Best Sound. *Alien* wins the award for Best Visual Effects.

Boston Pops

April 29: John Williams conducts his first concert with the Boston Pops Orchestra as conductor-in-residence after replacing Arthur Fiedler, whose 50-year tenure ended with his death the previous year. Two new compositions written by Williams for *The Empire Strikes Back* are premiered: "Yoda's Theme" and "Imperial March."

C-3PO (Anthony Daniels) attends John Williams's debut as the official conductor of the Boston Pops Orchestra.

MAY

"Gone with the Wind" Poster

Roger Kastel's painting for *The Empire Strikes Back* theatrical poster was inspired by the 1967 re-release poster for *Gone with the Wind*, which was designed by Tom Jung and painted by Howard Terpning.

Also in 1980...

Action Figures

Kenner produces 10 new action figures to coincide with the release of *The Empire Strikes Back*. To preserve the surprise of Yoda in the film, his action figure is postponed until the following year.

Han Solo (Hoth Outfit) — Lando Calrissian — Luke Skywalker (Bespin Fatigues) — Bespin Security Guard — Imperial Snow Trooper (Hoth Battle Gear) — IG-88 (Bounty Hunter) — Bossk (Bounty Hunter) — Rebel Soldier (Hoth Battle Gear) — Leia Organa (Bespin Gown) — FX-7 (Medical Droid)

MAY

Cover art for Empire soundtrack LP

LP Soundtrack

May 16: The two-LP soundtrack for *The Empire Strikes Back* is released by RSO Records. It quickly sells 800,000 copies. By this time, the *Star Wars* soundtrack has already sold 3 million copies.

TIME

May 19: *TIME* magazine features Darth Vader on the cover. In the main article, *TIME*'s show business writer Gerald Clarke describes *Empire* as "in many ways… a better film than *Star Wars*."

Benefit Premier

May 17: *Star Wars*: Episode V *The Empire Strikes Back* premieres at a benefit performance for the Special Olympics at the Kennedy Center in Washington, DC.

Royal Premiere

May 20: The Royal premiere of *Empire* takes place at the Odeon in London. David Prowse, who plays the body of Darth Vader, is among those who are completely surprised by Vader's paternal declaration to Luke Skywalker.

The Empire Strikes Back

May 21: *The Empire Strikes Back* begins its 70mm release in 127 theaters, and breaks 125 house records for opening day, a new industry achievement for the highest single-day per theater gross. A wider 35mm release is planned for June 18. Much to ILM's surprise, Lucas soon orders three new effects shots because he wants to clarify the location of Lando, Chewbacca, and the *Millennium Falcon* in relation to Luke and Leia in the Rebel medical frigate as the characters converse at the end of the film. The additional shots are completed in three weeks and cut into the 35mm prints in time for the wider release.

The Emperor's hologram in Empire

The Emperor Revealed

First viewed as a hologram in *Empire*, the Emperor is actually a composite image of a hooded, uncredited makeup assistant wearing prosthetic makeup, with chimpanzee eyes superimposed in postproduction into darkened eye sockets. Actor Clive Revill, who previously worked with director Irvin Kershner in *A Fine Madness* (1966), provides the Emperor's voice.

Imperial Diplomacy

China's Vice Premier Geng Biao

Shortly after the release of *Empire*, China's Vice Premier Geng Biao is in Washington, DC to talk about military equipment. President Jimmy Carter invites him to watch *Empire* with the First Family. "Geng Biao was on the edge of his seat all the way through the movie," Carter tells *TIME* magazine. "Fortunately, he did not ask me for any of the weapons he saw in the movie."

Star Wars fans wait in line to be among the first to see Empire.

Secrets of Boba Fett

Jeremy Bulloch lands the role of Boba Fett after his half-brother, *Empire* producer Robert Watts, encourages him to audition. When another actor becomes unavailable to play an Imperial officer on Cloud City, Bulloch is selected as a replacement, but then needs someone to cover for him as Fett for a sequence—filmed by a different unit—in which the bounty hunter confronts Vader while Han Solo is tortured. *Empire*'s second assistant director, Steve Lanning, notes that John Morton, who plays Rebel pilot Dak, is a similar size to Bulloch, and enlists Morton to play Fett for the sequence. Consequently, Bulloch appears in two different roles in concurrent sequences on Cloud City. In postproduction, Fett is voiced by an uncredited Jason Wingreen, whose many TV credits include appearances on *The Twilight Zone, Star Trek, Mission: Impossible,* and as Harry Snowden on *Archie Bunker's Place.*

Jeremy Bulloch as an Imperial officer with Princess Leia (Carrie Fisher) in Empire.

The Big Red One

May 28: *The Big Red One* premieres in France. Written and directed by Samuel Fuller, the movie stars Lee Marvin and Mark Hamill as members of the 1st Infantry Division of the United States Army during World War II.

Darth Vader (David Prowse), Lando Calrissian (Billy Dee Williams), and Boba Fett (John Morton) discuss Han Solo's fate.

Jeremy Bulloch as Boba Fett, escorting the carbonite-frozen Han Solo through the Cloud City corridors. In the background, actor Alan Harris plays a Bespin guard. Harris also plays the reptilian bounty hunter in Empire.

JUNE

Marvel's *Empire* Adaptation

June 3: *Star Wars* #39 (cover date September) begins Marvel's six-issue adaptation of *Empire* by writer/editor Archie Goodwin and artists Al Williamson and Carlos Garzon. Marvel simultaneously releases a small paperback version of the entire adaptation. *Empire* marks the first collaboration on *Star Wars* by longtime friends and frequent collaborators Goodwin and Williamson, who have recently ended a long run on the syndicated comic strip *Secret Agent Corrigan*. Lucasfilm had provided Ralph McQuarrie's initial concept art of Yoda as visual reference for the artists, and subsequently provides an up-to-date photo reference for Yoda, but not before the paperback version has gone to press.

Marvel's Empire paperback cover art by Bob Larkin

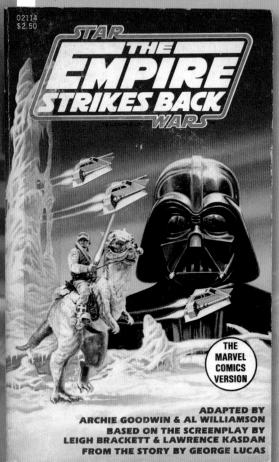

Star Wars #39 cover art by Al Williamson and Carlos Garzon

Yoda as he appears in Marvel's paperback adaptation (above left); Yoda in the corrected comic book version (above right).

Different Dialogue

Marvel's creative team uses dialogue from *Empire*'s screenplay in the comic book adaptation, which turns out to differ from lines in the film that are ad-libbed or changed during production.

In the film version of Empire, Leia declares her love for Han Solo, and Solo famously replies, "I know." Lucas did not approve Harrison Ford's ad-libbed line until after it tested favorably with audiences.

Our Kind of People

June 9: *People* magazine features Yoda on the cover. In an exclusive interview, Frank Oz admits that his work on *Empire* "was one of the hardest things I've ever done in 20 years of performing."

The Blues Brothers

June 20: *The Blues Brothers* is released. Directed by John Landis, the movie stars John Belushi and Dan Aykroyd, and features Carrie Fisher as the mystery woman, with cameos by Frank Oz and Steven Spielberg.

"Joliet" Jake Blues (John Belushi), Carrie Fisher, and Elwood Blues (Dan Aykroyd)

Empire Sketchbook

The Empire Strikes Back Sketchbook is published. Featuring concept and production sketches by Joe Johnston and Nilo Rodis-Jamero, the book also reveals the name of Vader's Star Destroyer as *Executor*.

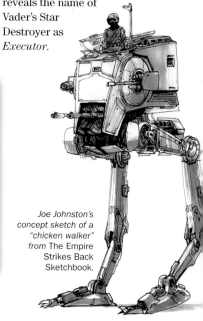

Joe Johnston's concept sketch of a "chicken walker" from The Empire Strikes Back Sketchbook.

Cover for The Empire Strikes Back Sketchbook, published by Ballantine Books.

US BOYCOTTS MOSCOW OLYMPICS ☯ IRAN-IRAQ WAR BEGINS ☯ SOLIDARITY BORN IN GDANSK

JULY

Burger King Raises a Glass

Burger King offers four different *Empire* glasses over the course of a four-week promotion. The restaurant franchise also offers three *Empire* posters illustrated by Boris Vallejo.

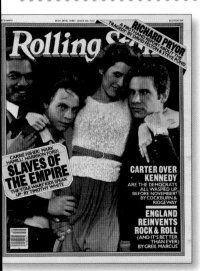

Limited edition Star Wars Burger King glass

Slaves of the Empire

July 24: *Rolling Stone* magazine features the cast of *Empire* on the cover. Interviewed by Timothy White, the veteran actors are subdued by a fame that has not translated into other starring jobs. Mark Hamill describes the surreal experience of visiting a Toys 'R' Us where all the *Star Wars* costumes had sold out except for "boxes and boxes of me." Carrie Fisher comments, "When we all kick off, we will be [known as] the princess and Luke and Han." Asked how she feels about that prospect, Fisher replies, "Helpless."

Rolling Stone cover photo by Annie Leibovitz

AUGUST

Close Encounters Revised

August 1: *Close Encounters of the Third Kind: The Special Edition* is released. Columbia Pictures allowed director Steven Spielberg—who had been dissatisfied with the original release of *Close Encounters*—to re-cut the picture and shoot additional sequences, provided that he include new footage of the alien mothership.

To lure audiences, Columbia Pictures heavily promotes the new footage of Roy Neary (Richard Dreyfuss) entering the alien mothership in Close Encounters of the Third Kind: The Special Edition.

August 17: *Empire* has grossed more than $145 million at the box office.

Record Success

August 31: The *Empire* soundtrack album has already sold 1 million copies.

SEPTEMBER

Exploring FX

September 22: *SPFX: The Empire Strikes Back* airs on CBS. Directed by Robert Guenette and hosted by Mark Hamill, the documentary focuses on *Empire*'s special effects.

Also in 1980...

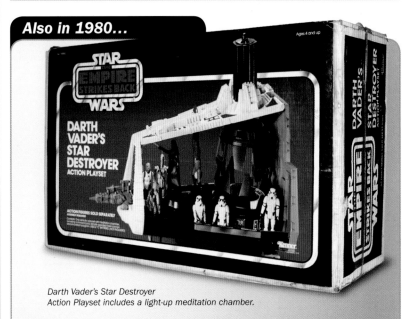

Darth Vader's Star Destroyer Action Playset includes a light-up meditation chamber.

Darth Vader's Star Destroyer

Darth Vader's Star Destroyer Action Playset is released by Kenner. Although the *Empire Sketchbook* identifies Vader's flagship as the *Executor*, the name is not mentioned in the movie itself, and Kenner—reportedly concerned that most toy-buyers would not know that an executor is a person who carries out a will or policy, and is not a synonym for assassin—was hesitant to use the name for toy packaging. Kenner's ad agency produced a list of 153 potential alternative names, including *Starbase Malevolent*, *Black Coven*, *Hephaestus VII* and *Cosmocurse*. Kenner finally opted to call the toy Darth Vader's Star Destroyer.

OCTOBER

GEORGE LUCAS and FRANCIS FORD COPPOLA
present
A FILM BY AKIRA KUROSAWA

Kagemusha
THE SHADOW WARRIOR

Press release signed by
Lucas and Coppola
publicizing Kagemusha

Cover of the press kit for Kagemusha

Kagemusha

October 6: *Kagemusha* (*The Shadow Warrior*) is released. It is director Akira Kurosawa's first Japanese production in 10 years. *Kagemusha* almost went unfinished until two great admirers, George Lucas and Francis Ford Coppola, convinced Twentieth Century-Fox to finance the rest of the picture and secure international distribution rights.

The Elephant Man

October 10: *The Elephant Man* is released. Directed by David Lynch, produced by Mel Brooks, and starring John Hurt, the story is inspired by the life of Joseph Merrick, a severely deformed man in 19th century London. The film shares the same title as Bernard Pomerance's stage play, which premiered on Broadway in 1979. George Lucas admires Lynch's films, and approaches him about directing the third *Star Wars* movie. Preferring to work on his own projects, Lynch respectfully declines.

John Hurt as the Elephant Man

NOVEMBER

Jingle Droids

Christmas in the Stars: Star Wars Christmas Album is released by RSO Records. Produced by Meco, the *Star Wars* themed Christmas album features original songs written by Maury Yeston, the vocal talent of Anthony Daniels as C-3PO, and Ben Burtt's sound effects for R2-D2 and Chewbacca. The album spawns the single "What Can You Get a Wookiee for Christmas (When He Already Owns a Comb)?" backed with "R2-D2 We Wish You a Merry Christmas." The latter tune's lead singer, making his recording debut, is 18-year-old Jon Bon Jovi (credited as "John Bongiovi").

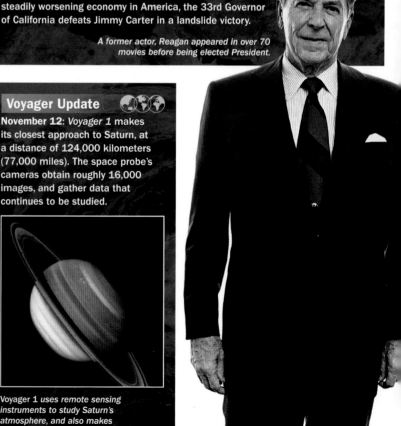

Christmas In The Stars
STAR WARS CHRISTMAS ALBUM

Featuring the Original Cast: R2-D2 · Anthony Daniels as C-3PO

Album cover art by Ralph McQuarrie

President Reagan

November 4: Ronald Reagan is elected the 40th President of the United States. Aided by the Iran hostage crisis and a steadily worsening economy in America, the 33rd Governor of California defeats Jimmy Carter in a landslide victory.

A former actor, Reagan appeared in over 70 movies before being elected President.

Voyager Update

November 12: *Voyager 1* makes its closest approach to Saturn, at a distance of 124,000 kilometers (77,000 miles). The space probe's cameras obtain roughly 16,000 images, and gather data that continues to be studied.

Voyager 1 uses remote sensing instruments to study Saturn's atmosphere, and also makes a close fly-by of the moon Titan.

⊙ UK PM THATCHER SAYS "THE LADY'S NOT FOR TURNING" ⊙ POLISH GOVERNMENT RECOGNIZES

DECEMBER

Lightsaber Mystery

December 2: Marvel Comics' *Star Wars* #45 ships (cover date March). Written by Archie Goodwin, with art by Carmine Infantino, Gene Day, and Chic Stone, "Death Probe" features Luke Skywalker in an adventure set right after the events of *Empire*. Luke wields a lightsaber, without any explanation for how he obtained it (he had lost his at the end of *Empire*).

GREAT!

WITH YOU TO HANG ONTO, MY *LIGHTSABER* CAN DO THE REST!

Luke uses a lightsaber of unidentified origin in Star Wars #45.

Flash Gordon

December 5: *Flash Gordon* is released. Directed by Mike Hodges and based on the classic comic strip by Alex Raymond, the Dino De Laurentiis production stars Sam J. Jones as Flash Gordon, Max von Sydow as Ming the Merciless, and features Timothy Dalton, Brian Blessed, William Hootkins, John Morton, John Hollis, and a soundtrack by the British rock group Queen.

PATHETIC EARTHLINGS... WHO CAN SAVE YOU NOW?

Music by QUEEN

DINO DE LAURENTIIS Presents FLASH GORDON
SAM J. JONES ★ MELODY ANDERSON ★ ORNELLA MUTI ★ MAX VON SYDOW ★ TOPOL ★ TIMOTHY DALTON
MARIANGELA MELATO as Kala ★ BRIAN BLESSED ★ PETER WYNGARDE ★ Screenplay by LORENZO SEMPLE, JR.
Produced by DINO DE LAURENTIIS ★ Directed by MIKE HODGES ★ Filmed in TODD-AO ★ A UNIVERSAL RELEASE

Flash Gordon poster artwork by Richard Amsel

John Lennon Assassinated

December 8: A stalker shoots John Lennon outside the musician's home in New York City. The killer is immediately apprehended. Lennon is survived by his widow, Yoko Ono, their son Sean, and Julian Lennon, his son from his former marriage to Cynthia Lennon (née Powell).

John Lennon met artist Yoko Ono in 1966. The couple released an album, Double Fantasy, on November 17, just three weeks before Lennon was killed.

Also in 1980...

More Merchandise

In 1980 *Star Wars* merchandise becomes even bigger business. Lucas sees his *Star Wars* brand appear on ice creams, underwear, and lunchboxes, among other things.

Streets Ice Treats package art, with cut-out images on back.

Underoos line of children's underwear includes a Princess Leia tank top and panty.

Luke Skywalker fatigue jacket is an exclusive item from the Official Star Wars Fan Club.

Switcheroo illuminated C-3PO switch plate cover by Kenner

Empire lunchbox by King Seeley Thermos

Yoda cap by the Thinking Cap Co.

1981

AFTER *EMPIRE* exceeds critical and financial expectations, many speculate whether Frank Oz might be nominated for industry awards for his performance as Yoda. However, the Screen Actors Guild dismisses this possibility because it does not regard puppeteers as actors. Meanwhile, Lucas searches for a new director for the next *Star Wars* movie, *Revenge of the Jedi*.

Alfred E. Neuman embodies Yoda.

> "Name the top-billed actor in the first and third highest-grossing movies of all time. It's me! But even my family guesses wrong. My cousin said Richard Dreyfuss."

Mark Hamill
People *magazine, 1981*

JANUARY

DeLorean DMC-12

January 21: The first DeLorean DMC-12 sports car rolls out of the factory in Dunmurry, Northern Ireland. Conceived by American engineer and automobile executive John DeLorean, the gull-wing vehicle's body is paneled in brushed stainless steel.

MAD

MAD #220 features the satire *The Empire Strikes Out*. After Lucasfilm's attorneys threaten a lawsuit, *MAD* replies with a copy of a fan letter they have received from George Lucas himself, who praises artist Mort Drucker and writer Dick Debartolo as "the Leonardo Da Vinci and George Bernard Shaw of satire."

FEBRUARY

New Team for Comic Strip

February 9: Writer Archie Goodwin and artist Al Williamson begin their run on the *Star Wars* comic strip, which Russ Manning must abandon after he is diagnosed with cancer. To avoid continuity problems with the upcoming *Revenge of the Jedi*, Goodwin and Williamson set their stories after *Star Wars* and before *Empire*.

The first Star Wars comic strip by Goodwin and Williamson

First Draft

February 20: Lucas completes his first draft for *Revenge of the Jedi*. The draft includes mention of the Galactic Empire's capital, a planet completely covered by cities, which Lucas names Had Abbadon.

Cover of Lucas's handwritten first draft for Revenge

Only cartoonist Mort Ducker knows if that is Lucas in the background.

Vader Confronts Leia

February 24: Marvel Comics' *Star Wars* #48 ships (cover date June). In "The Third Law," Leia, C-3PO, and R2-D2 come face-to-face with Darth Vader on the planet Aargau, where it is unlawful for non-citizens to possess weapons, and conversely unlawful for citizens to be unarmed.

Detail of Star Wars #48 cover art by Carmine Infantino and Bob Wiacek

MARCH

Radio Drama

National Public Radio begins broadcasting a 13-episode dramatization of *Star Wars*. Directed by John Madden and scripted by Brian Daley, the drama is 6.5 hours long and contains new and expanded sequences from the movie. Mark Hamill and Anthony Daniels reprise their roles as Luke and C-3PO. Other actors include Perry King as Han Solo, Ann Sachs as Leia, and Brock Peters as Darth Vader. NPR listenership increases 40 percent.

Bounty Hunter

March 4: In the *Star Wars* comic strip, Goodwin and Williamson expand upon dialogue from *Empire* to concoct a story of Han Solo having a close call with a bounty hunter on the planet Ord Mantell.

Promotional poster for the Star Wars radio drama

Soon after arriving on Ord Mantell, the Rebels encounter a bounty hunter named Skorr and his henchman Gribbet.

53rd Academy Awards®

March 31: *The Empire Strikes Back* is nominated for four Academy Awards®. Lucas and Twentieth Century-Fox had submitted Ben Burtt's name along with *Empire*'s sound team, but the Academy refuses to recognize Sound Designer as a credit.

Best Sound: **Bill Varney**, **Steve Maslow**, **Gregg Landaker**, **Peter Sutton**; Special Achievement Award for visual effects: **Brian Johnson**, **Richard Edlund**, **Dennis Muren**, **Bruce Nicholson**; Best Art Direction-Set Decoration: Norman Reynolds, Leslie Dilley, Harry Lange, Alan Tomkins, Michael Ford. Best Music, Original Score: John Williams.

(Bold indicates winners)

APRIL

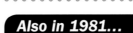

The revised "opening crawl" of A New Hope

Episode IV

April 10: *Star Wars* is re-released for the third time, now with the extended title Episode IV *A New Hope*. The release accidentally omits C-3PO's line: "The power beam holding the ship is coupled to the main reactor in seven locations. A power loss at one of the terminals will enable the ship to leave."

Space Shuttle Into Orbit

April 12: *Columbia* launches from Kennedy Space Center and becomes the first Space Shuttle to make a manned orbital test flight, orbiting Earth 37 times before returning to land at Edwards Air Force Base on April 14. At NASA's invitation, Lucas watches *Columbia*'s maiden flight. "I was awed," Lucas said afterward. "I stood a mile away when astronauts John Young and Robert Crippen floated that 86-ton spacecraft to a touchdown as perfect as a dream come true. I had a lump in my throat just like everyone else."

The Space Shuttle Columbia launches.

April 19: Hayden Christensen (the teenage Anakin Skywalker) is born in Vancouver, Canada.

Also in 1981...

Naming Dengar

A bounty hunter named Zuckuss is first mentioned in the early drafts of *The Empire Strikes Back*. Although Lucasfilm initially designates Zuckuss as the bandaged-headed human bounty hunter, Kenner releases the character's action figure with the name Dengar, and transfers the name Zuckuss to the droid bounty hunter with the bulbous head and tarnished protocol droid body.

Kenner's Dengar action figure

MAY

George Lucas and Richard Marquand clown around during filming of Jedi.

Revenge Director Announced

Lucasfilm announces that Richard Marquand will direct *Revenge of the Jedi*. Marquand's few credits include *The Legacy* (1978), the TV movie *Birth of the Beatles* (1979), and the upcoming *Eye of the Needle*. Lucas hears advance buzz for *Needle*, views an advance rough cut, and is impressed that Marquand delivered the picture on time and on budget. In a 1983 interview with *OMNI* magazine, he explains why he hired Marquand. "He liked *Star Wars*. He wanted to work with me. Finally, it's a very good career move for him: He will be catapulted into the top directors' category, and his salary will skyrocket."

JUNE

June 9: Natalie Portman, the future Padmé Amidala, is born in Israel.

Hamill's Broadway Debut

June 9: Mark Hamill assumes the role of John Merrick in Bernard Pomerance's play *The Elephant Man* at the Booth Theatre in New York City. He is reportedly appalled by the play's publicity department, which promotes his appearance with the tag: "And the Force continues… on Broadway!" Despite favorable reviews for Hamill's performance, the play closes on June 28.

Booth Theatre in NYC, where Hamill first plays Broadway

Production still from Raiders. From left to right: Harrison Ford, Steven Spielberg, William Hootkins, Denholm Elliot, and Don Fellows.

Raiders of the Lost Ark

June 12: *Raiders of the Lost Ark* is released. Directed by Spielberg and executive produced by Lucas, the film stars Harrison Ford as adventurous archaeologist Indiana Jones. The screenplay is by Lawrence Kasdan, based on a story by Lucas and Philip Kaufman. Other *Star Wars* veterans on staff include Robert Watts, Norman Reynolds, John Williams, and Ben Burtt. *Raiders* becomes the highest grossing movie of 1981.

Indiana Jones (Harrison Ford) swaps a bag filled with sand for a gold statue in Raiders.

JULY

Eye of the Needle

July 24: *Eye of the Needle* is released. Directed by Richard Marquand, and based on the novel by Ken Follett, the film stars Donald Sutherland as a secret agent during World War II.

Royal Wedding

July 29: Twenty-year-old Diana Spencer marries Prince Charles at St Paul's Cathedral in London, watched by a global television audience of 750 million.

Just married, Princess Diana and Prince Charles wave to the crowds.

Empire Re-Release

Theatrical re-release poster art by Tom Jung

July 31: *The Empire Strikes Back* is re-released for the first time. By October, *Variety* reports that the top four box office champs are *Star Wars*, *The Empire Strikes Back*, *Jaws*, and *Raiders of the Lost Ark*.

. . . .

Under the Rainbow

July 31: *Under the Rainbow* is released. Directed by Steve Rash, the film stars Chevy Chase and Carrie Fisher in a comedy set during the making of *The Wizard of Oz*.

Carrie Fisher and Chevy Chase in Under the Rainbow

. . . .

AUGUST

Body Heat

August 28: *Body Heat* is released. Written and directed by Lawrence Kasdan, and executive produced by an uncredited George Lucas, the film stars William Hurt and Kathleen Turner.

. . . .

OCTOBER

Introducing Shira Brie

October 20: *Star Wars* #56 ships (cover date February). Written by David Michelinie and illustrated by Walt Simonson and Tom Palmer, "Coffin in the Clouds" introduces a female Rebel pilot, Lt. Shira Brei (sic), a new romantic interest for Luke Skywalker, and an apparent source of concern for Princess Leia. In the following issue, Shira's last name is spelled Brie, a change that sticks. In subsequent issues, Shira claims that she joined the Rebellion after her entire family was slaughtered by the Empire on the planet Shalyvane.

Cover art for Star Wars #56 by Walt Simonson

Leia, Shira, and Luke meet at a Rebel base on the planet Arbra in Star Wars #56.

NOVEMBER

Time Bandits

November 6: *Time Bandits* is released. Directed by Terry Gilliam, the movie stars John Cleese and Sean Connery, and features *Star Wars* and *Empire* actors Kenny Baker (R2-D2), Jack Purvis (Chief Jawa and Chief Ugnaught), and Declan Mulholland (cut-scene Jabba).

. . . .

David Rappaport, Kenny Baker, Malcolm Dixon, Mike Edmonds, Jack Purvis, and Tiny Ross in Time Bandits

DECEMBER

Russ Manning Dies

December 1: After battling cancer, comic strip artist Russ Manning dies at the Long Beach Veteran's Hospital in California. The following year, Comic-Con International honors his memory with the addition of the Russ Manning Most Promising Newcomer Award to the annual award ceremony.

. . . .

Also in 1981...

AT-AT

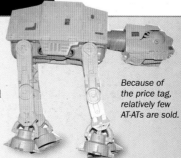

Kenner releases an AT-AT toy vehicle. With many moveable parts and priced at nearly $50.00, the Imperial walker is one of the more expensive *Star Wars* collectibles on the market.

Because of the price tag, relatively few AT-ATs are sold.

The AT-AT comes with two chin guns.

1982

UNLIKE THE PRODUCTION of *The Empire Strikes Back*, *Revenge of the Jedi* is not delayed by horrendous weather conditions or a burned-down sound stage. From studios in England to locations in Arizona and California, the biggest troubles while filming *Jedi* involve overheated costumed actors and malfunctioning robots. *Jedi* is ultimately completed on budget and on schedule.

The three directors: Irvin Kershner, George Lucas, and Richard Marquand on the Elstree Studio set of Jedi

"Artoo-Detoo is probably the most egocentric, wild, headstrong, and trying piece of machinery that any director could ever be cursed with on a set."

Richard Marquand
director of Return of the Jedi

JANUARY

Jedi Begins Filming

January 11: Principal photography begins for *Revenge of the Jedi* at Pinewood Studios in England. The first filmed scene has the Rebel heroes preparing to leave Tatooine during a sandstorm. Production includes a partial reconstruction of the full-size, steel-framed, and plywood-sheathed mock-up of the *Millennium Falcon*—previously used in *Empire*—that had been built by a firm of maritime engineers at Pembroke Docks in Wales. When filming is complete, the *Falcon* mock-up is broken down and sold for scrap. The sandstorm scene is ultimately cut from *Jedi*, but a few frames of footage appear in the trailer.

Enter the Ewok

Jedi introduces the Ewoks, natives of Endor. Kenny Baker is assigned to play the principal Ewok, Wicket, but takes ill and is replaced by 11-year-old Warwick Davis, who stands 89 centimeters (2 feet 11 inches) tall. *Jedi*'s first assistant director David Tomblin—who also worked on *Superman*, *The Empire Strikes Back*, and *Raiders of the Lost Ark*—directs Davis in an improvised movie that is filmed concurrently with *Jedi*, and is eventually titled *Return of the Ewok*.

Jabba's New Look

Although Jabba had appeared as a biped alien in Marvel's *Star Wars* comics, the character is re-imagined as an enormous animatronic puppet for *Jedi*. ILM's Phil Tippett works from sketches by concept artists Ralph McQuarrie and Nilo Rodis-Jamero to design the puppet. The completed Jabba the Hutt (now with two "t"s) is performed by three puppeteers: David Barclay (right hand and mouth), Toby Philpott (left hand, head, and tongue), and Mike Edmonds (tail).

FEBRUARY

Koo Stark

Prince Andrew meets Koo Stark—Camie from the deleted scenes in *Star Wars*—in a London disco. The tabloids monitor the pair until they part ways 18 months later.

A behind-the-scenes shot of actress/ model Koo Stark on the set of Star Wars, dressed as the character Camie.

APRIL

Unfinished Comic

Formerly titled *Star Wars Weekly*, Marvel UK's *The Empire Strikes Back* #155 presents the five-page story "Dark Lord's Conscience" by nascent comic book writer Alan Moore and artist John Stokes. Unfortunately, Marvel provides Stokes with an incomplete script, and the published result is a "story" without a conclusive ending.

Cover of Marvel UK's The Empire Strikes Back #155

A convoy of British vehicles drives through Port Stanley, August 1982.

Falklands War 🌐

April 2: The Argentine armed forces invade and occupy the Falkland Islands and South Georgia, which are under sovereignty of the United Kingdom. Britain launches an attack to retake the islands. The war ends with Argentine surrender 74 days later, on June 14.

Blue Harvest

After five months of covert set construction, *Jedi* begins filming in Buttercup Valley, near Yuma, Arizona, under the cover name *Blue Harvest*. Because the location is popular with dune-buggy riders, the set is surrounded by a chain link fence and patrolled by round-the-clock security guards. After an infiltrator takes photographs of a model and leaks them to the press, producer Howard Kazanjian continues to insist that he is not working on a *Star Wars* movie. "'This is *Blue Harvest*', I'd be saying. 'It's about horror beyond imagination!'"

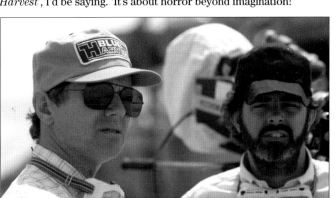

Director Richard Marquand (wearing Blue Harvest cap) and George Lucas on the set of Jedi

Endor Location

Production continues from late April through May near Smith River on Miller-Rellim Redwood Company land, and in the giant redwood forest near Crescent City in northwestern California, locations which serve as the Forest Moon of Endor. The forest terrain is especially difficult for the costumed actors, and those playing Ewoks jokingly tell production assistant Ian Bryce that they have left for the airport before they arrive on set wearing "Revenge of the Ewok" T-shirts.

The main cast pose on the set of Endor.

Also in 1982...

Revenge or Return?

Numerous members of production work under the impression that the title is *Revenge of the Jedi*. Producer Howard Kazanjian favors *Revenge*, and stickers with that title and Yoda's image are used to tag equipment and film cans.

Yoda Revenge sticker. The same design is used for a patch worn by cast and crew.

Filming Jedi's desert battle sequence in Buttercup Valley, California

ISRAEL WITHDRAWS FROM SINAI PENINSULA IN LINE WITH EGYPTIAN-ISRAELI PEACE TREATY 🌐

MAY

Double Feature

British theaters feature a double-bill of *Star Wars* and *The Empire Strikes Back*. The re-release poster combines elements from Tom Chantrell's *Star Wars* poster and Tom Jung's *Empire* poster.

Conan

May 14: John Milius's *Conan the Barbarian*, co-written by Oliver Stone, is released, starring Arnold Schwarzenegger and James Earl Jones. When Jones's character, Thulsa Doom, refers to a character as "my son," the line evokes Darth Vader from *Empire*.

Bodybuilder-turned-actor Arnold Schwarzenegger as Conan

Star Wars/Empire theatrical double-bill quad poster

Jedi Filming Wraps

May 20: Photography on *Jedi* is completed—on schedule and on budget—with the speeder bike scene at ILM in California.

Filming of the speeder bike scene in Jedi

Fox didn't want VHS sales to compete with the ongoing theatrical run.

Rental Video

May 27: *Star Wars: A New Hope* is released on VHS and Betamax, but Twentieth Century-Fox stipulates that all cassettes made available to the public are for rental only until September 1, when they can be sold for around $80.00. Cagey retailers offer the *Star Wars* cassette as a "lifetime rental," and charge customers up to $120 to keep the video at home indefinitely. *Star Wars* quickly becomes the first video to earn more than $1 million in rentals. Jack Valenti, the president of the Motion Picture Association of America, tells Congress that video cassette recorders will devastate the movie industry.

Shira Brie Lives

May 25: *Star Wars* #63 (cover date September) ships. In "The Mind Spider," written by David Michelinie and Walt Simonson, and illustrated by Tom Palmer, Luke discovers that Shira Brie—presumed killed in a starfighter crash—was really an Imperial secret agent, raised in the "palace of Emperor Palpatine." The story includes the very first rendering of the "Empire Capitol," and concludes with the revelation that Shira survived the crash.

Star Wars #63 cover art by Tom Palmer

"Empire Capitol" is on an unnamed world.

On the Executor, Darth Vader monitors Shira in a bacta tank.

Also in 1982...

Zuckuss and 4-LOM

After Kenner gave the name Dengar to the bounty hunter that Lucasfilm had previously designated Zuckuss, Kenner uses the latter name for another hunter, the one who appears in *Empire* as a rifle-wielding humanoid droid. Unfortunately, Lucasfilm has already named that character 4-LOM, a semi-acronym for "for love of money." As *Empire*'s other bounty hunters—Boba Fett, IG-88, and Bossk—have already been released as action figures, Kenner gives the name 4-LOM to the robed figure with the insectoid head.

Zuckuss action figure

4-LOM action figure

THE WEATHER CHANNEL LAUNCHES IN THE US ⊕ FIRST ISRAEL-LEBANON WAR ⊕ RALLY AGAIN

Also in 1982...

Pay-Per-View

Star Wars begins airing on pay-per-view television subscription services across the US. Long used in remote areas, cable TV and subscription services have existed since the late 1940s, but fewer than half a million households are wired for cable. *VIEW* magazine offers a cover feature on the TV premiere of *Star Wars*.

Cincinnati Pops

May 31: The Cincinnati Pops Orchestra presents the First Annual John Williams *Star Wars* Festival. The event is co-sponsored by Kenner Products, which is based in Cincinnati. According to the poster's fine print, "Juggling, bullwhip demonstrations, mime performances, and star shows" are part of the program for this one-night concert conducted by Erich Kunzel. Despite the concert's promotion as an "annual" event, it is the only John Williams *Star Wars* Festival to date.

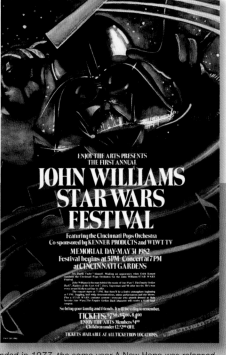

ENJOY THE ARTS PRESENTS
THE FIRST ANNUAL

JOHN WILLIAMS STAR WARS FESTIVAL

Featuring the Cincinnati Pops Orchestra
Co-sponsored by KENNER PRODUCTS and WLWT TV
MEMORIAL DAY·MAY 31 1982
Festival begins at 5PM · Concert at 7PM
at CINCINNATI GARDENS

The Cincinnati Pops Orchestra was founded in 1977, the same year A New Hope was released.

Blade Runner

June 25: *Blade Runner* is released. Directed by Ridley Scott and starring Harrison Ford and Rutger Hauer, the science-fiction film employs designer Syd Mead as "visual futurist," and features special photographic effects supervised by Douglas Trumbull. Visual effects include a miniature cityscape with a skyscraper made from a cannibalized *Millennium Falcon* model provided by ILM model-maker Bill George. Actor Kevin Thompson plays an animatronic teddy bear, and will subsequently appear as an Ewok in *Jedi*.

Anthony Daniels, Ann Sachs, Perry King, and Billy Dee Williams at a recording session

JUNE

THX Sound System logo

THX Sound

Lucasfilm launches the THX Sound System, a unique configuration of loudspeakers, originally integrated with the room acoustics of the Sprocket Systems dubbing stage but intended for cinema use. THX addresses problems such as interfering noise from adjacent theaters and the street, and marks the most significant improvement to cinema loudspeakers since World War II.

Poltergeist

June 4: *Poltergeist*, produced and co-written by Steven Spielberg, is released. A family is terrorized by supernatural forces in their own home. Spielberg ensures that the kids' bedrooms are decorated with *Star Wars* toys and posters.

ILM Groundbreaker

June 4: *Star Trek II: The Wrath of Khan* is released. Directed by Nicholas Meyer, the subtitle was originally *The Revenge of Khan*, but was changed to avoid confusion with *Revenge of the Jedi*. ILM works with Lucasfilm's Computer Division, headed by Ed Catmull, to produce the "Genesis sequence," the first fully computer-generated animated sequence ever put into a feature film.

Imperial Radio

The Empire Strikes Back radio dramatization, scripted by Brian Daley and directed by John Madden, is recorded over 10 days in a New York City studio. Frank Oz is unavailable to perform as Yoda, and Mark Hamill—who had previously demonstrated his ability to mimic Yoda on *The Muppet Show*—is briefly considered to voice the aged Jedi Master as well as Luke Skywalker. The role eventually goes to John Lithgow after he demonstrates his own ability to mimic Yoda to Madden, who had directed him earlier that year in Christopher Durang's Broadway play *Beyond Therapy*.

Mark Hamill in the studio, reprising his role as Luke Skywalker.

E.T.: The Extra-Terrestrial

June 11: *E.T.: The Extra-Terrestrial* is released. Directed by Steven Spielberg and with a screenplay by Melissa Mathison, the movie features music by John Williams and a spaceship designed by Ralph McQuarrie. In *E.T.*, a young boy shows off his collection of *Star Wars* action figures, and Williams incorporates a snippet of Yoda's theme music when an extra wearing an off-the-rack Yoda costume appears in a Halloween sequence. A scene featuring Harrison Ford as a school principal is deleted because Spielberg realizes audiences will find the increasingly famous Ford too distracting.

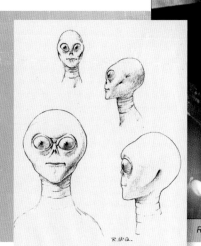

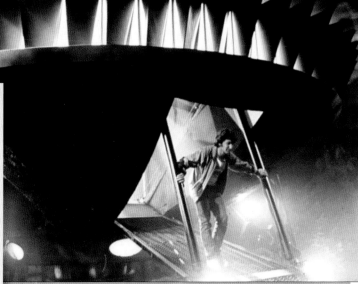

Ralph McQuarrie designed E.T.'s spaceship (above) and drew alien concepts (left).

For *Return of the Jedi*, Phil Tippett, who did stop-motion animation work on both *Star Wars* and *Empire*, becomes creature design supervisor. Tippett says, "It was George Lucas's intention to combine our experiences [from the previous movies] and bring it all together for *Jedi*. This was to be, in a sense, our graduate thesis." The mask for Klaatu—one of Jabba the Hutt's henchmen—is based on sketches by Ralph McQuarrie. Tippett also designs, sculpts, and paints the mask for the Mon Calamari Admiral Ackbar.

Klaatu mask

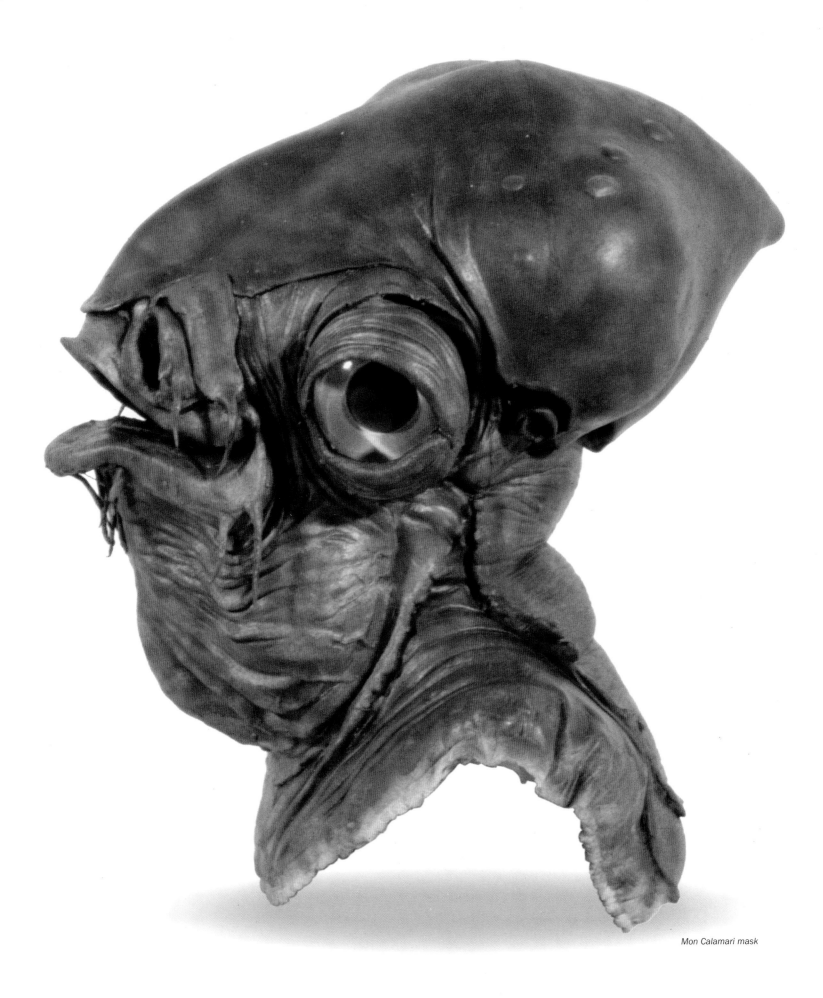

Mon Calamari mask

LaserDisc

June: *Star Wars* is released on LaserDisc. Because the Constant Linear Velocity (CLV) disc can only hold 60 minutes of playtime per side, the 121-minute-long film is time-compressed to fit on a single disc. It retails for $34.98.

LaserDiscs are 12-inch platters, the same size as LP records.

Also in 1982...

First Computer Game

Parker Bros. releases the first *Star Wars* computer game, *Star Wars: The Empire Strikes Back*, which is for the Atari 2600 VCS and Mattel Intellivision home consoles. The side-scrolling game is set on Hoth. One or two players assume the role of Rebel pilots to fly a snowspeeder and fire at advancing Imperial walkers to prevent them from reaching the Rebel base's shield generator.

Advertisement for the first Star Wars computer game

AUGUST

Meet Admiral Ackbar

Admiral Ackbar is introduced to members of the Official *Star Wars* Fan Club in *Bantha Tracks* #17. In *Jedi*, Ackbar is performed by puppeteer Timothy M. Rose, and voiced by Erik Bauersfeld.

Video Speed Limit

Star Wars is released on RCA SelectaVision's CED (Capacitance Electronic Disc) for $35.00. Like the LaserDisc released in June, the 121-minute-long *Star Wars* is slightly time-compressed, almost imperceptibly speeding up the movie to "fit" the disc.

JEDI PRODUCTION PART II

Introducing ADMIRAL ACKBAR

Admiral Ackbar

In STAR WARS, Princess Leia leads only a small part of the Rebel Alliance. The Commander of the entire Rebel Fleet is Admiral Ackbar—a member of the Mon Calamari race of highly intelligent master chess players from the water planet Dac. We'll see Admiral Ackbar and the amphibious Mon Calamari in the next chapter of the STAR WARS Saga: REVENGE OF THE JEDI.

Excerpt from Bantha Tracks #17

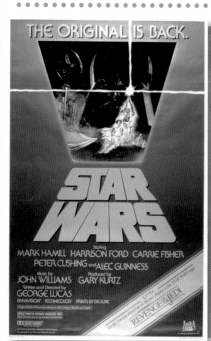

Poster for the fourth theatrical re-release of Star Wars.

Re-Release with *Revenge* Trailer

August 13: *Star Wars* is re-released for the fourth time in 1,070 theaters across the US, and debuts with a trailer for *Revenge of the Jedi*. The re-release grosses over $15 million. The trailer shows Luke wielding a blue-bladed lightsaber, the same color as the weapon he used in the previous movies, and also includes a few frames of the deleted sandstorm scene.

SEPTEMBER

Home Video

September 1: *Star Wars* is released on video in VHS and Betamax formats for the consumer market. All video formats—including the aforementioned LaserDisc and the RCA SelectaVision's CED—are edited as "pan-and-scan" versions of the movie, drastically cropping the film's wide picture plane to conform to the relatively square aspect ratio of most TV screens. The VHS and Betamax formats retail for approximately $80.

OCTOBER

Compact Disc

October 1: The first Compact Disc (CD) player, CDP-101, and the first album on CD, Billy Joel's *52nd Street*, are released by Sony in Japan. The player's retail price is around $900.

THE JEDI MASTER'S QUIZBOOK

425 Cosmic Questions & Answers About STAR WARS & THE EMPIRE STRIKES BACK

Compiled by Rusty Miller

The Jedi Master's Quizbook

October 12: Del Rey publishes *The Jedi Master's Quizbook*, compiled by Rusty Miller. It features 425 questions and answers about *Star Wars* and *The Empire Strikes Back*, which, according to Miller's foreword, range "from the obvious to the obscure."

Promotional poster from RCA

Free *Star Wars* Videodisc

October 21: RCA offers a free *Star Wars* CED videodisc with the purchase of any compatible RCA player. To advertise the promotion, RCA spends over $2 million on national television and in newspapers.

NOVEMBER

Teaser Poster

The *Revenge of the Jedi* advance poster is distributed to theaters. Painted by Drew Struzan, the poster incorporates photographic references from *Empire*. Oddly, Luke appears to be wielding a red-bladed lightsaber, while Darth Vader's is blue. In early December, Lucasfilm licensees are quietly told that the movie will be retitled *Return of the Jedi*.

Laverne and Shirley

November 9: Carrie Fisher guest stars on *Laverne and Shirley*, as does *Playboy*'s founder Hugh Hefner. Although Shirley's name remains in the show title, Cindy Williams has already left the series.

Comic Ackbar

November 14: The syndicated *Star Wars* comic strip promotes the upcoming appearance of Admiral Ackbar. In the subsequent serial by writer Archie Goodwin and artist Al Williamson, the Rebels meet the leader of their new allies, the Mon Calamari, who have agreed to help them evacuate from their Yavin base.

Goodwin and Williamson promote the new character.

Michael Jackson in his Thriller video

Thriller

November 30: Michael Jackson's album *Thriller* is released. Four days later, a 14-minute music video of the title track, directed by John Landis, premieres on television. *Thriller* becomes the best-selling album of all time.

THE SAGA CONTINUES.

STAR WARS
REVENGE OF THE JEDI

Coming May 25, 1983 to your galaxy.

THE REVENGE OF THE JEDI TEASER ONE SHEET

Revenge of the Jedi teaser poster

Also in 1982...

Micro Collection

Kenner introduces the *Star Wars* Micro Collection, a series of small-scale playsets that depict scenes from *Star Wars* and *Empire*, packaged with die-cast figurines. Playsets include various locations on the Death Star, Hoth, and *Millennium Falcon*. Although plans are made for additional playsets, low sales prompt Kenner to discontinue the Micro Collection before year's end.

Empire is Back

November 19: *The Empire Strikes Back* is re-released for the second time, grossing over $13 million.

Naming the *Executor*

November 19: Darth Vader officially dubs his Star Destroyer *Executor* in the *Star Wars* daily comic strip. As with the ongoing *Star Wars* Marvel Comics series, this mention popularizes the *Executor*, which goes unnamed in the film, novelization, and comic adaptation of *Empire*.

Detail from Star Wars comic strip by Goodwin and Williamson.

DECEMBER

The Dark Crystal

December 17: *The Dark Crystal* is released simultaneously in the UK, US, and Canada. Directed by Jim Henson and Frank Oz, who also perform various characters, the fantasy film features a cast of costumed performers and animatronic puppets, some of which use technology developed for the Yoda puppet in *Empire*. The film also features puppet-work by Tim Rose (Ackbar in *Jedi*) and Toby Philpott (Jabba's left hand, head, and tongue in *Jedi*).

Jen, a young Gelfling, in The Dark Crystal

Matte painting department supervisor Michael Pangrazio works on a glass matte painting—one of about 45 produced for *Star Wars*: Episode VI *Return of the Jedi*—for the interior docking bay on the Rebel headquarters frigate. The unpainted area at bottom right is where the live-action plate will be projected. Pangrazio says, "The final effect is magnificent, very convincing, like a 10 million dollar shot. It would be impossible to build a set anything like that."

1983

ON THE UPCOMING release of *Return of the Jedi*, Mark Hamill tells science-fiction movie magazine, *Starlog*, "With everything that's been set up, you can't bring the trilogy to a conclusion without disappointing some people. However, I'm sure many others will be surprised and pleased." *Return of the Jedi* opens in May to over 1,000 theaters and receives generally positive reviews, earning nearly $250 million by the end of December.

> "I think *Jedi* is the best *Star Wars* movie ever made, and it is definitely going to be the most successful."
>
> **Steven Spielberg**
> *TIME* magazine, May 23, 1983

INTERVIEWED BY *TIME* magazine before the release of *Jedi*, Lucas worries, "What if we have finally got to the end of the shaggy-dog story, and everybody says, 'That's it?' Technically and logistically, [*Jedi*] was the hardest of the three films to make, and all I see is the mistakes and the stuff that doesn't work." Before *Jedi*'s release, Lucas—exhausted by his work on the trilogy—announces his intention to take a two-year sabbatical from running Lucasfilm.

JANUARY

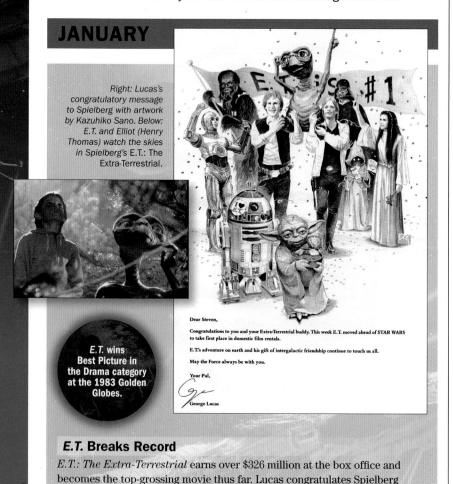

Right: Lucas's congratulatory message to Spielberg with artwork by Kazuhiko Sano. Below: E.T. and Elliot (Henry Thomas) watch the skies in Spielberg's E.T.: The Extra-Terrestrial.

Dear Steven,

Congratulations to you and your Extra-Terrestrial buddy. This week E.T. moved ahead of STAR WARS to take first place in domestic film rentals.

E.T.'s adventure on earth and his gift of intergalactic friendship continue to touch us all.

May the Force always be with you.

Your Pal,

George Lucas

E.T. wins Best Picture in the Drama category at the 1983 Golden Globes.

E.T. Breaks Record

E.T.: The Extra-Terrestrial earns over $326 million at the box office and becomes the top-grossing movie thus far. Lucas congratulates Spielberg via a full-page message in *Daily Variety* (above).

False Advertising?

Star Wars #71 ships (cover date May), with a story by Mary Jo Duffy, and art by Ron Frenz and Tom Palmer. Text and imagery on the cover suggest that the Rebels have finally located Han Solo, but the issue's final page reveals that the carbonite-frozen form in the background is definitely not Han Solo.

Star Wars #71 cover art by Ron Frenz and Tom Palmer

Lando Calrissian and Luke Skywalker discover that it is not Han frozen in the carbonite, but Chihdo, the Rodian.

Revenge Out *Return* In

January 27: Lucas officially announces that the title of his new movie has been changed to *Return of the Jedi*. The announcement prompts the price of *Revenge of the Jedi* teaser posters to skyrocket on the black market from $10 to $200. Lucasfilm supervises the destruction of the balance of *Revenge* posters at a warehouse, but reserves 6,800 of them for lucky members of the Official *Star Wars* Fan Club, who pay only $9.50. The posters sell out in three days.

Order form from Bantha Tracks #19

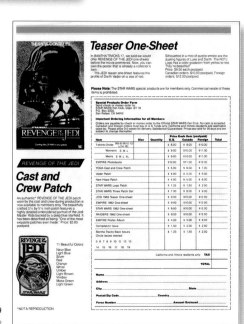

Teaser One-Sheet

Cast and Crew Patch

KILAUEA ON HAWII BEGINS SLOWLY ERUPTING ● FINAL EPISODE OF *M*A*S*H* IS WATCHED BY

Ackbar Action Figure

Kenner's latest mail-in offer, an Admiral Ackbar action figure who grips his "command stick," is shipped to collectors in advance of *Jedi*'s release.

Appearances in Bantha Tracks and the Star Wars comic strip also promote advance awareness of Ackbar.

SPECIAL OFFER!
FREE ADMIRAL ACKBAR
FIGURE FROM STAR WARS:
REVENGE OF THE **JEDI**
WITH SIX PROOFS-OF-PURCHASE

Now, get a special free action figure from the next chapter of the STAR WARS. saga, REVENGE OF THE JEDI., premiering in May 1983! Just purchase six Star Wars. Action Figures, send in the six proof-of-purchase seals with your name and address to the address below.

"REVENGE OF THE JEDI" FIGURE OFFER
P.O. BOX 909
YOUNG AMERICA, MINNESOTA 55399

• Offer expires January 31, 1983.
• Allow 10 to 12 weeks for processing.
• Offer void where prohibited, taxed or otherwise regulated.
• Offer good in U.S.A. only.

Mail-in offer as it appears on action figure cardbacks

FEBRUARY

ESB on NPR

February 14: National Public Radio broadcasts *The Empire Strikes Back* radio dramatization. Although the series does well and encourages talks for a radio drama of *Return of the Jedi*, the plans are scrapped because of Reaganomic cutbacks to NPR funding.

THE **EMPIRE STRIKES BACK**

COMING SOON TO A RADIO NEAR YOU

THE SAGA CONTINUES.
LISTEN AS LUKE SKYWALKER™ MEETS YODA, THE JEDI MASTER™ AND LEARNS THE SECRET BEHIND THE FORCE™
IN 10 EXCITING STEREO EPISODES.
EXCLUSIVELY ON NATIONAL PUBLIC RADIO MEMBER STATIONS NATIONWIDE

Empire on NPR poster by McQuarrie

MARCH

Soviet Empire

March 8: President Ronald Reagan, in his remarks at the Annual Convention of the National Association of Evangelicals in Orlando, Florida, refers to the Soviet Union as "an evil empire."

Reagan addresses the nation

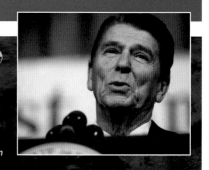

Reagan's Star Wars

March 23: President Reagan, in his address to the nation on defense and national security, proposes that the US could one day "intercept and destroy strategic ballistic missiles before they reached our own soil or that of our allies." Officially called the Strategic Defense Initiative, the proposal to use ground-based and satellite technology to create an antimissile shield quickly becomes known as "Star Wars." Lucasfilm notifies news bureaus that *Star Wars* is a trademark of Lucasfilm Ltd., and that the SDI should not be referred to as such (to no avail).

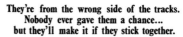

DEMILITARIZE SPACE
NO STAR WARS

Button protesting Reagan's plan to militarize space.

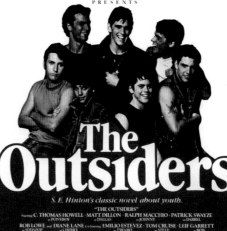

They're from the wrong side of the tracks. Nobody ever gave them a chance... but they'll make it if they stick together.

FRANCIS FORD COPPOLA
PRESENTS

The **Outsiders**

S. E. Hinton's classic novel about youth.

Coppola's *Outsiders*

March 25: *The Outsiders*, directed by Francis Ford Coppola, is released. Based on the 1967 novel by S.E. Hinton, the movie is actor C. Thomas Howell's second after *E.T.*, and features an early performance by Tom Cruise.

An Australian movie poster for the release of The Outsiders, which features (L–R) Emilio Estevez, Patrick Swayze, Karate Kid Ralph Macchio, Matt Dillon, C. Thomas Howell, Rob Lowe, and Tom Cruise.

Also in 1983...

A New Apprentice

Marvel Comics publishes *Star Wars Annual* #3. Written by Mary Jo Duffy and drawn by Klaus Janson, "The Apprentice" introduces Flint, son of a dead Jedi Knight, who is recruited by Darth Vader for "special training."

Cover art by Klaus Janson

STAR WARS ANNUAL

APRIL

Tokyo Disneyland

April 15: Tokyo Disneyland opens in Urayasu, Chiba, Japan. Constructed by Walt Disney Imagineering, the 465,000 square meter (115 acre) theme park is modeled after Disneyland in California and Magic Kingdom in Florida.

Kimono-clad Minnie and Mickey Mouse at Tokyo Disneyland

MAY

Hamill in *Amadeus*

Mark Hamill plays Wolfgang Amadeus Mozart in the Broadway production of Peter Shaffer's *Amadeus* at the Broadhurst Theater. Hamill had already spent 30 weeks in the role as *Amadeus* traveled the United States on its first national tour. He won the part after auditioning for the New York production in 1982.

Mark Hamill in Amadeus. *When Gary Kurtz learns Hamill is to play Mozart, he gives a gift: piano lessons.*

Jedi Preview

May 7: An advance screening of *Return of the Jedi* is held for Lucasfilm employees and their families at the Coronet Theater in San Francisco.

The Coronet Theater also screened the Blade Runner *premiere in 1982.*

Return of the Jedi Novelization

May 12: The novelization of *Return of the Jedi* is released. Author James Kahn previously authored *Poltergeist*'s novelization (1982). The novel reveals Luke's relationship to Leia, and includes an idiosyncratic detail of Luke hearing Ben Kenobi's spirit explain: "I took you to live with my brother Owen on Tatooine… and your mother took Leia to live as the daughter of Senator Organa on Alderaan." It becomes the bestselling book of 1983.

Also in 1983…

Message from Yoda

Yoda spreads the good word about reading on a poster for the American Librarian Association (ALA). The keeper of ancient wisdom also serves as "spokescreature" for National Library Week, April 17–23. The poster is translated into several languages, and widely distributed to public libraries, schools, and hospitals.

READ

and The Force is with you.

The ALA's Yoda poster remains in production for more than 20 years.

Lucas on *TIME*

May 23: Lucas is on the cover of *TIME* magazine. *TIME*'s San Francisco Correspondent Dick Thompson observes, "Lucas seemed every bit as nervous about *Jedi* as he was about *Star Wars*. He is a compulsive worrier, a nonstop perfectionist. Maybe that is why his movies are so good."

Jedi theatrical poster art by Tim Reamer. The same artwork is also used for the novelization's cover.

Opening Day

May 25: *Return of the Jedi* is released in 1,002 theaters. It breaks an industry record with the largest opening day gross, $6.1 million. *Jedi* earns $45 million by the end of the first week, and proceeds to become the year's highest-grossing film, earning more than $252 million. In interviews, Lucas admits he is "burned out" from spending nearly a decade on the trilogy. In *TIME* magazine, he announces his intention to take a two-year sabbatical after he finishes his duties as co-executive producer of the next *Indiana Jones* movie. As for more *Star Wars* films, Lucas maintains that if he makes any more, they will likely be the "prequels," the three episodes that precede the events of Episode IV *A New Hope*.

As with previous Star Wars films, the release of Jedi brings long lines to movie theaters, including the Loews Astor Plaza, the largest single-screen theater in New York.

JUNE

Lucasfilm's secrecy surrounding Anakin Skywalker's "reveal" results in a discreet unmasking in the comic adaptation.

Cover art by Bill Sienkiewicz

Comic Adaptation

Marvel Comics simultaneously releases the first of a four-issue adaptation of *Jedi* and a collected "super special" edition of all four issues. Written by Archie Goodwin and drawn by Al Williamson and Carlos Garzon, the adaptation's idiosyncrasies include the apparent survival of Yoda (Luke leaves the elderly Jedi "to much-needed rest"), Ben Kenobi's spirit claiming that he delivered the newborn Leia to "foster parents" on Alderaan, and no Jedi spirits appearing on Endor at the story's end.

Dalton's Bestseller

B. Dalton Bookstores, the largest book retailing chain in the US, announces that the *Jedi* novelization has sold more copies than any other book the chain has ever carried.

Also in 1983...

Jedi Figures

Continuing its well-established action figure line, Kenner brings out a whole host of new toys to tie in with *Return of the Jedi*.

No. 70690: Chief Chirpa

No. 70670: Gamorrean Guard

No. 70680: Emperor's Royal Guard

No. 70790: Bib Fortuna

No. 71240: The Emperor (released the following year)

First Lando Novel

June 12: *Lando Calrissian and the Mindharp of Sharu* by L. Neil Smith is published by Del Rey. The story is set prior to the events of *A New Hope*, after Lando acquires the *Millennium Falcon*. A gambler and adventurer, Lando is coerced into searching for the legendary Mindharp, a mine of ancient alien knowledge. The novel introduces Lando's new ally, the droid Vuffi Raa. Smith's previous novels include *The Probability Broach* and *The Venus Belt*.

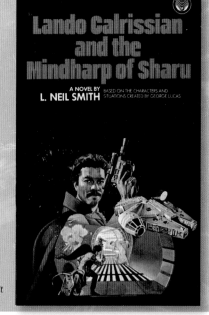

Cover art by William Schmidt

Pioneer Update

June 13: *Pioneer 10* becomes the first man-made object to leave the solar system as it passes the orbit of Neptune, which—because of Pluto's eccentric orbit—is presently the outermost planet in the solar system.

Crossing Neptune's orbit, Pioneer 10 is 4.52 billion km (2.81 billion miles) from the Sun.

⊕ SALLY RIDE IS FIRST US WOMAN IN SPACE

JULY

Jedi Adventure Centers

One hundred and thirty Jedi Adventure Centers are sent out to malls across the US. Devised by distributor Twentieth Century-Fox to promote the release of *Return of the Jedi*, each Center is a 91-kilogram (200-pound) modular walkthrough display that fills a 4.25 meter (14-foot) square area, measures about 2.44 meters (eight feet) tall, and features three separate activity areas: a Jedi Hall of Fame, Photo Center, and Communication Center. It is the most ambitious movie promotion Fox has ever staged at shopping venues.

The fully assembled Jedi Adventure Center

Newspaper ad for Fox's Jedi promotion

Death Star Battle

Star Wars: Return of the Jedi—Death Star Battle is released by Parker Bros. for the Atari 2600. Set in the Endor system, the game offers players the chance to pilot the *Millennium Falcon* against many TIE fighters before entering the second Death Star's main reactor to destroy the battle station.

Package art for Death Star Battle by Parker Bros.

Rolling Stone cover photograph by Aaron Rapoport.

Rolling Stone

Summer: Carrie Fisher, Darth Vader, an Ewok, and a Gamorrean guard are on the cover of *Rolling Stone*. In the interview inside, Lucas reiterates his intent to take off at least two years work. "All the prequel stories exist," Lucas says. As for Luke Skywalker's adventures beyond *Jedi*, "I have a tiny notebook full of notes on that. If I'm really ambitious, I could proceed to figure out what would have happened to Luke."

SEPTEMBER

Second Lando Novel

September 12: *Lando Calrissian and the Flamewind of Oseon* by L. Neil Smith is published by Del Rey. Lando and Vuffi Raa must fly the *Falcon* through the Flamewind, a massive stream of radiation that is an annual phenomenon in the Oseon system.

Flamewind of Oseon cover art by William Schmidt

Also in 1983...

Merchandise

Return of the Jedi roller skates made by Brookfield Athletic

Metal lunchbox made by King Seeley Thermos

LUKE SKYWALKER™ rescues PRINCESS LEIA™

Kellogg's cereal promotion from Australia: breakfasters rub off the silver spot on "decoder discs" to see if they have won one of 2,620 Toltoys Return of the Jedi prizes.

OCTOBER

Mad Jedi

MAD magazine features the satire *Star Bores: Re-Hash of the Jeti*. Written by Dick DeBartolo and illustrated by Mort Drucker, the satire confirms that Darth Vader is a sadist, but not a mathematician.

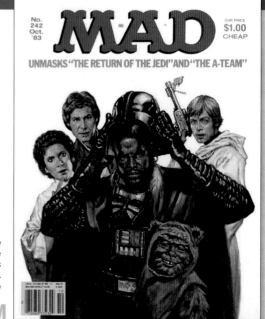

MAD also satirizes the television series The A-Team, which features actor Mr. T as B.A. Baracus.

Back to Bond

October 7: *Never Say Never Again* is released. The non-EON Productions remake of *Thunderball* (1965) returns Sean Connery to the role of James Bond, which he left after *Diamonds Are Forever* (1971), and reunites him with director Irvin Kershner.

Poster art by Rudy Obrero

Ord Mantell Revisited

Star Wars: Rebel Mission to Ord Mantell is released on Buena Vista records. It is written by Brian Daley, author of the Han Solo novels and *Star Wars* radio dramas, and features music and sound effects from the movies, along with a cast of unidentified voice actors as the Rebel heroes. Like the syndicated *Star Wars* comic strip, *Rebel Mission* expands on Han Solo's mention (in *Empire*) of his encounter with a bounty hunter on Ord Mantell while the Rebel base on Hoth is still under construction. Because *Rebel Mission*'s version of events on Ord Mantell differs from previously published stories, fans are left to ponder the continuity issues.

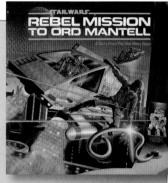

Ord Mantell is an Outer Rim scrap heap planet, home to many illegals.

NOVEMBER

Classic Creatures

November 21: *Classic Creatures: Return of the Jedi* airs on CBS. Directed by Robert Guenette, the documentary about the making of *Jedi* is hosted by Carrie Fisher and Billy Dee Williams, and features interviews with numerous cast and crew members.

After Endor

November 22: *Star Wars* #81 ships (cover date March). Written by Mary Jo Duffy and drawn by Ron Frenz, Tom Palmer, and Tom Mandrake, "Jawas of Doom" is the first *Star Wars* story set after the events of *Return of the Jedi*. The Jawas discover an unconscious Boba Fett in the desert, and mistake the armored bounty hunter for a derelict droid. Meanwhile, Han Solo returns to Tatooine, unaware that Boba Fett—last seen falling into the maw of the Sarlacc in *Jedi*—is still alive. After Solo confronts Fett again, Fett appears to meet his end a second time.

Boba Fett awakens in a Jawa sandcrawler in Star Wars #81.

Lando Calrissian and the Starcave of ThonBoka
A NOVEL BY L. NEIL SMITH
BASED ON THE CHARACTERS AND SITUATIONS CREATED BY GEORGE LUCAS
Ballantine / 31164 / $2.50

Starcave of ThonBoka cover art by William Schmidt

Third Lando Novel

November 12: *Lando Calrissian and the Starcave of ThonBoka* by L. Neil Smith is published. Lando and Vuffi Raa have a final confrontation with their nemesis, Rokur Gepta, the last sorcerer of Tund.

Twice Upon a Time begins a limited release. Produced and directed by John Korty and Charles Swenson, and executive produced by Lucas, the animated film uses stop-motion techniques for cut-out plastic pieces on a light table, a process that Korty calls "Lumage" animation (an abbreviation for "Luminous image"). Although the film is a commercial failure, its whimsical story and pioneering techniques become well known to many animation aficionados.

Early concept art for Twice Upon A Time

DECEMBER

Saga Documentary

December 3: *From Star Wars to Jedi: The Making of a Saga* is broadcast on PBS. Written and directed by Richard Schickel, and narrated by Mark Hamill, the documentary film is an overview of the entire *Star Wars* trilogy, with numerous interviews and behind-the-scenes clips from the movies.

1984-1996

BETWEEN THE TRILOGIES

WILL STAR WARS survive without the movies? For fans, the answer is an emphatic "Yes." After a dip in the late 1980s, *Star Wars* roars back to relevance with record-breaking TV projects, comics, video games, and music releases. This era is marked by innovative effects work from ILM and the debut of *The Young Indiana Jones Chronicles*, while *Star Wars* also arrives at Disney's theme parks. This period also sees the rise of the Expanded Universe—a unified narrative running through *Star Wars* spin-off stories and novels.

1984

DESPITE THE REALITY of no new movies on the horizon, *Star Wars* continues its winning streak. George Lucas is immortalized at Hollywood's famous Chinese Theatre, while *The Ewok Adventure* brings *Star Wars* to television. Ewoks also abound in spin-off books as the Licensing arm of Lucasfilm caters to younger fans. Meanwhile, Lucas and Steven Spielberg keep the *Indy* franchise humming along with the darker sequel *Indiana Jones and the Temple of Doom*.

> "We wanted to be the first people to have tennis shoe prints at Mann's Chinese Theatre."

Steven Spielberg
on his and George Lucas's prints in the theater's cement sidewalk

JANUARY

Droids at the Smithsonian

Lucasfilm donates an R2-D2 and C-3PO unit to the Smithsonian Institution's National Museum of American History. The famous droids are a popular exhibit.

Game On for Lucasfilm

A new computer games division, Lucasfilm Games (later LucasArts), is announced. Ballblazer and Rescue on Fractalus! are showcased at the 1984 Consumer Electronics Show.

The donated models had been used in Jedi.

FEBRUARY

Thousands Join the Club

Membership in the Official *Star Wars* Fan Club peaks at 184,046 members.

Touchdown

February 11: The space shuttle *Challenger* completes its 10th mission—designation STS-41-B—with the first-ever touchdown at the Shuttle Landing Facility at Kennedy Space Center in Merritt Island, Florida.

The mission, which commenced on February 3, saw the first untethered space walk using the Manned Maneuvering Unit by astronauts Bruce McCandless and Robert L. Stewart.

Apple Branches Out

January 24: Apple launches its first computer to bear the name "Macintosh." The revolutionary machine introduces the mass market to the combination of a graphical user interface and a mouse. It is revealed in an advertisement directed by Ridley Scott at the US Superbowl in January. One of the first people to buy the computer is the father of John Knoll (who will later create Photoshop with his brother Thomas and join ILM).

Apple Computer founder Steve Jobs and CEO and chairman John Sculley present the Mac.

As well as a graphical interface and mouse, the first Macintosh has a nine-inch screen, a floppy disc drive, and 128k of RAM.

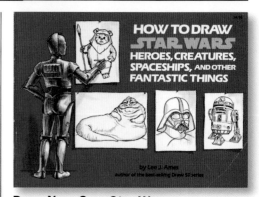

Draw Your Own *Star Wars*

February 12: Youngsters can now create their own *Star Wars* pictures with *How To Draw Star Wars Heroes, Creatures, Spaceships, and Other Fantastic Things*, an 80-page drawing tutorial by Lee J. Ames, published by Random House.

Big Film on the Small Screen

February 26: CBS's network premiere of *Star Wars: Episode IV A New Hope* draws 35 percent of the total television audience.

US MARINES PULL OUT OF BEIRUT, LEBANON ☻ SIEGE AT THE LIBYAN EMBASSY IN LONDON

MARCH

Comic Stripped

March 11: After five years in newspapers, the final *Star Wars* comic strip is published by the *Los Angeles Times* Syndicate. The last story marks the end of the fruitful pairing of writer Archie Goodwin and artist Al Williamson, who brought careful craftsmanship to the comics page in compact daily installments syndicated throughout Canada and the US. The wrap-up storyline is titled "The Final Trap" and centers around R2-D2 and C-3PO discovering a mysterious messenger drone and then accidentally triggering a telepathic ambush set up by Darth Vader.

The final installment of the Star Wars comic strip, which ran from March 1979 to March 1984

APRIL

The Marvel Comics Factor

Marvel Comics' *Star Wars* #86 (cover date August) is released. The story "The Alderaan Factor" centers on Princess Leia's mission to the alien world of Yinchor and her test of wills against an Alderaanian stormtrooper there. "The Alderaan Factor" is the one and only Marvel *Star Wars* comic story written by Randy Stradley, though he goes on to write other stories when the title moves to Dark Horse Comics.

The cover of Star Wars #86

Chemical Weapons

April 4: US President Ronald Reagan calls for an international ban on chemical weapons. Negotiations lead to the Chemical Weapons Convention, which prohibits the production, possession, and use of such weapons.

The Chemical Weapons Convention is signed in 1993.

Return of the Academy Awards®

April 9: At the 56th Academy Awards®, Richard Edlund, Ken Ralston, Dennis Muren, and Phil Tippett receive a Special Achievement Award for Best Visual Effects for their work on *Return of the Jedi*. The movie is nominated for Best Set Direction (Norman Reynolds, Fred Hole, James L. Schoppe, and Michael Ford), Best Sound (Ben Burtt, Gary Summers, Randy Thom, and David Parker), Best Sound Effects Editing (Ben Burtt), and Best Original Score (John Williams).

Academy Award® winners for Best Visual Effects: (L–R) Richard "Cheech" Marin (presenter), Richard Edlund, Ken Ralston, Dennis Muren, Phil Tippett, and Tommy Chong (presenter).

MAY

Spielberg and Lucas sign their names in the cement before leaving their hand and footprints.

Cemented in History

May 16: Continuing a Hollywood tradition, George Lucas and Steven Spielberg put their hand and footprints into the cement at Mann's Chinese Theatre (previously Grauman's). Their cement block is adjacent to the one that features the prints of Darth Vader, R2-D2, and C-3PO.

Computer Lift-off

The Last Starfighter is released. Directed by Nick Castle, it is one of the earliest films to use computer graphics to depict starships and battle scenes in a storyline that blurs computer games and real life.

The Adventures of Teebo is written and illustrated by Lucasfilm's art director, Joe Johnston.

Ewok Tales

Teebo, one of the Ewoks from *Return of the Jedi*, becomes the focus of his own adventures in a new illustrated book published by Random House. *The Adventures of Teebo: A Tale of Magic and Suspense* tells the tale of Teebo's struggle to rescue his sister from Duloks despite Yuzzum warriors and a giant Grudakk. In fact, the furry creatures venture beyond their forest moon en masse into bookstores as Lucasfilm makes the most of the kid-friendly aspects of *Return of the Jedi*. Titles include *How the Ewoks Saved the Trees*, *Wicket Finds a Way*, *Three Cheers for Kneesaa*, *The Ewoks' Hang-Gliding Adventure*, and *The Baby Ewoks' Picnic Surprise*.

Indy Strikes Back

May 23: *Indiana Jones and the Temple of Doom* is released. Executive produced by George Lucas and directed by Steven Spielberg, the sequel has a darker tone which echoes that of *The Empire Strikes Back*. "I wasn't okay with that," Spielberg says. "I kind of resisted, but George was tenacious that he wanted the second one to be darker. This is what he wanted to do, and I was his director for hire." ILM's effects work includes a mine-car chase that accounts for one third of the film's 140 special effects shots. Many *Star Wars* alumni contribute to the film, including visual effects supervisor Dennis Muren, producer Robert Watts, and sound designer Ben Burtt. In addition, the film features a score by John Williams and is shot at Elstree Studios in England.

The Royal European Premiere of Temple of Doom sees Lucas, Spielberg, Kate Capshaw, and Jonathan Ke Quan meet Diana, Princess of Wales, in London.

Busy Computer Bees

The Adventures of André and Wally B may be a simple story of a vengeful bee, but the short is a breakthrough demonstration of computer-synthesized, motion-blurred full-character animation by the Lucasfilm Computer Graphics Project team. It is directed by John Lasseter, formerly of Walt Disney Feature Animation.

JULY

Salyut 7

July 25: Soviet cosmonaut Svetlana Savitskaya becomes the first woman to walk in space. She performs an extra-vehicular spacewalk (EVA) and walks into the history books by spending over three hours outside the Soviet space station Salyut 7.

AUGUST

EditDroid

The science magazine *Discover* explores the emerging phenomenon of digital filmmaking with a cover story about Lucasfilm's revolutionary "EditDroid"— a machine that heralds the beginning of non-linear editing. The article also discusses Lucas's other pioneering projects: An audio signal processor (ASP) for sound editing, and Pixar, a computer graphics machine for creating digital images.

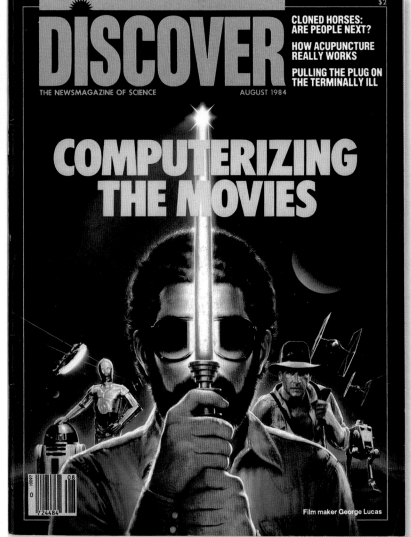

DISCOVER
THE NEWSMAGAZINE OF SCIENCE   AUGUST 1984
$2

CLONED HORSES: ARE PEOPLE NEXT?
HOW ACUPUNCTURE REALLY WORKS
PULLING THE PLUG ON THE TERMINALLY ILL

COMPUTERIZING THE MOVIES

Film maker George Lucas

George Lucas grasps a lightsaber as well as the future of filmmaking. He says, "Anybody who's worked with film realizes what a stupid 19th century idea it is."

Star Wars #90 cover art by Tom Palmer and Bob McLeod

Choosing or Losing?

Marvel Comics' *Star Wars* #90 (cover date December) is published. Written by Mary Jo Duffy, "The Choice" centers on Luke and Leia as they try to cool rising tensions among their Rebel friends. In doing so, they miss the First Conference of Free Peoples, chaired by Admiral Ackbar and Mon Mothma, thus losing their opportunity to make decisions as part of the new galactic government.

A Voyage of *Discovery*

August 30: The *Discovery* space shuttle blasts off from Kennedy Space Center, Florida. Its first mission—STS-41-D—is the 12th of NASA's Space Shuttle Program.

SEPTEMBER

Enter

Children's computer and technology magazine *Enter* runs a feature on the pioneering special effects developed by Lucasfilm and ILM, focusing on the effects mastery displayed in the *Star Wars* films.

September 21: *Until September* is released. The romance is directed by *Return of the Jedi* director Richard Marquand, and stars Karen Allen, who starred as Marion in *Raiders of the Lost Ark*.

Badge of Honor

At the 42nd World Science Fiction Convention (aka L.A.con II), badges reading, "I Sat Through the Trilogy," are handed out to those who watch a marathon *Star Wars* screening.

1,100 dedicated fans receive the badge after watching the entire trilogy back to back.

I SAT THROUGH THE TRILOGY
SEPT. 2-3, 1984
L.A. con II

OCTOBER

Terminator Begins

October 26: The science-fiction movie *The Terminator* is released. It begins the now classic story of a time-traveling cyborg assassin whose mission will go on to feature in three more films with visual effects by ILM.

Arnold Schwarzenegger as the eponymous cyborg from a future where robots battle humanity.

THE EWOKS
and the Lost Children

#6

Based on the television movie THE EWOK ADVENTURE.
Random House.

NOVEMBER

Book Tie-In With TV

To coincide with the two-hour television special, *The Ewok Adventure*, which airs this month on ABC, Random House publishes an adaptation of the story in a book called *The Ewoks and the Lost Children*.

The novelization of the movie is written by Amy Ehrlich, an author of over 30 books for young readers.

Home Video Technology

CBS/Fox Home Video releases *The Empire Strikes Back* on VHS cassette. The tape is priced at $79.95 and shoots up the sales charts, where it alternates with *Police Academy* for the number one spot. Although CBS/Fox paid $15 million for the video cassette rights, it benefits from a home video boom: Of the 17 million home VCRs in the US at the time, more than 40 percent are less than a year old.

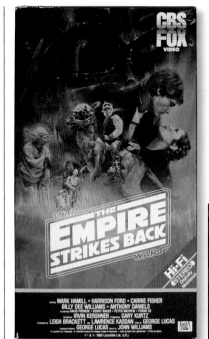

Landslide for Reagan

November 6: In the US presidential election, Ronald Reagan defeats Walter Mondale with 59 percent of the popular vote. Reagan carries 49 states in the Electoral College; Mondale wins only his home state of Minnesota and the District of Columbia.

Artwork from Star Wars: Droids, where C-3PO and R2-D2 continue their adventures, this time in an animated galaxy far, far away.

Cartoon Time

Everything is animated as production begins at Canada's Nelvana Studios on two new animation shows to premiere the following year. *Star Wars: Ewoks* presents more tales of the Ewoks while *Star Wars: Droids* follows the adventures of R2-D2 and C-3PO. Each episode is 30 minutes long and the two shows will air back-to-back, creating one full hour of *Star Wars* animation every Saturday morning. The initial order is for 13 episodes of each show.

Development artwork for Kneesaa a Jari Kintaka, Princess of Bright Tree Village, and her love interest, Wicket Wystri Warrick.

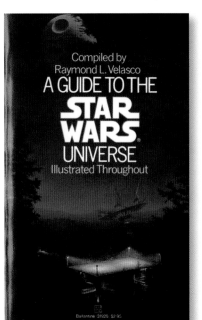

An Encyclopedic Universe

Fans take an encyclopedic look at everything *Star Wars* when Ballantine publishes *A Guide to the Star Wars Universe* by Raymond L. Velasco. It is the first guide to incorporate elements of spin-off material such as the novel *Splinter of the Mind's Eye* and the Han Solo novels by Brian Daley. To resolve how to list strange alien monikers, the book lists all characters alphabetically by their first names.

The 215-page book has nearly 1,000 entries and combines both in- and out-of-universe references.

Drew Struzan's poster concept art for The Ewok Adventure—ABC's highest rated movie of the season and the second highest rated movie on all networks for the whole of 1984.

On set: (L–R) Catarine Towani (Fionnula Flanagan), Kaink (Margarita Fernandez), Cindel Towani (Aubree Miller), and Jeremitt Towani (Guy Boyd).

Cindel Towani (Aubree Miller), Logray (Bobby Bell), and Mace Towani (Eric Walker) consult the crystal image spinner to see what's happening elsewhere on the forest moon.

As Easy as ABC

November 25: *The Ewok Adventure* airs as "The ABC Sunday Night Movie" to great success. The feature is directed by John Korty. Eric Walker—who plays young castaway Mace Towani—tells *Star Wars Insider* magazine: "A lot of people don't realize Lucas directed the reshoot... When he was on the set, the pace was a hundred times faster." *The Ewok Adventure* ushers in a wave of Ewok-themed merchandise and spin-off stories as *Star Wars* enters an era without the prospect of any new theatrical movies.

DECEMBER

Boeing...Boeing...Gone

December 1: In the Controlled Impact Demonstration (CID), NASA crashes a remote-controlled Boeing 720 into the desert of Edwards, California, in an experiment to measure crash survivability.

The controlled experiment helps to establish guidelines on fire regulations and retardant materials for air travel.

Also in 1984...

Star Wars Cereal

There's "a new Force at breakfast" with the first *Star Wars*-branded breakfast cereal: C-3PO's from Kellogg's. Ewoks and glue are a match made in heaven when the Italian company UHU gives away free Ewok figurines with its glue sticks.

1985

IT'S THE LAST HURRAH for *Star Wars* toys, as Kenner releases its final action figures. Meanwhile, *Star Wars* continues its move onto the small screen with three separate television projects. The TV movie *Ewoks: The Battle for Endor* excites fans with a blend of fantasy and action, while the twin Saturday morning cartoon series *Droids* and *Ewoks* breathe new life into *Star Wars* via the medium of animation. Things come full circle when *Droids* and *Ewoks* provide inspiration for new toy lines from Kenner.

> "The effects we did were pretty primitive... George just told us to go out there and have some fun."
>
> **Joe Johnston**
> *on making the live-action Ewoks movies*

MARCH

Gorbachev

March 11: Mikhail Gorbachev becomes General Secretary of the Soviet Communist party and leader of the Soviet Union. He succeeds Konstantin Chernenko and brings in a policy of glasnost ("openness").

Gorbachev at the 26th Party Congress

March 26: Keira Knightley is born in England. She will play Sabé, Padmé Amidala's decoy Queen, in Episode I.

Triple Bill

For the first time since the private screening at L.A.con II, the entire *Star Wars* trilogy is screened on a triple bill. The event is held at nine theaters across the US as well as in Canada, the UK, France, Germany, and Australia.

TOGETHER!

STAR WARS THE EMPIRE STRIKES BACK RETURN OF THE JEDI

ALL THREE ON THE ONE PROGRAMME

Strategic Star Wars

In his remarks at the National Space Club Luncheon, President Reagan says, "The Strategic Defense Initiative has been labeled 'Star Wars,' but it isn't about war; it's about peace. It isn't about retaliation; it's about prevention. It isn't about fear; it's about hope. And in that struggle, if you'll pardon my stealing a film line: The Force is with us."

Also in 1985...

Yak Face

When Kenner's *Star Wars* action figure line is axed, one final figure has not yet been distributed. Yak Face, who appears briefly in Jabba's palace in *Jedi*, never retails in the US, and will become a much sought after collectors' item.

🌐 **FIRST SUCCESSFUL ARTIFICIAL HEART TRANSPLANT** 🌐 **THE DISCOVERY CHANNEL LAUNCHES** 🌐

APRIL

Victory over Coke

April 23: Coca-Cola changes its formula and releases "New Coke." Consumers respond negatively to the sweeter concoction and rivals Pepsi seize the opportunity to declare "V-C Day," for Victory over Coke. A humbled Coca-Cola brings its original formula back in less than three months.

A consumer expresses her dissatisfaction with "New Coke" two months after its launch.

MAY

Latino

Latino, directed by *American Graffiti* alumnus Haskell Wexler, is screened at the 1985 Cannes Film Festival. The film depicts the Nicaraguan conflict between the Sandinistas and Contras. In addition to helping his friend Wexler obtain a distribution deal, Lucas serves as a consultant on the film. Lucas says, "On the one hand I'm doing these huge productions and at the same time I'm helping on these little productions, for my friends. But in most of the interviews with me, they're passed right over as though they never existed. But those movies may be closer to what I am than *Star Wars*." Ultimately, Lucas serves as executive producer on *Latino*, but declines a credit.

Haskell Wexler directing on the set of his film Latino

May 25: *Return of the Jedi* is re-released to theaters.

May 27: Basketball superstar Kareem Abdul-Jabbar leads the LA Lakers to victory over their arch-rivals, the Boston Celtics, in the NBA Final.

JUNE

They call themselves "The Goonies."

The secret caves. The old lighthouse. The lost map. The treacherous traps. The hidden treasure. And Sloth…

Join the adventure.

THE GOONIES PG

The Goonies

June 7: Richard Donner's adventure *The Goonies* is released. The film is co-produced by Steven Spielberg, features 18 visual effects by ILM under the supervision of Michael McAlister, and co-stars Jonathan Ke Quan from *Indiana Jones and the Temple of Doom*.

"Weird Al" Yankovic

June 18: "Weird Al" Yankovic releases *Dare to Be Stupid*, featuring the parody song "Yoda" set to the tune of the Kinks classic "Lola."

Cocoon

June 21: Ron Howard's warm-hearted sci-fi movie *Cocoon* debuts, with visual effects based on designs by Ralph McQuarrie. McQuarrie, Ken Ralston, Scott Farrar, and David Berry receive an Academy Award® for Best Visual Effects for ILM's work on the film.

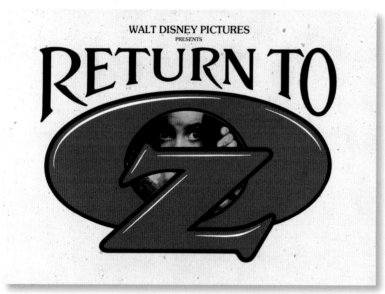

Press kit cover for Return to Oz

Return to Oz

June 21: *Return to Oz*, a semi-sequel to the 1939 classic, *The Wizard of Oz*, is released. The directorial debut of Lucas's USC classmate Walter Murch, the sound designer on *THX* and *Graffiti*, *Return* features Brian Henson, son of Muppets creator Jim Henson. During production, Lucas assists when the film runs over budget, commuting between San Francisco and London for no salary or credit.

JULY

Back to the Future

July 3: USC alumnus Robert Zemeckis's *Back to the Future* is released. Produced by Steven Spielberg, the time-travel adventure features effects work by ILM. In one scene, where Marty McFly is stranded in 1955, he poses as an alien visitor named "Darth Vader."

Back to the Future becomes the most successful film of 1985.

AUGUST

Japan's National Space Development Agency reveals its first astronauts. Takao Doi, Chiaki Mukai, and Mamoru Mohri are selected as payload specialist candidates for one of NASA's upcoming space shuttle missions.

Real Droids

August 5: *Fortune* magazine publishes a story on Lucasfilm's EditDroid and SoundDroid, which automate film and sound editing with software designed to replace traditional editing tools. The SoundDroid retails for $175,000 and the EditDroid for $93,000. Also mentioned among Lucasfilm's new ventures is Pixar, a computer animation company (named after the Pixar Image Computer), which is under consideration for a public offering.

The EditDroid has three screens and a controller called the Touchpad.

Only one prototype of the SoundDroid is ever made.

Titanic Found

August 31: Oceanographer Robert Ballard finds the wreck of the RMS *Titanic*, which has lain undiscovered in the North Atlantic since 1912.

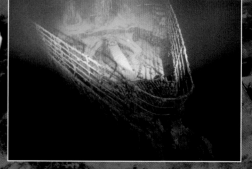

Over 5,000 artifacts are recovered from the rediscovered wreck of the Titanic.

SEPTEMBER

The Ewoks *and Droids* Adventure Hour *shows repeat episodes of* Ewoks *and* Droids.

Ewok and *Star Wars Droids* Adventure Hour

September 7: The *Ewoks* and *Droids* Adventure Hour premieres on ABC's Saturday morning cartoon block. The first installment consists of the *Ewoks* episode "The Cries of the Trees" and the *Droids* episode "The White Witch." Produced by Canadian animation studio Nelvana, *Droids* is inspired in part by the art of French comic artist Moebius, while the influences on the *Ewoks* animators include Walt Kelly's *Pogo*, *The Lord of the Rings*, and Carl Barks's *Uncle Scrooge*. Peter Sauder and Ben Burtt write the majority of the *Droids* episodes, while Paul Dini and Bob Carrau tackle most of the scripts for *Ewoks*.

Your new sales force premieres this fall on ABC-TV.

ABC press release for potential advertisers

ABC markets its new Star Wars programming with a reference to Jedi's forthcoming re-release.

"**A**s we rehearse our upcoming adventures for ABC-TV, the original adventure returns to a theatre near you."

RETURN OF THE JEDI returns to over 1200 theatres March 29

Home Sweet Home

Realizing Lucas's dream of an independent filmmaking retreat, the Main House group of buildings at Skywalker Ranch is finally completed. Lucasfilm officially moves its headquarters from San Anselmo to the Ranch, beginning the process during the first week of September and finalizing the move in early October. Approximately 100 employees in the marketing, publishing, licensing, legal, and administrative divisions occupy the Main House and four ancillary buildings. Still operating in their own buildings in San Rafael are Sprocket Systems, ILM, and Lucasfilm Games.

The Main House of Skywalker Ranch

Also in 1985...

Kenner Releases New Figures

Kenner launches a new line of action figures tying in with the animated *Droids* and *Ewoks* episodes. The *Droids* figures include all-new characters such as Thall Joben and Tig Fromm, as well as animation-styled interpretations of C-3PO and R2-D2. Kenner rebrands its A-wing vehicle under the *Droids* brand. *Ewoks* figures include King Gorneesh, Wicket Warrick, and the Dulok Shaman.

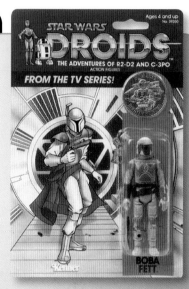

The Ewoks and Droids action figures come with collectible coins. Boba Fett's coin reads, "Boba Fett Bounty Hunter."

Speeder racer Thall Joben is the new owner of the droids after they become separated from Raymus Antilles.

Stephen Ouimette narrates the *Droids* cartoon series.

OCTOBER

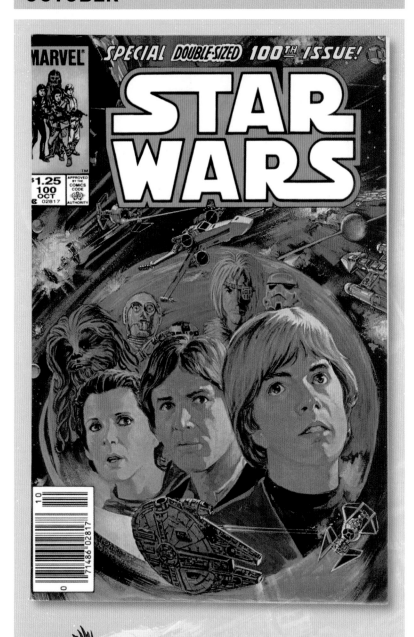

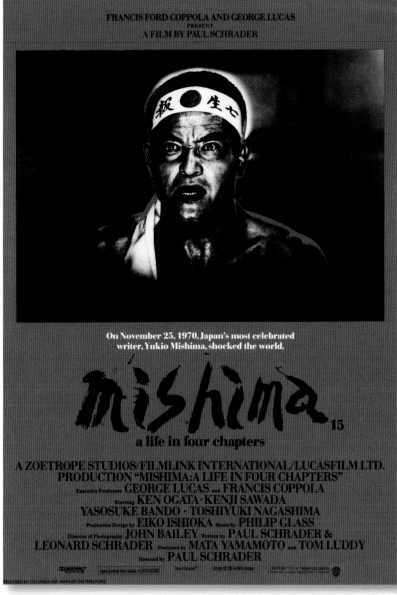

Mishima

October 4: *Mishima: A Life in Four Chapters*, produced by George Lucas and Francis Ford Coppola, is released. Directed by Paul Schrader, it tells the story of famed Japanese writer Yukio Mishima, who committed a ritual seppuku (suicide) in 1970. Mishima's suicide is suggested through the imagery of blood on paper optically composited with titles by ILM.

100th Issue

Marvel Comics' *Star Wars* series hits a centennial milestone with issue #100. The story, "First Strike," involves an attack on the Rebel base on the Forest Moon of Endor by a new threat—the extragalactic invaders known as the Nagai.

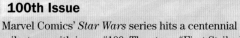

Luke fights Maccabree during the defense of Endor.

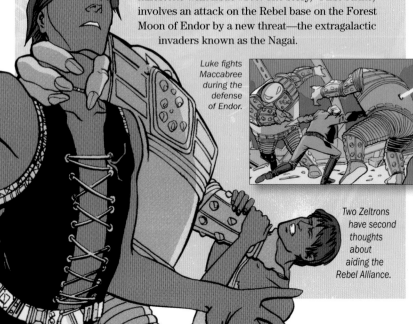

Two Zeltrons have second thoughts about aiding the Rebel Alliance.

Free Software Movement

October 4: Richard Stallman founds the Free Software Foundation (FSF), a non-profit organization to promote the free software movement; the idea that computer software should be free for anyone to modify and distribute.

NES Released

October 18: The 8-bit Nintendo Entertainment System (NES) is released, ushering in the next generation of home console gaming. The NES brings a much needed boost to the video game industry.

In Asia the NES is known as the Family Computer, or "FamiCom."

NOVEMBER

Spreading the Magic
November 5: ILM takes center stage in an episode of the PBS series *Nova* entitled "The Magic of Special Effects."

Leaders Meet
November 19: In a significant step towards the end of the Cold War, President Ronald Reagan meets with Soviet leader Mikhail Gorbachev for the first time. Their meeting in Geneva results in a pledge to seek a 50 percent reduction in nuclear arms.

Magazine advertisement for Ewoks: The Battle for Endor

Battle for Endor
November 24: The two-hour *Ewoks: The Battle for Endor* debuts on ABC. A sequel to 1984's *The Ewok Adventure* (also known as *Caravan of Courage*), it features a darker tone, with the family of Cindel Towani being killed off at the start of the film and a gigantic ground battle with an army of evil Marauders. Directed and co-written by brothers Jim and Ken Wheat, the film stars Wilford Brimley (of the summer hit *Cocoon*) as a gruff spacer. Joe Johnston is the movie's production designer and second unit director, while Phil Tippett is the creature supervisor. Many of the monsters in *The Battle for Endor*, including a winged condor dragon and a number of dinosaur-like blurrgs, are brought to life through traditional stop-motion animation. ILM's Michael McAlister wins an Emmy for Outstanding Visual Effects on *The Battle for Endor*.

Strategic Defense Lawsuit
November 25: Lawyers representing Lucasfilm meet with US District Judge Gerhard Gesell to seek a preliminary injunction stopping groups from using the phrase "Star Wars" in advertisements about President Reagan's Strategic Defense Initiative. Lawrence Hefter states, "*Star Wars*, your Honor, is a fantasy. It's something that doesn't exist." Hefter also claims that ads which associate the film series with the missile program "will cause children and parents to tend to shy away from *Star Wars*."

DECEMBER

Stained-Glass Knight
December 4: Barry Levinson's *Young Sherlock Holmes* is released. Working with Lucasfilm's Pixar Computer Animation Group, ILM creates its first-ever computer-generated character: The stained-glass knight. Final composites of the CG knight's animated shadows and a background stained-glass matte painting are printed directly onto film with a laser scanner. Other effects, including a swarm of attacking harpies and an array of living pastries, are achieved through go-motion and puppetry. Dennis Muren, Kit West, John Ellis, and Dave Allen are nominated for a Visual Effects Academy Award®.

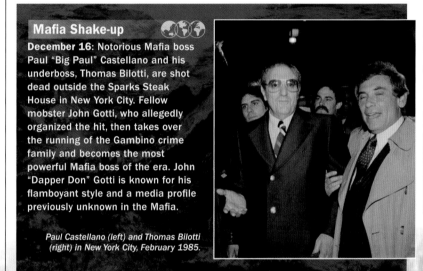

Mafia Shake-up
December 16: Notorious Mafia boss Paul "Big Paul" Castellano and his underboss, Thomas Bilotti, are shot dead outside the Sparks Steak House in New York City. Fellow mobster John Gotti, who allegedly organized the hit, then takes over the running of the Gambino crime family and becomes the most powerful Mafia boss of the era. John "Dapper Don" Gotti is known for his flamboyant style and a media profile previously unknown in the Mafia.

Paul Castellano (left) and Thomas Bilotti (right) in New York City, February 1985.

When Cindel's family is killed by a group of Marauders, she is comforted by her Ewok friend Wicket.

Star Wars has had an immense cultural impact over the decades, as demonstrated by its coverage in a wide range of magazines. *Star Wars* related subjects have graced the covers of everything from *Dirt Bike* to *Disney News*.

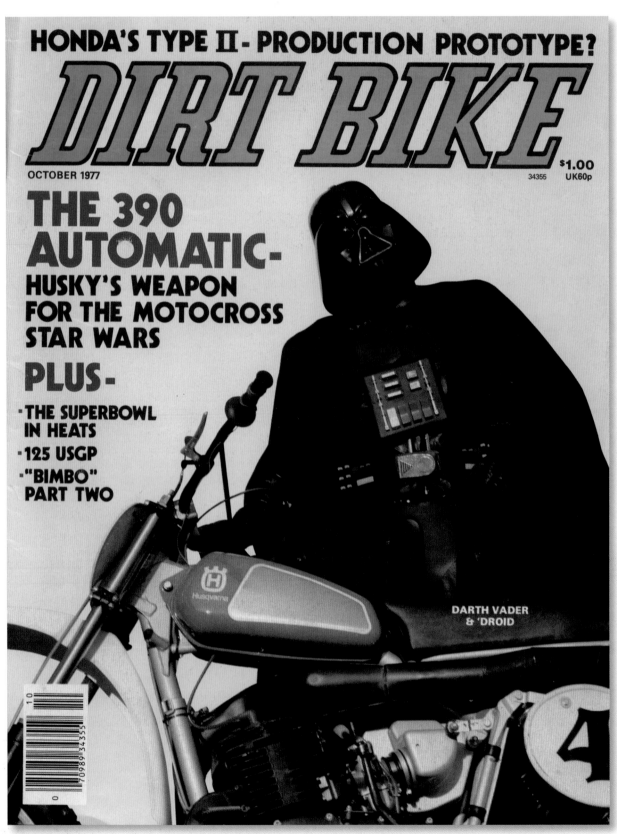

Dirt Bike, *October 1977*

SPRING 1987   *PRICE $1.75*

**George Lucas Shares His Galaxy
Inside the Magic Kingdoms' Magic Shops
Sherman Brothers — Music and Memories**

A rare glimpse of George Lucas without his beard: Disney News, Spring 1987

1986

STAR WARS SHOWS signs that it is beginning to fade from the public consciousness and revenue from *Star Wars* toys and merchandise continues to decline. Lucasfilm sells off its Pixar division. The long-running *Star Wars* comics series folds, and new Lucasfilm ventures like *Howard the Duck* fizzle. But bright spots remain, including the 3-D film *Captain Eo* at Walt Disney World.

Logo for the 3-D film starring Michael Jackson

> "If I hadn't been identified with the project, the reviews might have been a little gentler at least." **George Lucas** *on Howard the Duck*

JANUARY

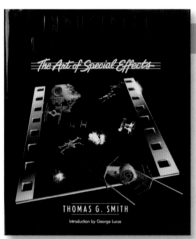

Magic Book
Del Rey publishes *Industrial Light & Magic: The Art of Special Effects* by Thomas G. Smith (ILM manager). The first of its kind, the book features an introduction by Lucas.

Industrial Light & Magic: The Art of Special Effects takes an in-depth look at the history of the company since its formation in 1975.

An Ewoks on Ice segment is included in the Ice Capades, a traveling entertainment show directed by Robert Turk, which features theatrical skits set to ice skating.

Ewoks on Ice pennants are now rare collectibles.

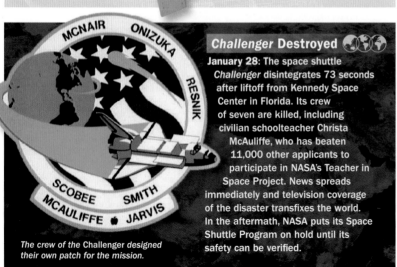

Challenger Destroyed 🌍
January 28: The space shuttle *Challenger* disintegrates 73 seconds after liftoff from Kennedy Space Center in Florida. Its crew of seven are killed, including civilian schoolteacher Christa McAuliffe, who has beaten 11,000 other applicants to participate in NASA's Teacher in Space Project. News spreads immediately and television coverage of the disaster transfixes the world. In the aftermath, NASA puts its Space Shuttle Program on hold until its safety can be verified.

The crew of the Challenger designed their own patch for the mission.

FEBRUARY

February 1: *The Empire Strikes Back* premieres on HBO.

Birth of Pixar
February 3: Apple CEO Steve Jobs purchases Lucasfilm's Computer Division for $10 million. He renames the graphics company Pixar, after their most promising piece of technology, the Pixar Image Computer.

Halley's Comet 🌍
February 9: Halley's Comet reaches its perihelion, the closest point to the sun, during its second visit to the solar system in the 20th century.

Also in 1986...
The first *Star Wars* soundtrack is released for the compact disc format by Polydor Records. It includes 75 minutes of the original 88-minute soundtrack.

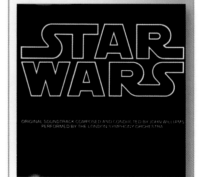

Alec Guinness publishes his autobiography, *Blessings in Disguise*.

Mir Launched 🌍
February 19: The Soviet Union launches the Mir space station, which is designed for continuous habitation. Its name means "peace."

Return of the Jedi on VHS
February 25: *Return of the Jedi* is released on video cassette. It is priced at $79.98 and is advertised to the public through full-page magazine ads, which call it "The Movie Everybody's Been Waiting For."

🌐 **CHERNOBYL NUCLEAR PLANT DISASTER** 🌐 **HANDS ACROSS AMERICA: 7 MILLION LINK HANDS**

MARCH

March 7: The modern-day fantasy *Highlander* is released, starring Christopher Lambert and Sean Connery and featuring Hugh Quarshie (Captain Panaka) as the immortal Sunda Kastagir.

. . . .

March 24: *Peter Cushing: An Autobiography* is published.

. . . .

APRIL

Pixar's Premiere

The Pixar Image Computer is introduced at the National Computer Graphics Conference. The computer has a medical application—producing high-resolution 3-D images for analysis and diagnosis.

The original Pixar Image Computer (displayed by Ed Catmull) is sold for $135,000.

Droids Comic

Under its kid-focused Star Comics imprint, Marvel publishes *Star Wars: Droids*, based on the successful cartoon series. The first issue carries an April cover date and details the adventures of R2-D2 and C-3PO.

Star Wars: Droids runs for eight issues.

. . . .

April 13: "Hell Toupee," an episode of the Steven Spielberg-produced television anthology series *Amazing Stories*, airs on NBC. The episode is directed by *The Empire Strikes Back*'s Irvin Kershner.

MAY

Final Issue

Marvel Comics ends its *Star Wars* series with issue #107 (cover date September). Titled "All Together Now," the comic hastily wraps up an extragalactic invasion plotline that has been running for the better part of a year. The end of the series brings about a hiatus in *Star Wars* comics publishing.

Cover of Star Wars #107

A shirtless Luke surveys his friends, the towering half-breed Bey, and several pale Nagai in the issue's final panel.

JUNE

The Great Heep

June 7: The *Droids* cartoon returns to television in the form of the primetime special *The Great Heep*. The program is written by Ben Burtt, directed by Clive A. Smith, and executive produced by Miki Herman (unit production manager on *Return of the Jedi* and production coordinator on *The Empire Strikes Back*.) Airing on ABC, the one-hour special pits R2-D2 and C-3PO against a monstrous droid the size of a a warehouse and brings back several characters from the 1985 animated series.

The Great Heep sees C-3PO and R2-D2 travel to Biitu and take on the evil android called the Great Heep.

The titular Great Heep is designed by Joe Johnston.

Labyrinth

June 27: Jim Henson's *Labyrinth* premieres, starring David Bowie as the sinister Goblin King. The dark fantasy adventure is executive produced by Lucas and features performances by Frank Oz and *Return of the Jedi*'s Warwick Davis. Shot at Elstree Studios, it proves to be Henson's final film. Says Davis, "It was a very crazy shoot. The script was written one way, but once the puppeteers added their input and all the crazy things they could do with their characters, it would change. But Jim Henson was a true master of the art, and that's the way he liked to work, to recognize the ad-libs."

David Bowie as the Goblin King and Jennifer Connelly as Sarah in Labrynth

AUGUST

Howard the Duck movie poster

Howard the Duck

Howard the Duck is released, directed by Willard Huyck and co-written by Gloria Katz, the duo who have helped Lucas write several scripts. Produced by Universal Studios and Lucasfilm, the adaptation of the Marvel comic book created by Steve Gerber is poorly received at the box office, earning only $16 million against its estimated $37 million production budget. Though Lucas expressed reservations about the story and the direction in which Universal wanted to go, he stayed on board in the hope that he could help his friends Huyck and Katz. "The die had been pretty much cast when I got involved," says Lucas, "so I endeavored to help Bill bring his version to the screen."

SEPTEMBER

Captain Eo (Michael Jackson) and his fellow space travelers are captured by the Supreme Leader (Anjelica Huston) on her dark, unwelcoming planet. Using music as a weapon, Eo and gang transform the Supreme Leader into a beautiful woman, and her planet into a lush paradise.

Captain Eo

September 12: The 3-D film *Captain Eo* premieres at Walt Disney World's EPCOT Center. Directed by Francis Ford Coppola and produced and co-written by Lucas, the 17-minute movie stars Michael Jackson in the title role and Anjelica Huston as his nemesis, the Supreme Leader. Two original Jackson songs, "We Are Here to Change the World" and "Another Part of Me," are performed as Captain Eo defeats his enemies through music. The film costs $10 million, which, in light of its short running time, makes it one of the most expensive films per minute ever made. The *Los Angeles Times* reports, "According to one Disney executive, [George Lucas] stuffed more special effects into these 17 minutes than there were in two hours of *Star Wars*."

HRH PRINCE ANDREW MARRIES SARAH FERGUSON ⊙ PAN AM FLIGHT 73 HIJACKED IN KARACHI

The All New Ewoks
September 13: Featuring an all-new introductory sequence and theme song, the *Ewoks* television cartoon returns for its second season on ABC. Now called *The All New Ewoks*, it launches with a Paul Dini episode, "The Crystal Cloak." Overall the second season of the series feels more child-friendly, with character motivations simplified and plotlines shortened. A total of 13 half-hour episodes are aired, ending on December 13 with Stephen Langford's "Malani the Warrior."

Teebo, Latara, and Kneesaa search for Wicket in the episode "Gone with the Mimphs."

On A Plate
The Hamilton Collection company releases its collectible *Star Wars* plates. Han Solo is the first in the initial set of eight. Images on the plates include Princess Leia, Darth Vader, and a montage of other *Star Wars* characters.

The Han Solo collectible plate depicts the smuggler in the Mos Eisley Cantina.

Also in 1986...
Darth Vader Cathedral
Lucas receives word that a sculpture of Darth Vader's head is to become a gargoyle on the north-west tower of the National Cathedral of Washington, DC.

The Vader gargoyle, sculpted by Jay Hall Carpenter and carved by Patrick J. Plunkett, awaits installation.

Also in 1986...
Ewok Toys
Ewok toys are released worldwide with products differing by country.

This Chief Chirpa mask is sold in France by César.

These Ewok figures, sold by Kehl in Germany, make a sound when squeezed.

DECEMBER
Lucasfilm sends out its last *Star Wars*-themed Christmas card until 1994. It depicts three Ewoks building and decorating a snowman.

Lucasfilm is well-known for sending out special holiday cards that feature various characters from the Star Wars films.

Little Shop of Horrors
December 19: The movie version of the off-Broadway musical *Little Shop of Horrors* opens. Directed by Frank Oz, the film stars Rick Moranis and the carnivorous plant Audrey II, built by the Jim Henson Company.

Voyager Returns
December 23: The aircraft *Voyager*, piloted by Dick Rutan and Jeana Yeager lands in the Mojave Desert, California, having completed the first nonstop circumnavigation of the Earth by air without refueling in 9 days, 3 minutes, and 44 seconds.

🌐 DESMOND TUTU BECOMES THE FIRST BLACK ANGLICAN CHURCH BISHOP IN SOUTH AFRICA 🌐

1987

AS THE *STAR WARS* phenomenon turns 10 years old, Star Tours at Disneyland becomes the first theme-park attraction to be set in a galaxy far, far away. Disney head Michael Eisner praises the motion-simulator, calling Lucas "the next generation of a 'Walt Disney,'" and fans line up to be among the first to rocket to the moon of Endor. Meanwhile, the first official fan convention takes place amid a flood of anniversary-themed merchandise including metal coins, plates, mugs, posters, and pins.

> "I wanted to make sure that it was done right, and it was maintained right, and that it was operated correctly. Disney is the only place in the world where that can happen."
>
> **George Lucas**
> *on Star Tours*

JANUARY

Star Tours Opens

January 9: Star Tours opens at California's Disneyland theme park. George Lucas and Michael Eisner cut the ribbon at the opening ceremony, and the ride attracts record-breaking lines. Eisner jokingly describes the opening crowds as "Nine thousand people who should be in school!" The ride contains ILM's longest visual effects shot to date—four and a half minutes of continuous effects footage simulating an uninterrupted view through the StarSpeeder viewport. Star Tours features the conceptual work of George Lucas, Disney Imagineers Tom Fitzgerald and Tony Baxter, and ILM's Dennis Muren.

In celebration of the debut, Disneyland remains open for a 60-hour marathon from 10 a.m. on January 9 to 10 p.m. on January 11.

On opening day, thousands of Star Wars fans turn up to see George Lucas and Michael Eisner (with red tie) open the Star Tours attraction.

Star Tours uses four military-grade flight simulators in its structures.

FEBRUARY

Farewell to *Bantha Tracks*

Bantha Tracks publishes its final issue with #35. At this point, Fan Club membership has dwindled to about 5,000. Lucas says, "Lucasfilm has taken a break from the *Star Wars* Saga to complete new film projects. The Fan Club is going to take that break, too."

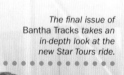

The final issue of Bantha Tracks takes an in-depth look at the new Star Tours ride.

APRIL

The Simpsons 🌐🌐🌐
April 19: *The Simpsons* debuts as a cartoon segment on *The Tracey Ullman Show*, and will be featured throughout the show's first three seasons.

The Simpson family

Principal photography begins on *Tucker: The Man and His Dream* in Marin County, California. Lucas puts up the initial money for Francis Ford Coppola to begin production, with Paramount as the backer and distributor.

April 27: Alec Guinness is honored by The Film Society of Lincoln Center at its 16th Annual Tribute to Film Achievement. Film Society President Alfred R. Stern says, "Over the years, no one has given us more pleasure than Sir Alec Guinness." Prior to the event, Carrie Fisher and Mark Hamill join Guinness at the restaurant Tavern on the Green in New York City.

MAY

Seasons of Change
May 21: George Lucas talks in the *The New York Times* about the anniversary of *Star Wars* and his new fantasy adventure *Willow*. The film opens on Memorial Day (the last Monday of May); two weeks earlier than is usual for blockbusters. Tom Sherak, president of distribution at Twentieth Century Fox, says, "George Lucas effectively moved the summer forward two weeks, from the middle of June to the end of May. The Wednesday before Memorial Day is called George Lucas Day."

First Celebration
May 23–25: In conjunction with *Starlog* magazine, the first Lucasfilm-sanctioned fan convention is held at the Stouffer Hotel in Los Angeles. The three-day event honors the Saga's first 10 years. In addition to an exhibit of *Star Wars* models and artifacts, ILM's Lorne Peterson, Bruce Nicholson, Steve Gawley, and Dave Carson make presentations on special effects. Guest speakers include Howard Roffman for Lucasfilm and Kim Strub for THX. In addition, special appearances are made by Anthony Daniels and George Lucas, plus R2-D2 and Darth Vader, who appear in character. Paying special tribute to George Lucas are *Star Trek* creator Gene Roddenberry, Irvin Kershner, Lucasfilm VP Sid Ganis, Lucasfilm marketing director Charles Lippincott, and producer Gary Kurtz.

Pin celebrating the first 10 years of Star Wars

The Star Wars 10th anniversary convention includes personal appearances, film screenings, and presentations from ILM. Here, George Lucas stands with the droids.

10th Anniversary
A number of products are released for *Star Wars*'s 10th anniversary, including the John Alvin poster "The First Ten Years" and a set of Rarities Mint 10th anniversary coins.

Special Star Wars 10-year anniversary commemorative pin badges

"The First Ten Years" poster includes many elements from the first three Star Wars films.

STAR WARS

T H E   F I R S T   T E N   Y E A R S

A   L O N G   T I M E   A G O   I N   A   G A L A X Y   F A R ,   F A R   A W A Y

The 10th anniversary coins feature popular characters from the Star Wars films.

🌐 **TERRY WAITE, SPECIAL ENVOY OF ARCHBISHOP OF CANTERBURY, KIDNAPPED IN BEIRUT** 🌐

JUNE

Spaceballs

June 24: Mel Brooks's *Spaceballs* is released. The satire spoofs the *Star Wars* trilogy with such characters as Dark Helmet and Pizza the Hutt. The production team sent a copy of the script to George Lucas, who was happy to approve it.

Bill Pullman, Daphne Zuniga, Lorene Yarnell, and John Candy in Spaceballs

Star Wars, The Empire Strikes Back, and *Return of the Jedi* are re-released on video for the 10th anniversary of *Star Wars*.

June 31: *The Living Daylights*, the 15th installment in the James Bond movie series, reinvigorates the Bond franchise and introduces Timothy Dalton as the agent known as 007.

JULY

Innerspace

July 1: Joe Dante's *Innerspace* is released, starring Martin Short and Dennis Quaid. The comedy involves a miniaturized trip through a human body, a concept popularized by 1966's *Fantastic Voyage*. ILM's work on the film earns Dennis Muren, Bill George, Harley Jessup, and Kenneth Smith the Academy Award® for Best Visual Effects. Steven Spielberg is the movie's exect**ive** producer.

Jack Putter (Martin Short) is injected with a miniature human as part of a risky experiment in Innerspace.

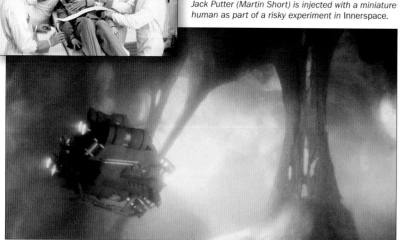
A pod carrying a miniaturized human travels through the body of its host in Innerspace.

AUGUST

Carrie Fisher publishes *Postcards from the Edge*. The bestselling book tells the story of an actress struggling with drug addiction and the stresses of Hollywood, and is drawn from Fisher's own life.

OCTOBER

Star Wars Roleplaying

Star Wars: The Roleplaying Game is published by West End Games. A wealth of sourcebooks and adventure modules associated with the game soon follow, providing fans with new details on the aliens, starships, and planets of *Star Wars*.

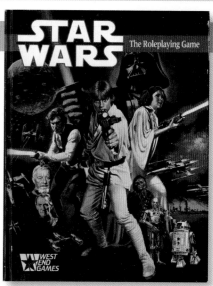

Star Wars: The Roleplaying Game produces some of the most authoritative Star Wars *guides.*

Maniac Mansion

Lucasfilm Games releases the graphical adventure Maniac Mansion for the Commodore 64 and Apple II. Developed by Ron Gilbert and Gary Winnick, it tasks the player with investigating a mansion and rescuing a kidnapped cheerleader. Praised for its puzzles, humor, and multiple possible endings, Maniac Mansion uses Lucasfilm Games's proprietary SCUMM (Script Creation Utility for Maniac Mansion) engine, which proves to be a strong foundation for similar graphical adventure games under development.

Screen shot from Maniac Mansion

Joseph Campbell Dies

October 31: Mythologist and lecturer Joseph Campbell dies at the age of 83.

First Fan Club Magazine

The premiere issue of the *Lucasfilm Fan Club* magazine is released. With a cover featuring C-3PO holding a cake for *Star Wars*'s 10th birthday, the issue features an interview with Anthony Daniels and an advance look at *Willow*.

First edition of the Lucasfilm Fan Club *magazine.*

Also in 1987...

Thomas Knoll, brother of ILM's John Knoll, develops a computer program to display grayscale images. His work attracts the attention of his brother John, and the two collaborate on developing the program that becomes the massively influential Adobe Photoshop.

WORLD POPULATION REACHES FIVE BILLION ⊕ STOCK MARKET LEVELS PLUMMET ON BLACK

NOVEMBER

The Star Wars Sourcebook

The Star Wars Sourcebook is published by West End Games. As the first-ever sourcebook published on the *Star Wars* Saga, it introduces a wealth of new background material on the trilogy for gamers hoping to flesh out their roleplaying campaigns. Among the secrets revealed in the book are profiles of alien species from the Mos Eisley Cantina, statistics on Imperial walkers and TIE fighters, and a blueprint of the interior of the *Millennium Falcon*. Concept art from the *Star Wars* trilogy is used throughout.

The Star Wars Sourcebook *is written by Curtis Smith and Bill Slavicsek.*

DECEMBER

Channel Tunnel

Eleven boring machines begin drilling from both sides of the English Channel to start construction on the Channel Tunnel connecting England and France.

The Eurotunnel stretches 35 miles under the English Channel.

Treaty Signed

December 8: In a step of thawing relations in the Cold War, the Intermediate-Range Nuclear Forces Treaty is signed in the East Room of the White House by Ronald Reagan and Soviet General Secretary Mikhail Gorbachev. It eliminates a mid-range class of ground-launched, nuclear and conventional, ballistic and cruise missiles.

3-D Comic

Blackthorne Publishing releases *Star Wars 3-D*, a comic series with a total of three quarterly issues. The independent company had previously released 3-D comics based on such diverse properties as *Rambo*, *Transformers*, and *Rocky & Bullwinkle*, and its *Star Wars* issues represent the first time the Saga has ever been depicted using the red-and-blue overlapping lines common to 3-D comics. Issue #1 features Luke Skywalker's return to Tatooine to find an owner for his aunt and uncle's moisture farm. The two remaining installments, entitled "Havoc on Hoth" and "The Dark Side of Dantooine," include the story of how the Rebels located the site for their frozen base in *The Empire Strikes Back*. The comics are released with little fanfare and many fans are unaware of their existence, making them a rarity for collectors.

Also in 1987...

Star Tours Milk

Carnation Milk releases a limited edition milk carton in partnership with Star Tours.

A spread from the Star Wars 3-D comic

1988

WITH FEW NEW PROJECTS in the pipeline, *Star Wars* goes back to explore its mythological roots. A television documentary series, featuring the late Joseph Campbell, explains how George Lucas's *Star Wars* characters sprang from the universal monomyth, which includes a hero who wins a victory over supernatural forces. The magic of myth has its appeal in other projects like Lucas's epic *Willow* that demonstrates many of the same ideals within a world of mysticism and monsters.

> "It's not a simple morality play. It has to do with the powers of life and their inflection through the actions of man."
>
> **Joseph Campbell**
> *on the appeal of* Star Wars

MARCH

Stephen Hawking

Physicist Stephen Hawking publishes the seminal *A Brief History of Time*, which explores the origins of the universe and the underpinnings of time and space.

APRIL

THE MOST VISUALLY HYPNOTIC EXPERIENCE ON FILM TODAY

Powaqqatsi

April 29: Godfrey Reggio's *Powaqqatsi* is released. The dialogue-free documentary is executive produced by George Lucas and Francis Ford Coppola, and serves as a sequel to 1982's *Koyaanisqatsi*. Featuring a score by Philip Glass, *Powaqqatsi* (a Hopi word meaning "life in transformation") focuses on the effects of industrialization on the third world. Lucas helped Reggio obtain distribution for the project through Cannon Films.

The poster for Powaqqatsi

Also in 1988...

The article "Star Wars: An Imperial Myth" by Koenraad Kuiper is published in the spring issue of the *Journal of Popular Culture*.

C-3PO and R2-D2 appear in *Robots in Space*, a special program for New York's Hayden Planetarium. The short film, which takes visitors through a tour of the galaxy, is shot at ILM with Skywalker Sound mixing the dialogue and adding the sound effects.

MAY

Willow

May 5: The fantasy adventure *Willow* kicks off the summer movie season. Produced and co-written by Lucas and starring *Jedi*'s Warwick Davis, the movie is directed by *American Graffiti*'s Ron Howard. Says Lucas, "I wanted somebody with a sense of humor and somebody who would be good with the human side of this. It's so easy to get overwhelmed with the effects and the logistics." Other members of the cast include Val Kilmer, as the roguish Madmartigan, and Jean Marsh, as the villainous Queen Bavmorda. Shot on location in Wales and New Zealand, the film features postproduction work by ILM. Dennis Muren calls it "an awful lot of work under the most difficult possible conditions," though ILM is able to complete the first computer morphing sequence in which a goat is transformed on screen into an ostrich, a turtle, a tiger, and finally a human.

Above: Ron Howard and Lucas join the cast of Willow for a photo opportunity. Top: VHS cover art

PERESTROIKA BEGINS IN THE USSR ✪ **WINDOWS 2.1 RELEASED** ✪ **POISON ATTACK ON HALABJ**

Also in 1988...

Rare Collectibles

Dairylea produces limited edition *Ewoks* and *Droids* packaging, while a rare series of action figures is released in Brazil.

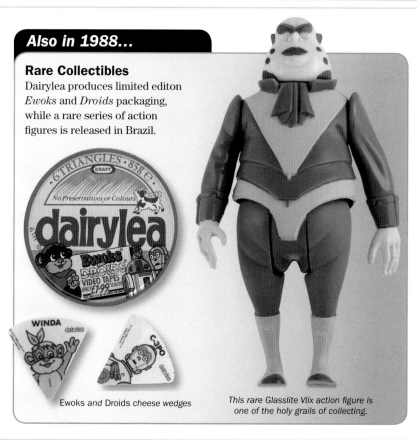

Ewoks *and* Droids *cheese wedges*

This rare Glasslite Vlix action figure is one of the holy grails of collecting.

ILM films a tiger and other animals for transitional shots to be used in the transformation sequence in Willow.

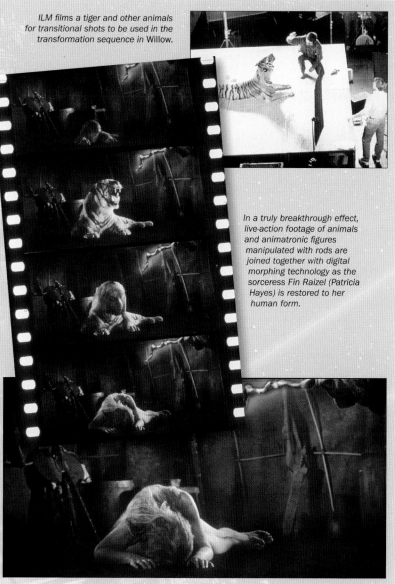

In a truly breakthrough effect, live-action footage of animals and animatronic figures manipulated with rods are joined together with digital morphing technology as the sorceress Fin Raizel (Patricia Hayes) is restored to her human form.

Windows 2.1

May 27: Microsoft releases Windows 2.1; a new operating system that is specifically designed to take advantage of the new Intel processors.

The adventure scenario *Tatooine Manhunt* is published by West End Games. Featuring four bounty hunters, it includes the first-ever map of Mos Eisley and the interior layout of the Mos Eisley Cantina.

Cover art (right) is a recycled McQuarrie painting.

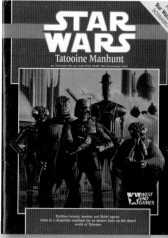

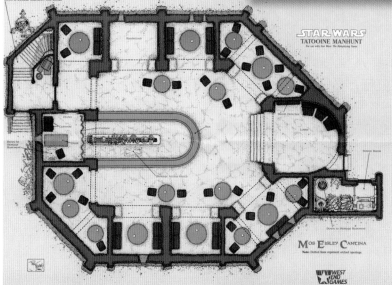

Map of the Mos Eisley Cantina

JUNE

Strike Force: Shantipole is released for West End Games' *Star Wars: The Roleplaying Game*. In the adventure, gamers delve into the development history of the B-wing starfighter.

Cover of Strike Force: Shantipole

The Power of Myth

June 21: The six-part documentary series *Joseph Campbell and the Power of Myth* premieres on PBS. It incorporates interviews with Bill Moyers filmed at Skywalker Ranch prior to Campbell's death. In the first episode of the series, "The Hero's Adventure," Moyers and Campbell discuss the characters of *Star Wars* and how they are echoes of the archetypes presented in Campbell's most famous work *The Hero With a Thousand Faces*. Other episodes include "The First Storytellers" and "Sacrifice and Bliss," both of which deal with humanity's relationship to the Earth. A companion book, *The Power of Myth* (above), is released by Doubleday at the same time and covers the topics in more detail.

AUGUST

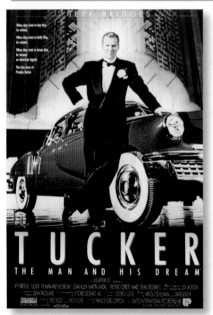

Marlon Brando was originally going to play the lead role, Preston Tucker.

Tucker

August 12: *Tucker: The Man and His Dream* premieres. Directed by Francis Ford Coppola and executive produced by Lucas, the biographical film stars Jeff Bridges as Preston Tucker and Martin Landau (*Space: 1999*) as financier Abe Karatz. The story of Tucker's fight against the Big Three automobile manufacturers, as he struggles to bring the 1948 Tucker Sedan to market, is shot in California's Marin County. *Tucker* receives positive critical reviews and lukewarm box-office results, though Landau does earn an Academy Award® nomination for Best Supporting Actor. Lucas acquires one of the surviving Tucker automobiles for his own personal collection.

Only 51 Tucker 1948 Sedans were ever made.

SEPTEMBER

Star Walking (the *Star Wars* appreciation society of Australia) is launched.

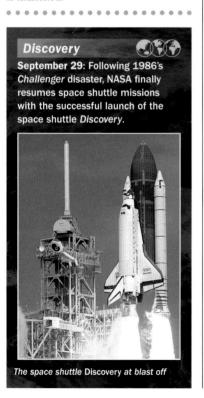

Discovery

September 29: Following 1986's *Challenger* disaster, NASA finally resumes space shuttle missions with the successful launch of the space shuttle *Discovery*.

The space shuttle Discovery at blast off

The ceiling of the Skywalker Library is a 12 m (40 ft) stained glass dome.

OCTOBER

Assault on Hoth is released by West End Games. This board game re-creates the epic struggle of Rebel snowspeeders versus Imperial walkers.

Assault on Hoth is a two player Star Wars board game.

NOVEMBER

Tibet

A group of Tibetan monks visit Skywalker Ranch to use the Scoring Stage's unique acoustics to record an album of chants. The 21 monks are members of the Gyuto order.

Gyuto order of Tibetan monks during their visit to Skywalker Ranch

Skywalker Library

The Skywalker Ranch Research Library acquires Paramount's own library when the studio can no longer maintain the budget for proper library maintenance. The acquisition triples the overall size of the Skywalker Ranch collection. The Ranch library also acquires the personal audio tape collection of Joseph Campbell, which contains lectures recorded throughout his career.

The Paramount collection includes the copy of Ben-Hur that was checked out by legendary film director Cecil B. DeMille in 1927.

George H.W. Bush

November 8: Ronald Reagan's former vice president, George H.W. Bush, defeats Democratic challenger Michael Dukakis for the presidency of the United States. Bush wins 53 percent of the popular vote and an overwhelming 40 states in the Electoral College.

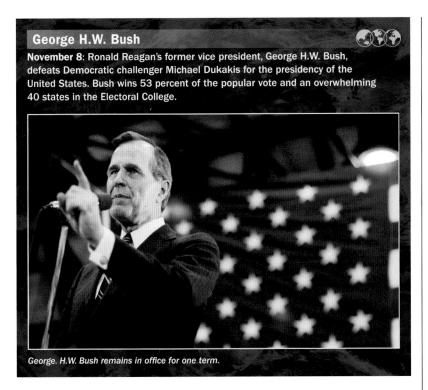

George. H.W. Bush remains in office for one term.

The Land Before Time

November 18: The animated dinosaur adventure *The Land Before Time* is released to theaters. Directed by Don Bluth and executive produced by Lucas and Spielberg, the film follows five young dinosaurs on a quest to reach the safety of the "Great Valley." Bluth, a maverick who had left behind the Disney studio system to open up his own competing animation shop, had previously collaborated with Spielberg on 1986's *An American Tail*. Says Lucas, "Steve had an idea about baby dinosaurs and he wanted me to executive produce it with him." Since its first release there have been 12 *Land Before Time* sequels.

Spanish release poster for The Land Before Time, *which grosses over $84 million worldwide.*

Also in 1988...

This advert showing Yoda and Lucas levitating is one of many Panasonic adverts that feature Star Wars characters in Japan.

Kenner's toy line is revitalized in Brazil years after it ended in the US.

DECEMBER

December 14: Frank Oz's *Dirty Rotten Scoundrels* is released. The dark comedy stars Steve Martin and Michael Caine, and features Ian McDiarmid (Emperor Palpatine) in a small role.

Michael Caine and Steve Martin play two con artists in Dirty Rotten Scoundrels.

Skywalker Ranch is a filmmaker's retreat nestled in the hills of California's Marin County, all but invisible from its access point on Lucas Valley Road (which was named "Lucas" long before George Lucas expressed an interest in the land). Most cars are hidden from view in underground parking lots, and its contemplative settings include an observatory, a fitness center, a vineyard, state-of-the-art editing and screening facilities (in the Tech Building, right), and even its own fire department.

The Main House is the centerpiece of Skywalker Ranch.

The Brook House at Skywalker Ranch

The Skywalker Ranch Fire Brigade was organized in 1985 and has 12 full-time firefighters as well as volunteers.

The Inn at Skywalker Ranch houses guests in themed, modern rooms.

The whimsically named Lake Ewok highlights the Ranch's harmony with the natural environment.

1989

WHILE ALL IS quiet on the *Star Wars* front, ILM is busier than ever. The visual effects specialists lend their talents to a number of 1989 films, including Lucas and Spielberg's *Indiana Jones and the Last Crusade*, which provides opportunities to test new technologies for future projects.

Sean Connery (center) among the cast of The Last Crusade *in the role of Indy's scholarly, obstinate father.*

> "There's a certain discipline that is established when you get into sequels. It's like a sonnet or a haiku."

George Lucas
on Indiana Jones and the Last Crusade

GEORGE LUCAS'S approach to the *Indiana Jones* sequel gives a hint of how he might approach the *Star Wars* prequels: "I prefer to roam around creatively, but once you develop a certain style and genre you have to be faithful to it."

JANUARY

Peter Cushing poses as the mad scientist Victor Frankenstein from Curse of Frankenstein (1957).

Miniatures Battles

West End Games releases the core rulebook for *Star Wars Miniatures Battles*. The game wins the 1991 Origins International Game Expo award for "Best New Miniatures Rules."

OBE for Cushing

Peter Cushing (Grand Moff Tarkin) is made an Officer of the Order of the British Empire (OBE) by Queen Elizabeth II for services to film.

FEBRUARY

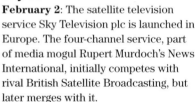

Sky TV

February 2: The satellite television service Sky Television plc is launched in Europe. The four-channel service, part of media mogul Rupert Murdoch's News International, initially competes with rival British Satellite Broadcasting, but later merges with it.

Less than two years after its launch, Sky Television will merge with British Satellite Broadcasting to create British Sky Broadcasting.

February 8: Lucas shoots a two-minute video explaining the magic of editing to be shown during the "Backstage Tour" at Disney-MGM Studios.

February 14: The first of 24 Block II Global Positioning System (GPS) satellites is placed into orbit.

MARCH

Dreams

Ken Ralston and an ILM crew travel to Japan to shoot background plates for Akira Kurosawa's film *Such Dreams I Have Dreamed*, or *Dreams*. The occasion marks the first time Kurosawa has worked directly with ILM.

Galaxy Guide 1

West End Games releases *Galaxy Guide 1: A New Hope* for the *Star Wars* roleplaying game. It is the first sourcebook to explore one of the *Star Wars* films in detail.

West End Games releases new information for its roleplaying game, becoming one of the biggest publishers of Star Wars material.

Above: Kurosawa (top left) directs Dreams. *The poster (right—Spanish version), by Intralink Film Graphic Design, shows a matte painting by ILM, reflecting the movie's magical realism.*

STEVEN SPIELBERG Presenta

LOS SUEÑOS
de *Akira Kurosawa*

⊕ **SERIAL KILLER TED BUNDY EXECUTED** ⊕ **FATWA AGAINST SALMAN RUSHDIE** ⊕

March 4: Warner Communications and Time Inc. announce plans to merge.

March 5: Jake Lloyd is born in Fort Collins, Colorado. The child actor goes on to play Anakin Skywalker in Episode I.

Exxon Valdez

March 24: The oil tanker *Exxon Valdez* spills 10.8 million gallons of oil after running aground in Alaska's Port William Sound, covering around 2,080 kilometers (1,300 miles) of coastline.

The Exxon Valdez is en route from Alaska to California when it strikes Bligh Reef.

APRIL

Lucasfilm Commercial Productions opens its doors. Its first advertisement is a spot for USAir.

MAY

May 21: Lucas is interviewed by *The New York Times* on film technology and the development of interactive educational systems. "I'm going to devote more and more of my time to that now," he says. "I'm trying to create programming for television that hasn't been invented yet."

Perfected Aging

May 24: In *Indiana Jones and the Last Crusade*, the villainous Walter Donovan (played by Julian Glover) gets his comeuppance by aging so rapidly he crumbles to dust. The transformation is conceived as one continuous shot, and requires extensive makeup and three articulated, motion-controlled puppet heads in varying stages of decomposition. Computer morphing is employed to blend the three-stage photography. The shot is the first-ever digital composite of a full-screen, live-action image; all of the elements are scanned in, digitally composited, and scanned back out to film.

JUNE

Ghostbusters II

June 16: This sequel to the smash 1984 supernatural comedy features the return of director Ivan Reitman and the original cast, as well as 180 effects shots from ILM under the supervision of Dennis Muren. The film's finale shows a living Statue of Liberty—a performer in a suit filmed against miniatures and bluescreen backgrounds.

Ghostbusters II has one of the biggest grossing opening weekends in cinema history.

Batman

June 23: Tim Burton's *Batman* is released, starring Michael Keaton as the caped crusader and featuring Billy Dee Williams (Lando Calrissian) as district attorney Harvey Dent.

In Batman lore, Harvey Dent eventually becomes the scarred, psychotic Two-Face.

Panasonic

Several *Star Wars* characters, including Chewbacca, the Ewoks, and even George Lucas, appear in television ads for Panasonic that air in Japan.

Advertisements, such as this one with C-3PO and R2-D2, are not distributed internationally and become rare curiosities for many fans.

JULY

THE ULTIMATE STAR WARS ADVENTURE
究極の スター・ウォーズ アドベンチャー

STAR TOURS

FROM THE
CREATIVE FORCES
OF DISNEY AND
GEORGE LUCAS

ディズニーとルーカスの.
フォースが生んだ
スペースマジック

PRESENTED BY

National/Panasonic

Visitors travel aboard a 40-passenger "StarSpeeder" along a frenzied course for four and a half minutes.

TOMORROWLAND トゥモローランド

Tokyo Disneyland.

Depicted on the Japanese poster for Star Tours Tokyo is the StarSpeeder 3000 vehicle and pilot droid RX-24, flanked by the familiar faces of R2-D2 and C-3PO. Although Star Tours promises "convenient daily departures to the Forest Moon of Endor," the poster seems to depict Earthly neighbors Jupiter and Saturn in the background.

The Star Tours press kit bag

Star Tours Tokyo

July 12: Star Tours opens at Tokyo Disneyland in Urayasu, Chiba. The Tokyo site incorporates six simulators —two more than the the Disneyland attraction in Los Angeles—plus a "Pan Galactic Pizza Port" that features an animatronic alien chef named Tony Solaroni.

Game Boy

July 31: Nintendo releases the 8-bit Game Boy portable video game system in North America. Despite its monochrome screen, it outsells competitors such as the Atari Lynx, which has a full-color screen.

AUGUST

The Opening of *The Abyss*

August 9: James Cameron's underwater sci-fi adventure *The Abyss* is released. A watery pseudopod created by ILM for one scene is considered the first entirely CG three-dimensional character. For their efforts, Hoyt Yeatman, Dennis Muren, John Bruno, and Dennis Skotak go on to win the Academy Award® for Best Visual Effects.

ILM's new computer graphics department worked for eight months to produce a total of 20 effects shots on The Abyss.

COLUMBIA'S 5-DAY "STS-28" MISSION ☼ **LOMA PRIETA EARTHQUAKE SHAKES SAN FRANCISCO**

Voyager 2

August 25: NASA's *Voyager 2* probe makes its closest pass to the planet Neptune and its moon Triton.

Due to Voyager 2's flight path, Neptune is the last object the spacecraft can visit on its way out of the solar system.

SEPTEMBER

Making History at the National Film Registry

September 19: *Star Wars* is one of the first 25 films to be inducted into the National Film Registry by the Library of Congress. *Star Wars* is the most recent movie to be included on the list, which includes D.W. Griffith's 1916 silent film *Intolerance* (the oldest film on the list) and classics such as *Citizen Kane, Casablanca, The Searchers, The Wizard of Oz,* and Walt Disney's *Snow White and the Seven Dwarfs.*

Lucas meets McCallum

Star Wars and *Indiana Jones* producer Robert Watts introduces Rick McCallum to Lucas during discussions about *The Young Indiana Jones Chronicles.* McCallum says about the meeting, "The question for *Young Indy* was, can you make a series as a normal network TV show on location, with huge production values, and be able to shoot three times as long?"

NOVEMBER

Timothy Zahn

November 6: Novelist Timothy Zahn receives a phone call from his agent confirming that he has been hired to write an authorized tale of the post-*Jedi* adventures of the *Star Wars* heroes. He begins work on *Heir to the Empire* shortly after.

East Meets West

November 9: Jubilant German citizens begin tearing down the Berlin Wall following a concession made by the East German government.

A man uses a pick-ax to attack the wall. Within days, the East-West border is declared completely open.

DECEMBER

Skywalker Sound

Skywalker Sound leases 30,000 square feet and commences groundbreaking work on a state-of-the-art sound facility in Santa Monica's Lantana Center.

OCTOBER

More ILM at Disney World

The Body Wars simulator attraction opens at Disney World's EPCOT Center. The ride, which takes visitors on a tour through the human respiratory and circulatory system, features effects work by ILM.

The ILM model shop tackles Body Wars after making a similar biological journey with their effects work on Innerspace in 1987.

To accurately mirror the movements of the ride simulator, the sets are photographed using motion control.

VELVET REVOLUTION IN CZECHOSLOVAKIA • FIRST FULL-LENGTH *SIMPSONS* EPISODE AIRS

1990

APART FROM A NEW venue for Star Tours and a few commemorative items for the 10th anniversary of *The Empire Strikes Back*, *Star Wars* is a thing of the past to the general public by 1990. However, comments by George Lucas and Irvin Kershner in *The Lucasfilm Fan Club* magazine encourage the probability—not just the possibility—of more *Star Wars* movies. While some fans are wondering what to do with their *Star Wars* toys, others are still avidly collecting.

"Now people can stop asking. They can just come and ride Star Tours all day long."

Mark Hamill
on fans who keep asking him when the next Star Wars movie will be released

JANUARY

This early LucasArts logo didn't last long and was soon supplanted by the popular "gold guy."

Doug Norby is president of Lucasfilm Ltd. from 1985 until 1992.

LucasArts Entertainment

January 11: Lucasfilm president Doug Norby announces that Lucasfilm Ltd. has consolidated nine of its business units under a new subsidiary named LucasArts Entertainment. The new organization is made up of Industrial Light & Magic, the THX Group, LucasArts Licensing, the Skywalker Group, LucasArts Attractions, LucasArts Luminaire, Lucasfilm Commercial Productions, Lucasfilm Games, and Lucasfilm Learning Systems.

Star Tours concept art illustrates a spacecraft simulator, in which guests are taken on a galactic tour by a droid guide.

Star Tours

January 13: Walt Disney World's new Disney/MGM Studios Theme Park celebrates the grand opening of the third Star Tours attraction. Like the Tokyo attraction, the Disney World version features six simulators, but its entrance is decorated by an Ewok village dominated by a 10.5-meter (35-foot) AT-AT walker. The grand opening's special guests include Lucas, Mark Hamill, Carrie Fisher, and Anthony Daniels. Says Disney CEO Michael Eisner, "Walt Disney is not here anymore, and none of us pretend to be as creative as he was. Today it is imperative that we make relationships with people like George Lucas, otherwise we will not move forward." Asked during a press conference when the next *Star Wars* film will be made, Lucas answers, "Five or six years."

The Saturn Award

January 21: The Saturn Award for Best Special Effects is awarded to Ken Ralston and ILM for *Back to the Future II*.

EditDroid

January 25: The EditDroid staff hosts an open house to demonstrate its digital editing system at the Santa Monica office and training facility, attended by more than 500 producers, directors, editors, and studio heads.

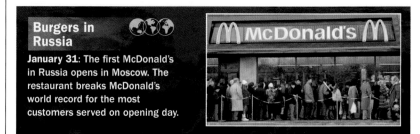

Burgers in Russia

January 31: The first McDonald's in Russia opens in Moscow. The restaurant breaks McDonald's world record for the most customers served on opening day.

Stealing Ewok

January 18: The *Los Angeles Times* reports on a Calgary writer who has accused Lucas of stealing the name and concept for the Ewoks. Lucas responds that he created the Ewoks in his original 1974 draft of *The Star Wars*, and came up with the name by reversing the syllables of the character he called a Wookiee and rhyming it with the northern California Indian tribe known as the Miwok (pronounced me-walk).

Above: Concept art for an Ewok. Left: The final version as seen in Jedi.

NELSON MANDELA RELEASED AFTER 27 YEARS IN PRISON ⊕ **GORBACHEV ELECTED FIRST SOVI**

MARCH

First Digital Recording

March 19–20: For a recording at Skywalker Sound, Lucasfilm's state-of-the-art recording facility at Skywalker Ranch, John Williams conducts the Skywalker Symphony Orchestra—a newly-formed group of 95 musicians from the Bay Area—in a performance of Williams's *Star Wars* music. Using 20-bit technology for "high definition sound," the recording is released as *John Williams Conducts John Williams: The Star Wars Trilogy* by Sony Classical. It is the first digital recording of the *Star Wars* music.

APRIL

Lucas vs. Luke

April 20: *Entertainment Weekly* reports on a $300 million trademark infringement lawsuit filed by Lucasfilm against Luke Skyywalker, aka Luther Campbell, leader of the controversial Florida rap group 2 Live Crew. Lucasfilm's attorney says, "The confusion could be very damaging to the company." The rapper later gives up the name and pays Lucasfilm an undisclosed sum.

Alex McCrindle

April 20: Alex McCrindle (General Dodonna) dies aged 78.

Alex McCrindle as General Dodonna in Star Wars. Dodonna is the first character in the Saga to use the phrase, "May the Force be with you."

Hubble Problems

April 24: The space shuttle *Discovery* places the Hubble Space Telescope into orbit. After failing to achieve sharp focus, it is discovered that the telescope's primary mirror has been ground incorrectly.

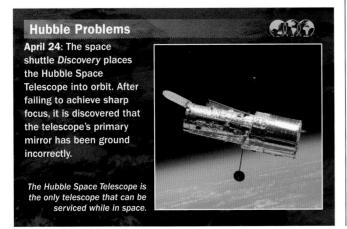

The Hubble Space Telescope is the only telescope that can be serviced while in space.

MAY

Jurassic Park

Based on Steven Spielberg's interest, Universal acquires the movie rights for *Jurassic Park*, Michael Crichton's science-fiction novel about a theme park populated by cloned dinosaurs. Crichton is inspired by the dinosaur drawings of William Stout, an uncredited storyboard artist on *Raiders of the Lost Ark*.

Lawrence Noble

To honor the 10th anniversary of *The Empire Strikes Back*, an unused piece of artwork by Lawrence Noble—originally designed for the first *Empire* poster campaign—is brought back and printed as a Fan Club exclusive.

Yoda in Bronze

To commemorate the 10th anniversary of *The Empire Strikes Back*, the Fan Club offers for sale a bronze Yoda sculpture by artist Lawrence Noble, a professional illustrator who had previously worked on poster concepts for the movie. Limited to an edition of 50 and priced at $500, the bronze is cast from Noble's clay sculpt of Yoda—his very first effort at sculpture—that he'd made 10 years earlier.

Noble's 23-cm (9-inch) tall bronze Yoda is cast from a 10-year-old uncommissioned clay sculpture.

JULY

Williams Celebrates the Discovery

July 4: John Williams conducts the Boston Pops Esplanade Orchestra in the premiere of his composition *Celebrate Discovery*, which commemorates Christopher Columbus's arrival in America.

"Style B"

May: The "Style B" silver mylar *The Empire Strikes Back* 10th anniversary poster features Luke riding on a tauntaun inside a stylized number 10.

From Game to Screen

July 23: Lucasfilm Ltd. Television joins with Atlantis Films Limited and The Family Channel to start production on *Maniac Mansion*, a comedy series based on Lucasfilm Games' 1987 computer adventure. It is produced by Eugene Levy and stars Joe Flaherty, who are both alumni of the SCTV comedy troupe. After its September premiere, the program is hailed by *TIME* magazine as the "looniest, sweetest family comedy of the year."

The show is not directly based on the game of the same name, but is inspired by its mad-scientist vibe and offbeat humor.

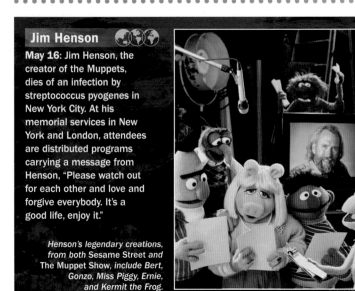

Jim Henson

May 16: Jim Henson, the creator of the Muppets, dies of an infection by streptococcus pyogenes in New York City. At his memorial services in New York and London, attendees are distributed programs carrying a message from Henson, "Please watch out for each other and love and forgive everybody. It's a good life, enjoy it."

Henson's legendary creations, from both Sesame Street and The Muppet Show, include Bert, Gonzo, Miss Piggy, Ernie, and Kermit the Frog.

Presumed Innocent

July 27: Alan J. Pakula's drama *Presumed Innocent* is released. Starring Harrison Ford, it features a musical score by John Williams.

AUGUST

August 2: Iraq invades Kuwait, overrunning its military in only two days. The action leads directly to the Gulf War.

Darkman

August 24: Sam Raimi's *Darkman* is released, starring Liam Neeson (Qui-Gon Jinn) in the title role. This film brings the 38-year-old Neeson much wider public recognition.

Movie poster for Darkman, designed by John Alvin.

Red Tails

Issue #12 of the *Lucasfilm Fan Club* magazine announces that Lucasfilm will soon begin production of the motion picture *Red Tails*. The movie will tell the story of the Tuskegee Airmen—a group of African-American fighter pilots who provided escort for bombing missions in Europe during World War II. According to the article, the movie is "scheduled for release sometime in 1992."

Lucasfilm Fan Club #12 also contains features about Maniac Mansion *and* Back To the Future II.

The Adventurer

The first issue of Lucasfilm Games' magazine *The Adventurer* is released. The ongoing mag provides information about upcoming products and company news for customers and fans. The first cover story shines a spotlight on the WWII flight simulator Secret Weapons of the Luftwaffe.

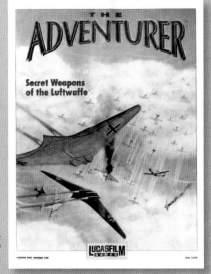

The first issue includes a teaser version of Secret Weapons of the Luftwaffe.

The Adventurer provides advance looks at a number of early games, including Star Wars for the Nintendo Entertainment System.

OCTOBER

The Secret of Monkey Island is the first in a series of five graphical adventure games.

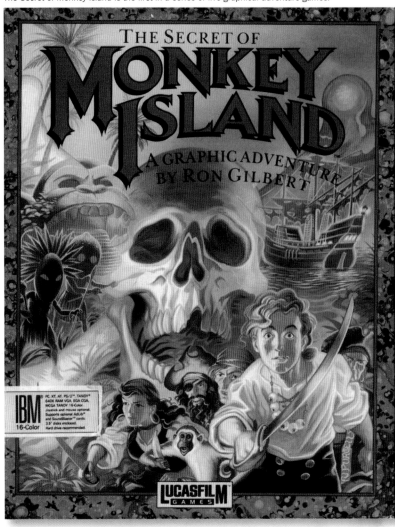

The Secret of Monkey Island

Lucasfilm Games releases the graphical adventure game The Secret of Monkey Island, designed by Ron Gilbert. It wins accolades for its humor, as the player controls young Guybrush Threepwood through a series of challenges that pit him against the villainous ghost pirate LeChuck. Monkey Island employs an updated version of the SCUMM engine originally introduced for Maniac Mansion. Lucasfilm Games also releases the fantasy adventure game Loom at the same time, and several references to Loom are included as in-jokes in the Monkey Island storyline.

Jurassic Park

Michael Crichton's novel *Jurassic Park* hits bookshelves. Universal's decision to snap up the movie rights in May is justified when the book becomes a bestseller.

Blue Planet

The IMAX feature *Blue Planet* premieres. Directed by Ben Burtt and produced by the IMAX Space Technology Corporation for the National Air and Space Museum, it features views of the Earth filmed from orbit on space shuttle missions. The narrative, written by Toni Myers, focuses on our planet's origins and its ecological fragility.

1991

TIMOTHY ZAHN'S novel *Heir to the Empire* surprises everyone by going to the top of *The New York Times* bestseller list. The book taps into a reservoir of fan enthusiasm that many were convinced had long since dried up, and it paves the way for what will take shape as the modern *Star Wars* Expanded Universe. In theaters, ILM wows moviegoers by conjuring up *Terminator 2,* and *Star Wars* makes a return to the comics medium in the visually stunning epic *Dark Empire*.

> "The only rules they gave me was that I was to start three to five years after *Jedi*, and that I could use anybody who had not been killed in the movies."
>
> **Timothy Zahn**
> *author of* Heir to the Empire

JANUARY

The Gulf War
January 17: The Gulf War officially begins with Operation Desert Storm. The United States and other allied nations launch an air campaign against Iraqi radar sites and other strategic targets. More than 1,000 air sorties are launched per day during the massive assault.

FEBRUARY

Hasbro Tonka
February 1: Hasbro acquires the Tonka Corporation for $516 million in the wake of Tonka's dismal holiday sales. This gives Hasbro control of Kenner Parker Toys, which had been purchased by Tonka in 1987. The Kenner Products and Parker Bros. divisions bring with them such venerable names as *Clue* and *Monopoly*.

Star Wars Echo
The *FidoNet Star Wars Echo* is established. This early method of online communication involves a network of dial-up bulletin board systems (BBS) linked through the "echomail" message forum. *The Star Wars Echo* is one of the first electronic methods for discussing and encouraging *Star Wars* fandom.

Return of the Star Wars
President Bush reveals in his State of the Union address a revision of the Strategic Defense Initiative ("Star Wars") missile defense system. The new Global Protection Against Limited Strikes (GPALS) will include 1,000 space-based "Brilliant Pebbles" interceptors, 750 to 1,000 long-range ground-based interceptors at six sites, space-based and mobile sensors, and transportable ballistic missile defenses. It will never be deployed, and will lose funding once Clinton becomes President.

MARCH

March 1: Dark Horse Comics secures publishing rights for spin-offs of *Star Wars*, *Indiana Jones*, and *The Young Indiana Jones Chronicles*. Dark Horse has already had great success with spin-offs of other popular movies, including *Alien*, *Predator*, and *Terminator*.

MAY

THE SAGA CONTINUES.
STAR WARS
FIRST IN A THREE BOOK CYCLE OF ALL-NEW ADVENTURES
HEIR TO THE EMPIRE
The vanquished Imperial fleet returns to destroy the Republic... and a voice from the past brings a warning to Luke Skywalker...
NOW AT A BOOKSTORE NEAR YOU!
BY TIMOTHY ZAHN — BANTAM HARDCOVERS

Heir to the Empire
Set five years after *Return of the Jedi*, Timothy Zahn's *Heir to the Empire* introduces charismatic villain Grand Admiral Thrawn. Lucas Licensing had previously vetoed Zahn's idea to include an insane clone of Obi-Wan Kenobi and to name his alien Noghri assassins "the Sith."

The book's cover, illustrated by Tom Jung, is reproduced in this promotional advertisement.

⊙ POLICEMEN INDICTED FOR RODNEY KING BEATING ⊙ BORIS YELTSIN ELECTED RUSSIAN LEADER

Backdraft

In Ron Howard's *Backdraft*, ILM produces a quarter-scale rooftop model and matte painting for a shot of a chemical plant inferno.

William Baldwin, Kurt Russell, and Scott Glenn in Backdraft

STS-40

June 5: The space shuttle *Columbia* goes on its 11th mission, carrying the Spacelab research module into orbit. The module is for spacelab sciences and is the first of its kind to be solely dedicated to biology.

Space shuttle Columbia on launch day

JUNE

Jungle Fever

June 7: Samuel L. Jackson (Mace Windu) appears in *Jungle Fever* as a crack cocaine addict. Having struggled with drug use in the past, he had urged director Spike Lee, "Don't recast me—I've done all the research." His performance is so acclaimed that the 1991 Cannes Film Festival awards a special Supporting Actor jury prize just for him.

Samuel L. Jackson as Gator Purify in Jungle Fever

The Rocketeer

From director Joe Johnston, this historical adventure is adapted from the comics by Dave Stevens. ILM's Ken Ralston leads the visual effects effort, which includes a 10-m (34-ft) scale zeppelin.

JULY

Terminator 2: Judgment Day

July 3: James Cameron's *Terminator 2: Judgment Day* is released, starring Arnold Schwarzenegger, Linda Hamilton, and Robert Patrick, who, as a liquid-metal T-1000, is occasionally portrayed as a computer effect. Industrial Light & Magic is responsible for the revolutionary CG work on display in scenes where the T-1000 reforms its body from shards and morphs into view after disguising itself as black-and-white floor tiles. For their efforts on the film, Dennis Muren, Stan Winston, Gene Warren Jr., and Robert Skotak win the Academy Award® for Best Visual Effects.

In several scenes, the T-1000 effect morphs into live-action footage of actor Robert Patrick.

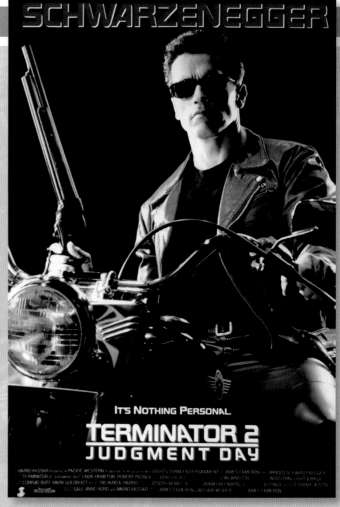

Also called T2, the film becomes a Schwarzenegger smash.

Also in 1991...

Comic Strips

Limited-edition copies of Al Williamson and Archie Goodwin's 1981–1984 black-and-white *Star Wars* newspaper comic strips make their way into collectors' hands via a three-volume hardbound set from Russ Cochran.

The Russ Cochran set reproduces the newspaper strips in their original format. Included is the tale of "The Bounty Hunter of Ord Mantell," first published in early 1981 (below).

AUGUST

Super Nintendo

August 13: The Super Nintendo Entertainment System (SNES) is released, shipping to stores with the game Super Mario World. The 16-bit console is the next-generation replacement for the Nintendo Entertainment System (NES), which is still widely in use.

The SNES (European version—above) is an advantage for Nintendo in the console wars with Sony and Sega.

SEPTEMBER

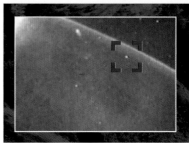

UFOs Caught on Camera

September 15: A camera positioned on the cargo bay of the space shuttle *Discovery* records footage of supposed UFOs. NASA says the objects are ice particles, but others claim their movements suggest controlled craft. One news headline reads, "*Star Wars* Over Australia?"

WARSAW PACT DISSOLVED ☀ RECORD SOLAR ECLIPSE ☽ LENINGRAD RENAMED ST PETERSBU

OCTOBER

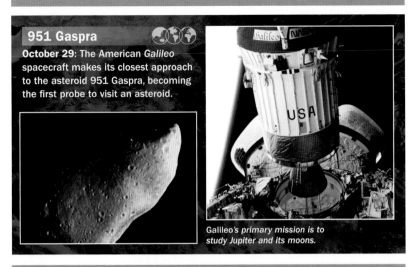

951 Gaspra

October 29: The American *Galileo* spacecraft makes its closest approach to the asteroid 951 Gaspra, becoming the first probe to visit an asteroid.

Galileo's primary mission is to study Jupiter and its moons.

NOVEMBER

JVC's gameplay is light years more sophisticated than the Star Wars games for the Atari platform.

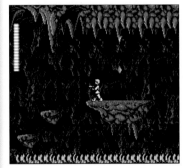

Star Wars enters the side-scrolling action game genre.

JVC *Star Wars*

Lucasfilm Games' *Star Wars* is released by JVC for the Nintendo Entertainment System (NES), Sega Master System, Game Boy, and Sega Game Gear. It is the first *Star Wars* game that allows players to play as the main characters, including Luke, Han, and Chewbacca. Its plot closely follows the events of Episode IV *A New Hope*, with levels that involve fighting Sand People on Tatooine, piloting the *Millennium Falcon* to the Death Star, and rescuing Princess Leia from the space station's detention block.

DECEMBER

Hook

December 11: Steven Spielberg's *Hook* is released. The tale of a grown-up Peter Pan is one that Spielberg had long wanted to tell, and the movie stars Robin Williams as Peter and Dustin Hoffman as Captain Hook. Among ILM's visual effects work is a breakthrough camera shift, achieved by texture-mapping a matte painting of Neverland Island onto a 3-D wireframe model.

Hook finishes the year as the #5 top-grossing film in the US.

A Dark Empire

Dark Empire #1 is published by Dark Horse Comics. The six-issue series by writer Tom Veitch and artist Cam Kennedy portrays a bleak post-*Jedi* galaxy ruled by Emperor Palpatine in a cloned body. Luke Skywalker gambles that he can turn to the dark side and defeat it from within, and Boba Fett reappears because the Sarlacc found him "somewhat indigestible." *Dark Empire* was originally scheduled for a late '80s release from Marvel Comics, but instead becomes the first *Star Wars* comic published by Dark Horse in its capacity as Lucasfilm's new comics licensee. "Cam Kennedy was the perfect artist for *Dark Empire*," says Dark Horse publisher Mike Richardson. "He had spectacular painted scenes of the ships, characters, and action. It was gorgeous, like watching a Technicolor film of the movie frames."

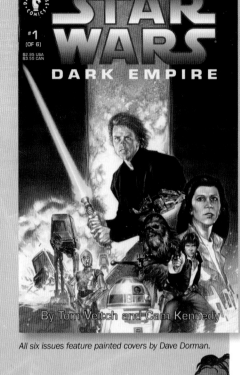

All six issues feature painted covers by Dave Dorman.

AT-AT armor is no match for the punch of the Falcon's quad cannons in this scene by artist Cam Kennedy.

GOT HIM!

December 26: The Supreme Soviet dissolves the Soviet Union of Socialist Republics following the resignation of President Gorbachev the day before.

WAR IN CROATIA ● TIM BERNERS-LEE ANNOUNCES WORLD WIDE WEB ● TERRY WAITE FREED ●

1992

LUCASFILM'S BIGGEST TV project to date debuts in 1992 with *The Young Indiana Jones Chronicles*, which follows Indy—aged 10 and in his late teens—as he interacts with famous figures of the early 20th century. The result of Lucas's desire to create educational and engaging television, *Young Indy* makes use of digital replications of extras, digital matte paintings, and digital compositing, which earn the series an Emmy Award for visual effects, and pave the way for a relaunch of *Star Wars*.

> "I think people need to be exposed to all kinds of information, hopefully in entertaining form, so they have an opportunity to understand the larger world of ideas."
>
> **George Lucas**
> *on* The Young Indiana Jones Chronicles

FEBRUARY

Defenders of Dynatron City

February 22: An animated TV special, *Defenders of Dynatron City*, airs on Fox Children's Network. The project is spearheaded by LucasArts Licensing, working with concept creator Gary Winnick of Lucasfilm Games and producer DiC Entertainment. The special follows a group of oddball superheroes including Ms. Megawatt, Jet Headstrong, and Monkey Kid as they protect their eponymous home. Though it does not get picked up as a regular series, the special is released on VHS in October. Lucasfilm Games releases a game version for the Nintendo NES in July.

MARCH

Young Indy Pilot

March 4: The first *Young Indiana Jones Chronicles* episode—the feature-length "Young Indiana Jones and the Curse of the Jackal"—airs on ABC. It is followed by five one-hour weekly episodes, which collectively comprise season one.

Sean Patrick Flanery as the young Indy.

Lloyd Owen (Henry Jones Sr.), Ruth de Sosa (Anna Jones), and Corey Carrier (Henry "Indiana" Jones Jr.)

Thalberg Award

March 30: At the 64th Academy Awards® ceremony, Spielberg presents Lucas with the Irving G. Thalberg Life Achievement Award from the Academy of Motion Picture Arts and Sciences. The award is given only in years when the Board feels there is a deserving recipient. Noting that Lucas's leadership in encouraging motion picture exhibitors to upgrade their sound and projection quality is an incalculable service to motion picture art, Academy governors praise Lucas for carrying the producer's role "beyond the postproduction phase of movie-making into the theaters."

🌐 **BOSNIAN WAR & THE SIEGE OF SARAJEVO BEGIN**

APRIL

Windows 3.1

The Windows 3.1 operating system is released by Microsoft. Partly thanks to a TV advertising campaign, the Windows platform becomes the most widely adopted graphical operating system.

Euro Disney

April 12: Euro Disney (later known as Disneyland Resort Paris) opens in Marne-la-Vallée, France. Its version of the Star Tours attraction features an animatronic character named ROX-N in the post-ride area, who is capable of speaking English, French, and Italian.

Celebrations at the opening of Euro Disney

MAY

A Second Season for *Indy*

May 13: Principal photography begins for the second season of *The Young Indiana Jones Chronicles*. Shooting locations include Africa, Italy, England, Israel, Ireland, and Czechoslovakia.

JUNE

The Glove of Darth Vader

The Glove of Darth Vader is the first book in a new series of Bantam novels aimed at young readers. Set after *Return of the Jedi*, the six-book series introduces colorful characters including Palpatine's mutant heir and the devious (and bearded) father of Jabba the Hutt.

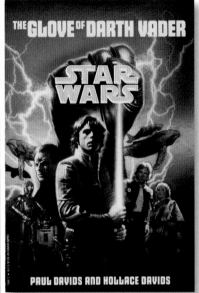

Cover art by Drew Struzan

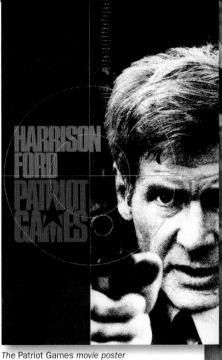

The Patriot Games movie poster

Patriot Games

June 5: Harrison Ford stars in *Patriot Games*, replacing Alec Baldwin as CIA agent Jack Ryan in the latest film based on the novels of Tom Clancy. The movie also features James Earl Jones and Samuel L. Jackson.

Dark Force Rising

Bantam publishes Timothy Zahn's bestselling novel *Dark Force Rising*, the sequel to *Heir to the Empire* and the second book in the *Thrawn* trilogy. The plot thickens and the New Republic's fate becomes increasingly dire as Grand Admiral Thrawn gets his hands on a fleet of Clone Wars-era warships.

Dark Force Rising cover art by Tom Jung

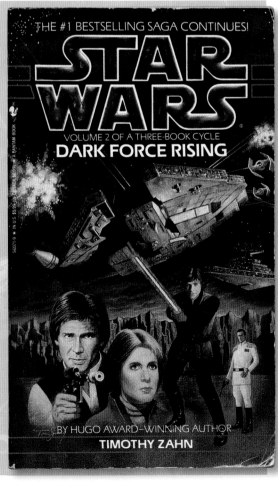

MERYL STREEP · BRUCE WILLIS · GOLDIE HAWN

A ROBERT ZEMECKIS FILM

Death Becomes Her

JULY

Death Becomes Her

July 31: *Death Becomes Her* debuts. Directed by Lucas's USC classmate Robert Zemeckis, the film marks the first time that CG effects capture realistic human skin texture. ILM's work is recognized when Ken Ralston, Doug Chiang, Douglas Smythe, and Tom Woodruff Jr. receive the Academy Award® for Best Visual Effects.

Meryl Streep is nominated for a Golden Globe for her performance in Death Becomes Her.

Olympics

July 25: The Summer Olympics open in Barcelona, Spain. South Africa takes part for the first time in 32 years, and a united Germany competes for the first time since 1964. The lifting of the amateur status rule produces the US basketball "Dream Team," featuring Michael Jordan, Magic Johnson, Larry Bird, and others, who easily win gold.

SEPTEMBER

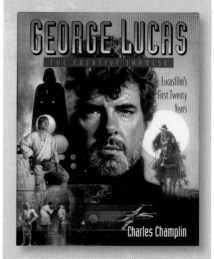

GEORGE LUCAS
THE CREATIVE IMPULSE

Lucasfilm's First Twenty Years

Charles Champlin

Lucas's Creative Impulse

Abrams publishes *George Lucas: The Creative Impulse*. Written by Charles Champlin, the hardcover book chronicles Lucasfilm's first 20 years, and includes a filmography and a look at Skywalker Ranch.

Indy Back on the Small Screen

September 21: Season two of *The Young Indiana Jones Chronicles* opens with the episode "Austria 1917," detailing Indy's misadventures as a spy during World War I. The 17 subsequent episodes are a mix of both new installments and episodes produced for the first season, and take Indy from Ireland to Princeton to Petrograd. Among the historical figures crossing paths with Indy in season two are Pablo Picasso, Eliot Ness, Sigmund Freud, and Ernest Hemingway.

AUGUST

Classic Star Wars

Classic Star Wars #1 is released by Dark Horse Comics. The series reprints the daily *Star Wars* newspaper strip produced from 1981 to 1984 by Al Williamson and Archie Goodwin, but reformats it for the four-color comic-book format by trimming credit boxes, dropping redundant dialogue balloons, and varying the panel size and layout. Williamson comes aboard to contribute original covers and provide fill-in art. "Al had a very obvious paternal attachment toward the presentation of the series as a whole, and basically provided a stamp of approval on each issue," says editor Bob Cooper.

In Classic Star Wars #1, Imperial troops pursue Luke and Leia.

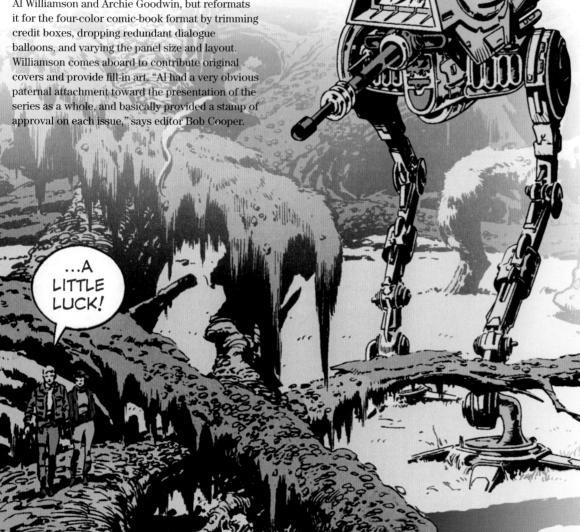

...A LITTLE LUCK!

Sean Patrick Flanery stars as the teenage Indy working undercover in Austria, 1917.

OCTOBER

Peekskill Meteorite

October 9: A 13-kilogram (29-pound) meteorite lands in the driveway of the Knapp residence in Peekskill, New York, destroying the family's Chevrolet Malibu. It becomes known as the Peekskill Meteorite.

YITZHAK RABIN ELECTED

THE GREAT DARTH VADER WAS A SICK MAN IN AN IRON MASK!

YES, THAT MASK INSPIRED *TERROR* THROUGHOUT THE GALAXY...

...BUT THE FEEBLE HEART WITHIN WAS FOREVER POSSESSED BY THE *IMPOTENT* SIDE OF THE FORCE!

End of the Empire

Dark Horse Comics completes the initial six-issue series of *Dark Empire*. Sales are so strong that the company commissions the same writer/artist team for a sequel.

Dave Dorman's cover of a lightsaber-wielding Leia

A Book to Collect

Chronicle Books releases Steve Sansweet's *Star Wars: From Concept to Screen to Collectible*. Its rare artwork and photos of unproduced toys tap into a resurgence of interest in *Star Wars* collecting.

STAR WARS #6 (OF 6) DARK EMPIRE
By Tom Veitch and Cam Kennedy

NOVEMBER

Super *Star Wars*

Super *Star Wars* is released for the Super Nintendo Entertainment System. The side-scrolling platform game incorporates John Williams's musical score (in an improvised 16-bit style) and Mode 7 effects to create a sense of 3-D during the vehicle sequences, and to smoothly scale backgrounds for scenes like the approach on the Death Star. Loosely based on *Star Wars*: Episode IV *A New Hope*, players can control Luke, Han, and Chewie, with the game culminating in a Death Star trench run. Super *Star Wars* quickly becomes a best-selling game, and *Electronic Gaming Monthly* names it the Best Action/Adventure Game of 1992.

Super Star Wars's gameplay is smooth but unforgiving, with tough enemies and no save features.

Clinton for President

November 3: Democrat Bill Clinton defeats incumbent Republican George H.W. Bush and independent challenger Ross Perot for the presidency of the United States. In his victory speech, he promises to tackle "the conversion of our economy from a defense to a domestic economic giant."

Bill Clinton, Vice President-elect Al Gore, and Hillary Clinton celebrate at an election night rally.

Batman battles the Joker in the 22-minute long holiday episode.

The Voice of Hamill

November 13: Mark Hamill makes his voiceover debut as the Joker in "Christmas with the Joker," a season-one episode of *Batman: The Animated Series* (co-produced by *Ewoks*'s Paul Dini).

The Letterbox Trilogy

Twentieth Century Fox Video releases the *Star Wars* Trilogy Special Letterbox Collector's Edition. Packaged in a slipcase with a hologram of the original movie poster adorning the front, the set contains letterbox VHS cassettes for each of the *Star Wars* films, a fourth cassette of *From Star Wars to Jedi: The Making of a Saga*, a 48-page special edition of the book *George Lucas: The Creative Impulse*, and a certificate of authenticity featuring a message from Lucas.

DECEMBER

Pinball Wizard

A *Star Wars* pinball machine is launched by Data East. It features speaker cutouts in the shape of the Death Star and an animated R2-D2.

1993

STAR WARS BEGINS to dominate electronic entertainment in 1993, as LucasArts moves into new territory. Critical and commercial smashes X-Wing and Rebel Assault excel at original storytelling. X-Wing is marketed as a "space combat simulator," and uses the same game engine as popular flight simulator Secret Weapons of the Luftwaffe. Rebel Assault is LucasArts' first game exclusively on CD-ROM and features a new proprietary video streaming engine.

> "Robin Williams called once. He said he and his son were playing, and he wanted to ask for some hints."
>
> **Amanda Haverlock**
> *LucasArts receptionist, on the public appeal of Rebel Assault*

FEBRUARY

Star Wars: X-Wing

LucasArts' *Star Wars: X-Wing* is released on floppy disc for PC. Programmed by flight simulator expert Larry Holland, the game uses a fully 3-D graphical engine and asks players to pilot their way from flight training to the attack on the Death Star. Among its innovations is the iMUSE dynamic music system, which changes the background score to reflect victories, losses, and the arrival of enemies. With the success of X-Wing, LucasArts releases two expansion discs—Imperial Pursuit and B-Wing—that continue the story and introduce new classes of the ships.

In addition to the X-wing, players can pilot Y-wing and A-wing starfighters.

World Trade Center

February 26: In New York City, the explosion of a van bomb damages the North Tower of the World Trade Center, killing six and injuring more than a thousand.

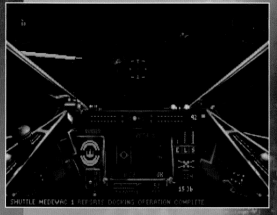

The game has a steep learning curve, requiring careful management of lasers, engines, and shields.

All scenes in *Star Wars:* X-Wing are original but inspired by the first *Star Wars* movie.

MARCH

The Return of *Young Indy*

March 13: After a five-month hiatus, *The Young Indiana Jones Chronicles* returns with the episode "Young Indiana Jones and the Mystery of the Blues." Its framing sequence (set in 1950) features Harrison Ford, who is bearded due to his work on the movie *The Fugitive*. "George called Harrison and he agreed to do it if we could shoot at his home," says Rick McCallum. "We shot it in a day." Seeing Ford again, Lucas gets an idea for an *Indy IV*, set in the 1950s.

Harrison Ford and George Lucas on a chilly Young Indiana Jones set

Pentium Chip

March 22: Intel ships the first Pentium computer chips. The revolutionary chip greatly increases the capabilities of personal computers, including their utility as gaming platforms.

The Pentium replaces the i486 chip as the computing standard.

APRIL

Super Live Adventure

April 27: *George Lucas's Super Live Adventure*, a $25 million live-entertainment show, opens in Japan. Produced by Kenneth Feld (of *Ringling Brothers* fame), the production features 60 performers in sequences referencing *American Graffiti*, *Willow*, and the *Star Wars* and *Indiana Jones* trilogies. Movie clips, crashing bridges, laser lights, and audience participation help "good triumph over evil." Despite the fact that the cast had only two months to rehearse, the show debuts in Yokohama and tours four Japanese cities over the course of 22 weeks. At launch, half a million tickets have already been sold for the 7,000-seat Yokohama auditorium.

This inclusive poster touches on all Super Live Adventure elements.

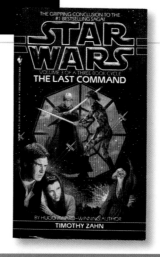

The Last Command

Timothy Zahn's *The Last Command* wraps up the popular *Thrawn* trilogy by revealing the fates of villains Grand Admiral Thrawn and Joruus C'baoth. It also features the birth of Han and Leia's twins, Jacen and Jaina. Former Imperial assassin Mara Jade emerges from the trilogy as a romantic foil for Luke Skywalker.

All volumes in the Thrawn trilogy feature painted covers by Tom Jung.

JUNE

June 1: Super *Star Wars: The Empire Strikes Back* is released for the Super Nintendo. Like its predecessor, it offers 12 megabits of action and advanced Mode 7 technology for its vehicular sequences.

Luke fights Vader in a final boss battle.

Jurassic Park

June 11: Spielberg's *Jurassic Park* is released, stunning moviegoers with raptors, brachiosauruses, and a T-rex brought to life through ILM's pioneering use of CG. For the first time, digital technology is able to render realistic skin and muscles and animate movements that look truly natural. Software breakthroughs permit unprecedented freedom in compositing these CG creations with live action film—for the first time in ILM's history, all restrictions on camera movement are removed thanks to such tools as SoftImage. The *Jurassic Park* effects win Dennis Muren, Stan Winston, Phil Tippett, and Michael Lantieri the Academy Award® for Best Visual Effects.

The T-rex breaks loose at Jurassic Park and chaos ensues.

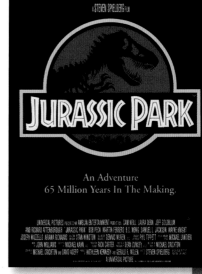

The poster for the monster-sized hit movie that finishes 1993 in the #1 spot

The Super Live Adventure special-edition light-up lightsaber is available only at the show in Japan.

AUGUST

Bend-Ems

Just Toys releases a set of *Star Wars* Bend-Ems figures, the first new *Star Wars* figures to be released since the Power of the Force line in 1985. Toy-hungry collectors snap these up, as Hasbro still has not announced anything regarding plans for a new wave of action figures.

The Bend-Ems release includes figures of Luke, Leia, Obi-Wan, Chewie, R2-D2, and others.

Mars Unobserved

August 22: In a disappointing setback, NASA loses contact with the Mars Observer before it can enter orbit above the red planet.

The Mars Observer was to study the planet's geography and climate.

SEPTEMBER

Hayden Christensen (Anakin Skywalker) makes his television debut on the Canadian television series *Family Passions* aged 12.

Twentieth Century Fox releases the laserdisc set *Star Wars Trilogy: The Definitive Collection*, which comes with a hardcover edition of the book *George Lucas: The Creative Impulse*.

September 24: *Entertainment Weekly* reports on the prequels, speculating that a new trilogy will be released "between 1995 and 2000" and will tell the story of Obi-Wan and Anakin "from their days as friends and fellow Jedi Knights."

Abrams publishes *Monsters and Aliens from George Lucas.* Written by Bob Carrau (*The Ewok Adventure*), the book provides humorous back stories for creatures illustrated in concept art.

Some of the aliens profiled in the book include Gamorreans and Ithorians.

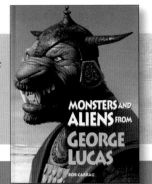

OCTOBER

May The Delta Force Be With You

October 3: Between 1983 and 1985, the US Defense Department had employed Chris Majer to try different techniques to improve the Special Forces' morale and training. In an unpublished interview, Majer said, "They wanted to be seen as the first incarnation of Jedi Knights." Their motto was "Vi Cit[Sit] Teccum"—or "May the Force Be With You." After achieving very good to spectacular results, the units were broken up. On October 3, 1993, two of the trainees—Master Sergeant Gary Gordon and Sergeant First Class Randy Shughart—are part of the 1st Special Forces Operational Detachment-Delta (1SFOD-D), or "Delta Force," sent into Mogadishu, Somalia. After two Black Hawk helicopters are downed, Gordon and Shughart, in the third helicopter, insist upon being inserted into the desperate situation in order to save surviving troops. Despite their incredible heroism, skill, and fight, both men are killed by overwhelming numbers. On May 23, 1994, Gordon and Shughart posthumously receive the Medal of Honor.

Also in 1993...

Cards are the Topps

Topps releases the *Star Wars Galaxy* set of trading cards. Among the card images are concept sketches, rare poster art, and original illustrations from top comics professionals.

The trading cards are purchased in packets of eight.

Each packet contains a random assortment of cards.

Packaging for a retailer box that contains packs for individual sale

Tales of the Jedi

The first issue of *Tales of the Jedi* is published by Dark Horse Comics. Written by Tom Veitch with art by Chris Gossett, it takes place 4,000 years before the events of the *Star Wars* movies—the first time that any Expanded Universe story has been set in such an exotic timeframe. *Tales of the Jedi* introduces Jedi Knight Ulic Qel-Droma and kicks off a string of related comics projects set during the history of the Old Republic.

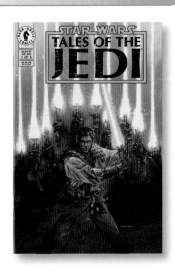

Editing the Future

Avid Technology acquires the EditDroid and SoundDroid technologies, joining forces with Lucasfilm to develop and produce the next generation of digital picture and sound editing systems. Ultimately, the Avid Media Composer system will become the standard in digital editing.

NOVEMBER

In addition to its flight sequences, Rebel Assault includes several ground-combat missions.

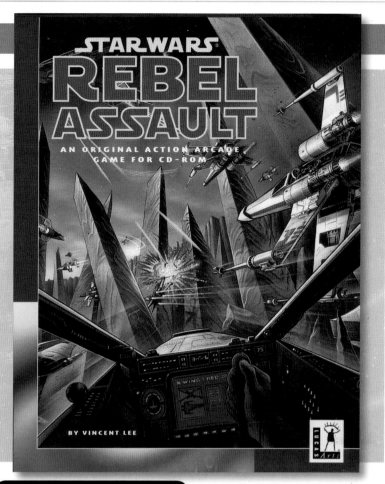

BY VINCENT LEE

Rebel Assault

LucasArts releases Rebel Assault on CD-ROM for the PC. The space shooter is the company's first CD-ROM game and can store more than 500 megabytes of data, allowing for extensive speech and digitized movie footage. Rebel Assault features the proprietary video streaming engine INSANE (or Interactive Streaming Animation Engine). Although the "on rails" gameplay doesn't allow the player to veer away from a predetermined flight path, the superb graphics and mission variety are hits with fans. Within two months of its release, Rebel Assault becomes the best-selling CD-ROM entertainment title to date, with over one million units sold worldwide.

THE ORIGINAL SOUNDTRACK ANTHOLOGY

Anthology

November 23: After the *Star Wars* movie soundtrack licenses revert to Lucasfilm, a comprehensive re-issue of them is released through Twentieth Century Fox Film Scores. Under the name *Star Wars Trilogy: The Original Soundtrack Anthology*, the four-disc set consists of the complete soundtrack from each of the three films and a disc of rare bonus tracks and source music, all packaged inside a collectible box.

Also included in the Soundtrack Anthology is a booklet with an essay on Williams's music by Nicholas Meyer.

Also in 1993...

MicroMachines

Galoob introduces the *Star Wars* MicroMachines line, which features small plastic models of the *Millennium Falcon* and other ships. The toys help feed the growing fan demand for new *Star Wars* merchandise.

A Star Wars MicroMachines 3-Pack with the Millennium Falcon, a Star Destroyer, and an X-Wing

DECEMBER

December 10: The wildly popular first-person shooter Doom hits the computer games market. Produced by id Software, its first nine levels are made available as free shareware.

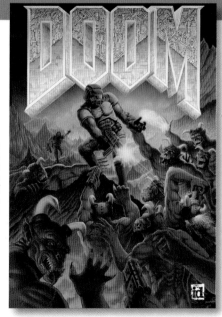

Doom's action centers on a space marine who is thrown into battle against ferocious demons while defending Phobos, one of the moons of Mars.

December 15: *Schindler's List* is released, starring Liam Neeson (Qui-Gon Jinn) as German businessman Oskar Schindler in Spielberg's Holocaust drama.

LO SIGN THE OSLO PEACE ACCORD ✪ DRUG LORD PABLO ESCOBAR KILLED IN COLUMBIA ✪

1994

THE FIRST STEPS toward the Prequel Trilogy renew public interest in *Star Wars* and the franchise moves up a gear with new novels, comics, and games. Producer Rick McCallum and production designer Gavin Bocquet embark on recces for film locations and rumors that Lucas may direct the films—something he hasn't done since 1977—fuel industry excitement. As one studio executive says, "Somebody else doing *Star Wars* means nothing. George Lucas doing it means everything."

> "I've got the stories done, but I have to write the screenplay— so that's a deterrent."
>
> **George Lucas**
> *on the Star Wars Prequel Trilogy*

JANUARY

January 22: *The Young Indiana Jones Chronicles* television series receives a 1993 Golden Globe nomination for Best Dramatic Series, but loses out to the police drama *NYPD Blue*.

FEBRUARY

Jedi Search

The first novel of the *Jedi Academy* trilogy by Kevin J. Anderson, is published by Bantam. Set seven years after *Return of the Jedi*, it chronicles Luke Skywalker's attempt to rebuild the Jedi Order.

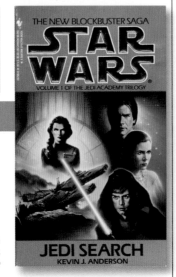

Admiral Daala debuts in Jedi Search as an Imperial villainess.

MARCH

A Fair Parody

March 7: in *Campbell v. Rose Music Inc.*, the US Supreme Court rules that parodies of an original work are generally covered under "fair use."

March 21: At the 66th Annual Academy Awards®, *Schindler's List* wins seven Oscars, including Best Picture, Best Director for Steven Spielberg, and Best Actor for Liam Neeson.

"The best drink of water after the longest drought of my life."—Spielberg wins his first two Oscars in one night.

APRIL

Dark Horse Droids # 1

April 1: The first issue of Dark Horse's *Star Wars: Droids* debuts. The series stars R2-D2 and C-3PO as they bounce between masters in adventures. The stories are written by Anthony Daniels (C-3PO), Jan Strnad, Dan Thorsland, and Ryder Windham.

Issue #1 of Star Wars: Droids—"The Kalarba Adventures"

A Match Made at Bantam

Bantam's novel *The Courtship of Princess Leia* by Dave Wolverton is published. Set four years after *Return of the Jedi*, it ends with the wedding of Han Solo and Princess Leia. The union between the two is a crucial development in the Expanded Universe, and their three children will star in their own adventures.

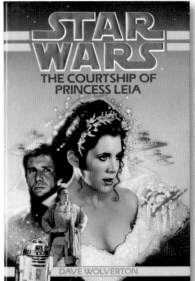

Han and Leia's relationship is threatened by the presence of Prince Isolder. Abducting his beloved, Han plunges them both into danger on the planet Dathomir.

KURT COBAIN IS FOUND DEAD ☻ **NELSON MANDELA ELECTED PRESIDENT OF SOUTH AFRICA** ☻

The Search Begins

Rick McCallum kicks off an extensive search for Episode I conceptual artists, which will stretch on for six months. His efforts net artists Terryl Whitlatch and Iain McCaig, among others.

A conceptual drawing of one of Padmé Amidala's headdresses by Iain McCaig.

One of Terryl Whitlatch's many fantastical creatures.

MAY

May 6: Ewan McGregor (younger Obi-Wan Kenobi) makes his feature film debut in Bill Forsyth's comedic drama *Being Human*, starring alongside Robin Williams.

Doctor George Lucas

May 6: George Lucas receives an honorary Doctor of Fine Arts degree from the University of Southern California, the school where he met a slew of future filmmakers, including Walter Murch and John Milius. In his acceptance speech, Lucas uses the theme of a symbiont circle to illustrate how his friends shaped his career. "Symbiosis is two dissimilar organisms living together, especially when the association is mutually beneficial," Lucas says. "It is the most important thing that I learned from my friends here at the film school."

In his acceptance speech, Lucas says, "I know how I got here. I got here with a lot of help from my friends."

JUNE

Super *Star Wars: Return of the Jedi* is released by LucasArts for the Super Nintendo system, wrapping up the trilogy of titles in the popular Super *Star Wars* series.

Classic *Star Wars*

June 28: Issue #1 of *Classic Star Wars: A New Hope* is published by Dark Horse Comics. This two-part series reprints the original 1977 Marvel movie adaptation.

The first planning meeting takes place to discuss the multimedia project *Shadows of the Empire*, which is slated to become Lucasfilm's tent-pole property for 1996.

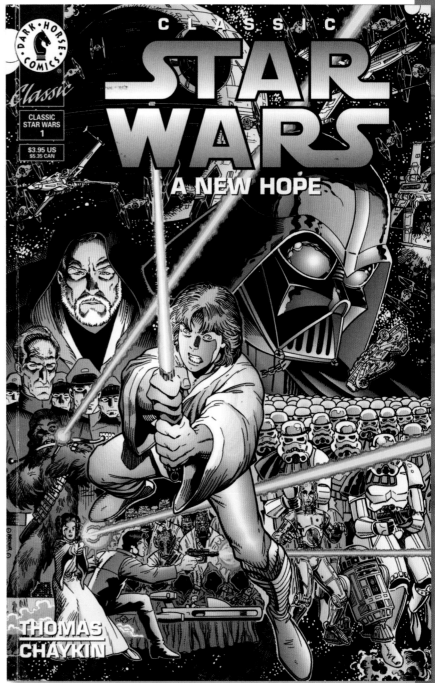

The all-new cover for issue #1 of the reprint series is illustrated by Arthur Adams.

BETWEEN THE TRILOGIES

JULY

Shoemaker-Levy 9

July 15: Comet Shoemaker-Levy 9 breaks apart near Jupiter, sending fragments of itself into the gas giant's atmosphere over a six-day period to the delight of Earthbound astronomers.

Star Wars: TIE Fighter

Star Wars: TIE Fighter is released on floppy disk for PC and Macintosh. A space-combat sequel to 1993's X-Wing, it features extensive combat missions and new craft, including TIE defenders and missile boats. For the first time in a *Star Wars* story, the plot is told from the Empire's perspective. Players control a TIE recruit as he rises through the ranks and uncovers treachery from Imperial factions that wish to overthrow Emperor Palpatine. TIE Fighter is warmly welcomed by fans and critics, receiving a perfect five out of five review in the September issue of *Computer Gaming World*.

TIE Fighter spawns two expansions: Defender of the Empire and Enemies of the Empire.

Time Warner Audio Books releases the *Dark Empire* audio dramatization on cassette, with plans to do the same for the *Tales of the Jedi* comics.

July 31: Tomart Publications releases the first edition of its *Price Guide to Worldwide Star Wars Collectibles*.

AUGUST

August 11: Peter Cushing dies at the age of 81. In addition to his role as Grand Moff Tarkin, Cushing is remembered for playing Victor Frankenstein and Van Helsing in the Hammer horror films.

Dark Horse Classics

Dark Horse releases the first installment of *Classic Star Wars: The Early Adventures*. The nine-issue, full-color comic book series collects the 1979–1980 newspaper strips by the influential Russ Manning and reprints them for a new audience.

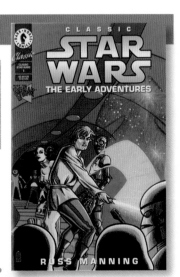

Issue #1 features an original cover by Mike Allred.

Kenner releases Action Masters, a line of small die-cast metal figurines.

Among the 1994 releases are figures of C-3PO, Princess Leia, R2-D2, and Obi-Wan Kenobi.

SEPTEMBER

In light of the growing interest in *Star Wars*, the Lucasfilm Fan Club magazine is renamed *Star Wars Insider* with issue #23.

The Star Wars Insider debut features an Expanded Universe timeline and an interview with Denis Lawson (Wedge Antilles).

OCTOBER

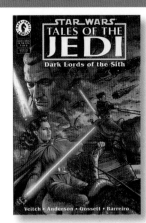

Tarik, a black bear whose grunts were recorded by Ben Burtt for use in Chewbacca's vocalizations, dies of congestive heart failure, liver disease, and cancer at Happy Hollow Zoo in San Jose.

The first issue of *Tales of the Jedi: Dark Lords of the Sith* is published by Dark Horse. This six-part series recounts the rise of villain Exar Kun.

Cover art by Dave Dorman

Young Indiana Jones Season Three

October 15: The third and final season of *The Young Indiana Jones Chronicles* premieres with the episode "Young Indiana Jones and the Hollywood Follies." Unlike previous seasons, season three consists of four television movies, which air on the Family Channel between 1994 and 1996. Unlike previous formats, the television movies do not feature the "Old Indy" bookend segments. Looking back over the *Young Indy* experience, producer McCallum remarks, "We ended up shooting over 170 weeks—more than three years—on locations in 25 countries." This made the series the longest sustained period of shooting in the history of film or television.

Indy's Hollywood adventures bring him into conflict with film director John Ford (Stephen Caffrey).

CLINTON SIGNS ASSAULT WEAPONS BAN

NASA LOSES

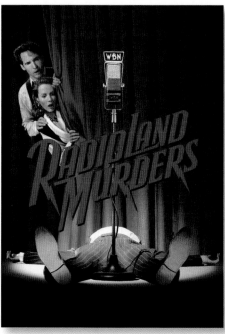

Radioland Murders

October 21: *Radioland Murders* is released. Produced and co-written by Lucas, this 1939 murder mystery had been on Lucas's mind since the filming of *American Graffiti*. "I wanted to do something off-the-wall and crazy, in the tradition of Abbott and Costello," he remembers. The trailblazing production of *Young Indy* permits Lucas to scale up similar techniques for use on a feature film. Despite disappointing box office numbers, Lucas remains upbeat. "I still enjoy *Radioland* a lot. It's lively, it's funny, and it's about a subject I like."

Radioland Murders employs budget-stretching visual tricks including digital sets and computer-cloned crowds.

Doug Chiang, an ILM art director who had been submitting sketches to Rick McCallum in his free time, officially begins work as the design director for Episode I.

Chiang is responsible for much of the film's craft, including the Naboo starfighter and the Queen's ship. Here, he talks to Lucas and Fay David, the art department coordinator.

Brainstorming

An early *Shadows of the Empire* brainstorming session takes place between Lucasfilm, LucasArts, and Bantam Books. Novelist Steve Perry introduces a new character, Dash Rendar, who will star in the 1996 project. After the meeting, a 25-page story outline circulates between Skywalker Ranch and Bantam editor Tom Dupree's New York offices.

DECEMBER

The novel *The Crystal Star* by Vonda McIntyre, is released by Bantam. The storyline prominently features Han and Leia's children Jacen, Jaina, and Anakin.

December 23: Sebastian Shaw (the figure of Darth Vader in *Jedi*) dies aged 89. His body of work includes films dating back to 1930.

Aboard a space station, the heroes face off against the other-worldly Waru.

NOVEMBER

November 1: After dropping his kids off at school, Lucas arrives at his home office to begin writing the screenplay for Episode I.

November 3–4: More than 50 *Star Wars* licensees and international agents converge at Skywalker Ranch for the first-ever *Star Wars* Summit. The two-day conference, held in the Technical Building, outlines Lucasfilm's future plans for the franchise.

November 18: Aged 13, Natalie Portman (Padmé Amidala) makes her feature film debut as a child who befriends a middle-aged assassin in Luc Besson's *Léon* (also known as *The Professional*).

Jean Reno plays hitman, Léon, in Luc Besson's acclaimed film.

The Art of *Star Wars*

December 27: The Art of *Star Wars* opens at the Yerba Buena Center for the Arts in San Francisco. The exhibit of props, costumes, artwork, and models is the first major presentation of Lucasfilm artifacts in the United States and follows a year-long tour in Japan. By the time the doors open, more than 1,200 people are waiting, some of them in line since 5:00 a.m. By early afternoon, there is a one-hour wait just to get into the gift shop. The next morning *The Today Show* devotes a segment to the exhibit and its popularity. Says Renny Pritikin, the facility's artistic director, "Popular culture is tremendously influential. People who don't take this stuff seriously are cheating themselves."

A matte painting of the Death Star's core shaft adorns the Art of Star Wars's exhibit poster.

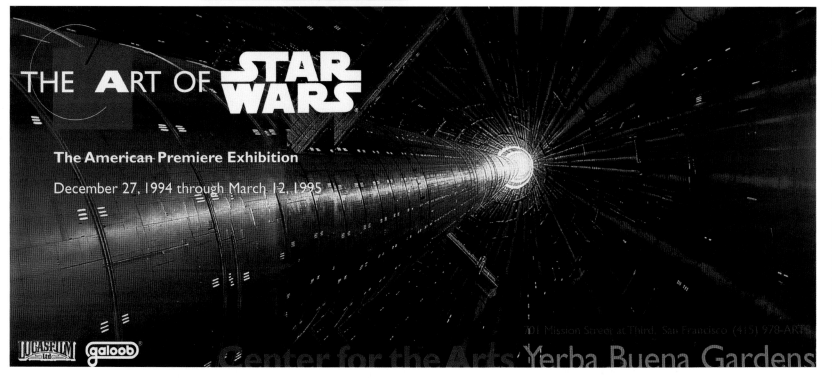

THE **A**RT OF **STAR WARS**

The American Premiere Exhibition

December 27, 1994 through March 12, 1995

LUCASFILM Ltd. galoob

Center for the Arts Yerba Buena Gardens

701 Mission Street at Third, San Francisco (415) 978-ARTS

CONTACT WITH **MAGELLAN SPACECRAFT** 🌐 **PRESIDENT YELTSIN SENDS TROOPS INTO CHECHNYA** 🌐

1995

STAR WARS TOYS STRIKE BACK! Though the Prequel Trilogy is still a far-off dream for fans, Hasbro taps into the renewed enthusiasm with the first *Star Wars* action figures, vehicles, and playsets since the mid-1980s. *Dark Forces* makes a splash among gamers, while the launch of new fiction finds appeal among young and old readers. As work proceeds on Episode I, fans are given one last chance to own the original versions of the Original Trilogy on home video during a promotional blitz.

> "There's a very definite older market for action figures."
>
> **F.A.O. Schwartz store manager**
> *during 1995's action-figure mania*

The early figures have beefed-up muscles, a feature toned down in later sculpts.

FEBRUARY

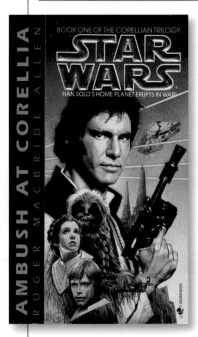

Ambush at Corellia cover art by Drew Struzan

New York Toy Fair

February 13: *Star Wars* makes a splash at New York's annual Toy Fair. Using the event to mark the rebirth of the Saga as a toy license, *Star Wars* licensees put products on display in more than a dozen showrooms. At Kenner's display, an Imperial officer escorts buyers into what resembles a Death Star conference room, while MicroMachine maker Galoob reports that their showroom has quadrupled in size from the previous year.

Ambush at Corellia

Ambush at Corellia by Roger MacBride Allen debuts and spends six weeks on the *New York Times* bestseller list. As volume one of the *Corellian* trilogy, it represents the first time that any Expanded Universe source has explored Han Solo's home planet in detail.

JANUARY

***From Star Wars** to Indiana Jones: The Best of the Lucasfilm Archives* is published by Chronicle Books (reprinted from the Japanese edition published by Hata). All-new photographs document everything from the Emperor's cane to the Ark of the Covenant.

The book's first half features props from the Star Wars trilogy, while its second half spotlights the Indy trilogy.

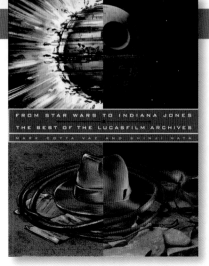

Spacewalk

February 9: Bernard Harris, Jr. (right) and C. Michael Foale (left) become, respectively, the first African American and the first British-born man to walk in space. They set these records while testing new insulation for extravehicular activity from the space shuttle *Discovery*.

⊕ **WORLD TRADE ORGANIZATION CREATED** ⊕ **EARTHQUAKE NEAR KOBE, JAPAN, KILLS THOUSANDS**

Star Wars: Dark Forces

February 15: *Star Wars*: Dark Forces is released for the PC platform. This first-person shooter action game, following in the footsteps of groundbreaking shooter Doom, introduces Kyle Katarn on his quest to uncover and shut down the Empire's plan to build an army of robotic Dark Troopers. Dark Forces uses LucasArts' Jedi game engine—developed specifically for this release—and has a number of new features, including the ability to jump, crouch, and look in all directions. It becomes one of the year's best-reviewed and most successful games, with LucasArts reporting 300,000 copies accounted for at launch.

Dark Forces villains include stormtroopers, sewer-dwelling dianogas, and Boba Fett.

Boba Fett as he is rendered on screen in Star Wars: Dark Forces.

Once Were Warriors

February 24: Lee Tamahori's *Once Were Warriors* has its US premiere. Starring Rena Owen and Temuera Morrison (Jango Fett) as urban Maoris, the movie is a smash and becomes the top-grossing film in New Zealand's history.

Movie poster for Once Were Warriors

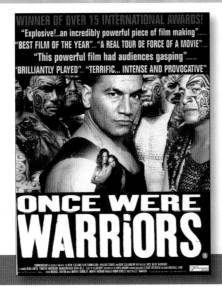

MARCH

A Unique Experience

The adventure ride Indiana Jones and the Temple of the Forbidden Eye opens at Disneyland in Anaheim, California. "For those ride aficionados who have been going to parks across the country, it will be different from anything they've ever experienced," promises Lucas, who came up with the concept. "It is not a rollercoaster and it's not a simulated movie. It's a unique experience."

A Night at the Cantina

March 3: In conjunction with the successful Art of *Star Wars* exhibit, a charity fund-raiser is held at the Center for the Arts at Yerba Buena Gardens in San Francisco, California. Labeled "A Night at the Cantina," the gala's $250-per-plate proceeds go to the Center for the Arts' Arts and Education program. The event is attended by Lucas, Kenny Baker, Anthony Daniels, and Ralph McQuarrie.

Indiana Honors

March 11: The Museum of Television honors *The Young Indiana Jones Chronicles* at the Television Festival in Los Angeles, where it joins other programs selected for artistic value, cultural impact, or historical significance. The ceremony, which is attended by Lucas and Rick McCallum, includes a screening of the episode "Paris 1919."

APRIL

Location, Location, Location

Archaeologist and fan Dr. David West Reynolds travels to Tunisia to track down the original filming locales used for Tatooine in the *Star Wars* trilogy. Armed with a knowledge of French, Arabic, and Berber, Reynolds finds the sites for the Lars Homestead, Mos Eisley's downtown, and the "*Star Wars* canyon" where the Jawas ambushed R2-D2. His efforts attract the attention of Rick McCallum.

Chott el Jerid, a salt lake in southern Tunisia, is the location for the Lars Homestead exterior.

Children of the Jedi by Barbara Hambly is published by Bantam and remains on the *New York Times* bestseller list for four weeks.

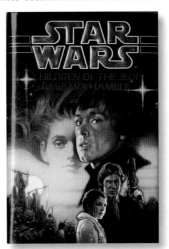

Cover art by Drew Struzan

Skywalker Summit

April 20: Lucasfilm holds a second *Star Wars* Summit at Skywalker Ranch for its licensees. Lucas jokes that he's been "dragged from my writing room," tells attendees about his progress on the Prequel Trilogy, and announces that he might direct the first one.

Full Throttle

April 30: LucasArts releases Full Throttle, a computer adventure game developed in-house using the SCUMM game engine. Mark Hamill provides voiceover work for the game's main villain, Adrian Ripburger.

Also in 1995...

Star Walking

Issue #23/24 of the Australian *Star Wars* Fan Club newsletter has Boba Fett on the cover.

MAY

Spielberg is honored with a Lifetime Achievement Award by the American Film Institute. Lucas speaks at the ceremony, calling his friend the "T-rex of directors."

JUNE

Young Jedi Knights: Heirs to the Force, by Kevin J. Anderson and Rebecca Moesta, is Lucas Licensing's first young adult novel to make the *New York Times* bestseller list.

Cover art by Dave Dorman

JULY

The first issue of the new comic book series *X-Wing Rogue Squadron* (written by *X-Wing* novelist Michael Stackpole) is published by Dark Horse.

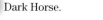

The debut storyline is titled "The Rebel Opposition."

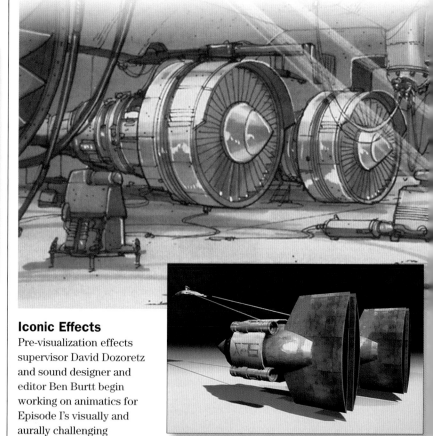

Iconic Effects

Pre-visualization effects supervisor David Dozoretz and sound designer and editor Ben Burtt begin working on animatics for Episode I's visually and aurally challenging Podrace sequence.

The Podracers—seen here in an animatic model—were developed after a research visit by the design team to a jet junkyard.

The landspeeder model features shift-action-running gear and a pop-open hood.

Chewbacca comes packaged with his trademark bowcaster and heavy blaster rifle.

The Princess Leia Organa figure features a molded plastic cape.

Luke's "Red 5" X-wing comes with weathering and battle damage.

Power of the Force

Hasbro's Power of the Force collection hits stores and becomes the top-selling boys' toy of 1995. The first wave of figures includes Luke Skywalker, Han Solo, Chewbacca, Darth Vader, R2-D2, Ben (Obi-Wan) Kenobi, C-3PO, Princess Leia Organa, and a stormtrooper. Many of the figures are much more muscular than their original Kenner counterparts, and the lightsaber accessories have unusually long blades that are shortened in subsequent assortments. Also released are an X-wing fighter, TIE fighter, landspeeder, Imperial AT-ST, and an electronic *Millennium Falcon*.

ACTOR CHRISTOPHER REEVE PARALYZED IN ACCIDENT ASTRONAUT NORMAN THAGARD BREAK

Old airplane parts were analyzed in preparation for this concept art.

Tales from the *Mos Eisley Cantina* is published by Bantam. This short-story anthology provides backstories for the bizarre barflies from Episode IV *A New Hope*, including Greedo the bartender, and the members of the band.

Cover art by Stephen Youll

Star Wars Website

July 15: To promote the upcoming re-release of the *Star Wars* trilogy on home video, Twentieth Century Fox launches the first official *Star Wars* website. At www.tcfhe.com/starwars, visitors can view video clips and scripts, brush up on filmographies of the stars, download images of props, preview an interview with Lucas, and participate in trivia quizzes. The site's URL is prominently featured on billboards promoting the re-release, and serves as a test for future web-based projects.

San Diego Comic-Con

July 28: At the San Diego Comic-Con, Friday is designated "*Star Wars* Day." An estimated 30,000 attendees take in the *Star Wars* displays on the show floor, including teasers for next year's *Shadows of the Empire* project and a giant Apple Jacks cereal box, which is at the booth of Dark Horse Comics to promote a special mail-in offer for an X-wing comic book.

The Mandalorians fight on the side of the Sith in this saga from Kevin J. Anderson and artist Dario Carrasco, Jr.

Tales of the Jedi: *The Sith War* #1 is published by Dark Horse. This six-issue limited series represents the first time a battle between the ancient Jedi and Sith is depicted in the Expanded Universe.

Star Wars Trilogy Re-Released

August 29: Twentieth Century Fox re-releases the *Star Wars* trilogy on home video. *Star Wars*, *The Empire Strikes Back*, and *Return of the Jedi* are the first home videos to feature the THX Digital Mastering Process, making the audio and video quality as close to the original motion picture experience as possible. Those who purchase the trilogy as a set also receive a three-part interview between Lucas and film critic and historian Leonard Maltin that provides inside information about the development of the Prequel Trilogy. Jeff Yapp, president of Fox Home Entertainment states, "The quality of the tape the consumer is getting is the best that's ever been available." The huge initial sell-through has Fox projecting overall sales of 13 million units.

Half-face art is used to promote each film: Vader for A New Hope, *a stormtrooper for* The Empire Strikes Back, *and Yoda for* Return of the Jedi.

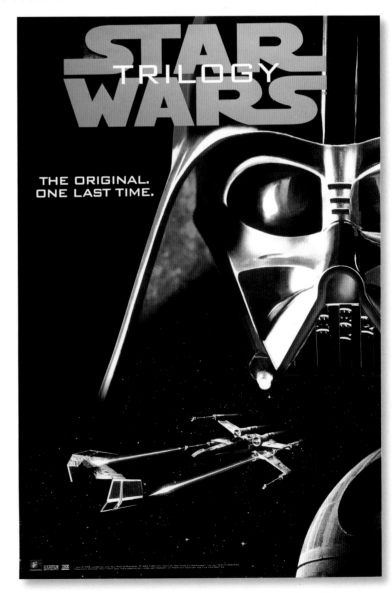

AUGUST

Shadow Moon

Shadow Moon, the first book in the *Shadow Wars* trilogy, is published in hardcover by Bantam. With a story by Lucas and Chris Claremont (known for his work on *Uncanny X-Men*), it continues the adventures of the characters introduced in the movie *Willow*, and is followed by *Shadow Dawn* and *Shadow Star*.

In Shadow Moon, *Willow Ufgood returns from a life of farming to become a hero.*

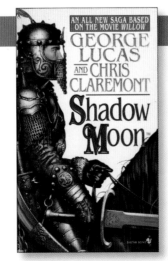

August 30: ILM alumnus Ken Ralston is named president of Sony Pictures Imageworks, the studio's visual effects branch.

SEPTEMBER

Hasbro releases toy vehicles scaled for its new action figure line, which re-uses the vintage tooling from the original line of Kenner toys.

OCTOBER

Junior Jedi Knights: The Golden Globe is the first installment in a six-book series intended for junior readers, starring Anakin Solo, the 11-year-old son of Han and Leia.

Nancy Richardson writes the first three volumes, with Rebecca Moesta finishing the series.

The first issue of the two-part *Empire's End* is published by Dark Horse comics. Wrapping up the *Dark Empire* saga, *Empire's End* features the final death of the cloned Emperor.

Artist Jim Baike replaces Cam Kennedy for Empire's End.

Essential Characters
The Essential Guide to Characters is published by Del Rey. The 200-page book covers everyone from Luke Skywalker to Expanded Universe creations such as Prince Isolder, and is the first in a series of guidebooks to explore the in-universe underpinnings of the *Star Wars* galaxy.

Written by Andy Mangels, the guide covers characters from Ackbar to Zuckuss.

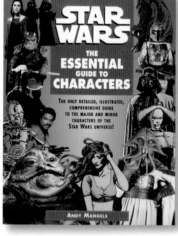

Obi-Wan is made of a near-solid piece of translucent plastic.

Star Wars Potato Chips
Promoted on packages of Lays potato chips, a see-through "Spirit of Obi-Wan" figure is made available to fans through an exclusive mail-in offer.

Kellogg's Promotion
Cereal boxes from Kellogg's promote a *Star Wars* mail-in offer for an exclusive "Han Solo in Stormtrooper Disguise" action figure.

The figure comes with a removable helmet, but no gun.

The advertising campaign sees the bunny battling against classic villains such as the Wicked Witch of the West.

Vader's "supervolt" batteries are his downfall.

Energizer Wars
A new television commercial for Energizer batteries is unveiled. In this *Star Wars* crossover, Darth Vader attempts to defeat the unstoppable Energizer Bunny, but is foiled when his lightsaber runs out of power due to his reliance on an inferior battery brand. It is the first new *Star Wars* moving image in almost 10 years, and the first time a *Star Wars* character has been used to sell a non-licensed product in the US.

October 29: For its work on Dark Forces, LucasArts receives the 1995 Sci Fi Universe Reader's Choice award for Best Achievement in Multimedia in a ceremony at the Universal Hilton in Los Angeles.

NOVEMBER

Darksaber, **by Kevin** J. Anderson, is published by Bantam Spectra and becomes a bestseller. It centers on a plot by the Hutts to build their own Death Star.

Darksaber sees Luke's romance with Callista develop.

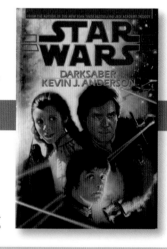

Mardji, the Asian elephant from Marine World Africa, who starred as the bantha in *Star Wars*: Episode IV *A New Hope*, is euthanized at the UC-Davis veterinary center after suffering from chronic bone inflammation.

Mardji, seen here being dressed in her bantha costume, also appeared in television commercials for peanut butter.

November 17: The new James Bond movie *GoldenEye* is released after legal disputes forced a six-year hiatus in the series. Pierce Brosnan debuts as the new Bond.

Brosnan is the fifth screen Bond after Sean Connery, George Lazenby, Roger Moore, and Timothy Dalton.

Toy Story

November 22: Pixar's *Toy Story* is released during the Thanksgiving holiday. Directed by John Lasseter, it is the first feature film to use only CG animation. *Toy Story* makes household names out of its buddy-comedy stars Buzz Lightyear (Tim Allen) and Woody the Cowboy (Tom Hanks). It features the voice of *The Empire Strikes Back's* John Ratzenberger (Bren Derlin) as Hamm the Piggy Bank. Made for an estimated $30 million, the film grosses more than $360 million worldwide and earns Lasseter a Special Achievement Academy Award®.

Illustrating the Universe

The Illustrated Star Wars Universe is published. Written by Kevin J. Anderson, it features profiles of planets throughout the galaxy accompanied by many new artworks by Ralph McQuarrie.

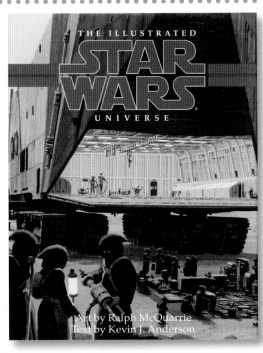

The Illustrated Star Wars Universe *(right) includes new artworks by McQuarrie that illustrate previously unseen aspects of the Star Wars galaxy, including a snowy base on Hoth (below) and the interior of Jabba's Palace on Tatooine, where Bib Fortuna, Salacious Crumb, and a Twi'lek are visible (bottom).*

Rebel Assault II

LucasArts releases Rebel Assault II: The Hidden Empire, the sequel to 1993's Rebel Assault. The gameplay is built around a plot by Imperial forces to develop a cloaking device, and contains 15 land, air, and space missions with a variety of *Star Wars* vehicles, including speeder bikes and a *Millennium Falcon*-style transport. Rebel Assault II features the first live-action in-universe *Star Wars* footage to be shot since *Return of the Jedi*, incorporating props and costumes borrowed from the Lucasfilm Archives.

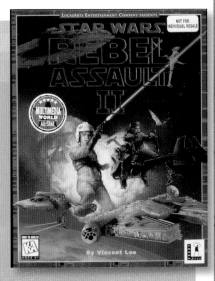

Protagonist Rookie One is played by Jamison Jones in the live-action cutscenes.

DECEMBER

More from Hasbro

A second wave of action figures is released from Hasbro, including Lando Calrissian, Luke in X-wing gear, and the ever-popular Boba Fett.

Luke in his X-wing pilot outfit.

Jumanji

December 15: *Jumanji*, directed by Joe Johnston, debuts. It features another breakthrough for ILM in the form of the first realistic CG hair and fur.

American Graffiti Honored

December 27: *American Graffiti* is honored by the Library of Congress as an inductee to the National Film Registry for its "cultural, historic, or aesthetic significance." Other films inducted in 1995 include Alfred Hitchcock's *North by Northwest* (1959) and the sci-fi classic *The Day the Earth Stood Still* (1951).

1996

SHADOWS OF THE EMPIRE is the "movie without a movie" in a year that sees many of Lucasfilm's key licensees unite to tell the story of what happened between Han Solo's carbonite-freeze in *The Empire Strikes Back* and his thaw in *Return of the Jedi*. A novel, comic book series, video game, soundtrack, trading card set, action figure line, and other elements tell different parts of the story, propelling the multilayered tale of smuggler Dash Rendar and his efforts to help Leia, Luke, Lando, and Chewbacca outwit Prince Xizor.

"Xizor is a classic villain; he's like the Godfather with a reptilian overlay."

Howard Roffman
vice president of Lucas Licensing, on the villain of Shadows of the Empire

JANUARY

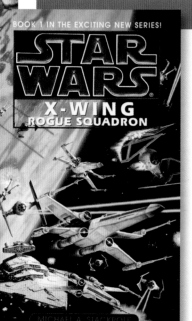

X-Wing: Rogue Squadron

X-Wing: Rogue Squadron, the first installment in a new series of X-wing novels, is published by Bantam. Written by Michael A. Stackpole, the book puts minor movie character Wedge Antilles at the head of Rogue Squadron during the New Republic's liberation of Coruscant and the ongoing war against renegade Imperial warlords. Two more novels (*Wedge's Gamble* and *The Krytos Trap*) follow in 1996, and *The Bacta War* is published in early 1997.

In a break from the norm, the X-Wing covers feature space battles rather than character portraits.

Silicon Graphics Onyx

LucasArts, at work on the *Shadows of the Empire* video game, learns that an actual Nintendo 64 won't be on hand until July. Instead they write software using Silicon Graphics Onyx systems to emulate the Nintendo 64's capabilities. "It was an interesting challenge developing a game for a machine that didn't exist," says technical lead Eric Johnston.

Record VHS Sales

January 31: On the last date for retailers to order videos of the original version of the *Star Wars* trilogy, 22 million cassettes are shipped in North America with another 8 million shipped to other countries.

FEBRUARY

Deep Blue

February 10: IBM computer Deep Blue defeats world chess champion Garry Kasparov for the first time in their multigame matchup.

Brian Daley

February 11: Brian Daley, writer of the NPR radio adaptations of the *Star Wars* films, dies of pancreatic cancer at age 49. Friend and author James Luceno scatters some of his ashes in Palenque, Mexico.

Joel McNeely

A *Shadows of the Empire* recording session takes place in Scotland with conductor Joel McNeely and the Royal Scottish National Orchestra and Choir. One unusual addition is an Imperial language created by Ben Burtt. "Ben came up with an ancient epic poem, the words from which I used for the lyrics of the music. I asked Ben to make the language Germanic with hard syllables, very harsh and guttural," explains McNeely. The recording sessions are mastered at England's Abbey Road Studios.

Joel McNeely (right) conducts the Royal Scottish National Orchestra at the Shadows of the Empire recording session.

⊕ **DUNBLANE SCHOOL MASSACRE** ⊕

MARCH

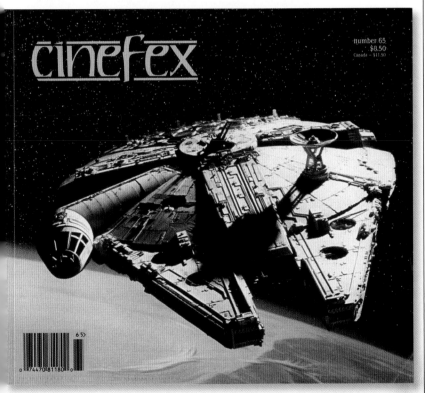

Unlike the 1980 figure, this Yoda doesn't come with a snake.

Luke in Dagobah Fatigues

Han In Hoth Gear

Third Wave of New Action Figures

The third wave of Hasbro's new *Star Wars* action figures hits shelves. The figures include Yoda, Luke in Dagobah Fatigues, Han in Hoth Gear, and a TIE Fighter Pilot.

cinefex

number 65
$8.50
Canada – $11.50

Cinefex

Issue #65 of *Cinefex* is a 20th anniversary salute to ILM. It features a year-by-year filmography and overview of the company's effects work as well as extensive interviews with both Lucas and Dennis Muren.

APRIL

Before the Storm

Michael P. Kube-McDowell's *Before the Storm* is released. The first book in the *Black Fleet Crisis* trilogy, it features a subplot in which Luke Skywalker searches for his birth mother. The object of Luke's focus proves to be an imposter—a resolution that sidesteps any potential conflicts with the upcoming Prequel Trilogy.

STAR WARS

BOOK 1 OF THE BLACK FLEET CRISIS
BEFORE THE STORM
MICHAEL P. KUBE-McDOWELL

The New Republic faces a terrifying threat from the darkest depths of the Empire

The Black Fleet Crisis trilogy's plot revolves around a brushfire war with the alien Yevetha.

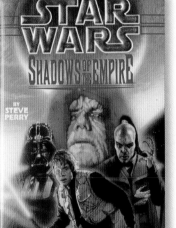

Shadows of the Empire Novel

Steve Perry's *Shadows of the Empire* novel hits bookstores. The book is the heart of a multimedia *Shadows* narrative that extends through a comic book series and a game. "Part of the idea of using three different media was not to simply retell the same story but to look at the events from different perspectives," says Lucasfilm's Howard Roffman. "The novel looks at things from the overall Rebel-Imperial situation, the comics have more of a bent for Boba Fett and the bounty hunter side of the story, and the game focuses on the action sequences. Basically, it was a case of looking at which aspect of the story best suited each medium."

MAY

Dragonheart

May 31: Rob Cohen's *Dragonheart* is released. ILM's proprietary facial animation software is used to bring the digital character of Draco to life, incorporating the voice and facial physique of Sean Connery. It is the most sophisticated CG character realized to date.

JUNE

Hasbro's Shadow Figures

Hasbro's *Shadows of the Empire* figures go on sale. Among the new releases are Prince Xizor, Dash Rendar, Luke in Imperial Guard Disguise, Chewbacca in Bounty Hunter Disguise, and Leia in Boushh Disguise. Other figures released at the same time include two-packs of Boba Fett vs. IG-88 and Prince Xizor vs. Darth Vader. *Shadows of the Empire* also has its own vehicle line including a swoop bike and Dash Rendar's Outrider. Other summer figures (not part of the *Shadows* wave) are such oddities as Han with Smuggler Flight Pack and Crowd Control Stormtrooper.

Smuggler-hero, Dash Rendar comes with a heavy weapons pack.

Xizor brandishes twin energy-blade shields.

Sourcebook

West End Games releases the *Shadows of the Empire Sourcebook*, a roleplaying guide to the people, places, and things of *Shadows*. Written by Peter Schweighofer, the sourcebook doubles as an encyclopedia for non-gaming fans of the *Star Wars* Expanded Universe.

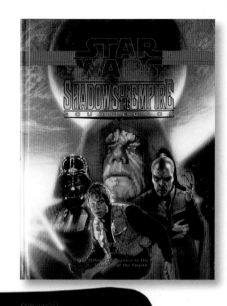

N64 Released

The Nintendo 64 gaming system is released in Japan, with a North American release following in September. The N64, named after its 64-bit CPU, replaces the company's previous Super Nintendo console.

The Ninentdo 64 game console

JULY

Age of the Sith

The preview issue #0 of *Tales of the Jedi: The Golden Age of the Sith* appears. This advance peek at an all-new era of *Star Wars* history is set 5,000 years before the events of the first movie and introduces brother and sister hyperspace explorers Gav and Jori Daragon.

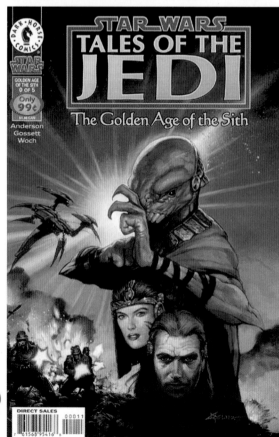

Landing on the Sith tombworld of Korriban, the Daragons drop into a nest of infighting as the Sith Lords vie for supremacy.

SPACE ROCKET *ARIANE* EXPLODES ❂ BOMBING AT OLYMPICS IN ATLANTA, GEORGIA, KILLS ON

New Footage for Board Game

Parker Bros. enlists 82-year-old cinematographer Gilbert Taylor to capture new footage for *Star Wars: The Interactive Video Board Game*. The shoot uses the film's original costumes and props, and David Prowse dons Vader's suit once more. James Earl Jones records new lines for Vader's speaking parts.

Gilbert Taylor (above, left) was director of photography for the original Star Wars film.

Independence Day

July 3: Roland Emmerich's alien invasion movie *Independence Day* is released. It is produced and co-written by Hollywood producer Dean Devlin. The film is a big hit at theaters, becoming one of the top-grossing movies of 1996.

Dolly the Sheep

July 5: Scottish researchers at the Roslin Institute near Edinburgh are the first to clone a mammal, Dolly the Sheep, from an adult cell.

AUGUST

Hasbro Figures with Removable Clothes

A new line of 12-inch figures are released from Hasbro. These figures contain removable clothing and accessories such as weapons and gun belts. The initial release includes Luke Skywalker, Han Solo, Darth Vader, and Obi-Wan Kenobi.

Each 12-inch figure comes packaged in a special window box.

Life on Mars

August 6: NASA announces that the Mars meteorite ALH 84001 could contain evidence of primitive life, after electron microscope scanning reveals structures that could be fossilized bacteria.

Gavin Bocquet

Gavin Bocquet and a small art department arrive at Leavesden Studios in London. There, they begin the actual construction of the production elements for Episode I.

Royal Divorce

August 28: Charles, Prince of Wales, and Princess Diana officially divorce.

Gavin Bocquet and Lucas examine a set model at Leavesden Studios.

OCTOBER

Radio Series

The *Return of the Jedi* Original Radio Drama airs on NPR. The script, an adaptation and expansion of the movie storyline written by novelist Brian Daley before his death, includes scenes deleted from the original cut of the movie, such as the sandstorm as the *Millennium Falcon* departs Tatooine. Produced by Highbridge Audio, the radio drama features Ed Asner as Jabba the Hutt and Ed Begley, Jr. as Boba Fett.

Anderson • Carrasco • Heike

Golden Age of the Sith

The first issue of *Tales of the Jedi: The Golden Age of the Sith* is published, kicking off a six-part mini-series with art by Dario Carrasco, Jr.

ILM Goes Digital

Del Rey publishes *Industrial Light & Magic: Into the Digital Realm* by Mark Cotta Vaz, which chronicles the history of ILM and its evolving body of work in the booming field of digital effects.

NOVEMBER

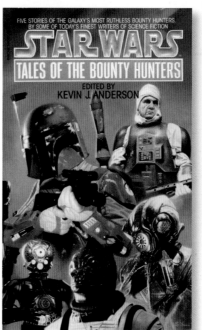

New Novels

Two new *Star Wars* novels hit the shelves: Kristine Kathryn Rusch's *The New Rebellion* and the short story collection *Tales of the Bounty Hunters*, edited by Kevin J. Anderson.

Bill Clinton Re-Elected

November 5: Incumbent Bill Clinton defeats Republican challenger Bob Dole to win re-election to the US presidency. With a margin of more than 8 million in the popular vote, Clinton becomes the first Democrat since Franklin Delano Roosevelt to win presidential re-election.

Star Wars: **Dark** Forces is released by Sony for the PlayStation platform.

Also in 1996...

The Skywalker Lightsaber resembles the weapon Luke receives in Obi-Wan's hut.

Jedi Weapons

Icons releases several prop replica lightsabers in 1995–1996, including the sabers used by Vader, Obi-Wan, Luke in *A New Hope*, and Luke in *Return of the Jedi*.

Jake Lloyd's character only wants one thing for Christmas: A Turbo Man action figure.

Jingle All the Way

November 22: The future Anakin Skywalker Jake Lloyd stars in *Jingle All the Way* opposite Arnold Schwarzenegger.

Arnold Schwarzenegger plays a mattress salesman with guilt issues who vows to give his son the best Christmas ever.

Trading Card Set

A trading card set and a book by renowned fantasy artists, the Brothers Hildebrandt, are released for *Shadows of the Empire*.

The Millennium Falcon and Prince Xizor's Virago appear on this Hildebrandt card.

Lucas Kenner Figure

At a *Star Wars* licensee summit, Kenner presents Lucas with a one-of-a-kind 12-inch doll of himself, made in appreciation of Kenner's long-standing toy license with Lucasfilm. The figure is actually a 12-inch Obi-Wan Kenobi with a unique sculpted head. In addition, a customized Han Solo is presented to Lucasfilm president Gordon Radley, and a customized Luke Skywalker is given to vice president of licensing Howard Roffman.

Star Wars Website Launch

November 26: StarWars.com is launched. The site is initially quite sparse, with basic facts about the Original Trilogy films, trivia questions, screenshots, descriptions of locales and characters, and printout coloring pages for kids. Interest on the site grows for the Special Edition—restored versions of the *Star Wars* films featuring updated special effects, to be released in 1997.

Also in 1996...

Not the *Falcon*

With Han Solo in carbon-freeze, smuggler Dash Rendar takes over the *Shadows of the Empire* storyline. This action figure scaled vehicle is Dash's ship, the *Outrider*.

The Outrider can swivel its cockpit and blaster cannon.

The Shadows soundtrack is released on CD by Varese Sarabande.

DECEMBER

Shadows becomes a must-have holiday game for the new Nintendo 64 console.

Shadows of the Empire

The Shadows of the Empire video game debuts for the Nintendo 64 home console. Players control Dash Rendar through shooter and vehicle modes that feature such enemies as IG-88 and Boba Fett.

Dash Rendar watches the Falcon blast off after battling his way through Hoth's Echo Base.

Card Game Tournament

Decipher Games invites the world's best *Star Wars* customizable card game players to Vail, Colorado, for the first annual SWCCG World Tournament. Out of 32 regional finalists, winner Raphael Asselin of Quebec receives a paid trip with Dr. David West Reynolds to visit the original *Star Wars* filming sites in Tunisia.

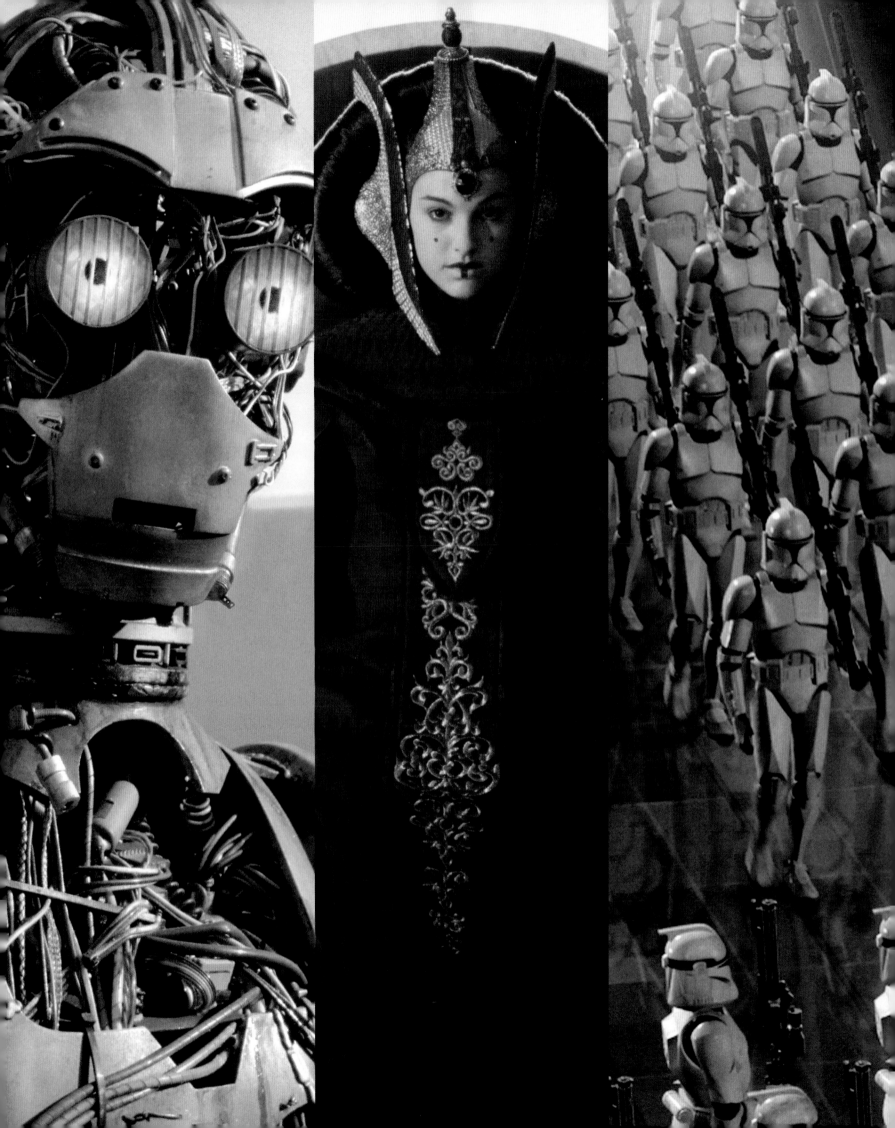

THE RETURN OF the original *Star Wars* trilogy to theaters exceeds all box office expectations. Fans cheering these old favorites, and their spirited discussion regarding the changes made to the Special Edition cause *Star Wars* to make headline news around the world once again. But the re-release is only the start. In 1997, Lucas returns to the director's chair for the first time since 1977 for a new trilogy of *Star Wars* movies that, among other things, teaches the world the definition of the word "prequel."

1997-2005

THE PREQUEL TRILOGY

1997

INDUSTRY INSIDERS do not know what to expect: They know *Star Wars* has a devoted following, but considering how many homes across America own VHS copies of the trilogy, will a theatrical release make any sizable impact on the usually sedentary months of the first-quarter box office?

Poster advertising Special Edition theatrical release.

"The idea of film as a dynamic, ever-changing medium puts it in the same category as all other art forms."

George Lucas
Star Wars Insider #33

THE MARKETING CAMPAIGN rightly heralds the *Star Wars* films as "three reasons why they build movie theaters." An entire generation has grown up watching *Star Wars* on television. The promise of a big screen picture, digitally revamped surround sound, and newly enhanced visual effects proves irresistible. Its opening weekend take is an impressive $35.9 million. Once again Hollywood execs have underestimated the *Star Wars* Saga, while Lucas rightly banked that audiences would return to a galaxy far, far away....

JANUARY

Scare Wars

January 1: In the spirit of R.L. Stine's *Goosebumps* series of juvenile horror books, Bantam Books publishes the first *Star Wars: Galaxy of Fear* novel, *Eaten Alive*. Pre-teen Alderaanian siblings Tash and Zak Arranda encounter Force ghosts, carnivorous planets, zombies, and mutated clones in the 12-book run.

The first few installments of the Galaxy of Fear series feature 3-D hologram covers, an eye-catching gimmick used frequently to draw attention in the late 1990s.

Original footage with human Jabba (Declan Mulholland) stand-in

Wireframe model of where digital Jabba will appear

Finished render of CG Jabba in Special Edition

Star Wars: Special Edition

January 31: *Star Wars: Special Edition* opens on 2,104 screens in the US. The re-release requires a concerted restorative effort to keep the original negative from degrading. Despite the best archival storage procedures, the film had suffered from extensive dirt damage, and some 62 shots had been recorded on defective stock. With film restoration experts from YCM Labs, Pacific Title, and Twentieth Century Fox, Lucasfilm is able to save the movie, as well as address visual effects shortcomings that have long rankled Lucas. ILM animators add droids and creatures to Tatooine. Han Solo meets with a slithering Jabba the Hutt. Newly animated digital X-wing and TIE fighters boast improved aerobatics, and Greedo shooting first in the Cantina sparks endless online fan debate. Accompanying this release is a renewed effort to move *Star Wars* to the forefront of the public consciousness with new merchandise celebrating 20 years of the Saga.

George Lucas, Carrie Fisher, and Mark Hamill are joined by costumed characters at the January 21 Westwood Village Special Edition premiere of Star Wars.

⊕ **MADELEINE ALBRIGHT BECOMES FIRST**

Albin Johnson

January 31: Fan Albin Johnson wears full stormtrooper armor to a *Star Wars* premiere. The reaction he receives sparks his interest in gathering armored fans to form a Legion known as the 501st.

FEBRUARY

Star Wars Chronicles

February 1: Chronicle Books imports (and translates) an impressive Japanese tome filled with rare behind-the-scenes production and prop stills, and presents it as the lavish coffee-table book, *Star Wars Chronicles*.

Time of Your Life

February 10: *Star Wars* once again graces the cover of *TIME* magazine. Inside is an interview with Lucas and McCallum about the return of the Saga.

Ewoks and Droids

February 11: Fox Video makes available edited versions of the *Ewoks* and *Droids* animated series cut together into VHS movies: *The Pirates and the Prince* and *The Haunted Village*.

E.T. vs. R2-D2

February 14: As the Special Edition release continues to bring in money, Spielberg acknowledges—with a Drew Struzan-illustrated ad in *Variety*—that *Star Wars* has reclaimed the number one spot as the highest-grossing film of all time.

Dear George, Congratulations for renewing the most enduring motion picture in cinema history.

Your pal, Steven

Cloud City

February 14: *The Empire Strikes Back: Special Edition* premieres. New scenes include expanded wampa cave footage and a dramatic flight into Cloud City. Its $22.3 million opening weekend sets a February record.

Dolly the Sheep

February 22: Scientists in Scotland announce the successful birth of a cloned sheep, Dolly. Actually born in July of 1996, Dolly's public introduction as the first mammal to be cloned from an adult somatic cell sparks a media frenzy and endless rounds of debate—both informed and otherwise— on the merits and perils of cloning.

Disneyland Star Tours

February 28: During a 10th anniversary celebration at Disneyland in Anaheim, officials mention a hoped-for revamp of Star Tours (something that would prove to be very slow to materialize).

Spectators watch the fireworks over Disneyland during the 10th anniversary of Star Tours.

FEMALE SECRETARY OF STATE IN THE US

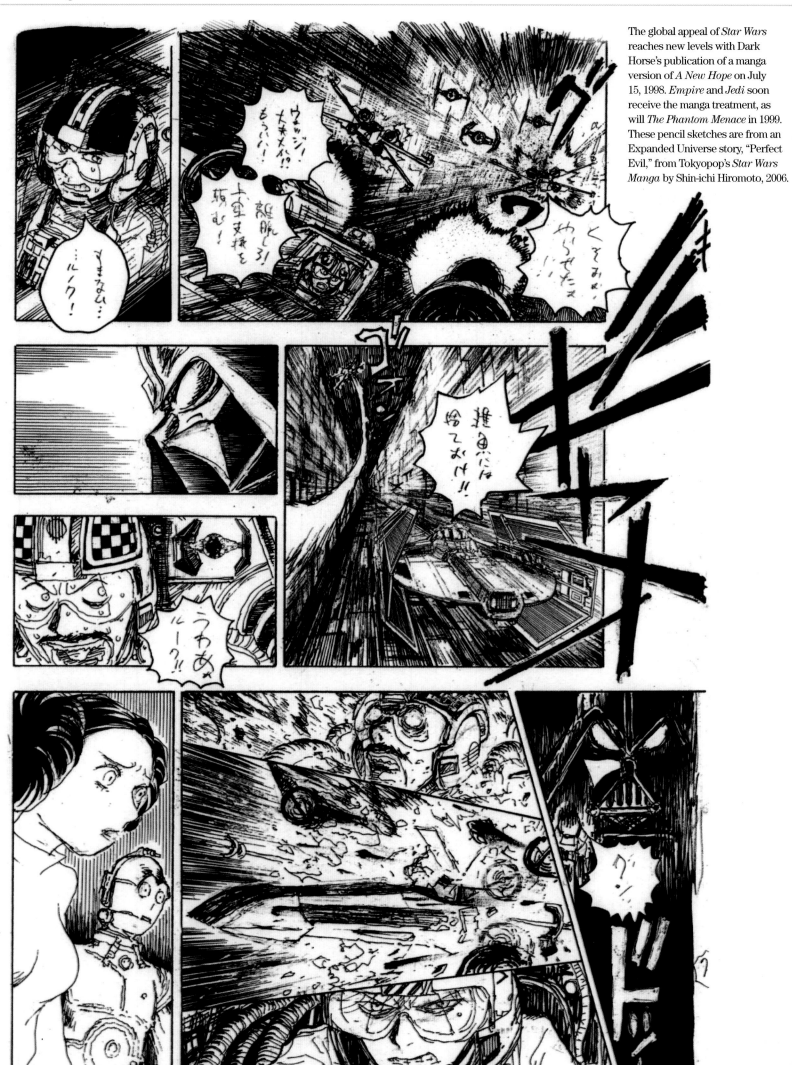

The global appeal of *Star Wars* reaches new levels with Dark Horse's publication of a manga version of *A New Hope* on July 15, 1998. *Empire* and *Jedi* soon receive the manga treatment, as will *The Phantom Menace* in 1999. These pencil sketches are from an Expanded Universe story, "Perfect Evil," from Tokyopop's *Star Wars Manga* by Shin-ichi Hiromoto, 2006.

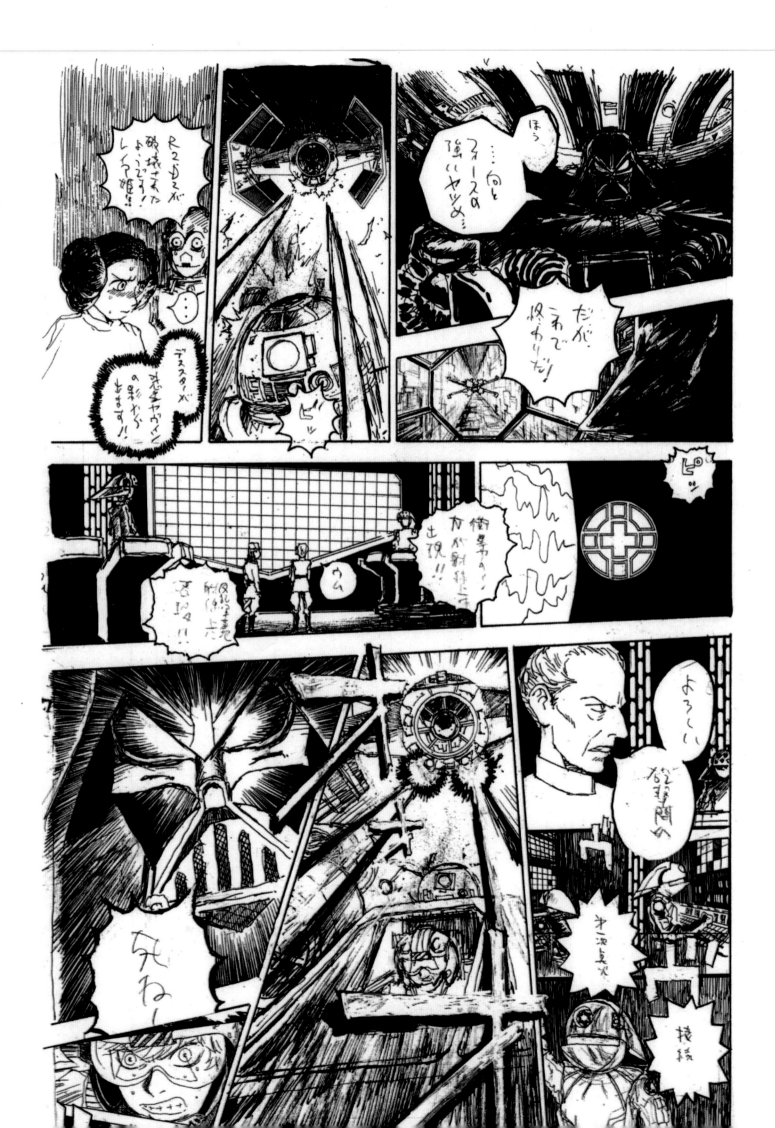

MARCH

Coruscant Celebration

March 14: *Return of the Jedi* returns to theaters. Updated visuals include a new Sy Snootles musical number, a more animated Sarlacc, and a planet-hopping celebration with the first cinematic look at the city-planet Coruscant.

The Coruscant cityscape is screened as part of a montage of various alien worlds celebrating the fall of the Empire.

APRIL

Casting Rumors

Reports circulate throughout the entertainment press and online that actors Liam Neeson, Ewan McGregor, and Natalie Portman are in the top spots as leads in the new, untitled *Star Wars* Prequel. Though Lucas and casting director Robin Gurland have indeed selected the talented trio, protocol dictates that no public comments be made until the ink of final signatures on their respective deal memos are dry. As such, the actors' involvement in *Star Wars* is talked about for weeks—in some cases, months—before Lucasfilm offers any official confirmation or denial.

Liam Neeson's role is described only as a "venerable Jedi."

Natalie Portman is said to be in the role of "a young queen."

Ewan McGregor is listed as young Obi-Wan Kenobi.

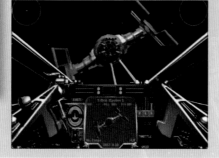

X-Wing vs. TIE Fighter

April 29: LucasArts releases X-Wing vs. TIE Fighter, the third game in Lawrence Holland's popular X-wing series. The game is designed expressly for multiplayer combat.

Increasing online connectivity finally allows players to dogfight in virtual space.

MAY

The Lost World

May 23: Spielberg's *The Lost World: Jurassic Park* features amazing effects, such as digital dinosaurs and a miniature freighter collision, supervised by ILM's Dennis Muren, Pablo Helman, and Lorne Peterson.

JUNE

Samuel L. Jackson

Entertainment Weekly reports that Samuel L. Jackson will have a "cameo" appearance in Episode I. This is a culmination of a rather public crusade of Jackson's to appear in the *Star Wars* prequels. On December 6, 1996, the actor said on the British TV talk show *TFI Friday* that "I just want to get in a room with George Lucas and tell him I'm interested!" Jackson would be cast as Mace Windu, a member of the Jedi Council, whom Lucas would describe as "an emerging character" throughout the Prequel Trilogy.

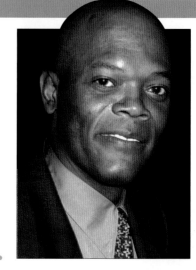

HALE-BOPP COMET COMES CLOSE TO EARTH ☻ TONY BLAIR ELECTED BRITISH PRIME MINISTER

Wookiee Awards

June 10: "I know this is a clichéd thing to say, but I'm going to say it anyway. This guy is one of the reasons I became an actor," says a visibly moved Mike Myers, host of the MTV Movie Awards, as he presents the Lifetime Achievement Award to Chewbacca, beloved Wookiee hero. Then Carrie Fisher finally bestows upon Chewie the award he never got in *A New Hope*. The idea is the brainchild of the MTV Awards producers, and it is Peter Mayhew underneath the yak fur costume, reprising his most famous role.

Peter Mayhew as Chewbacca towers over tiny Carrie Fisher at the MTV Movie Awards. Chewbacca delivers a prepared acceptance "speech."

The award is accompanied by a video retrospective of Chewbacca's life, set to Carly Simon's "Nobody Does It Better."

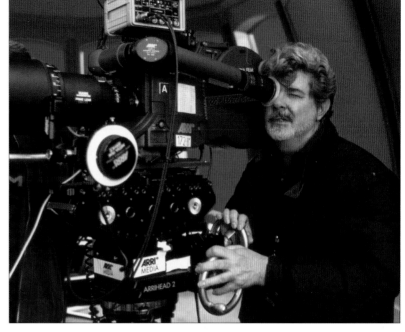

Principal Photography

June 26: The first day of principal photography on Episode I. After a lengthy hiatus, cameras once again roll on *Star Wars* with George Lucas back in the director's chair. At this early stage, the movie is only known as "The Beginning." The production has leased the entirety of the 286-acre Leavesden Studios—a former Rolls Royce aircraft engine factory—for two-and-a-half years. This allows for sets to remain standing during the lengthy postproduction stage and be revisited for pick-up photography. For months, production designer Gavin Bocquet's art department has been preparing for this day with the construction of sets, while costume designer Trisha Biggar's team has created an unprecedented wardrobe for the galactic citizenry. The first scene captured revolves around Sith Lords Darth Sidious and Darth Maul as they conspire on a Coruscant balcony.

JULY

Men in Black

July 2: Memorable digital aliens, including a man-sized cockroach, feature prominently in the action-comedy movie, *Men in Black*, the result of Rob Coleman's animation team, along with other departments at ILM.

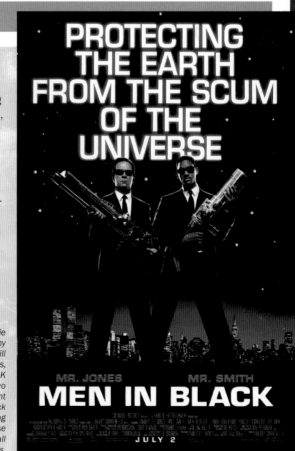

PROTECTING THE EARTH FROM THE SCUM OF THE UNIVERSE

MR. JONES   MR. SMITH
MEN IN BLACK

JULY 2

Men In Black's movie poster depicts Tommy Lee Jones and Will Smith in their roles as, respectively, Agent K and Agent J, two top-secret government officials who track down Earth-dwelling aliens and erase the memories of all human witnesses.

JULY

Images captured by the Sojourner include shots of itself on the surface of Mars.

Pathfinder

July 4: After a seven-month voyage, the Mars Pathfinder lander arrives on Mars and its *Sojourner* rover explores the alien landscape. NASA's public website, which tracks the mission, becomes one of the most heavily visited in this early period of the Internet.

Lucas Plaza

July 11: Modesto, California, honors hometown hero George Lucas by dedicating a downtown plaza to him, complete with a bronze sculpture depicting two fun-loving American teens reclining on a fender of a '57 Chevy. Lucas's teenage years spent driving about Modesto inspired his first smash hit, *American Graffiti*. Oakdale sculptor Betty Saletta returns the inspiration in kind with her tribute in the Lucas Plaza.

Lost Scenes Screened

July 19: Lucasfilm director of fan relations Steve Sansweet hosts a special 20th anniversary *Star Wars* presentation at Comic-Con International in San Diego, California. The fan audience is eager for any news about Episode I, but Lucasfilm remains tight-lipped about the production. Instead, Sansweet offers a treat from the past: The first ever—and only—public screening of the fabled lost Biggs Darklighter scenes at the Anchorhead power station from *A New Hope*.

Luke Skywalker (Hamill) and Biggs Darklighter (Garrick Hagon) in the cut scenes.

The Naboo Palace, Italy

July 22: The Episode I production moves to Caserta, Italy, to shoot interiors for the Naboo Royal Palace scenes. While there, Lucas holds the first press conference about Episode I.

The opulent Reggia di Caserta is the largest 18th-century palace in Europe, with 1,200 rooms.

Lucas directs Silas Carson as Nute Gunray in the Reggia di Caserta.

THE UK CEDES HONG KONG BACK TO CHINA ✤ MOTHER THERESA OF CALCUTTA DIES IN INDIA

Desert Storm

July 29: The Episode I production moves to Tozeur, Tunisia, where it is met by a ferocious thunderstorm. Early the next day, the crew discovers that the Mos Espa and Podrace arena sets are devastated. Dressing room tents have been ripped apart, equipment trucks battered, and props and costumes tossed about by gale-force winds. Rick McCallum's production team scrambles to rearrange the shooting schedule to allow for these assets to be repaired and rebuilt, while Lucas continues shooting on the areas of set that remain intact. Thanks to the resilience and resourcefulness of the crew, the production stays on schedule. Ever-optimistic, Lucas remarks to McCallum that the same thing happened over 20 years ago in Tunisia during the original *Star Wars* shoot—so it is a sign of good luck.

Casting Confirmed

Star Wars Insider #34 compiles casting information and confirms Jake Lloyd as young Anakin and Pernilla August as his mother, Shmi. The magazine lists some supporting roles, including Ray Park, Terence Stamp, and Adrian Dunbar (whose role as Bail Organa is ultimately cut from the finished film, and later recast).

AUGUST

Digital Dewbacks

August 11: StarWars.com, the official Lucasfilm site, begins streaming *Anatomy of a Dewback*, a five-part behind-the-scenes daily documentary on the making of the digital creatures for the Special Edition release of *A New Hope*. This is one of the first behind-the-scenes video series produced by a movie studio specifically for Internet distribution.

Online fans have to wait for their dial-up connections to stream the latest installments of the new StarWars.com web video series, Anatomy of a Dewback.

The cinematic sandstorm (left) is nothing compared to the real tempest that ravages the Episode I set in Tunisia (below).

VHS

August 26: Lucasfilm and Twentieth Century Fox Home Entertainment release *The Star Wars Trilogy: Special Edition* on VHS in both widescreen and pan-and-scan format. As an extra incentive, they announce that the sets will be available at retail for only 97 days.

Princess Diana

August 31: Diana, Princess of Wales, her boyfriend Dodi Fayed, and driver Henri Paul are killed when their car crashes in the Pont de l'Alma tunnel of Paris in a bid to avoid paparazzi photographers. An 18-month investigation determines that Paul was under the influence of alcohol and antidepressants, though rumors persist that other forces were in play. Her tragic death grabs headlines the world over, prompting a massive outpouring of sympathy and grief.

SEPTEMBER

Photography Wraps

September 29: The first phase of principal photography wraps on Episode I, though stunt coordinator Nick Gillard continues to shoot second-unit action scenes.

OCTOBER

Shadow Boxing

LucasArts adds more *Star Wars* games to its roster. The fighting game, *Masters of Teräs Käsi*, pits characters against one another in hand-to-hand combat. Hero Kyle Katarn returns in *Jedi Knight: Dark Forces II*, a PC release that incorporates live actors and full motion video cutscenes. Also available is the rather tardy PC release of the *Shadow of the Empire* video game, a port of the 1996 Nintendo 64 game.

Only in Masters of Teräs Käsi would Luke Skywalker fight a Tusken Raider on Hoth.

Ray vs. Ewan

October 1: On the FS1 Stage at Leavesden Studios, Ewan McGregor (Obi-Wan Kenobi) and Ray Park (Darth Maul) film their incredibly fast-paced lightsaber duel under the supervision of stunt coordinator Nick Gillard.

No camera trickery was used to speed up this lightsaber combat.

Future of Toys

October 14: Lucas Licensing announces a long-term partnership with Hasbro, Inc. and Galoob Toys, Inc. for the creation of toys tied to the *Star Wars* Prequel Trilogy. This agreement allows Hasbro to continue production of action figures, adding new prequel characters to its already robust line of Original Trilogy toys. Galoob's agreement covers small-scale figures, vehicles, and playsets—a continuation of its current license that saw the creation of popular MicroMachines incarnations of *Star Wars* characters and vehicles. By the following year, both companies would produce preview toys for Episode I.

Future of Novels

October 15: Lucas Licensing grants Ballantine Publishing Group the rights to publish all the new adult fiction as well as a major portion of the nonfiction books stemming from the *Star Wars* prequels. In addition to the Prequel Trilogy novelizations, Ballantine's imprint, Del Rey Books, will publish spin-off *Star Wars* novels featuring Original Trilogy characters. Prior to the Ballantine run, Bantam had held the license for *Star Wars* novels since 1991.

Star Wars Exhibition

October 29: *Star Wars*: The Magic of Myth exhibition opens at the Smithsonian's National Air & Space Museum in Washington, DC. It showcases not only the mythic underpinnings of the *Star Wars* Saga and their connections to real world cultures, but also the ingenuity required to realize *Star Wars* on the screen. Over 200 props, costumes, and models from the Lucasfilm Archives are placed on display, along with interpretive text that compares the fantastic elements with their real-world historical counterparts. A Tusken Raider gaffi stick, for example, equates to a Fijian war club, while the bright jumpsuit of an X-wing pilot finds an analog in a Navy crew man's "international orange" flight suit. Lucas attends the opening in Washington, which would go on to welcome over a million visitors by January 1999. A companion book, written by exhibition curator Mary Henderson, is published by Bantam Spectra.

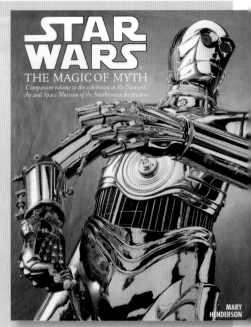

The companion trade-paperback book to the Magic of Myth exhibition at the Smithsonian.

Studio photography of some of the props and costumes on display at the exhibition.

Ticket for the October 29 opening. Visitors may have spotted Lucas at the event.

NOVEMBER

Actor Jack Purvis, who played the Jawa chief in Episode IV, an Ugnaught chief in Episode V, and Teebo the Ewok in Episode VI, dies at the age of 60.

Starship Troopers

November 7: Paul Verhoeven's *Starship Troopers* opens in theaters, with some starships effects supplied by ILM. The terrifying insects are realized by Tippett Studio (founded in 1984 by Phil Tippett and Jules Roman).

DECEMBER

The Crimson Empire *series features painted covers by Dave Dorman.*

Crimson Empire

December 18: *Crimson Empire* #0, the first *Star Wars* web comic, debuts on StarWars.com as a lead-in to the print series that soon follows. Set several years after the events of *Return of the Jedi*, and immediately after the events of the landmark Dark Empire comic series, *Crimson Empire* is written by Dark Horse Comics founders Mike Richardson and Randy Stradley and illustrated by Paul Gulacy and P. Craig Russell. Notable for its introduction of Kir Kanos, a rogue red guard, the series finally delivers on the implied deadliness projected by the imposing red robes and visored helmet of the Emperor's Royal Guards (first seen in *Return of the Jedi*). Running for six issues, the series would prove popular enough to spawn a sequel.

The sleek and deadly Kir Kanos will prove to be an extremely popular Expanded Universe character.

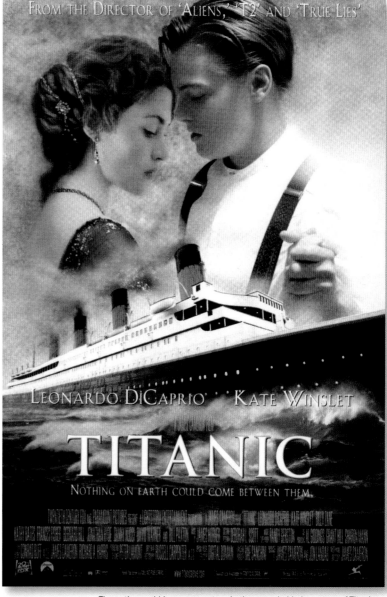

FROM THE DIRECTOR OF 'ALIENS,' 'T2' AND 'TRUE LIES'

LEONARDO DiCAPRIO · KATE WINSLET

TITANIC

NOTHING ON EARTH COULD COME BETWEEN THEM.

The entire world is soon swept up in the remarkable love story of Titanic.

Titanic

December 19: James Cameron's motion picture *Titanic* is released. Years in the making with a ballooning budget reputed to exceed $200 million, the movie has been pegged as a potential disaster that would live up to its namesake. When unveiled to the public, however, *Titanic* becomes a critical and commercial success. The movie boasts approximately 500 visual effects shots, mostly supplied by Digital Domain, though ILM did contribute as well. Skywalker Sound handled the sound mix and sound editing.

Also in 1997...

Star Wars Food Promotions

A company from South Africa, called Nature's Source, runs a *Star Wars* promotion giving away free cardboard discs with breakfast cereal. In Spain, ice-cream company Frigo releases limited-edition plastic *Star Wars* popsicle sticks.

Limited edition Star Wars popsicle sticks sold in Spain.

Banana Bitz Star Wars cereal promotion

191

The 501st Legion—a fan group founded in 1997 following Albin Johnson's costumed tribute to *Star Wars*—appear at events in full stormtrooper armor and other Imperial attire. Over the next decade, thousands of fans would join the Legion. Above, 200 members take part in the annual Tournament of Roses Parade in Pasadena, California, January 1, 2007. George Lucas is the 501st's Grand Marshal.

1998

EPISODE I CONTINUES its lengthy postproduction phase. Editors Ben Burtt and Paul Martin Smith take full advantage of the digital medium to gather disparate takes that can then be stitched and smoothed together. A massive workload lies ahead for ILM, as the three visual effects supervisors—John Knoll, Dennis Muren, and Scott Squires—must finish 2,000 effects shots.

John Knoll with the "skinless" C-3PO puppet.

"Having developed this whole different way of making movies... I decided I'd better do it first to figure it all out."

George Lucas
on returning to the director's chair

ROB COLEMAN leads the animation team in creating digital thespians that must hold their own opposite flesh and blood actors, while Steve Gawley supervises construction of hundreds of practical miniatures. The inroads of digital effects have not spelled the end of the model shop. In fact, more models are built for Episode I than the entire Original Trilogy put together.

Rob Coleman, animation supervisor for Episode I, in his office.

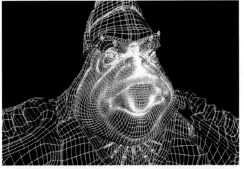

Gungan leader, Boss Nass, is perhaps one of the most challenging characters for Rob Coleman and his team to create. Because of the Gungan's heavy cloak, ILM develops a special cloth simulator that makes it move just like real fabric.

🌐 THE UNABOMBER PLEADS

Dennis Muren, visual effects supervisor at ILM, and Steve Gawley, model supervisor, with a tank from Episode I.

A controlled explosion of a Gungan shield generator carried out by ILM.

JANUARY

That's No Moon...

January 29: Space agency representatives from 15 countries sign agreements in Washington establishing the framework for design and cooperation to build the International Space Station. The US, Russia, Japan, Canada, and nations of the European Space Agency unite in this aerospace engineering effort that begins construction in November.

An artist's impression of how the finished space station will look.

Players Get Jaded

January 31: LucasArts releases Jedi Knight: Mysteries of the Sith, an expansion to its popular 1997 first-person shooter. Rather than full-motion video cutscenes, this game instead relies on animation to move the story forward. The popular Expanded Universe anti-hero Mara Jade serves as the player character.

Cover art for Jedi Knight: Mysteries of the Sith

In-game footage of Jedi Knight: Mysteries of the Sith

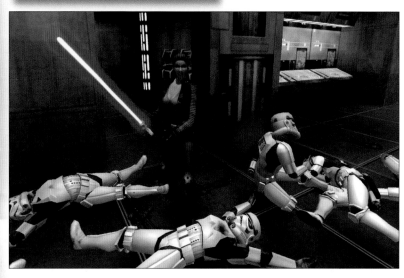

GUILTY AND RECEIVES LIFE IMPRISONMENT

FEBRUARY

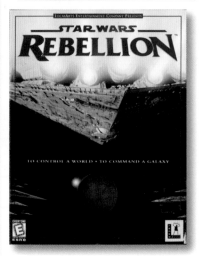

Padawan Publishing

February 9: Lucasfilm announces Scholastic, Inc. and Random House as publishers of young reader *Star Wars* books. Scholastic will focus on digest-format books, including novelizations of the upcoming prequels and an original middle-grade fiction series. Random House will publish beginning reader, novelty, picture books, and other young reader fare.

The cover art to Rebellion incorporates the famously imposing overhead Star Destroyer design introduced in A New Hope.

February 28: LucasArts releases the galaxy-spanning real-time strategy game *Star Wars: Rebellion*. It goes by the name *Star Wars: Supremacy* in the UK and Ireland.

MARCH

Archie Goodwin

March 1: Comics writer, editor, and artist Archie Goodwin dies at the age of 60. While at Marvel Comics, he was known for founding the Epic imprint of creator-owned titles. He was a major contributor to the early *Star Wars* Expanded Universe, writing the long-running newspaper strip with Al Williamson as artist.

Lucas talks to the Episode I crew at Leavesden Studios.

March 2: Lucas returns to Leavesden for a round of Episode I pick-up photography. Rather than full scenes, the shoot involves mostly specific shots to fill out the story.

King of the World

March 14: *Titanic* breaks the $460 million box office record set by *Star Wars*, which had only just retaken it in early 1997 with its re-release. This top spot has been handed back and forth between Spielberg and Lucas, as their films *Jaws*, *E.T.*, and *Star Wars* have each held the record. James Cameron is now welcomed into this elite club by Lucas, who takes out a full-page ad in *Variety*—an illustration of *Star Wars* characters bailing from the sinking ocean liner.

The Variety ad is illustrated by Episode I concept artist Iain McCaig.

JIM
CONGRATULATIONS!
GEORGE

IAIN McCAIG

APRIL

Jar Jar's Genesis

George Lucas approves the first shot of Jar Jar Binks. Throughout principal photography of Episode I, actor Ahmed Best wore a detailed rubber Jar Jar Binks suit to allow ILM the possibility of retaining his on-set performance and enhancing it with a digital Jar Jar head. Matching an animated head onto a live-action body ultimately proved too limiting and time-consuming an approach, though the suit provided invaluable lighting reference for the fully computer-generated character.

Ahmed Best wearing the Jar Jar Binks costume.

Jar Jar Binks as he appears in Episode I.

Fox Fanfare

April 2: Ending much industry speculation, Lucasfilm announces that Twentieth Century Fox will distribute the *Star Wars* Prequel Trilogy theatrically and on home video. Says Peter Chernin, Chairman and CEO of the Fox Group, "The biggest thrill of any motion picture executive is to touch greatness. At Twentieth Century Fox, it has been a tremendous joy to have been a part of George Lucas's groundbreaking *Star Wars* trilogy. It is one of the privileges of my career that Fox will join George Lucas and Lucasfilm to bring the first three chapters in this incredible Saga to the world." Meanwhile, traditionalist *Star Wars* fans breathe easy knowing that the snare drums and horns that accompany the studio logo will continue to precede each movie.

MAY

Sales and fan reaction proves that LEGO and Star Wars snap perfectly together.

Another Brick in the Wall

April 30: LEGO systems acquires its first-ever license, bringing its world-famous building block toys to another creative property: The *Star Wars* Saga. The agreement grants LEGO global rights to produce construction toy sets for the *Star Wars* prequels as well as the original *Star Wars* trilogy. The first of these toys would arrive on shelves in 1999: the classic X-wing fighter. In years to come, the success of *Star Wars* products would prompt LEGO to seek out and acquire additional licenses, such as *Harry Potter*, *Batman*, *Indiana Jones*, and *Toy Story* sets.

May 8: ILM unleashes global destruction in Mimi Leder's *Deep Impact*, one of two asteroid-collision movies in theaters this year. Scott Farrar and Bill George serve as visual effects supervisors.

JUNE

Popularity Contest

Star Wars Insider #38 lists the top 20 characters as voted by readers. As the Prequel Trilogy is as yet unseen, the list consists of classic trilogy characters with one notable exception: Mara Jade (first seen in Timothy Zahn's *Thrawn* trilogy) at #20. Han Solo is #1.

"He has the right looks to make any woman wish they were Princess Leia," testifies one voting fan.

Lynne's Diaries

June 22: StarWars.com begins posting a series of behind-the-scenes production videos chronicling the making of Episode I. The short, in-depth videos start with the November 1994 moment when Lucas first sat down to write the script for Episode I. Hosted by Lynne Hale, director of publicity, and shot by documentarian Jonathan Shenk, the series lasts 11 chapters, and covers all aspects of the production, as documentary cameras are rolling throughout the making of the movie.

Lucas at his desk on his first day of writing the Episode I script, November 1, 1994.

Definitive Reference

June 30: Del Rey publishes the 384-page hardcover book, *The Star Wars Encyclopedia* by Stephen J. Sansweet. The definitive reference book of its time, it collects all the elements introduced into the *Star Wars* canon by two decades of Expanded Universe publishing, the *Ewoks* and *Droids* animated series, and the Original Trilogy. With the Prequel Trilogy in development, the book does include some careful edits to reflect the evolving *Star Wars* storyline, such as revealing that Emperor Palpatine was a Dark Lord of the Sith, and excising any reference that Owen Lars and Obi-Wan Kenobi were brothers.

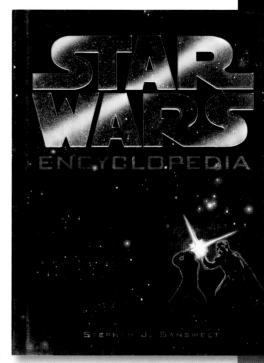

The cover art for the Encyclopedia incorporates elements from Drew Struzan's Revenge of the Jedi poster.

JULY

A Failed Role Indeed

West End Games declares bankruptcy despite the popularity of its *Star Wars* roleplaying game. For 10 years, the publisher greatly added to the Expanded Universe. The license for the tabletop game goes into limbo, leaving avid fans unsure about the future of their beloved hobby.

July 17: The Academy of Motion Pictures Arts & Sciences hosts a 25th anniversary screening of *American Graffiti* in Los Angeles, with Lucas and cast-members in attendance.

AUGUST

Filling In the Gaps

August 10: Cameras roll in Leavesden for another five days of Episode I pick-up photography. In the evolving edit, Lucas has inserted placeholder footage created by David Dozoretz's animatics team. Most of this previsualization is intended to map out ILM visual effects shots, but a small number are for live-action elements that clarify action, cover edits, and expand new ideas. In mostly bluescreen-filled stages, Lucas shoots such scenes as the Queen telling Anakin that Padmé has been sent on an errand, and Nute Gunray and Rune Haako being marched away as prisoners.

Senator Palpatine (Ian McDiarmid) and Queen Amidala (Natalie Portman) film a Coruscant scene.

SEPTEMBER

End of an Era

September 1: Timothy Zahn's *Vision of the Future* is released, essentially ending the story era covered by Bantam Books. The novel finally brings Luke Skywalker and Mara Jade together after their many adventures apart, and positions them for a future as husband and wife. This union is echoed in the Empire and the New Republic signing a peace accord that brings the Galactic Civil War to a peaceful end.

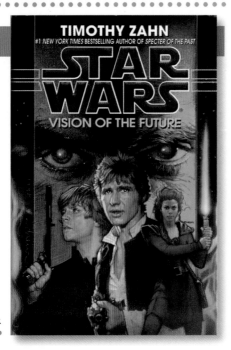

The familiar Han and Luke are joined by Mara Jade and Thrawn on the novel's cover.

September 4: Google Inc., the company that would redefine how content is found on the Internet, is founded in Mountain View, California.

September 6: Legendary filmmaker Akira Kurosawa, a key influence on George Lucas, dies at age 88. His last script, *After the Rain*, is produced posthumously and released a year later.

Akira Kurosawa with Francis Ford Coppola and George Lucas on the set of Kagemusha, 1980.

The Height of Multi-Media

September 18: Before the rise of broadband Internet connections revolutionized the availability of video and other "rich media" content, interactive CD-ROMs prove a popular entertainment and educational outlet. *Star Wars* contributes to this arena with the definitive information trove, *Star Wars: Behind the Magic*. Produced by LucasArts, this two-disc set includes scene-by-scene overviews of the three films, deleted scenes from *A New Hope*, encyclopedic guides to characters, vehicles, and creatures, and interactive activities that explore the vastness of the *Star Wars* universe. The CD-ROM release is named the multi-media item of the year by *Entertainment Weekly*.

With the rise of the Internet and the DVD format, Behind the Magic represents a last hurrah for Star Wars CD-ROM entertainment.

⊕ YANGTZE RIVER FLOODS KILLING THOUSANDS ⊕ US EMBASSY BOMBINGS LINK TO BIN LADEN ⊕

A Menacing Title

September 25: StarWars.com announces *The Phantom Menace* as the name of Episode I, bringing an end to rumored titles, such as *Balance of the Force, Children of the Force, Star Wars: Genesis, Red Tails,* and *Jedi Squad.* Immediately, fan speculation shifts from "what is the title?" to "is that really the title?," as rumors of bogus titles, meant to throw off bootleggers, gain credence among those who cite the whole *Revenge of the Jedi* scenario as credible precedent. Some fan sites speculate that the revelation is really a stealthy way of testing a prospective title. The title, an oblique reference to Darth Sidious and the shadowy Sith conspiracy, comes as a surprise to many particularly when presented without the context of a story.

September 29: Hasbro Inc. buys Galoob Toys, Inc., makers of MicroMachines, adding to the toy giant's already impressive roster of acquired companies like Kenner, Playskool, Tonka and Tiger Electronics.

Also in 1998...

Bantha Figure

Kenner produces the long-awaited Bantha toy for The Power of the Force action figure line, complete with Tusken Raider rider.

OCTOBER

Episode I Preview Toys

October 8: Collectors eagerly anticipating Episode I toys get an early holiday gift from Hasbro. The Mace Windu action figure is an exclusive mail-away available for $2.99 and six Kenner proofs-of-purchase. The STAP and Battle Droid combo is available on toy store shelves. Galoob will make available a Naboo mini-playset in November.

The Single Trooper Aerial Platform (STAP) will only be briefly seen in Episode I, yet becomes the first toy from the movie.

October 15: Lucasfilm and Dolby Laboratories announce the launch of a new theatrical digital 6.1-channel surround sound technology—Dolby Digital-Surround EX, with the release of *The Phantom Menace.*

October 21: Lucas Learning launches the educational game DroidWorks. It will later receive the Codie award as the "Best New Home Education For Pre-Teens" by the Software & Information Industry.

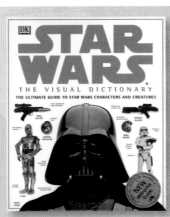

The Visual Dictionary includes new fabrications constructed specifically for the book, including this cutaway view of a stormtrooper helmet completed by ILM modelmaker Don Bies.

Cover art for The Visual Dictionary

A Saga in Meticulous Detail

October 22: DK Publishing produces two landmark *Star Wars* reference books written by Dr. David West Reynolds: *Star Wars: Incredible Cross-Sections* and *Star Wars The Visual Dictionary.* The first book features painstakingly researched and rendered cutaway illustrations of famed *Star Wars* vehicles by artists Richard Chasemore and Hans Jenssen. The second is a detailed pictorial guide to key characters and artifacts from the movies.

Cover art for Incredible Cross-Sections

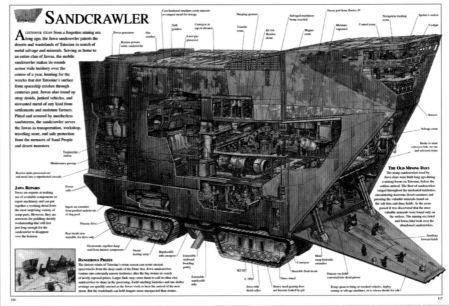

Richard Chasemore's meticulous cutaway of a Jawa sandcrawler features all the droids glimpsed in the auction sequence in Episode IV.

Also in 1998...

Expanded Universe Action Figures

For the first time, Kenner makes action figures of characters from the novels and comics in addition to new figures of movie characters. "3-D playscenes" or "Freeze Frame action slides" are bundled within the packaging.

Space Trooper action figure   EV-9D9 action figure

NOVEMBER

Poster Revealed

November 1: The Episode I teaser poster is unveiled at Mann's Chinese Theatre in Hollywood, an event covered on television by *Entertainment Tonight*. Designed by Ellen Lee of the Episode I Art Department under the supervision of Jim Ward, vice president of marketing, the stark image captures the idea that Episode I is the start of a larger saga, and that Anakin Skywalker will someday become Darth Vader. The poster stands apart from the previous trilogy posters as being photo-based as opposed to the older painted style.

The poster art literally foreshadows Anakin's fate. The horizontal design of the banner more naturally lends itself to the image of a cast shadow than the vertical one-sheet.

Fox Studios stands on the site of the former agricultural exhibition venue, the Sydney Showgrounds in Moore Park.

Star Wars Moving Down Under

November 3: Lucasfilm announces that Episodes II and III will be shot at the new Fox Studios Australia in Sydney. This comes after a year of discussions between Rick McCallum and the studios. Previous studio productions include *The Matrix* and *Babe: Pig in the City*.

Every Saga Has a Beginning...

November 17: After more than 15 years of waiting, the first moving images from a new *Star Wars* movie appear on the silver screen. *The Phantom Menace* trailer debuts in select theaters in 26 cities. Theaters experience a crush of attendance, and many have to implement new rules to keep viewers from simply watching the trailer, skipping the feature, and requesting a refund on admission. StarWars.com posts the trailer, generating the biggest Internet event in its short history with more than 10 million downloads. This surpasses records previously set by the Mars Sojourner website and the online posting of the Kenneth Starr report. Fan sites scrutinize the trailer in minute detail, breaking down the 70-odd shots into paragraph long examinations of their potential content and impact on the story.

EPISODE I

November 19: The Episode I trailer appears on television, on the show *Entertainment Tonight*. Lucasfilm insists that the trailer be shown in its entirety, unedited.

November 20: The trailer moves beyond the 26 cities and goes to theaters across North America. It most often plays in front of *The Waterboy* or *Meet Joe Black*.

Pixar's Second Hit

November 25: Pixar proves that the success of *Toy Story* was not a fluke with its well received follow-up, *A Bug's Life*. Pixar again turns to Skywalker Sound for the animated movie's rich sound design and editing, a tradition carried out with each Pixar movie henceforth.

The storyline to A Bug's Life mirrors The Seven Samurai in many ways, but with numerous comedic twists.

DECEMBER

Testament to its popularity, a stolen print of the Episode I trailer lands on the Internet auction site, eBay.

Star Wars #1

December 16: Eschewing the limited series format, Dark Horse begins a new *Star Wars* ongoing series, something absent from the comics market since the Marvel run ended in 1986. Simply called *Star Wars*, it is set during the prequel era and at first showcases Jedi Knight Ki-Adi-Mundi. The first arc, "Prelude to Rebellion," lasts six issues, and includes a bonus issue #0 that debuts on StarWars.com as an animated comic. The series would then concentrate on the heroes of the Jedi Council, as well as featuring the anti-hero bounty hunter, Aurra Sing.

"Prelude to Rebellion" is written by Jan Strnad.

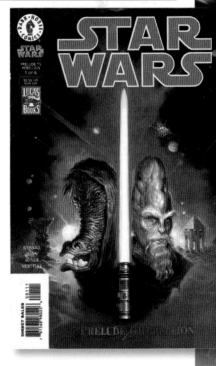

Luke Be A Jedi Tonight

December 20: Mark Hamill guest-stars on *The Simpsons* as himself. After saving Mark from a sci-fi convention gone awry, Homer finds a new career as a bodyguard. Hamill returns in the last act reprising his Luke Skywalker character in a crazed dinner theater production of *Guys and Dolls*. Hamill had long established himself as a prominent voice actor, having garnered acclaim as the voice of the Joker on the *Batman* animated series. Hamill also provides the voice of a bodyguard instructor in the episode.

🌐 CLINTON IMPEACHMENT HEARINGS BEGIN 🌐

D.CHIANG

As design director for *Star Wars*: Episode I *The Phantom Menace*, Doug Chiang envisions new technologies that are familiar yet distinct, including the rolling destroyer droids and the Queen's sleek starship. Chiang explains that, for Anakin's Podracer, "taking the engines out of the context of a jet and putting them into the deserts of Tatooine made for a stunning image."

1999

WHEREAS MOST movie studios are desperate to drum up excitement about upcoming releases, Lucasfilm and Twentieth Century Fox are kept busy managing expectations as anticipation for Episode I becomes a worldwide media phenomenon. Avid fans begin queuing at movie theaters weeks in advance, determined not to miss out on the movie event of the decade.

Die-hards rallied by various Star Wars fan websites line up for Episode I's theatrical release.

"I would say it's about 90 percent of what I wanted it to be."

George Lucas
On Star Wars: *Episode I* The Phantom Menace

THE OUTPLACEMENT firm Challenger, Gray & Christmas coins the term "*Star Wars* Flu" when it estimates that 2.2 million US workers will call in sick on May 19 in order to see the new movie. Though Episode I is the highest grossing movie of the year, its astounding $431 million (domestic) take falls short of the colossal box office of *Titanic*, a film many predicted Episode I would finally sink.

JANUARY

All's Fair in *Star Wars*

Vanity Fair runs a feature article on Episode I, built around an interview with Lucas. It is illustrated with shots by renowned photographer Annie Leibovitz. This early look at the movie kicks off its publicity push, a strategy that targets fence-sitters and people with casual *Star Wars* interest.

Fans wait in line outside the Senator Theater in Baltimore to see The Phantom Menace.

Starr Wars

MAD magazine #377 compiles the 20 stupidest things of 1998. Acknowledging the ongoing Kenneth Starr investigations into Bill Clinton's improprieties with intern Monica Lewinsky, it creates a *Star Wars* parody poster—which inexplicably surfaces some time later as a series of postage stamps in the disputed former Soviet Union region of Abkhazia.

MAD's parody crawl describes "a period of civil lawsuits" and makes reference to "The DEATH CIGAR, a bizarre sexual prop with enough power to destroy an entire Presidency."

Whither Celluloid?

January 25: A hot topic of discussion at this year's Sundance Film Festival is the abandonment of traditional photochemical film production for digital video. Lucas has already shot one scene of Episode I sans film, and is a leading advocate for the format. The transformation is mostly occurring in the documentary camp, as filmmakers are able to capture more footage more effectively and cheaply with digital video.

FEBRUARY

Encore

February 8: John Williams and the London Symphony Orchestra record the score to *The Phantom Menace* over an eight-day session at Abbey Road Studios. Williams introduces a tender new theme for Anakin Skywalker; fit for a 10-year old boy, but with a subtle nod to the future darkness to come.

John Williams's score includes the "Duel of the Fates" musical cue, which features a choral accompaniment.

February 28: X-Wing: Alliance arrives from LucasArts, the last entry in the venerable X-wing flight simulator series.

X-Wing: Alliance allows users to operate a Falcon-like space freighter.

MARCH

March 7: Perhaps the greatest filmmaker of all time, Stanley Kubrick dies at age 70. His *2001: A Space Odyssey* had an indelible influence on the look and feel of *Star Wars*.

Stanley Kubrick dies after completing Eyes Wide Shut.

Digital Theater

March 9: Digital Theater Systems announces its own enhanced surround cinema decoder—DTS-ES—to compete with Dolby Digital EX.

The Home Stretch

March 11: The full Episode I trailer debuts in theaters, focusing more on the central plot of the Trade Federation's invasion of Naboo, with more action and dialogue than the teaser trailer. The online version enjoys over 3.5 million downloads in five days on StarWars.com. Also in theaters is the movie's release poster illustrated by Drew Struzan. The collage of characters follows the format established by the Special Edition theatrical posters.

Darth Maul looms menacingly in the background of the Episode I release poster.

Episode I's trailer features more peeks at the groundbreaking ILM visuals Episode I has in store.

That '90s Sitcom

March 14: FOX's popular sitcom, *That '70s Show* is rife with *Star Wars* references, given that it follows the lives of a group of teenagers living in Wisconsin in the late 1970s. In an episode titled "A New Hope," the gang rushes out to see *Star Wars* and becomes obsessed with the film phenomena, which fittingly airs as Episode I mania reaches a fever pitch.

March 20: At Leavesden Film Studios, the last pick-up shot for Episode I captures the moment in which Senator Palpatine meets young Anakin Skywalker.

March 25: Lucas donates $1.5 million to his alma mater, the USC School of Cinematic Arts, for the creation of a new digital studio.

March 28: Lucas talks to Leslie Stahl on *60 Minutes* about returning to *Star Wars*.

Keanu Knows Kung Fu

March 31: Audiences are blown away by the Wachowski Brothers' slick mix of Eastern philosophy, high-powered action sequences, and eye-popping visual effects in *The Matrix*. The old "Star Trek vs. Star Wars" debates are momentarily shelved as *The Matrix* is hailed as a worthy contender.

APRIL

Sneak Peek Gaming

LucasArts' PC game *Star Wars: Episode I—The Phantom Menace* is released shortly before the movie opens. The game closely follows the film's storyline and gives players a sneak peek at the new chapter in the *Star Wars* Saga.

April 7: Seventeen-year-old Daniel Alter becomes the first fan in line at the Village Theater in Westwood for *The Phantom Menace*, a whole month before the film is due to open.

Digital Filmmaking

April 19: Sony and Panavision announce a partnership forged by Lucasfilm to develop high-definition digital cameras for Episode II. The cameras will record imagery in 24-P (progressive)—24 distinct, non-interlaced frames of imagery per second—keeping them consistent with the standards set by film projection.

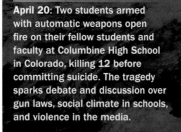

The Columbine Tragedy

April 20: Two students armed with automatic weapons open fire on their fellow students and faculty at Columbine High School in Colorado, killing 12 before committing suicide. The tragedy sparks debate and discussion over gun laws, social climate in schools, and violence in the media.

April 21: Del Rey Books publishes *The Phantom Menace* novelization by Terry Brooks.

Celebration Time

April 30: Lucasfilm holds its first official fan convention since the 1987 10th anniversary event, *Star Wars* Celebration. The Wings Over the Rockies Air and Space Museum in Denver, Colorado, welcomes over 30,000 fans for three days to celebrate the past and future of the *Star Wars* Saga. Torrential rains could not dampen the enthusiasm of die-hard fans eager to catch their first glimpses of Episode I scenes, actors, and behind-the-scenes production presentations. Uniting fans from far and wide, the event also raises over $30,000 in donations to memorial funds for the victims of Columbine.

A highly coveted selection of character badges from the first Star Wars Celebration sets a trend for badge collections at future conventions.

MAY

Star Wars: Episode I Racer, a LucasArts video game re-creating the thrill of Podracing, is released for N64 and PC.

Issue #73 of Game Informer magazine covers the launch of Star Wars: Episode I Racer.

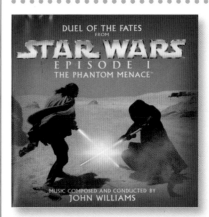

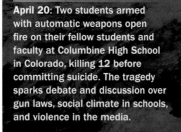

I Want My MTV

May 3: "Duel of the Fates," a music video produced for a single from the Episode I soundtrack, premieres on MTV and VH1. Featuring a John Williams orchestral score and a full choir, it is not the usual MTV fare, but is a huge hit. The video intersperses film clips from Episode I with behind-the-scenes footage of the making of the movie and the recording of the music.

Midnight Madness

May 3: Episode I merchandise arrives in stores. In response to overwhelming fan demand, a number of retailers, including Wal-Mart, Super Kmart, K-B Toyworks, F.A.O. Schwarz, and Media Play open selected stores at 12:01 a.m., coining the phrase "Midnight Madness." Among the must-have Episode I collectibles are Hasbro action figures equipped with small, encoded chips that, when read with a reader (sold separately), produce dialogue for the character; all new LEGO® *Star Wars*™ sets; and a slew of tie-in books for a wide range of ages.

A customer in Los Angeles pushes a cart loaded with just-released Episode I toys.

Left: Early Battle Droid action figure with encoded chip. Above: Toys "R" Us promotion

May 4: Sony Classical releases the Episode I soundtrack album. Fans trying to avoid spoilers are shocked to read tracks labeled "Qui-Gon's Noble End" and "The High Council Meeting and Qui-Gon's Funeral."

May 7: The movie *The Mummy* showcases ILM's cutting edge work on particle simulation through an immense sandstorm, as well as motion capture for the character of Imhotep.

Pre-Selling Episode I

May 12: In an era before online sales, Episode I tickets are made available for advance purchase at 3:00 p.m. Eastern Daylight Time at select theaters and outlets in the United States and Canada. Theater owners agree to make every reasonable effort to begin with those fans already standing in line. In a continuing effort to discourage profiteering, a maximum of 12 tickets can be purchased per customer.

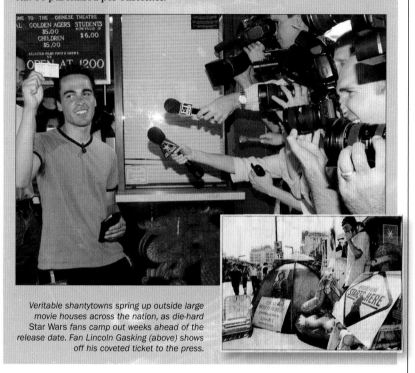

Veritable shantytowns spring up outside large movie houses across the nation, as die-hard Star Wars fans camp out weeks ahead of the release date. Fan Lincoln Gasking (above) shows off his coveted ticket to the press.

Also in 1999...

Bottle Cap Collection

Pepsi releases a *Star Wars* bottle cap collection and a large plastic stage for its display.

Charity Screenings

May 16: Episode I premieres in 11 cities in the US and Canada—three days early—to benefit local charities devoted to children's programs. At each premiere, portions of the theater seating are made available for disadvantaged children. The screenings raise $5.6 million.

Jake Lloyd (Anakin Skywalker) arrives for the premiere of The Phantom Menace in Westwood, organized to benefit the Elizabeth Glaser Pediatric AIDS Foundation.

The Prequel Has Landed

May 19: At long last, *The Phantom Menace* is released to theaters—an enormous production delivered on time and on budget. The long-awaited movie has the biggest opening day ($28.5 million) and opening week ($132.4 million) in box-office history. It also smashes opening weekend box-office records in 28 countries and ends the year with worldwide ticket sales of $924 million, becoming the second-highest worldwide grossing film ever released. Although the movie garners mostly favorable reviews, it does weather its share of criticism, as dizzying expectations make it an easy target.

An eager fan, dressed as Darth Maul, waits outside Mann's Chinese Theatre for the first screening of The Phantom Menace.

Star Wars in Colored Bricks

May: The first LEGO *Star Wars* sets are released to tie in with Episode I. The sets, including 7140 X-Wing Fighter, are the LEGO Group's first venture with a licensed property and mark the beginning of a long and successful collaboration between the LEGO Group and Lucasfilm.

Also in 1999...

Scholastic Inc. begins publishing the *Jedi Apprentice* novel series starring young Obi-Wan Kenobi. Dave Wolverton writes the first book, *The Rising Force*, with Jude Watson penning the rest (more than 20).

JUNE

A VFX Superstar

June 3: ILM senior visual effects supervisor Dennis Muren is given a star on the Hollywood Walk of Fame, the first for a visual effects artist. At the time of the ceremony, Muren has earned an impressive eight Academy Awards® for his work at ILM.

Dennis Muren with directors James Cameron and Lucas, and R2-D2 at his "walk of fame."

June 14: The Presidio Trust approves Lucasfilm Ltd.'s plan to create a new company headquarters within a campus-like setting at a former army base in San Francisco.

June 15: The hour-long special *From Star Wars to Star Wars* airs on FOX. Hosted by Samuel L. Jackson, it focuses on ILM's work on various movies, including Episode I.

The Digital Menace

June 17: Lucasfilm, CineComm Digital Cinema, and Texas Instruments present a digital presentation of Episode I footage for members of the media at AMC's Burbank 14 theater, in southern California. A six-minute segment from the climactic lightsaber duel is projected side-by-side with film examples to demonstrate the stability, durability, and clarity of the digital image. The whole movie is then publicly screened the next day in New York and Burbank.

The Power of Myth

June 21: *Star Wars: The Power of Myth* Experience, a traveling roadshow that blends original trilogy and Episode I characters and stories with classical mythology begins a three-month 13-city European tour in Dublin, Ireland. One of the show's highlights is the full-scale Naboo starfighter prop.

DK Publishing produces a book to accompany the show.

MAD Maul

June 21: *MAD* magazine #385 features Alfred E. Neuman as Darth Maul on the cover. Inside is a movie parody titled *The Fandumb Magazine*.

June 23: LucasArts releases the Episode I *Insider's Guide*, its last entry in the multi-media CD-ROM market, which is being eroded by the popularity of the Internet and DVD bonus features.

The Saga Begins

June 24: "Weird Al" Yankovic debuts the music video to "The Saga Begins," a song about Episode I sung to the tune of Don McLean's "American Pie." Yankovic goes so far as to turn his official website into a parody of StarWars.com.

JULY

A Royal Welcome

July 14: Episode I's European Premiere is at the 1999 Royal Film Performance to aid the Cinema and Television Benevolent Fund, with Prince Charles in attendance. The screening is at the Odeon Leicester Square. Lucas, Rick McCallum, and cast members appear.

Prince Charles meets Ewan McGregor and director George Lucas at the European premiere of Episode I in London.

Woman Commander

July 23: The space shuttle *Columbia*'s 26th flight, STS-93, is led by Air Force Colonel Eileen Collins, the first woman Shuttle Commander. The mission highlights the deployment of the Chandra X-Ray Observatory.

AUGUST

A Royal Ride From Hasbro

Hasbro releases the action-figure scale Electronic Naboo Royal Starship Blockade Cruiser Playset, a return to the large playsets of the Original Trilogy. The toy spans almost 92 centimeters (three feet) in length and is loaded with play features like a working droid lift, sounds, lights, and an enemy droid starfighter.

August 3: Bantam Books publishes its final new *Star Wars* novel, *X-Wing: Starfighters of Adumar* by Aaron Allston.

X-wings set off on a diplomatic mission, which proves to be a greater challenge for the pilots than even aerial combat.

August 11: Lucas Learning releases *Yoda's Challenge*, an Episode I CD-ROM designed to immerse children aged six and up in math, reading, and music.

Also in 1999...

Fit for a Queen

Queen Amidala is used on many high-end products, including an Yves Saint Laurent make-up campaign, a Limoges porcelain box, and Robert Tonner porcelain dolls (left). They have two costume variations: Senate Chamber and Celebration gowns.

Hasbro also produces an Amidala doll, who becomes the cover girl on August's Dolls magazine.

SEPTEMBER

September 7: Episode I props, including the full-sized Naboo fighter, are on display at the Generation 2000 Exposition in Galeries Lafayette, Paris.

September 15: LucasArts releases the *The Phantom Menace* video game for the PlayStation.

Strange Tales

September 29: Dark Horse Comics begins publishing *Star Wars Tales*. The quarterly anthology format allows for creative experimentation, including stories outside continuity. One popular example: "Skippy the Jedi Droid," a tale written by Peter David, reveals that the malfunctioning R5-D4, who blows his top in Episode IV, was in truth a Jedi in disguise.

Also in 1999...

Bricks and Pieces

The phenomenon of LEGO® *Star Wars* continues, with the release of 14 sets relating to Episodes I, IV, V, and VI, and one LEGO® Mindstorms® set (the 9748 Droid Developer Kit).

Anakin's N-1 comes in the set 7141 Naboo Fighter.

Anakin Skywalker minifigure from set 7141 Naboo Fighter.

Luke Skywalker minifigure from the set 7140 X-Wing Fighter.

Darth Vader's TIE Advanced IX ship comes in the set 7150 TIE Fighter & Y-Wing.

OCTOBER

Chewbacca Is Moonstruck

October 5: Del Rey publishes *Vector Prime* by R.A. Salvatore, the first book in *The New Jedi Order* series. Set 25 years after Episode IV, the series introduces the invading Yuuzhan Vong aliens as villains. In a shocking turn, Chewbacca dies in a cataclysm when an entire moon is dragged from orbit onto a planet. An outpouring of fan grief and disbelief fills up Internet message boards.

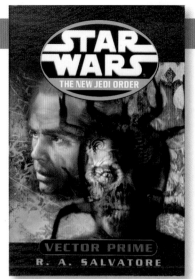

Cliff Nielsen's eerie Vector Prime cover art

A Model and Marriage for Mara

October 26: Mara Jade is played by model Shannon Baksa, who poses for official trading card photography. Her likeness is revealed on StarWars.com when the site posts the cover to *Star Wars Insider* #47. In November, Dark Horse tells the story of Mara's marriage to Luke Skywalker in the *Union* mini-series.

NOVEMBER

Casting Episode II

November 2: Casting director Robin Gurland begins work on Episode II; a casting breakdown describing the role of adult Anakin Skywalker is distributed to casting agencies. It reads, in part, "Self-determined, extremely intelligent and forthright... LEAD. Should resemble Jake Lloyd... at 19 years old." In the meantime, Ahmed Best is the first actor announced to return to Episode II on November 10.

Lucas with casting director Robin Gurland and Temuera Morrison, who is cast as Jango Fett.

Also in 1999...

Taco Bell Topper

Taco Bell sells *Star Wars: The Phantom Menace* cup toppers and limited edition cups for $2.99 with every drink purchased. As well as Darth Maul, other cup toppers include Yoda and a young Anakin.

This Darth Maul cup topper comes with flexible arms.

November 5: Episode I completes its staggered international release with a last major overseas stop, China.

November 7: Fox Studios Australia opens with a flashy public event that features C-3PO and R2-D2, as well as a near life-sized X-wing starfighter.

Spare Circuits or Parts?

November 11: C-3PO and R2-D2 serve as spokesdroids for the Canadian Association of Transplantation and the Kidney Foundation of Canada. A poster features the protocol droid quoting his line from Episode IV.

Jar Jar's Journey

November 15: Lucas Learning releases *Jar Jar's Journey*, an interactive CD-ROM storybook adventure that retells Episode I from Jar Jar's point of view, for kids aged four and up.

Jar Jar's cartoonish antics fit well with the whimsical illustration style of Jar Jar's Journey.

Also in 1999...

Pepsi and Episode I

Pepsi-Cola Company debuts 24 limited-edition can designs across various product lines, including Pepsi (Anakin, R2-D2), Mountain Dew (Darth Maul, Obi-Wan), Diet Pepsi (Queen Amidala, Shmi), and—in limited markets—Storm (Jar Jar, Qui-Gon). Pepsi also distributes random gold Yoda cans that customers can choose to keep or redeem for a $20 *Star Wars* check and a replacement can.

The huge Pepsi-Cola Star Wars promotion features customized vending machines and special TV spots.

High Definition Delivered

November 15: At the COMDEX conference, Sony President and CEO Nobuyuki Idei announces that Sony and Panavision will soon deliver the latest generation of digital camera to Lucasfilm so that testing can commence in preparation for shooting Episode II without film. The collaboration couples the new digital camera developed by Sony with a special new series of lenses and accessories specifically developed and manufactured by Panavision to meet the needs of cinematographers.

The unprecedented collaboration between Sony, Panavision, and Lucasfilm results in the Sony HDW-F900 camera being used on Episode II.

Clear Your Mind of Questions

November 22: StarWars.com fields questions from fans via its new "Ask the Lucasfilm Jedi Council" feature. Concept design director Doug Chiang, animatics supervisor David Dozoretz, production designer Gavin Bocquet, and others offer their insights into movie production.

DECEMBER

Lost on Mars

December 3: NASA loses radio contact with the *Mars Polar Lander*, moments before the spacecraft enters the Martian atmosphere. Having been traveling on an interplanetary journey since January, the lander becomes the first to explore the southern polar regions of the red planet. The lander and its probes presumably crash on the Martian surface.

Back in Theaters

December 3: *The Phantom Menace* is re-released for one week in the US and Canada with 100 percent of the proceeds going to charities selected by theater owners, raising more than $2.1 million. The first time the entirety of box-office revenue has been allocated for charity in a theatrical release of this scale, more than 350 cities host the return of Episode I, with over 180 charities benefitting.

December 9: Wizards of the Coast becomes a *Star Wars* licensee, securing the rights to publish roleplaying and miniature games, filling the void left by West End Games's departure in 1998 (see p.197).

December 17: John Dykstra (visual effects supervisor on *Star Wars*) serves as visual effects supervisor for Sony Pictures Imageworks on *Stuart Little*, a feature with a computer-generated lead character who requires exacting cloth and fur simulation.

Stuart Little stars a furry character wearing soft clothes—a digital simulation challenge.

Y2K Hysteria

December 31: Many around the world nervously await the arrival of January 1, 2000. Aside from culturally rooted fears of apocalyptic events that accompany a millennial transition (even though the true millennial rollover happens at the end of 2000), the media latches onto the Y2K computer bug as a practical fear. A shortcoming in a computer's two-digit year notations can cause systems to become confused that the year "00" is supposed to follow "99." Despite prognostications of widespread chaos, the calendar rolls over with little incident.

2000

WITH THE 1900s left behind, the future has arrived. An increasingly every-day convenience, the Internet sparks a fevered rush of investment into online companies, resulting in an economic boom that peaks in March. Leading this shifting paradigm, Lucasfilm leaves behind the photochemical legacy of film for a purely digital production of *Star Wars:* Episode II *Attack of the Clones*.

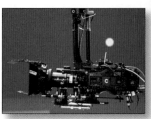

The Sony 24-P digital camera.

> "In order to get anything to happen you have to... go into an area where you're not sure you're going to be able to pull it off."

George Lucas *on digital cinematography*

THE NEW *STAR WARS* MOVIES continue to consume large chunks of Internet chatter, drawing praise, criticism, and conjecture. Websites peg dozens of young actors as front-runners for teen Anakin Skywalker. Despite the pointed opinions of many web-wags, Lucas sticks to his Gungan, even penning the script to Episode II with the humorous title "Jar Jar's Great Adventure."

JANUARY

January 4: John Williams's score to Episode I is nominated for a Grammy Award. In the February 23 ceremony, it loses to Thomas Newman's score for *American Beauty*.

January 12: Spielberg presents Lucas with the Women in Film, American Jewish Committee's Sherrill C. Corwin Human Relations Award at a ceremony in Beverly Hills.

Looking through Sony's 24-P digital camera, Lucas is on location at the Naboo Lake Retreat for Episode II with (L–R) Julie D'antoni (visual effects plate coordinator), Calum McFarlane ('B' camera operator), Rick McCallum (producer), and Dave Nichols (key grip).

A Wookiee Remembered

January 20: Dark Horse publishes a Chewbacca mini-series as tribute to the fallen Wookiee warrior, who died in the 1999 novel, *Vector Prime*. The story takes the form of memorials told by Chewie's friends and enemies, featuring a team of different artists for each tale written by Darko Macan.

The cover of Star Wars Chewbacca #1, with artwork by Sean Phillips.

Tojjevvuk, the mad albino Wookiee, falls to Chewbacca in #2 (February 16, 2000).

January 27: StarWars.com launches the *Homing Beacon*, a biweekly email newsletter. It will eventually go weekly and have over two million subscribers.

FEBRUARY

Episode I Nominations

February 15: *The Phantom Menace* is nominated for three Academy Awards®. Rob Coleman, John Knoll, Dennis Muren, and Scott Squires for Visual Effects; John Midgley, Gary Rydstrom, Tom Johnson, and Shawn Murphy for Sound; Ben Burtt and Tom Bellfort for Sound Effects Editing. In all three categories, *Episode I* is beaten by *The Matrix*.

Lucas at Berkeley

February 16: Lucas is the featured guest for the Herb Caen/*San Francisco Chronicle* Lecture on media and journalism at the Zellerbach Hall on the campus of the University of California at Berkeley. "Some of us are in occupations and professions that allow us to have louder voices than other people," says Lucas. "And therefore we should be doubly aware of what we're saying because it does influence people, and it's especially true of the media as much as it is of the entertainment business."

Costumes on Display

February 21: A selection of Trisha Biggar's amazing Episode I costumes go on display as part of the 8th Annual Art of Motion Picture Costume Design exhibit at the Fashion Institute of Design & Merchandising (FIDM) in Los Angeles, including Queen Amidala's Senate and Coruscant gowns, Captain Panaka's uniform, Chancellor Valorum's robes, Naboo handmaiden outfits, and Darth Maul's robes.

The fan around Padmé's head in her End Parade costume (from Episode I) is designed to give the impression of an angelic halo.

February 21: The trustees of the American Film Institute select Harrison Ford to receive the 28th Lifetime Achievement Award.

MARCH

Your Own Slice of StarWars.com

March 9: StarWars.com partners with Homestead.com to offer fans an online space with a fans.starwars.com domain name. Of the several hundred that immediately sign up, many create tribute sites to their favorite characters or their particular expression of fandom. (This service is discontinued on November 27, 2001, when the partnership terminates.)

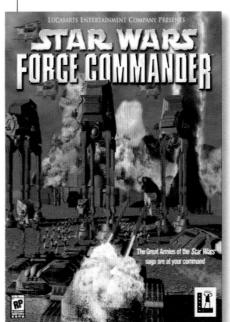

March 9: At ShoWest, Lucas presents John Williams with the Maestro Award, an honor specifically invented to recognize Williams's achievements.

March 17: LucasArts announces that it will partner with Verant Interactive Inc. and Sony Online Entertainment to create the first multiplayer *Star Wars* online roleplaying game. The title promises to immerse thousands of game players into the classic *Star Wars* galaxy. The game will be distributed and sold at retail by LucasArts, and available for play online exclusively at Sony.

March 22: LucasArts and Ronin Entertainment release *Star Wars: Force Commander*, a 3-D real-time strategy game.

APRIL

The One to Own

April 3: Episode I begins its worldwide release on VHS. In the first 48 hours of its release, enthusiastic video purchasers snap up more than 5 million copies. The movie is available in a pan-and-scan format or a deluxe widescreen collector's edition.

Lucasfilm opts for a photo collage for the video packaging of Episode I, rather than the theatrical poster artwork.

April 3: LucasArts releases *Star Wars: Episode I Jedi Power Battles* for the PlayStation. The game allows one or two players to pit Jedi characters against Trade Federation enemies.

Another Kind of Year by Year

April 4: *The Essential Chronology* is published by Del Rey Books. Written by Kevin J. Anderson and Daniel Wallace, it is the first narrative to attempt to put all the events of the Expanded Universe into a chronological, historical order.

The Essential Chronology features black-and-white pencil artwork by Bill Hughes.

For the Padawans

April 5: Lucas Online launches www.StarWarsKids.com, the official online destination for young *Star Wars* fans. At launch, the site includes educational articles offering insight into the history of the Saga for young new fans introduced to *Star Wars* by Episode I. It also features interactive games, letting kids customize their own Podracer or guide R2 units through mazes.

April 9: After extensive testing, Lucas signs off on the use of the Sony HDW-F900 24-P digital camera to capture the live-action photography of Episode II.

Lucas poses with Sony's revolutionary digital camera.

An International Museum Tour

April 13: While the Magic of Myth exhibit travels across the US, Europe gets its own traveling display of *Star Wars* props and costumes with the Art of *Star Wars* tour. It opens at the Barbican Centre in London.

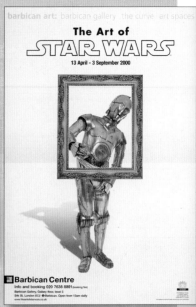

The Art of Star Wars exhibit showcases props and artwork from all four movies (left) and its promotional poster features the inquisitive C-3PO (right).

A New Scribe

April 13: Screenwriter Jonathan Hales joins Episode II production to help Lucas refine the final drafts of the script. Hales had previously worked with Lucas on *The Young Indiana Jones Chronicles*, where he wrote or co-wrote "The Curse of the Jackal," "The Scandal of 1920," and "Tales of Innocence."

April 15: Lucas is one of 15 celebrity drivers in the 24th annual Toyota Pro/Celebrity Race in Long Beach, California. He doesn't win, but the event raises $120,000 for charity.

Jonathan Hales on the set of Padmé's dining room.

MAY

Grand Conjunction

May 3: A rare "Grand Conjunction" occurs in the heavens, as Mars, the moon, Saturn, Jupiter, Mercury, and Venus align in a rough line within 30 degrees of sky as seen from Earth.

Certain Points of View

May 5: Over the decades, *Star Wars* has had an enormous cultural impact, as the many books dedicated to its discussion testify. St. Martin's Griffin press publishes *The Science of Star Wars*, an unlicensed book by astrophysicist Jeanne Cavalos. This is an early example of a cottage industry that arises during the Prequel Trilogy, which produces independently published works that use *Star Wars* as a springboard for academic discussion on a wide array of topics.

Further reading?

Topics explored include philosophy, in The Tao of Star Wars *by John M. Porter (Humanics Trade Group, June 2003),* Star Wars and Philosophy *edited by Kevin S. Decker (Open Court, March 2005),* The Dharma of Star Wars *by Matthew Bortolin (Wisdom Publications, April 2005); religion in* Finding God in a Galaxy Far, Far Away *by Timothy Paul Jones (Multnomah Books, October 2005),* Star Wars Jesus *by Caleb Grimes (WinePress Publishing, December 2006),* The Gospel According to Star Wars *by John C. McDowell (Westminster John Knox Press, March 2007); mythology in* The Journey of Luke Skywalker *by Steven A. Galipeau (published by Open Court, April 2001),* Star Wars: The New Myth *by Michael J. Hanson (Xlibris Corporation, April 2002); and cultural impact in* Empire Triumphant *by Kevin J. Wetmore, Jr. (McFarland & Company, September 2005),* Finding the Force of the Star Wars Franchise *by Matthew Wilhelm Kapell (Peter Lang Publishing, July 2006),* Culture, Identities and Technology in the Star Wars Films *by Carl Silvio (McFarland & Company, Inc. January 2007),* Wizards, Wardrobes and Wookiees *by Connie Neal (IVP Books, May 2007).*

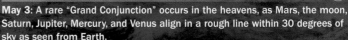

The Force in Orlando

May 5: Every weekend in May, the Disney-MGM Studios theme park in Orlando, Florida, stages *Star Wars* Weekends. Special events, parades, exclusive merchandise, and celebrity guests such as Carrie Fisher, Jake Lloyd, Peter Mayhew, and Jeremy Bulloch delight *Star Wars* fans in what becomes an almost-annual tradition.

The New Anakin

May 12: When word reaches the Internet that Lucas will hold test-screenings for the role of Anakin Skywalker, just about every young actor in Hollywood is rumored to be in the lead. Winning the coveted role is 19-year old Canadian actor Hayden Christensen, who is announced on StarWars.com.

JUNE

June 8: Episode I's nine-and-a-half minute Podrace sequence on Tatooine wins the Best Action Sequence award at the MTV Movie Awards.

May The Furby With You

June 14: Tiger Electronic's Interactive Yoda is unveiled at F.A.O. Schwartz in New York. In the mold of the immensely successful Furby toy, Tiger's Yoda interacts via a series of sensors and has a vocabulary of over 800 words recorded by Frank Oz.

Training in how to use the included lightsaber is provided by the Interactive Yoda himself.

The Interactive Yoda can answer questions with pearls of Jedi wisdom.

The Next Journey Begins

June 26: Three years to the day after Episode I began principal photography in Leavesden Studios, digital cameras roll tape in Sydney's Fox Studios Australia on Episode II. The bluescreen draped Stage Six houses minimal set elements—a podium and a pod—that will eventually be turned into the enormous Galactic Senate chambers. In a scene cut from the final film, Ian McDiarmid reprises his role as Chancellor Palpatine, announcing word of Padmé's apparent death in an explosion. Also shot that day is the momentous motion by Jar Jar Binks (Ahmed Best) that grants Palpatine emergency executive power.

Producer Rick McCallum on the set of Episode II.

The "Twilight" story-arc also introduces popular Twi'lek character, Aayla Secura.

The Mighty Quin

June 28: The ongoing *Star Wars* comic series starts its "Twilight" arc in issue #19. Written by John Ostrander and illustrated by Jan Duursema, the storyline focuses on rogue Jedi Quinlan Vos, who would prove to be an extremely popular recurring character.

June 30: *The Perfect Storm* showcases ILM's breakthrough digital water effects. The extremely difficult work required a CG crew as big as Episode I's to deliver a fifth of the shots.

Episode II would benefit from the R&D done by ILM for The Perfect Storm.

(L–R) Mas Amedda (David Bowers), Chancellor Palpatine (Ian McDiarmid), and Sly Moore (Sandi Finlay) standing on a Senate speaking platform.

JULY

Jedi Master of the Macabre

July 11: StarWars.com announces that Christopher Lee will be part of the cast of Episode II. Lee's character "Count Dooku" goes unconfirmed; he is identified only as "a charismatic separatist."

Star of Hammer films and The Three Musketeers, Christopher Lee is a veteran of the industry.

Senator Organa

July 13: Jimmy Smits is announced as part of the Episode II cast. Unlike other casting decisions, no secret is made that Smits will be playing Bail Organa, Senator of Alderaan.

Smits starred on hit TV show L.A. Law between 1986 and 1992.

Insider Trading

July 14: *Star Wars Insider* publishes its 50th issue. Ironically, this milestone is the last issue from Fantastic Media, which has held the Fan Club license since 1987. The magazine and club switches hands to Wizards of the Coast, which resumes publishing after a slight transitional delay.

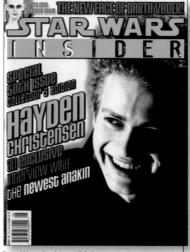

Not Quite a Hero

July 21: Harrison Ford stars in a role against type in Robert Zemeckis's Hitchcock-inspired *What Lies Beneath*. Rather than a hero, Ford plays a husband with a secret that haunts his wife from beyond the grave.

Star Wars Insider #50 features an extensive first interview with Hayden Christensen.

AUGUST

On Location

August 1: StarWars.com starts a series of weekly video reports on Episode II called "On Location," eventually adding 30 installments hosted by Ahmed Best. Best talks to many of the on-set crew who work behind the scenes in Australia, Tunisia, Italy, and Spain throughout the shoot.

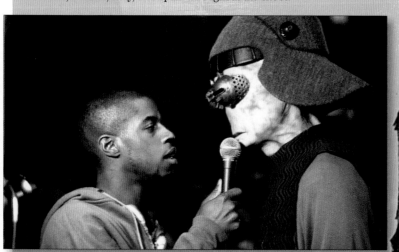

Ahmed Best interviews a Neimoidian extra on the set at Fox Studios Australia.

Sir Alec Guinness Remembered

August 5: Sir Alec Guinness dies of liver cancer at age 86 in West Sussex, England. From the set of Episode II, Lucas issues the statement, "He was one of the most talented and respected actors of his generation and brought an amazing range and versatility to his work." Guinness's storied career spanned a variety of genres, from the classic Ealing comedies of the post-World War II era, to Shakespeare, to David Lean epics such as *The Bridge on the River Kwai* and *Lawrence of Arabia*. Guinness's role as Ben Kenobi in *Star Wars* endeared him to a new generation.

Sir Alec Guinness on the set of Episode IV: A New Hope

August 25: Studio photography in Australia is completed on Episode II. Production packs up and moves to Lake Como, Italy.

SEPTEMBER

Undressed To Kill

September 6: Dark Horse publishes a *Darth Maul* mini-series written by Ron Marz, featuring Maul's mission to destroy the Black Sun criminal organization. To help artist Jan Duursema accurately depict a shirtless Maul, prequel concept artist Iain McCaig establishes Maul's torso tattoos.

The first of four installments of a comic book featuring Darth Maul

Concept art for Darth Maul by Iain McCaig

SECOND INTIFADA IN THE MIDDLE EAST · KURSK SUB SINKS IN BARENTS SEA

Also in 2000...

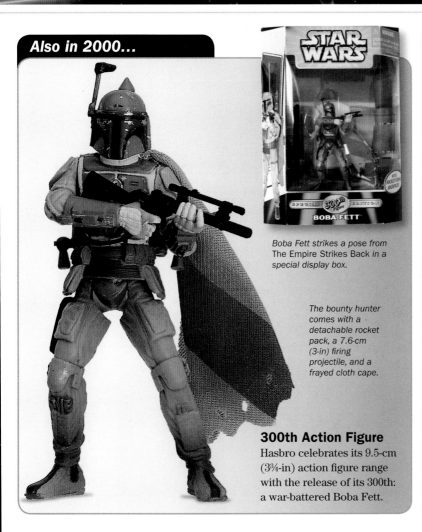

Boba Fett strikes a pose from The Empire Strikes Back in a special display box.

The bounty hunter comes with a detachable rocket pack, a 7.6-cm (3-in) firing projectile, and a frayed cloth cape.

300th Action Figure

Hasbro celebrates its 9.5-cm (3¾-in) action figure range with the release of its 300th: a war-battered Boba Fett.

Back to the Homestead

September 7: Production travels to the Chott El Jerrid, Tunisia, returning to the exterior of the Lars homestead. Aside from Episode II scenes, Lucas takes advantage of the location shoot to gather a single scene for Episode III—the delivery of the infant Luke Skywalker. (Lucas ultimately opts to reconstruct the scene in 2003 with actors against greenscreen.)

Hayden Christensen at the Lars homestead surface location, situated on the salt flat at Chott El Jerrid, Tunisia.

September 13: Shelagh Fraser, who played Aunt Beru in *A New Hope*, dies.

A Welcome in Spain

September 13: Production moves to La Plaza d'España in Seville, Spain. Cast and crew are greeted by hundreds of fans who crowd round the perimeter of the plaza in the hopes of catching a glimpse of Lucas, Ahmed Best, Hayden Christensen, or Natalie Portman.

Lucas shakes hands with enthusiastic fans in Spain.

September 20: Principal photography wraps on Episode II, after four days of shooting at Elstree Studios. Production ends a day and a half ahead of schedule. Rick McCallum and Lucas's production discipline keeps the movie on time and on budget throughout its development.

The LEGO Challenge

September 22: The LEGO® *Star Wars* Galactic Challenge World Championships brings 35 children from 18 countries to LEGOLAND® California. They are given 10 LEGO sets and two hours to construct their creations. Two children—David Michon (US) and Peter Nagy (Hungary) win the grand prize: a family trip to LEGO headquarters in Denmark, and a chance to participate in LEGO product development.

A splashy logo for the LEGO event

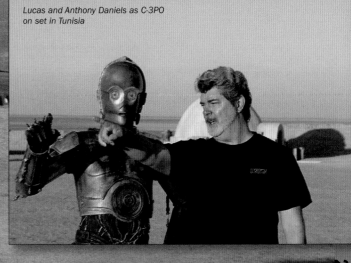

Lucas and Anthony Daniels as C-3PO on set in Tunisia

OCTOBER

October 13: The Art of *Star Wars* museum exhibit moves to the National Museum of Photography, Film, and Television in Bradford, England.

Eras of Adventure

October 26: LucasBooks establishes distinct "eras" in its publishing program, each with coded symbols. At launch, five eras are carved out: The Old Republic covers tales of ancient Jedi Knights and Sith Lords; The Rise of the Empire chronicles events around the Prequel Trilogy; The Rebellion covers the Original Trilogy; The New Republic chronicles events after *Return of the Jedi*; and The New Jedi Order, set 25 years after *A New Hope*, is the focus of a new series. Dates center on the Battle of Yavin in year 0, with years either before "BBY" or after "ABY" the battle.

The Old Republic Era
25,000–1,000 years before *Star Wars: A New Hope*.

The Rise of the Empire Era
1,000–0 years before *Star Wars: A New Hope*.

STAR WARS: **EPISODE I** *The Phantom Menace* – 32 years BBY

STAR WARS: **EPISODE II** *Attack of the Clones* – 22 years BBY

STAR WARS: **EPISODE III** *Revenge of the Sith* – 19 years BBY

The Rebellion Era
0–5 years after *Star Wars: A New Hope*.

STAR WARS: **EPISODE IV** *A New Hope* – 0 years

STAR WARS: **EPISODE V** *The Empire Strikes Back* – 3 years ABY

STAR WARS: **EPISODE VI** *Return of the Jedi* – 4 years ABY

The New Republic Era
5–25 years after *Star Wars: A New Hope*.

The New Jedi Order Era
25+ years after *Star Wars: A New Hope*.

Great Expectations

October 31: Del Rey publishes *Balance Point*, the second hardcover novel in *The New Jedi Order* series. Written by Kathy Tyers, it includes a crucial development in the story of Mara Jade: she discovers she is pregnant. Luke Skywalker will be a father.

Cliff Nielsen's cover art for Balance Point has a silhouetted Jacen Solo torn between opposing forces.

GEORGE W. BUSH IS ELECTED US

NOVEMBER

Fan Film Network

November 6: StarWars.com and AtomFilms.com partner to create the *Star Wars* Fan Film Network, giving fans a sanctioned arena to produce, display, and enter their fan films in competition for recognition by Lucasfilm. Participants are given access to a library of official *Star Wars* sound effects to include in their works, and finalists are given a share of revenue generated by site sponsorship. The partnership results in a wave of new documentaries, parodies, and animated shorts.

Too Close to Call

November 7: The US Presidential election between Republican candidate George W. Bush and Democratic candidate Al Gore proves controversially close. Premature verdicts result in a blow to the credibility of mainstream media with their inability to adapt with this changing story. The Supreme Court controversially declares George W. Bush the victor in a rare, but not unheard of situation, where the winner of the largest number of electoral votes is not the winner of the popular vote.

Republican supporters watch as the Florida race narrows to just 200 votes.

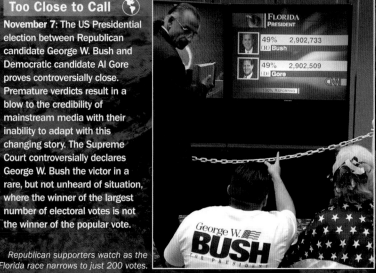

Sith Illustrated

November 14: Sith founder Darth Bane, introduced in the Episode I novelization, is pictured for the first time in Random House's *Secrets of the Sith*. The gruesome warrior has a torso covered in armored orbalisk creatures, and a cage-like helmet.

Darth Bane artwork by Jesús Redondo

Star Geeks tells the tale of two die-hard fans, Harry and Chris, who win tickets to see a special advanced screening of Episode I and run into a die-hard Trekkie on the way.

The RPG Roles On

November 11: Wizards of the Coast unveils its new *Star Wars* roleplaying game (RPG) line with a special gala event at Planet Hollywood in Seattle, Washington. Guests include actors Peter Mayhew and Jake Lloyd, and artists Drew Struzan and Adam Hughes.

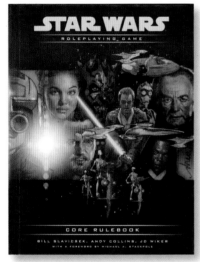

RPG rulebook cover art by Drew Struzan

November 14: LucasArts releases *Star Wars*: Demolition, a vehicle-on-vehicle combat game.

November 14: Lucas donates a lightsaber prop signed by Liam Neeson to the Movie Action for Children auction to benefit UNICEF.

November 15: Rick McCallum presents Episode II footage at the InterBEE 2000 conference in Chiba City, Japan, displaying the high quality of the digital format.

DECEMBER

December 2: The massive multiplayer online roleplaying game gets a name, *Star Wars*: Galaxies, as its official website launches.

December 14: *Star Wars*: Episode I The Battle for Naboo game is released by LucasArts.

The Battle for Naboo on Nintendo Gamecube

Also in 2000...

Power of the Jedi

Hasbro's Power of the Jedi series revisits many favorite characters, but also introduces some previously unseen in action-figure form, most notably Jek Porkins.

Jek Porkins, an X-wing pilot from the planet Bestine IV, is played by William Hootkins in A New Hope.

Role Play First

The *Star Wars*: Invasion of Theed roleplaying game comes with a Hasbro figure of Rhorworr.

Rhorworr is a young Wookiee from Naboo

Back on Video, Again...

November 21: Benefiting from the many new fans introduced to the Saga by Episode I, Lucasfilm releases the original *Star Wars* trilogy once again on VHS. These special-edition pan-and-scan and widescreen cassettes feature packaging designs that match the look of the recently released Episode I VHS.

The new Original Trilogy VHS packaging casts Episode V in an all black box.

2001

EPISODE II SPENDS the year in postproduction. Digital moviemaking affords Lucas unprecedented flexibility. The animatics team led by Dan Gregoire and the art department led by Ryan Church and Erik Tiemens help envision entirely new sequences that did not exist during preproduction or principal photography. Lucas then gathers the live-action elements he needs during stints of pick-up photography in England.

> "When we animated him in the computer, we had to put in all those little ear jiggles and rough puppet-like actions."
>
> **Rob Coleman**
> on making digital Yoda mirror the Yoda puppet

BY YEAR'S END, a multipart trailer campaign reveals glimpses of Episode II. Meanwhile, ILM busily toils away on its sizable workload. Despite Lucas's early suggestion that Episode II would be a smaller, more personal story, the number of effects shots increases as the galactic canvas expands.

A complex action sequence set in a droid factory is added to Episode II fairly late in postproduction, made possible through bluescreen live-action photography and digital environments.

JANUARY

January 11: Tests are underway for the release of a print version of Episode II. Although the movie was captured without film, the rarity of digital projection necessitates transference to film for distribution.

Citation Needed

January 15: Larry Sanger and Jimmy Wales launch Wikipedia, a publicly editable online encyclopedia incorporating wiki software: a content-creation tool that allows users to create collaborative websites. By year's end, Wikipedia will boast 20,000 articles.

January 21: Apple Inc. introduces iTunes, software for the organization and playback of digital music and video.

Concept art for Episode II depicts Anakin fighting droids in a Geonosis droid factory. It sets the tone for the sequence, detailing the fiery, mechanical, environment of the busy factory that will have to be recreated on screen.

FEBRUARY

Ben Burtt has access to footage, animatics, and effects via his Avid workstation.

Plan of Attack

Lucas, McCallum, and Burtt screen the first cut of Episode II. Lucas sees room for improvement. While some scenes are cut, big scenes—including a tense confrontation between Dooku and Obi-Wan, and an action set-piece inside a droid factory—are planned as additional photography. Throughout editorial, Burtt presents Lucas with initial iterations of scenes for examination and discussion. The Avid digital editing system enables Burtt to pull up the entire library of footage already gathered for the movie, as well as placeholder scenes constructed by Dan Gregoire's animatics team.

Faces Frozen in Data

February 11: At Toy Fair in New York, Lucas Licensing unveils busts that are amazing replicas of the cast in Episode II. They are the product of new laser-scanning techniques executed by Gentle Giant Studios, a rapidly growing company in Burbank, California. The digital information gathered by the scans can be used to create exacting video game models, visual effects, or toys and collectible figures.

Actor Temuera Morrison's features are scanned by Gentle Giant to become the foundation of this blank Boba Fett bust.

We Got Death Star

February 15: The animated short, *Star Wars Gangsta Rap*, is added to the Fan Film Network; becoming one of the most popular fan films ever produced. Sample lyrics include: "Uncle Owen, I know I'm on probation/ I cleaned the droids, can I go to Tosche Station?"

The short is created by Jason Brannon, Chris Crawford, and Thomas Lee.

February 15: The first *Star Wars* e-novella, *Darth Maul: Saboteur* by James Luceno is published virtually.

Starfighter

February 17: LucasArts holds a big premiere party at the Sony Metreon in San Francisco for the release of *Star Wars*: Starfighter on the PlayStation 2.

Star Wars: Starfighter introduces pirate character Nym, who will later star in his own comics series.

MARCH

March 2: Lucas attends the ribbon-cutting of the Zemeckis Center for Digital Arts at USC. Lucas funded the center's sound stage and advanced media classroom.

March 3: Aspen's annual US Comedy Arts Festival honors *American Graffiti* with a reunion featuring Lucas, screenwriters Gloria Katz and Willard Huyck, and various cast members.

Just the Facts

DeAgostini begins testing its new product, *Star Wars* Fact File, at newsagents and stores in the Harlech area of the UK. These information-packed weeklies are "partwork periodicals," a type of encyclopedia that comes in hole-punched magazine-style installments which are later sorted in binders.

The first installment of DeAgostini's ambitious partwork series

Adding to the Action

March 26: Episode II pick-up photography begins at Ealing Studio. The first day gathers reaction shots of Padmé and Anakin aboard the Naboo yacht as they watch Obi-Wan ambushed on Geonosis via hologram. Most of the shoot involves bluescreen-drenched sets, which visual effects supervisors John Knoll, Ben Snow, and Pablo Helman will transform into exotic worlds.

Hayden Christensen films the scene in which Anakin goes in search of his mother on Owen's speeder bike. The Tatooine landscape will be added by the visual effects team.

SPACE STATION MIR RE-ENTERS EARTH'S ATMOSPHERE AND FALLS INTO THE PACIFIC OCEAN ✈

APRIL

Phantom Television

Episode I begins airing internationally on pay television. FOX and Lucasfilm initially plan to broadcast the movie for free, as part of a "Thanksgiving in April" push to encourage family viewing. However, a tepid advertising and viewer market at the time causes it to switch gears, and instead target the real Thanksgiving holiday for broadcast.

Back in Time

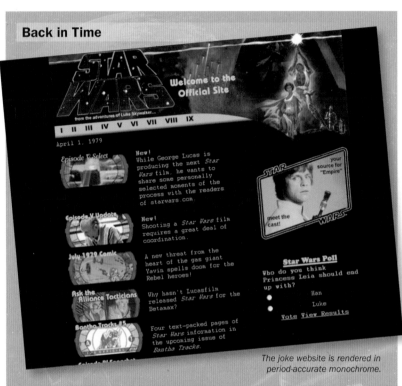

The joke website is rendered in period-accurate monochrome.

April 1: On April Fool's Day, StarWars.com changes its design to represent April 1, 1979, and breaks news on the making of "*Star Wars 2*," or *The Empire Strikes Back*.

C-3PO

The Jedi-Con exclusive is based around a 1995 C-3PO action figure, now in a unique box.

April 13: The Official German Fan Club holds Jedi-Con in Cologne. This event marks the first-ever action figure to be produced as a convention exclusive—a C-3PO with event-specific packaging, made by Hasbro.

April 28: Lucas Learning releases Super Bombad Racing, a madcap "big head" cart-racing style game.

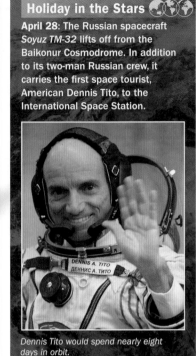

Dennis Tito would spend nearly eight days in orbit.

The Naboo Fighter Flies Again

April 28: A new museum exhibit, The Art of the Starfighter, opens at the Smithsonian Art and Industries building in Washington, DC. The centerpiece is the full-sized 11-meter (35-foot) Naboo starfighter used in the filming of Episode I. To mark its unveiling, the Smithsonian holds a *Star Wars* costume party.

As the only large-scale starship prop produced for Episode I, the Naboo fighter travels extensively, including to the Oakland Chabot Space & Science Center, California.

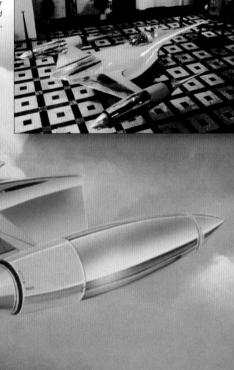

Doug Chiang's production painting of the Naboo N-1 becomes the signature image of The Art of the Starfighter exhibit.

Jedi Trials

April 29: Despite a viral email campaign urging people to fill out "Jedi Knight" as their religion in the UK census, it is not recognized as an official religion. Knowing of the campaign in advance, census officials created a code that translated a "Jedi Knight" entry as "other." Some media outlets misreported that the creation of the code in some way conferred official status to "Jedi Knight," but it was simply a bookkeeping measure.

The Chosen One

April 29: Hayden Christensen is honored as the "One to Watch" in the Third Annual Young Hollywood Awards at the House of Blues on Hollywood's Sunset Strip. The ceremony celebrates the industry's emerging talent.

MAY

Infinite Possibilities

May 2: LucasBooks unveils the "Infinities" brand for speculative storytelling outside of established *Star Wars* canon. First up is Dark Horse's *Star Wars: Infinities—A New Hope*, a four-part mini-series by Chris Warner, Drew Johnson, and Ray Snyder. In a manner not unlike DC Comics's "Elseworlds," or Marvel's "What If" titles, this series speculates what would have happened had Luke failed to destroy the first Death Star.

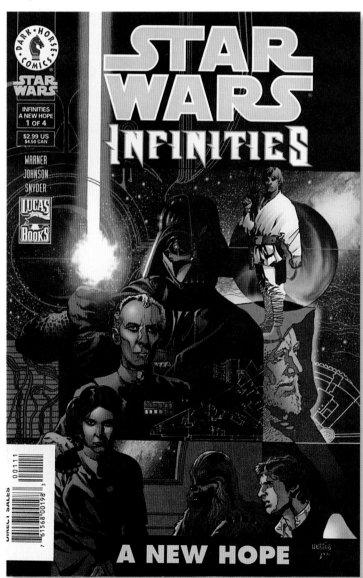

The cover art to Star Wars: Infinities #1 by Tony Harris

May 4: Another round of *Star Wars* weekends begins at Disney-MGM Studios with guests including Kenny Baker, Carrie Fisher, Peter Mayhew, Doug Chiang, and Phil Brown.

May 25: Michael Bay's *Pearl Harbor* features ILM effects. Eric Brevig supervises the creation of digital planes and battleships, as well as extensive miniature work to create complex war scenes.

Bay's production contains extensive practical effects and digital and miniature enhancements.

JUNE

June 8: StarWars.com begins syndicating headlines to fan-sites via RSS feeds.

Final Cut Amateur

June 15: Dissatisfied with Episode I, an anonymous fan re-cuts the movie removing elements he/she found objectionable. This version, nicknamed "The Phantom Edit," spreads via the Internet and on bootleg tapes at conventions. Its popularity causes Lucasfilm to issue a statement: "While we appreciate fan enthusiasm in general, creating, duplicating, and/or distributing any edited version of a *Star Wars* film is clear copyright infringement and is illegal."

Connecting at Conventions

June 19: Head of fan relations Steve Sansweet begins a run of convention appearances presenting exclusive behind-the-scenes video content from Episode II in "*Star Wars*: Connections." The presentation's overarching theme is that Episode II holds many ties to the beloved Original Trilogy.

Steve Sansweet signs exclusive Topps Cards at San Diego Comic-Con.

June 20: Lucas Learning redefines itself. No longer a creator of consumer products, the company instead focuses on direct-to-school educational products.

Also in 2001...

Lucas appears on the cover of *Cinema* magazine, which publishes an article about Lucasfilm going digital.

FIRST SAME-SEX MARRIAGE ACT ☉ TIMOTHY MCVEIGH EXECUTED FOR OKLAHOMA BOMBING ☉

JULY

July 2: The *Star Wars* Fan Club auctions off over 900 products from its archives on eBay, including some rarities dating back to 1977.

July 18: *Jurassic Park III* opens, directed by *Star Wars* alumnus Joe Johnston. ILM once again delivers digital dinosaur effects and more.

Once thought invincible, the T-rex meets its match in the spinosaurus.

In From the Darkness

July 24: The ongoing *Star Wars* comic series begins a story arc titled "Darkness" in issue #32. Written by John Ostrander with pencils by Jan Duursema, the grim story follows Jedi Knight Quinlan Vos as he is drawn to a prison world overrun by vampire-like Anzati. This story is notable for spotlighting Vos's apprentice, Aayla Secura, an attractive blue-skinned Twi'lek in an abbreviated outfit. Jon Foster's striking cover art of Aayla on issue #33 in particular catches Lucas's eye.

In "Darkness," Aayla Secura's amnesia leads her down a path where she intends to kill her Jedi Master, Quinlan Vos.

Not the Weapon of a Jedi

July 24: Lucasfilm files a lawsuit against Minrad Inc., a Buffalo, New York-based medical instruments company that has developed an energy-beam surgical device called a "Light Saber." As per the suit, the company is to drop the trademarked name to avoid any confusion with the weapon created in *Star Wars*.

The Car In Front Is a Toy Yoda

July 27: Jodee Berry, a server at Hooters in Florida, sues her employers after the prize "Toyota" she thought she was vying for in a workplace competition turned out to be a "toy Yoda" from Tiger Electronics. The suit is settled for an undisclosed amount of money.

Clone Wars

July 31: The US House of Representatives passes the Weldon-Stupak Human Cloning Prohibition Act by a vote of 265-162, banning human cloning to create embryos that would be used for medical research. The Bush administration had condemned the proposed cloning methods as allowing for "human embryo farms."

Rebirth

July 31: It's a boy! Mara Jade gives birth to Ben Skywalker in the pages of *Rebirth*, the second book of *The New Jedi Order* duology, *Edge of Victory*, by Greg Keyes.

Cover art by Therese Nielsen.

Jon Foster's artwork of Aayla Secura would convince Lucas to feature the blue-skinned Jedi in Episode II.

AUGUST

Topps releases a 90-card character-based *Star Wars* Evolutions collectible set, which includes actor autographs as chase cards.

Carrie Fisher's autograph card is one of the chase cards most in demand.

Attack of the Title

August 6: StarWars.com announces the full title of the next movie, *Star Wars: Episode II Attack of the Clones*. Unlike the more oblique *Phantom Menace*, this new title mirrors *The Empire Strikes Back* in its blunt promise of action.

Jedi Trials Redux

August 7: Following the example set by the UK in April, Australian fans are urged via email to enter "Jedi Knight" into their official census in an attempt to have it recognized as an official religion. However, the email campaign isn't successful and Jedi remains an unrecognized religion.

August 12: At SIGGRAPH in Los Angeles, an exhibition geared toward digital imaging and interactive technologies professionals, ILM makes available a souvenir Boba Fett T-shirt.

The SIGGRAPH T-shirt features a simple Boba Fett helmet.

Lucasfilm's Future Home

August 14: A long-stalled agreement on developing a new campus at the site of a former Army hospital between the Presidio Trust and Lucasfilm is finally signed, two years late. Razing operations begin within 60 days and continue through the spring; construction continues through 2005.

Long before construction begins, Lucasfilm asks its artists to create a convincing previsualization of what the Presidio campus environment would look like once completed.

SEPTEMBER

John Williams visits the editorial team at Skywalker Ranch to begin exploring ideas that will become the Episode II score the following year.

A New Apprentice

Scholastic publishes *The Path to Truth*, the first in the 11-book *Jedi Quest* series by Jude Watson. A follow-up to her popular *Jedi Apprentice* books, the *Jedi Quest* series focuses on the adventures of a teenage Anakin and his Master, Obi-Wan.

The Jedi Quest cover features an Anakin image morphed from the likenesses of Jake Lloyd and Hayden Christensen.

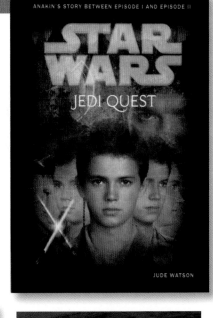

ANAKIN'S STORY BETWEEN EPISODE I AND EPISODE II

STAR WARS JEDI QUEST

JUDE WATSON

9-11-2001

September 11: Al Qaeda terrorists hijack commercial airliners to attack multiple targets in the US. Thousands die when two planes smash into the World Trade Center, destroying the iconic buildings. Another plane slams into the Pentagon, while a fourth crashes in a Pennsylvania field. The devastating attacks will profoundly affect culture, temperament, and the world for years to come.

September 12: The *Jedi Quest* comics series, a tie-in with the newly launched Scholastic book series, begins from Dark Horse Comics.

Anakin faces Darth Maul in a hallucination that occurs in Jedi Quest #1.

September 19: LucasArts and Sony Online Entertainment post a video preview of *Star Wars*: Galaxies game-play.

OCTOBER

The One To Own on DVD

October 15: At long last, a *Star Wars* movie arrives on DVD. Episode I is given the deluxe two-disc treatment with a pristine digital transfer and a trove of special bonus material. Included is an unblinking, feature-length behind-the-scenes documentary called "The Beginning." Lucas also has ILM complete visual effects on discarded sequences and presents them as deleted scenes. Episode I is the number-one selling DVD at Amazon.com for three months before release. It takes in $45 million in its first week, setting a new sales record. Consumers purchase an estimated 2.2 million units within the first two weeks.

The DVD has a retail price of $29.98 in the US.

A deleted scene from The Phantom Menace, *which appears as an Episode I DVD exclusive.*

iPod Arrives

October 23: Apple unveils the iPod, a portable music and data storage device with an eye-catching, minimalistic design. First-generation models come with five or 10 gigabyte capacities.

Shaken to the Core

October 30: Del Rey publishes the massive hardcover novel *Star by Star* by Troy Denning. This turning point in *The New Jedi Order* includes events such as Anakin Solo's death, Jacen Solo's capture, and the conquest of Coruscant by the Yuuzhan Vong.

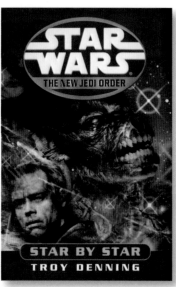

Cliff Nielsen's cover art for Star by Star

NOVEMBER

Once More With Ealing

November 1: Ealing Studios hosts a second round of Episode II pickup photography. Because Ewan McGregor shaved off his beard to film *Black Hawk Down*, he must wear a false one for his handful of scenes. Production wraps after five days of shooting.

Breathtaking

November 2: The first Episode II teaser trailer, titled "Breathing," is attached to Pixar's *Monsters, Inc.* A true tease, the 60-second trailer has no dialogue and only random images from the movie fading in and out of black accompanied by the sound of Darth Vader's mechanical wheezes.

The Episode II trailer, "Breathing", features scores of cloned boys (actor Daniel Logan).

November 9: An Episode II online exclusive trailer, called "Mystery," debuts on DVD.StarWars.com—a website reachable only through use of an Episode I DVD.

A Jedi Shall Not Know...

November 12: The Episode II advance theatrical poster is revealed online and in theaters. It showcases Anakin Skywalker and Padmé Amidala standing with their backs to each other, with the foreboding text: "A Jedi shall not know anger. Nor hatred. Nor love."

Star Wars fans are quick to theorize what the red lightsaber signifies—and point out that Anakin's Padawan braid is on the wrong side.

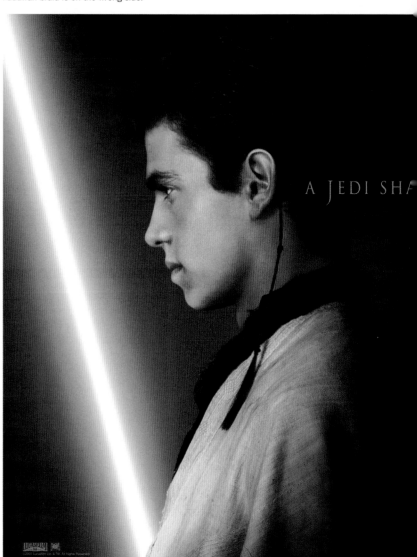

A JEDI SHA

Forbidden Love

November 15: The full Episode II teaser trailer, "Forbidden Love," debuts in theaters in front of *Harry Potter and the Sorcerer's Stone*, as well as on StarWars.com. This trailer's primary objective is to introduce Episode II as an unabashed love story, new territory for the Saga.

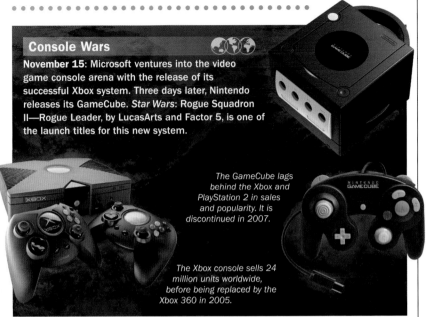

Console Wars

November 15: Microsoft ventures into the video game console arena with the release of its successful Xbox system. Three days later, Nintendo releases its GameCube. *Star Wars*: Rogue Squadron II—Rogue Leader, by LucasArts and Factor 5, is one of the launch titles for this new system.

The GameCube lags behind the Xbox and PlayStation 2 in sales and popularity. It is discontinued in 2007.

The Xbox console sells 24 million units worldwide, before being replaced by the Xbox 360 in 2005.

November 25: Episode I premieres on the FOX Television station, where it is presented as Thanksgiving Day family entertainment.

R2-D2: The Untold Story

November 25: StarWars.com begins posting the multi-part mockumentary, *R2-D2: Beneath the Dome*. Mischievously produced during the making of Episode II—and featuring all the key cast-members as well as surprising guests like Francis Ford Coppola and Richard Dreyfuss—the video tells the "true story" of R2-D2 as if he were a troubled actor climbing his way back to the top after sordid years spent in obscurity.

Photo-manipulation places R2-D2 in the thick of things, like New York City's Times Square.

November 27: Lucas's fantasy epic, *Willow*, directed by Ron Howard, is released on DVD and features, as bonus material, a full-length commentary by star Warwick Davis (also Wicket Warrick in *Return of the Jedi*).

DECEMBER

Auction for America

December 5: Lucasfilm takes part in the Auction for America fundraiser on eBay, donating a number of rare props from the Lucasfilm Archives and custom models from the ILM Model Shop to raise money for the September 11 Children's Fund.

ILM model makers pose with their one-of-a-kind creations.

December 20: StarWars.com announces that comic book Jedi Aayla Secura will appear as a live action character in *Attack of the Clones*.

ILM employee Amy Allen is cast as Aayla Secura.

...OT KNOW ANGER.

NOR HATRED.

NOR LOVE.

STAR WARS
ISODE II

2002

WITH THE IMPENDING May 16 release of Episode II, ILM starts the year completing a weekly average of 50 visual effects shots in order to deliver the movie's total of over 2,000 on time. The last two reels of the film include grueling challenges: For example, Geonosis is mostly a virtual environment that must be painstakingly created.

ILM chief grip Tom Cloutier looms large in the Geonosis arena miniature.

> "What I looked forward to the most in going back was the fact that I could deal with how the Empire was created."
>
> **George Lucas** *on the Episode II DVD commentary, 2002*

IN THE FINISHED PICTURE, an extensive miniature set crafted by the ILM Model Shop becomes an enormous execution arena populated by CG monsters and aliens. This explosive start to the Clone Wars includes thousands of troopers, droids, and vehicles in intricate battle scenarios. The toughest assignment, however, falls to Rob Coleman and his team of animators who have to turn the wizened Master Yoda into a nimble, acrobatic swordsman.

Computer graphics creature model supervisor Geoff Campbell (left) and animation director Rob Coleman tackle digitizing Yoda.

Chief pyrotechnics engineer Geoff Heron on the bluescreen stage shoot with the clone walker model.

JANUARY

January 2: Wizards of the Coast announces that Richard Garfield will create a new *Star Wars* Trading Card Game, effectively bringing an end to Decipher Inc.'s *Star Wars* CCG.

January 5: LucasArts releases the game *Star Wars*: Obi-Wan on Xbox.

January 7: At the MacWorld conference in San Francisco, animatics supervisor Daniel Gregoire shares the stage with Steve Jobs and demonstrates some of his work from Episode II.

Williams scores a Jedi Council scene.

January 18: John Williams and the London Symphony Orchestra begin scoring *Attack of the Clones* at Abbey Road Studios, London.

January 27: A&E airs the two-hour biography documentary, *George Lucas: Creating an Empire*. Three days later, Lucas appears on Carrie Fisher's *Conversations from the Edge* talk show on the Oxygen channel.

January 29: Hayden Christensen is nominated for the SAG award for Outstanding Performance by a Male Actor in a Supporting Role for his role as Sam Monroe in *Life as a House*.

Out of Sync Jedi

January 12: For weeks, an online rumor that the boy band N'Sync has shot a cameo appearance as Jedi Knights rankles fans. *Saturday Night Live* has fun with the idea with a sketch featuring "N'Sync" (the *SNL* cast) as all-singing and dancing Jedi, but ultimately N'Sync does not appear in Episode II.

⊙ PRESIDENT BUSH SIGNS THE NO CHILD LEFT BEHIN

FEBRUARY

February 4: The March-cover-dated issue of *Vanity Fair* features Episode II, with exclusive set and cast photography by Annie Leibovitz.

What's in a Name?
February 6: The ongoing investigation into corporate malfeasance by collapsed energy giant ENRON uncovers a host of dummy companies with familiar names: JEDI (Joint Energy Development Investment) LP; Chewco; Kenobe, Inc.; and Obi-1 Holdings LLC. Lucasfilm issues a statement that the use of the *Star Wars*–inspired names was done without its knowledge or permission.

The Enron logo in front of the Houston-based energy trading firm's headquarters

Thermal Mapping of Mars
February 19: NASA's *Mars Odyssey* space probe begins to map the surface of Mars from orbit using its thermal emission imaging system.

MARCH

HoloNet News, aka HNN would be the CNN of the Star Wars galaxy.

Countdown to Clones
March 10: The Episode II release trailer arrives, first appearing on FOX sandwiched between episodes of *Malcolm in the Middle* and *The X-Files*. The online version posted on StarWars.com includes a cryptic link to HOLONETNEWS.com. That website, stealthily launched a few days prior, appears as a news source from inside the *Star Wars* galaxy.

The release trailer is the first to show some of the complex computer-generated sequences of the Clone Wars courtesy of ILM.

March 10: LucasArts releases *Star Wars: Jedi Starfighter* for the PlayStation 2.

In-game action from Jedi Starfighter shows the gamer in a wider battle. The red circle indicates the next target.

March 12: Drew Struzan's Episode II release poster is unveiled in movie theaters and online.

E.T. Phones Back
March 22: *E.T.: The Extra-Terrestrial* is re-released to theaters for its 20th anniversary. ILM artists, led by Bill George, make a few effects changes at Spielberg's request. Digitally replacing federal agents' guns with walkie-talkies sparks some controversy, but the eventual DVD release includes both the original and the re-release versions.

March 26: The adventures of Jedi Kyle Katarn continue when LucasArts releases *Star Wars: Jedi Knight II—Jedi Outcast* for the PC.

ACT ☉ A LARGE PART OF ANTARCTICA'S ICE SHELF BREAKS OFF ☉ THE BRITISH QUEEN MOTHER DIES

The Prequel Trilogy expands the visual vocabulary of *Star Wars*, but fans pay special attention to the growing arsenal of lightsabers, the most iconic weapons in the Saga. Whereas several of the lightsabers for Episode IV were fashioned out of photographer flash clamps, the new generation of weapons is custom machined from scratch.

Preparing for Episode III, property master for the Prequel Trilogy Ty Teiger says, "Episode I was very tech-y, and the closer we get to Episode IV, we're having to sort of back off a bit. You can see it if you look at the lightsabers from Episode IV and you look at the lightsabers from Episode I. They're vastly apart as far as looks, so we're going to have to sort of marry that all together."

*Obi-Wan Kenobi's lightsaber
(Episode I)*

*Count Dooku's lightsaber
(Episode II)*

Yoda's lightsaber (Episode III)

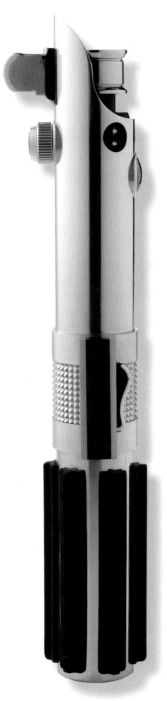

*Anakin Skywalker's lightsaber
(Episode III)*

*Darth Vader's lightsaber
(Episode III)*

*Luke Skywalker's lightsaber
(Episode VI)*

*Darth Maul's lightsaber
(Episode I)*

APRIL

Setting the Scene

Lucas begins imagining scenarios for Episode III, asking concept design supervisors Ryan Church and Erik Tiemens to develop seven new planets for a montage of Clone Wars battles.

Erik Tiemen's production painting depicts a crystallized iceberg world, the proposed site of a major Clone Wars battle.

RING PLANET
RYAN CHURCH
• 12 JUN 02
• SW3

Ryan Church's exploration of a world completely embraced by an artificial ring structure—a feat of engineering hubris and largesse fitting for the Neimoidian home world.

The Weapons of a Jedi Knight

April 2: A new licensee, Master Replicas, picks up where Icons left off and produces high-end *Star Wars* prop replicas—including blasters and lightsabers. In addition to its limited edition replica props, Master Replicas has a surprise hit with Force FX lightsabers that feature interactive sound effects.

Illuminated blades and rugged design make the Force FX lightsabers extremely popular.

April 4: *Variety* reports on half a dozen fans forming a line outside Grauman's Chinese Theater in Hollywood for *Attack of the Clones*, over a month before release.

April 12: Hayden Christensen and Natalie Portman appear on the cover of the magazine *Entertainment Weekly*.

Patricia C. Wrede's Episode II novelization published by Scholastic

Boba Fett on the Episode II soundtrack cover

Attack of the Collectibles

April 23: Episode II products hit retail. Following the admitted glut of Episode I merchandise, Lucas Licensing limits the number of products. Collectors nonetheless have much from which to choose. Sony Classical releases the soundtrack on CD. The Episode II novelization (by R.A. Salvatore) and the junior novel (by Patricia C. Wrede) both become bestsellers, the latter #1 on *The New York Times* list. Promotional partners such as Frito-Lay, Yoplait, and General Mills launch their tie-in products. In May, Kellogg's Episode II Cereal comes with a promotional life-sized clone trooper helmet.

A deluxe helping of cereal and clone trooper helmet, found only in Canada

DUTCH POLITICIAN PIM FORTUYN ASSASSINATED ⊙ QUEEN ELIZABETH II'S

MAY

Behind the Armor

May 1: Dark Horse Comics publishes issue #1 of *Jango Fett: Open Seasons*, a four-part comic series that tells the back story of the Episode II bounty hunters. Written by Haden Blackman with pencils by Ramón F. Bachs, the series is notable for shining a long overdue spotlight on Mandalorian culture. It also attempts to rectify a few missteps, explaining claims that Fett was once known as Jaster Mereel by creating the character of Mereel as someone in Jango's past.

The Open Seasons comic series explains how Jango Fett came to be in possession of his fabled Mandalorian suit of armor.

May 12: Once again foregoing celebrity red-carpet premieres, Episode II first arrives in 11 cities hosting screenings to benefit regional children's charities.

Samuel L. Jackson and Darth Vader at the Los Angeles charity premiere

When Clones Attack

May 16: Episode II opens in 3,161 theaters across North America and in almost 100 digitally projected presentations worldwide. Opening weekend ticket sales are $80 million and by the end of the month, it moves past the $200 mark. Its final gross is $302 million in North America and $635 million in worldwide box-office. (The Latin American release is pushed to later in the summer in deference to the soccer World Cup.)

Fans in stormtrooper gear gather for a Star Wars opening day at Grauman's Chinese Theatre.

Does Whatever a Spider Can

May 3: A long-awaited *Spider-Man* movie swings into theaters. Directed by Sam Raimi, the superhero movie from Sony has visual effects supervised by *Star Wars* veteran John Dykstra. It also has an enormous $114 million opening weekend.

The Spider-Man *release poster*

Ewan McGregor joins host Jay Leno on The Tonight Show.

Celebration II

May 3: Over 27,000 fans flock to Indianapolis for *Star Wars* Celebration II, an official fan convention held through May 5, with guests such as Hayden Christensen and emcee Anthony Daniels. Highlights include a digital theater showing of scenes from *Attack of the Clones*, a 25th anniversary *Star Wars* concert, and an exclusive action figure: Lucas as an X-wing pilot.

Costumed fans congregate in Indianapolis for Celebration II. A life-sized display of Hasbro packaging (left) allows fans to pose as a Star Wars action figure.

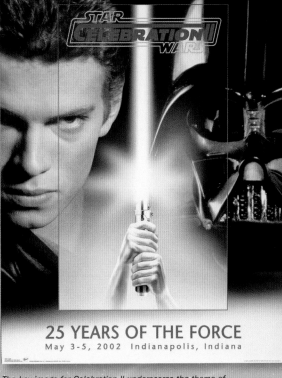

25 YEARS OF THE FORCE
May 3-5, 2002 Indianapolis, Indiana

The key image for Celebration II underscores the theme of connections uniting the image of Anakin and Darth Vader.

Water on Mars

May 28: The *Mars Odyssey* spacecraft finds enough frozen water underneath the Martian surface to fill Lake Michigan twice.

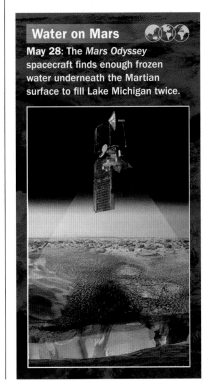

JUNE

The World Cup Runneth Over

Some parts of the world release *Attack of the Clones* slightly later than the worldwide May release date, because of the soccer World Cup. When the movie does open, it is accompanied by the "Beautiful Campaign" of unique outdoor posters—with text reflecting the soccer championship. The Brazilian Yoda poster, for example, calls out "Yodinho!" a reference to Ronaldinho. Other campaign posters include such sports-specific taglines as "Our Goalie Uses the Force," "Force-Force-Two," and "On Our Pitch, Size Matters Not."

YODINHO!

OUR GOALIE USES THE FORCE

June 2: Authorities seize approximately 5,000 bootleg copies of Episode II in Malaysia, days before the movie is to debut in Kuala Lumpur.

Never Tell Me The Odds

June 15: Near Earth Asteroid 2002 MN misses the planet Earth by a scant 120,000 kilometers (75,000 miles), a span equivalent to a third of the distance to the moon. The 79-meter (260-foot) long hunk of space rock would have devastated 2,000 square kilometers (772 square miles) on impact.

June 24: THX is spun off from Lucasfilm as its own company.

JULY

Mad About Episode II

MAD magazine #419 sports two Episode II covers, but the actual parody of the movie, *Star Bores: Epic Load II Attack of the Clowns* appears in September's issue #421. It chronicles the tale of young Mannequin Skystalker coming to terms with his love for PetMe AmaDilly, despite the admonitions of Jet-eye Knights like Oldie-Von Moldie, Lace Windows, and Master Yodel.

MAD *magazine recasts Alfred E. Neuman as Anakin Skywalker on both of its Episode II parody covers.*

The Beginning of the End

Lucas begins meeting weekly with concept design supervisors Church and Tiemens. In this early development of Episode III, the artists explore worlds that have long percolated in Lucas's imagination: A lava world, a sinkhole planet first envisioned by McQuarrie in 1976, and Kashyyyk, the arboreal home of the Wookiees. This creative process is charted by Lucasfilm nonfiction editor J.W. Rinzler, who will follow production throughout its three-year voyage in order to encapsulate it in later books.

Erik Tiemens sits in his sunny workspace on the third floor of the Main House at Skywalker Ranch, where the Prequel art department has worked since the mid-1990s.

Ryan Church's concept illustration depicts a tree-city on the Wookiee homeplanet of Kashyyyk.

Tiemens's early concept work exploring the hellish landscape of Mustafar.

Managing Magazines

July 2: The Fan Club and *Star Wars Insider* magazine change hands again, from Wizards of the Coast to Paizo Publishing. *Star Wars: Gamer* magazine, meanwhile, ceases publication after its 10th issue (having started in 2000).

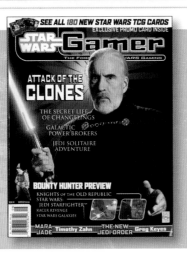

The final issue of Star Wars: Gamer magazine features Christopher Lee as Count Dooku on the cover.

July 3: Dark Horse begins reprinting the original run of Marvel *Star Wars* comics as thick trade paperback collections called *Star Wars: A Long Time Ago....*

July 13: Twentieth Century Fox Japan transmits Episode II digitally to five theaters via satellite. The encrypted data is stored locally at theater servers for projection at preset show times.

July 19: *K-19: The Widowmaker,* a drama about a doomed Russian nuclear submarine, is released. It stars Liam Neeson and Harrison Ford, allowing the heroes from the Prequel and Original Trilogies to meet face to face.

Two Russian captains are portrayed by Neeson and Ford in K-19.

AUGUST

On the Move

August 16: Outgrowing the available space at Skywalker Ranch, most of Lucasfilm—save for the chairman's office, JAK films, and Ranch Operations—moves down the road to Big Rock Ranch. The new headquarters are inspired by the architecture of Frank Lloyd Wright's Prairie-style.

Big Rock Ranch sits on a manmade lake in scenic Marin County.

August 22: The Episode I DVD wins four times in the fifth annual DVD awards. The awards are Viewer's Choice, Best Authoring, Best Menu Design, and Best Audio Presentation.

SEPTEMBER

September 4: Dark Horse begins publishing a new ongoing series, *Star Wars: Empire*, set in the Original Trilogy era.

The first story arc in Star Wars: Empire *is "Betrayal," written by Scott Allie.*

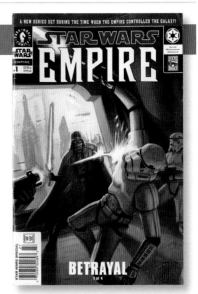

Magic Down Under

September 18: The traveling Magic of Myth exhibition leaves the US and arrives at The Powerhouse Museum in Sydney, Australia. To mark the opening, the city's Monorail dedicates a train to *Star Wars*.

With Episode II made in Sydney, locals are used to Star Wars *grabbing headlines.*

Where's the (Tiny) Fire?

September 19: Skywalker Ranch's remote location in the hills of Marin County necessitates its own fire department. Code 3 Collectibles, a new *Star Wars* licensee makes available a die-cast 1/32-scale replica of a Skywalker Ranch fire truck.

The truck boasts over 500 pieces in its construction and retails for $209.96.

Defining the Force

September 26: The words "Jedi," "dark side," and "the Force" find a place in the new edition of the Shorter Oxford English Dictionary. They are some of the 3,500 new words that have met the publisher's prerequisite of achieving a certain level of usage.

OCTOBER

Hasbro unveils its upcoming holiday action figures: a two-pack of R2-D2 with antlers and C-3PO dressed as Santa, based on an old Lucasfilm holiday card illustrated by Ralph McQuarrie (see p.72).

The Hasbro holiday figures come in a plastic bubble with a painted fireplace background on the cardback.

We'll Take The Blue One

October 2: Hasbro introduces the must-have toy of the holiday season: a fully automated, 38-centimeter (15-inch) tall, interactive R2-D2. The droid responds to over 40 voice commands, plays games, sings and dances, and even includes a drink holder.

The Interactive R2-D2 would be re-released in updated packaging in subsequent years.

Digital Trailblazing

October 5: Hollywood SMPTE & USC School of Cinema host an all-day seminar on digital cinema, with Rick McCallum one of the key speakers. He describes the trailblazing *Attack of the Clones* as a "hellish nightmare," but worth the effort. "Everything is developing fast," he says. "There's probably been more development in camera and lens technology in the last two years than in the previous 20."

October 16: Lucasfilm unveils a striking, illustrated poster for the forthcoming IMAX release of *Star Wars: Episode II Attack of the Clones*.

October 28: LucasArts releases Clone Wars for the Nintendo GameCube. Expanding beyond the Episode II Geonosis battle, the game follows a Separatist plot to harness an ancient superweapon.

Size Matters Not...Except in IMAX

October 31: Episode II returns to theaters as an IMAX experience. The digital image is enhanced through an IMAX process to fill an eight-storey screen and the sound is amped up to 12,000 watts of uncompressed signal. These early IMAX editions of feature films have to conform to projector specifications that will not allow for a film longer than two hours. As such, this version of Episode II is a unique edit not seen anywhere else. The big screen equals big business, as opening night adds $1.5 million to the theatrical gross.

Theatrical poster for the release of Attack of the Clones at the IMAX

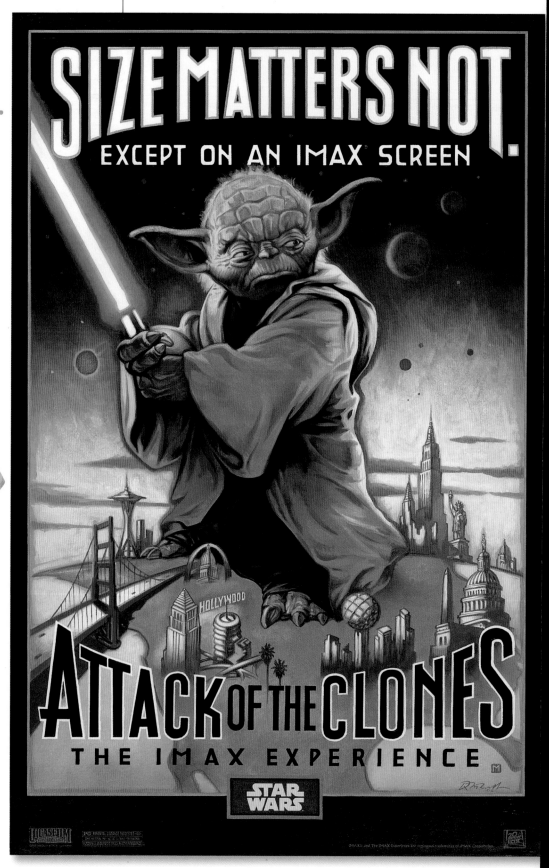

Number One in Toys

October 31: After a summer of fierce competition on retail shelves, *Star Wars* toys edge past *Spider-Man*, *Harry Potter*, and *Power Rangers* to emerge as the top-selling licensed brand of the year according to NPD Funworld, the research organization recognized as the leading source of toy industry data. Hasbro lightsabers sold more than double the huge numbers posted in 1999.

Darth Vader's Unleashed figure and a telescoping Obi-Wan lightsaber are some of the popular Hasbro releases this year.

NOVEMBER

November 1: The classic title *Bantha Tracks* is resurrected for a new fan-focused newsletter, the first issue handed out as a freebie at the IMAX premiere.

Reluctant Internet Star

November 8: Canadian teenager Ghyslain Raza video-records himself doing Jedi moves with a golfball retriever standing in as a double-bladed lightsaber. He inadvertently leaves the videotape behind, which is then spread by pranksters across the Internet the following spring. Branded as "The *Star Wars* Kid," Raza becomes a reluctant online sensation and pop culture punchline throughout 2002. As of today, the clip has had more than 900 million views.

November 11: Lucasfilm and MBNA (later acquired by Bank of America) team up to create a Galactic Rewards program and *Star Wars*-branded credit card.

November 15: LucasBooks announces its *Clone Wars* program, a branded effort across various publishers—adult novels, young reader books, and comics—to tell untold stories of the Saga.

November 28: A new tradition next to turkey and candied yams? *Star Wars: Episode I The Phantom Menace* again airs on FOX Television at Thanksgiving.

DECEMBER

Clone of the Attack

MAD magazine issue #424 features a full-color insert that redesigns the Episode II poster with George W. Bush, key members of his administration, and Saddam Hussein starring in *Gulf Wars: Clone of the Attack*. Intended as a withering satire of the march to war, pro-administration hawks actually love it. *MAD* magazine receives requests to provide issues to Defense Secretary Donald Rumsfeld and National Security Advisor Condoleeza Rice.

December 18: The *Star Wars* Fan Club brings back the classic Fan Club Kit, an annually mailed package of various flat goodies exclusive to members.

The Star Wars Fan Club membership card

December 26: The previous year's *R2-D2: Beneath the Dome* mockumentary is a Best Buy and Musicland store exclusive on DVD.

Be the Bounty Hunter

December 5: LucasArts releases the *Star Wars*: Bounty Hunter video game. Set between Episodes I and II, it explores how and why Jango Fett became the clone template, allowing gamers to play as the fearless bounty hunter.

An All Digital DVD

November 12: Episode II arrives in a widescreen two-disc DVD set, created directly from the digital source for unparalleled picture quality. Testament to the increasing popularity of DVD, Episode II is also released in a more neophyte-friendly "pan-and-scan" version. It is also the last *Star Wars* movie to come out on the moribund VHS format. The long-form documentary included on the DVD focuses on the creation of digital characters.

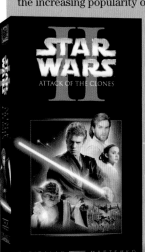

With the assumption that those who value widescreen presentation have made the switch to DVD, the VHS is released only in full frame.

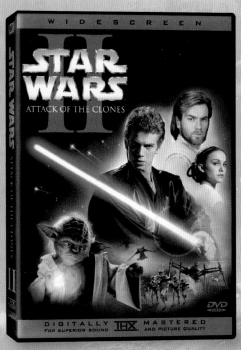

The widescreen and pan-and-scan sets are differentiated by a gold or blue color band on the DVD packaging.

RIKES FEAR IN THE DC AREA ✪ THE US DEPARTMENT OF HOMELAND SECURITY IS ESTABLISHED ✪

2003

ATTACK OF THE CLONES launched the first explosive volleys of the long anticipated Clone Wars, and audiences are hungry for more. Fortunately for avid fans, Lucasfilm has a curiosity for new types of storytelling. Teaming up with Cartoon Network, LFL taps Emmy Award-winning animation director Genndy Tartakovsky to produce a *Star Wars* micro-series.

An animated clone trooper from the 2-D Clone Wars animation series.

> "I actually cut a bunch of three-minute *Samurai Jack* clips just to see what we could do if we followed that type of pacing. You can actually do a lot."

Genndy Tartakovsky
Executive producer, Star Wars: Clone Wars

TARTAKOVSKY'S SERIES of three-minute-long programs telling original stories in traditional 2-D animation would do more than make the wait for Episode III bearable. Their critical and ratings success would prove the viability of animated *Star Wars* adventures on the small screen.

JANUARY

January 7: Lucas appears as himself on an episode of the NBC sitcom *Just Shoot Me*, starring Laura San Giacomo and David Spade.

January 27: Due to overwhelming demand, the Magic of Myth exhibit at the Powerhouse Museum in Sydney, Australia, is extended by three weeks.

January 31: Toymaker Hasbro agrees to pay Lucasfilm $200 million in cash and stock for the exclusive rights to make *Star Wars*-themed toys until 2018.

FEBRUARY

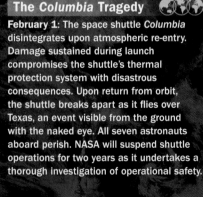

The *Columbia* Tragedy

February 1: The space shuttle *Columbia* disintegrates upon atmospheric re-entry. Damage sustained during launch compromises the shuttle's thermal protection system with disastrous consequences. Upon return from orbit, the shuttle breaks apart as it flies over Texas, an event visible from the ground with the naked eye. All seven astronauts aboard perish. NASA will suspend shuttle operations for two years as it undertakes a thorough investigation of operational safety.

The shuttle launches on January 16 for its 28th flight.

February 6: American Cinematheque begins a week-long celebratory tribute to ILM and George Lucas at the Egyptian Theater in Hollywood. Lucas attends the launch of the event.

February 11: John Knoll, Pablo Helman, Rob Coleman, and Ben Snow are nominated for the Best Visual Effects Academy Award® for Episode II, though *The Lord of the Rings: The Two Towers* will win.

Small Screen *Wars*

February 20: Lucasfilm and Cartoon Network announce the *Star Wars: Clone Wars* micro-series for the fall television season. "Genndy Tartakovsky and the team at Cartoon Network are tops in their field," says Howard Roffman, president of Lucas Licensing. "Their work on *Samurai Jack* shows that they can tell an epic story in a unique way, lavishing equal attention on dramatic battle scenes as well as dramatic development of the characters."

A long-time Star Wars fan, Genndy Tartakovsky is eager to lead his animation crew into a galaxy far, far away.

⊕ **LAST SIGNAL RECEIVED FROM** *PIONEER 10* ⊕ **WORLDWIDE ANTI-WAR PROTESTS** ⊕ **COALITION**

Clone Wars in Comics

February 26: LucasBooks begins filling in the Clone Wars era, first through Dark Horse Comics. The lightsaber-wielding villainess Asajj Ventress is introduced in *Jedi: Mace Windu*, a one-shot comic. Meanwhile, in the monthly *Star Wars: Republic* series, the Separatists target the Republic clone-hatcheries in the 64-page *The Defense of Kamino*.

Concept art by Dermot Power of a female Sith for Episode II

Based on the unused Episode II concept art, Asajj Ventress would prove to be a long-lasting and popular villain.

MARCH

Bridging the Saga

March 4: Del Rey publishes *Tatooine Ghost* by Troy Denning. Taking place after *Return of the Jedi*, the novel connects Prequel and Original Trilogy characters: Leia Organa Solo uncovers stories of young Anakin's early life with his mother, Shmi, as they lived as slaves on Tatooine.

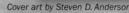

Cover art by Steven D. Anderson

The Great Han Solo Coat Debate

March 11: Unable to decide what is the correct color of Han's Hoth outfit due to conflicting reference photography, Hasbro produces the action figure in two versions: one with a blue coat and another with a brown coat.

Hasbro makes light of the "controversy" with this print ad, which cagily refuses to settle the coat dispute.

Collectors can choose their preferred coat color: blue, which echoes the original Han on Hoth 1980 action figure (see p.85), or brown, which matches most costume reference photography.

On-set photography of Harrison Ford as Han wearing the brown coat (Chewbacca's coat is indisputably brown).

FORCES INVADE IRAQ ⊕ SARS CASE IN VIETNAM LEADS TO GLOBAL ALERT ⊕ CRISIS IN DARFUR ⊕

APRIL

April 7: The latest digital cameras are ready for Episode III, with greater picture resolution and "undercranking" ability allowing for capture rates from one to 24 frames per second.

April 22: The Xbox version of *Star Wars*: Clone Wars by LucasArts and Pandemic Studios is released, supporting multiplayer online play via Xbox Live.

Chewie, Come Home

April 23: StarWars.com announces that Peter Mayhew will return for Episode III. "I'm delighted to return as Chewbacca," says Mayhew. "I think his re-appearance in this film is a fitting way to tie the whole Saga together, especially for Wookiee fans." Word of the return of this beloved character gets picked up worldwide by international media.

Peter Mayhew's yak-hair costume from the original trilogy is updated with a new, more durable, acrylic fiber costume and features an articulated mask with radio-controlled facial servos.

MAY

Guest Director

As Episode III continues its preproduction phase, animatics supervisor Dan Gregoire collaborates with Steven Spielberg to previsualize key action sequences, such as the duel on Mustafar and the Utapau chase involving General Grievous and Obi-Wan Kenobi. Spielberg explores these scenes for Lucas partly as a favor and partly to acquire experience with the latest previsualization methods, a tool he would employ extensively in the making of *War of the Worlds*.

The animatic cut of the chase through Utapau is originally much longer, and features audacious vehicle-related stunts worthy of an Indiana Jones movie—with good reason given that the director is Steven Spielberg.

A New Animation Studio

May 12: After the collapse of several studio-funded animation projects that were to be undertaken by ILM—including *Frankenstein* and *Curious George*—Lucas launches his own studio to develop computer-animated features and television. Lucasfilm Animation starts up at the Point Richmond Tech Center, in the San Francisco East Bay, a facility that at one time housed Pixar.

LUCASFILM ANIMATION
A LUCASFILM COMPANY

JUNE

A Winner, Yoda Is

June 2: For his duel with Dooku, Yoda wins an MTV Movie Award for Best Fight. A newly animated Yoda voiced by Frank Oz accepts the award. "Promise myself, cry I would not," says the visibly moved Jedi Master. In his acceptance speech, he thanks Christopher Lee, George Lucas, Samuel L. Jackson, Natalie Portman, Watto, Chewie, Taun We, Vin Diesel, R2-D2, C-3PO, Björk, Greedo, Steve Guttenberg, Ki-Adi-Mundi, Lama Su, Queen Latifah, and all the younglings at MTV.

Heart of Dark Side

June 3: Del Rey publishes *Shatterpoint* by Matthew Stover, the first of its Clone Wars-era novels. The novel follows Mace Windu's journey into the violent jungles of his homeworld to track down a fellow Jedi Master who has apparently gone rogue. With stark depictions of wartime violence, the book is heavily influenced by Joseph Conrad's *Heart of Darkness* and its associated movie *Apocalypse Now*.

Steven D. Anderson's cover to Shatterpoint features Mace Windu, while Jedi Master Depa Billaba is tucked into the background scenery.

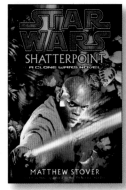

99% OF THE HUMAN GENOME MAPPED TO 99.99% ACCURACY ⊕ GEORGE W. BUSH PREMATUR

Make the Jump

June 5: StarWars.com unveils Hyperspace, a paid subscription service promising exclusive online content. The main benefit of its initial $19.95 annual fee is unprecedented access to the making of Episode III. Editor Pablo Hidalgo is "embedded" with the crew in Sydney and files daily reports from the set, anticipating the rise of movie production blogs. He also facilitates online fan chats with cast and crew, and plants a live webcam in the studio, letting fans peek at the production in progress. The first year of Hyperspace generates $1 million in revenue for Lucas Online.

Pablo Hidalgo (left) moderates an online chat between Star Wars fans and producer Rick McCallum from the production offices of Episode III in Fox Studios, Sydney.

Arrival Down Under

June 16: Lucas arrives on the Episode III set at Fox Studios in Sydney. He tours the seven active sound stages to see the sets under construction, and checks in with various department heads as the movie nears its production start date.

Lucas reviews the work of the Creature Shop with supervisors Rebecca Hunt and Dave Elsey.

June 18: Bruce Spence is announced as being in Episode III. With roles in *The Matrix: Revolutions*, *The Return of the King*, and *Mad Max Beyond Thunderdome*, Spence has featured in several epic trilogy conclusions.

Lucas prepares for a shoot on a greenscreen-lined Utapau landing platform set with Bruce Spence (Tion Medon).

The Final Journey Begins

June 30: The first day of principal photography on Episode III consists of scenes from early in the movie, when Obi-Wan Kenobi (Ewan McGregor), Anakin Skywalker (Hayden Christensen), and R2-D2, make their way through General Grievous's enormous star cruiser. The first productive day results in a total of 48 setups and 2 minutes, 28 seconds of script. At one point late in the day, Lucas tilts the Hyperspace webcam toward a monitor with Christensen's Episode III look, revealing it to the Internet.

Lucas and Hayden Christensen (Anakin Skywalker) between takes on the Separatist cruiser turbolift set on the first day of shooting Episode III.

Star Wars is one of the biggest merchandising success stories of all time, licensing everything from this book to pasta shapes. But it was not foreseen: Back in 1977, few properties were licensed and movies were not considered to have enough staying power for merchandise. It all began for *Star Wars* when toy manufacturer Kenner signed up — just a month before the release of the first movie—to produce a board game and a handful of action figures. By 1985, Kenner had sold over 250 million figures.

These days, you can eat, drink, play, read, and bathe *Star Wars*. And far from just wearing the T-shirt, you can wear the jewelry, the pajamas, the slippers, and the Yoda ears—and so can your dog. Yoda has been an enduring favorite: Over the years, he has been re-created in, among other things, driftwood, felt, wool, soap, chocolate, Play-Doh, and 24-karat gold. Here are just a few of the many Yoda-inspired creations out there.

Jedi Master Yoda, LEGO® Ultimate Collector Set, 2002

Plush Yoda on "Hover Chair," Clinton Cards, UK, 2005

Yoda the Jedi Master *board game, Kenner, 1981*

Bubble Bath and Shampoo Soakies, Omni Cosmetics, US, 1981

Yoda Plush Holiday Ornament,
Kurt S. Adler, 2005

Diet Pepsi Twist, Japan, 2005

Yoda Mouse Pad, Encore, 2005

Yoda Pet Costume (headpiece and
jumpsuit), Rubie's Costume Co., 2005

41-cm (16-in) Yoda Plush Doll, Tomy,
Japan, 2003

Limoges Porcelain Miniature Box, Atelier de Limoges,
France, 1998. Written inside is, "Try not. Do. Or do not.
There is no try."

Ceramic Candle Holder,
Sigma, 1983

ST5220 Mild-Formula Bubble Bath,
Cosrich Group Inc., 2005

Yoda Maquette, Attakus, France, 2000

JULY

Hasbro offers a retail toy pack-in booklet called *Star Wars: Clone Wars Short Story Collection*, featuring works by science-fiction authors Matthew Stover, Jude Watson, and Timothy Zahn.

A Galaxy Not Far Away....

July 7: LucasArts and Sony Online Entertainment launch the massively multiplayer online game *Star Wars: Galaxies—An Empire Divided*. In the first week, 125,000 customers sign up to live out a virtual life in the *Star Wars* universe. Players can choose from 10 species, and can explore 10 worlds: Tatooine, Corellia, Naboo, Talus, Rori, Dantooine, Lok, Yavin 4, Dathomir, and Endor's forest moon.

Star Wars: Galaxies will eventually expand its gameplay with interstellar combat and iconic starships.

July 9: Disney's big-budget movie *Pirates of the Caribbean: The Curse of the Black Pearl* is released and is a box office hit. *Star Wars* alumnus John Knoll supervises the thousand-plus ILM effects.

South of the Border

July 12: Mexico City hosts the first ever *Star Wars* Collectors Convention, sanctioned by Lucasfilm and organized by the Official *Star Wars* Fan Club in Mexico. A key collectible souvenir of the event is a set of badges based on vintage action figures.

A sampling of the Star Wars Collectors Convention badges, featuring Darth Vader, a vinyl-caped Jawa, and an original stormtrooper from the first assortment of vintage action figures.

Ancient Knights

July 15: LucasArts and BioWare release *Star Wars: Knights of the Old Republic* for the Xbox. Set in an ancient time when the Jedi and Sith were numerous, the game follows a group of heroes trying to thwart the plans of Darth Malak and the mysterious Darth Revan. Sharp writing, strong characterizations and vocal performances, and a stunning twist in the story cause Knights of the Old Republic to become a fan favorite. It wins Game of the Year awards from the Game Developers Choice Awards and BAFTA Games Awards, and Interactive Achievement awards for best console RPG and best computer RPG.

The player controls assassin droid HK-47 near the Jedi enclave on the plains of Dantooine.

July 17: *Pink Five*, a short about an X-wing pilot named Stacey, wins the George Lucas Select Award at the *Star Wars* Fan Film Awards at the San Diego Comic-Con International.

The Battle of Yavin is shown from Stacey's valley-girl point of view.

You Pick the Droid

July 31: Lucas allows subscribers to Hyperspace on StarWars.com to choose the paint scheme of Obi-Wan Kenobi's new astromech droid R4-G9 in Episode III. Four designs developed by the droid shop crew are posted on StarWars.com, and users select the brass-and-copper color scheme.

Brassy R4-G9, as he's depicted in the Star Wars: The Clone Wars animation

AUGUST

August 14: A period of water-tank shooting begins in Stage 2 at Fox Studios Australia for a fuel tank sequence that would ultimately be cut.

August 21: Hyperspace subscriber Amy Somensky wins a trip to the Episode III set through a writing contest. She guest-writes the August 25 Set Diary.

Eye in the Sky 🌎

August 25: A Delta II rocket launches from Cape Canaveral, carrying into orbit the Spitzer Space Telescope. The infrared space observatory begins capturing spectacular imagery of distant interstellar objects, including, in 2005, extrasolar planets.

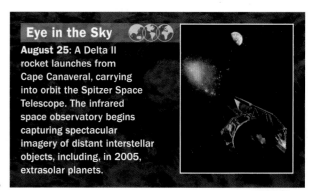

SEPTEMBER

Lord Vader Rises

September 1: A crowd gathers around Stage 4 in Sydney. "They should have sold tickets for this," jokes production designer Gavin Bocquet. Crew members from various departments—not all of them needed for the shoot— mill about, waiting. At 5:48 p.m., Hayden Christensen dons the dark armor of Darth Vader for his first take as the fully transformed Sith Lord. On a minimal set that includes a mechanical floor and the reclining bed of a rehabilitation chamber, Darth Vader bursts free of his shackles when Darth Sidious tells him the heartbreaking news that Padmé Amidala is dead.

An agonized Darth Vader (Hayden Christensen) is about to break free of his restraints while an amused Darth Sidious (Ian McDiarmid) watches.

September 16: *Star Wars*: Jedi Knight—Jedi Academy, the new installment in the first-person shooter saga, this time driven by the Quake III engine, is released for the PC.

It's a Wrap

September 17: Principal photography on Episode III wraps up at 6:42 p.m. with scene V177G: Darth Vader (Hayden Christensen), Darth Sidious (Ian McDiarmid), and Governor Tarkin (Wayne Pygram) stand on the bridge of a Star Destroyer. To date, the production has completed 144 scenes in 2,883 setups. Only 41 scripted scenes remain, but as always, the evolving edit may create new scenes needing additional photography to be scheduled later in production.

STAR WARS

JEDI KNIGHT: JEDI ACADEMY

ACTIVISION.

OCTOBER

Already a proven master of cinematic action, Yoda sees more combat time in Episode III.

Cutting Episode III

With the stateside return of Lucas, Episode III enters into the lengthy postproduction phase. During principal photography, editors Roger Barton and Ben Burtt have been assembling footage into a rough edit, which undergoes continual refinement. (The Hyperspace webcam is set up in Burtt's editorial station for a spell.) Lucas, meanwhile, hands over 98 Yoda shots to Rob Coleman's animation team.

Hasbro Gets to the Points

October 1: For years, Hasbro had been printing "Jedi Master Points" on its toy packaging, and yet offered no real way of redeeming them. Finally, the toy maker launches a 13-week online auction of toys and collectibles—with the printed cardboard points serving as currency.

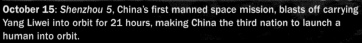

First for China

October 15: *Shenzhou 5*, China's first manned space mission, blasts off carrying Yang Liwei into orbit for 21 hours, making China the third nation to launch a human into orbit.

Yang Liwei completes 14 orbits and successfully lands back in China on October 16.

Yoda Yule

October 20: Hasbro once again produces an action figure based on an old Lucasfilm holiday card illustrated by Ralph McQuarrie: Yoda dressed as Santa Claus. The figure is first made available to members of the *Star Wars* Fan Club and then to general consumers.

The Holiday Yoda figure originally sells for $12.95.

The Yoda figure includes a re-creation of the 1981 Lucasfilm holiday card that inspired the toy (see p.72).

If Adventure Has a DVD...

October 21: The *Indiana Jones* trilogy arrives on DVD. Lucasfilm tasks the firm Lowry Digital to painstakingly restore the picture quality of the movies, a process that it will later apply to the *Star Wars* trilogy. Aside from the three movies, *Raiders of the Lost Ark*, *Indiana Jones and the Temple of Doom*, and *Indiana Jones and the Last Crusade*, the set includes a feature-length documentary produced by Laurent Bouzereau, which interviews key cast and crew members. Additional bonus material includes featurettes on the stunts, sound, music, and visual effects of *Indiana Jones*.

The box set is available in both widescreen and pan-and-scan editions.

The remastered DVDs are the best Indy has looked in home entertainment.

NOVEMBER

Epic Conclusion

November 4: Del Rey publishes *The Unifying Force* by James Luceno, the 19th and final book of the epic *The New Jedi Order* series. The hardcover comes bundled with a CD-ROM that includes an electronic version of the first book in the series, *Vector Prime*.

November 5: *The Matrix: Revolutions* debuts in theaters, bringing an end to the *Matrix* trilogy, which started alongside the Prequel Trilogy.

LAST COMMERCIAL CONCORDE FLIGHT ⊙ CAR BOMB ATTACKS IN ISTANBUL ⊙ GEORGIA'S ROS

Three-Minute Epics

November 7: The *Star Wars: Clone Wars* micro-series airs on Cartoon Network. The first three-minute shorts chronicle the adventures of Obi-Wan Kenobi and Anakin Skywalker as they attempt to route the Separatists on Muunilinst. Side stories include an underwater battle with Kit Fisto leading Mon Calamari Knights against the Quarren Isolationist League, and Count Dooku's recruitment of Asajj Ventress from a gladiatorial arena. Genndy Tartakovsky and his creative team infuse the shorts with a cinematic scale and nonstop conflict. Reviews and ratings are positive.

Mat Lucas provides the voice for Anakin Skywalker in Star Wars: Clone Wars, as well as for the video games Clone Wars, Episode III—Revenge of the Sith, and Battlefront II.

November 9: Mark Hamill provides the voice of Luke Skywalker in an episode of the FOX animated series *Family Guy*, "When You Wish Upon a Weinstein."

November 9: Actor Art Carney, seen in *The Star Wars Holiday Special*, passes away.

DECEMBER

December 8: A re-imagined *Battlestar Galactica* mini-series is broadcast on the Sci-Fi network, drawing critical acclaim and warranting a full series.

December 17: *The Lord of the Rings* movie trilogy is complete with the release of *The Return of the King*.

Making Episode III

December 23: The Episode III web documentary series begins months earlier than the previous incarnations—an early debut facilitated by Hyperspace. Documentary director Tippy Bushkin captures many hours of footage throughout the production of the final prequel, and the Lucasfilm Documentary team cuts together a total of 18 webdocs, covering such topics as General Grievous's art design, costume design, HD video production, pickups and reshoots, and actors.

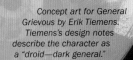

Actor Ian McDiarmid in full make-up as Sith Lord Darth Sidious. McDiarmid says, "When you're playing a character of solid blackness, that in itself is very interesting."

Concept art for General Grievous by Erik Tiemens. Tiemens's design notes describe the character as a "droid—dark general."

December 26: Hayden Christensen plays Stephen Glass, the amoral *New Republic* reporter, in the acclaimed feature film *Shattered Glass*, based on a true story.

Hayden Christensen as Stephen Glass, with Chloe Sevigny and Melanie Lynskey

2004

THE FOUR-DISC boxed set of the original *Star Wars* trilogy arrives on DVD. It includes digitally refurbished versions of Episodes IV, V, and VI, painstakingly cleaned up by Lowry Digital. The frame-by-frame restoration prompts Lucas to once again make a handful of changes.

Star Wars Original Trilogy DVD boxed set

"I have to be true to my vision, which is 30 years old, but I have to be true to it."

George Lucas
on the Prequel Trilogy

CHANGES made to the Original Trilogy films include Hayden Christensen replacing Sebastian Shaw as the spectral Anakin Skywalker in *Jedi* and a new CG Jabba the Hutt replacing the creaky 1997 version in *A New Hope*. The foundation of the bonus disc is a two-and-a-half-hour documentary by Kevin Burns, titled *Empire of Dreams*, featuring interviews with over 40 cast and crew members from the Original *Star Wars* Trilogy.

JANUARY

Spirit Mars Rover

January 4: *Spirit*, one of two rovers deposited on Mars, touches down. In three weeks, its sibling, *Opportunity*, will land on the opposite side of the red planet.

Concept artwork for the opening space battle of Revenge of the Sith, by Ryan Church

Episode III Opening Scene

January 8: Lucas hands over the opening Episode III battle sequence—coded OSB—to ILM. Painstakingly mapped out in animatics, the sequence includes a lengthy and continuous opening shot. John Knoll's digital artists work to create the biggest space battle ever seen in *Star Wars*.

⊙ FACEBOOK IS FOUNDED ⊕ SAN FRANCISCO ISSUES MARRIAGE LICENSES TO SAME-SEX COUPLE

Comic Book: The Movie

January 27: Mark Hamill's directorial debut, *Comic Book: The Movie*—a mockumentary about comic books and their fans—arrives on DVD.

FEBRUARY

Survivor's Quest

February 3: *Survivor's Quest* marks Timothy Zahn's return to the Expanded Universe. The Del Rey hardcover release features Luke Skywalker and Mara Jade investigating the ill-fated *Outbound Flight* exploratory mission, and establishes the fan-coined 501st Legion as a presence in the *Star Wars* galaxy.

Lucas's Lifetime

February 18: James Cameron presents Lucas with the first-ever Lifetime Achievement Award from the Visual Effects Society at the Hollywood Palladium.

MARCH

Clone Wars Continue

March 26: The next 10 installments of the *Star Wars: Clone Wars* micro-series begin airing on Cartoon Network. Season two's story arc features Mace Windu fighting single-handedly against a droid army on Dantooine; Padmé Amidala versus chameleon droids on the icy planet Ilum; Anakin dueling Asajj Ventress on Yavin 4; and a seven-minute finale that introduces the Episode III villain, General Grievous.

Obi-Wan Kenobi, Mace Windu, Yoda, and Anakin Skywalker have 2-D illustrated adventures.

APRIL

Release Date Announced

April 5: StarWars.com announces the Episode III release date: a mostly worldwide rollout on May 19, 2005, with the exception of Japan, which will release the movie in July 2005.

Big Miniatures

Stage photography begins for some of the largest *Sith* miniatures built by the ILM Model Shop led by Brian Gernand. These huge constructs include a Kashyyyk tree and the Utapau sinkhole. Many are photographed and scanned using the Zenviro process, which turns the models into virtual digital environments.

Modelmakers Phil Brotherton, Stephan Dupuis, and Daren Rabinovitch with the Wookiee tree miniature

Long Way Round

April 14: Ewan McGregor begins a motorcycle tour around the world with Charley Boorman, from New York to London. Their 19,000-mile (30,000-kilometer) journey through Europe and Asia will become the documentary series *Long Way Round*.

StarWarsShop.com

April 14: StarWars.com launches StarWarsShop, an in-house official store managed by Lucasfilm for online consumers. The store features an extensive collection of *Star Wars* collectibles and a number of exclusives available only from Lucasfilm.

Fan Club

April 28: The *Star Wars* Fan Club once again undergoes changes. The production of *Star Wars Insider* magazine moves from Paizo Publishing to IDG Entertainment and subscription to the magazine is coupled to the Hyperspace premium offering on StarWars.com.

Issue #77 is the first Star Wars Insider to be published by IDG.

MAY

Wookiee War

May 17: ILM animation supervisor Rob Coleman serves as director for a two-day live-action shoot of Wookiee performers in Sydney. The Wookiees are costumed Australian and New Zealand locals of towering height, shot against bluescreen to gather elements for the eventual Kashyyyk battle.

JULY

Conquering Comic-Con

July 21: Lucasfilm boasts a huge presence at San Diego Comic-Con International, including a *Star Wars* pavilion on the exhibit hall floor. On July 24, Steve Sansweet hosts a presentation featuring guests Rick McCallum and Hayden Christensen. In front of thousands of fans, Sansweet reveals the title of Episode III—*Revenge of the Sith*—and displays a T-shirt sporting the logo—a shirt whose availability on the pavilion floor sparks a fan stampede.

AUGUST

Animation Studio

August 3: Lucasfilm announces it will open an animation studio in Singapore to complement its Stateside studio in the creation of digital content for television, movies, and games.

Pick-up Photography

August 23: Episode III pick-up photography begins at Shepperton Studios outside of London. The Hyperspace webcam is there to capture the mostly bluescreen and greenscreen shooting.

September 13: The George Lucas Educational Foundation (GLEF) begins publishing *Edutopia* magazine, promoting positive change in education. The magazine will present a continual flow of fresh ideas and inspiring success stories.

SEPTEMBER

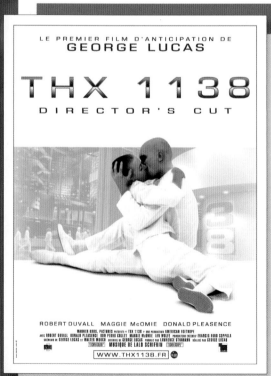

THX 1138 Re-Release

September 10: George Lucas and Warner Bros. re-release *THX 1138* as a director's cut in 20 select theatrical markets, and then on DVD on September 14. The film has undergone an extensive restoration, with several new ILM visual effects shots added to it.

French poster for THX 1138's re-release

Emmy

September 12: The *Star Wars: Clone Wars* micro-series wins an Emmy Award for Outstanding Animated Program.

Sky Captain

September 17: *Sky Captain and the World of Tomorrow* is released theatrically. A throwback to 1930s-style adventure serial films, it is executed with cutting edge digital cinematography techniques. *Star Wars* is a key influence on the design and tone of the movie.

Set in a robot-filled alternative 1939, Sky Captain and the World of Tomorrow sees Joe Sullivan (Jude Law) and Polly Perkins (Gwyneth Paltrow) investigate the mysterious Dr. Totenkopf with the help of Franky Cook (Angelina Jolie).

Battlefront

September 21: LucasArts and Pandemic Studios release *Star Wars*: Battlefront—based around the *Star Wars* battles—for Xbox, PlayStation 2, and PC gaming.

Trilogy Released

September 21: The Original Trilogy arrives on DVD in stores. It becomes the focus of a huge push of related products, such as Original Trilogy-branded action figures from Hasbro and the *Star Wars*: Battlefront video game. Shattering all records for entertainment franchise spending in a single day, fans around the world spend more than $115,000,000. Record-breaking sales will continue over the coming week as the DVDs and game debut internationally.

OCTOBER

Future of *Star Wars*

Lucasfilm Animation leaves its Point Richmond facility, moving to Skywalker Ranch. At this year's MIPCOM, the annual Cannes-based media content trade show, Lucasfilm representatives begin expressing their interest in moving into television.

The official tie-in to the exciting new *Star Wars* video game!
STAR WARS
REPUBLIC COMMANDO
HARD CONTACT
KAREN TRAVISS

Hard Contact

October 26: The *Republic Commando* novel series starts with the publication of *Hard Contact* by Karen Traviss.

Lightspeed Jump

October 27: The first expansion for *Star Wars*: Galaxies, the game Jump to Lightspeed, arrives, enhancing play by adding starship travel and combat.

The connection between Anakin and Darth Vader grows stronger, as hinted in the Episode III teaser poster.

Teaser Poster

October 28: The build-up of anticipation over the forthcoming Episode III continues with the release of a teaser poster that appears both in theaters and online. The poster depicts an intense Anakin Skywalker whose cape suggests the image of Darth Vader's mask.

NOVEMBER

George Bush Victory

November 2: George Bush defeats Democratic candidate John Kerry and is re-elected for a second term as US President.

Teaser Trailer

November 5: The *Sith* teaser trailer arrives in theaters and online. It is built around old Obi-Wan Kenobi's recollections of Anakin as told in Episode IV.

Polar Express

November 10: In June, former *Star Wars* concept design supervisor Doug Chiang had formed Iceblink Studios, developing concept art for a variety of projects, including collaborations with Robert Zemeckis and ImageMovers. In November, *The Polar Express* arrives in theaters, directed by Zemeckis and branded as a glimpse into the future of cinema due to its revolutionary process. Actors adorned with tracking dots are captured by specialized cameras, and their expressions and body language are then married to digital character models. This method gives the director and actors time to focus on performance. Later, Zemeckis constructs elaborate virtual camera shots and environments in the computer-generated picture. (Zemeckis's company is purchased by the Walt Disney Company in 2007, and shut down in 2010.)

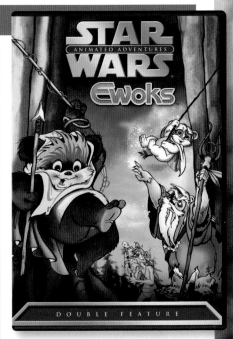

STAR WARS
ANIMATED ADVENTURES
Ewoks
DOUBLE FEATURE

Ewoks and *Droids* on DVD

November 23: Animated episodes of *Ewoks* and *Droids* are released as DVD movies, as are the *Ewoks* live-action TV movies.

DECEMBER

Closer

December 3: Natalie Portman stars in Mike Nichols's *Closer*. She would win a Golden Globe for Best Supporting Actress, and earn Academy Award® and BAFTA nominations.

Sith Lords

December 6: *Star Wars*: Knights of the Old Republic II—The Sith Lords, a follow-up to last year's acclaimed game, is released by LucasArts and Obsidian Entertainment for the Xbox.

2005

STAR WARS FANS are swept up in a bittersweet moment of triumph and reflection as the *Star Wars* Saga at long last concludes. For seemingly the last time, they don robes and armor and gather at movie theaters worldwide to cheer as the *Star Wars* logo recedes into infinity on the big screen.

Star Wars characters hit Sydney's streets to celebrate the release of Episode III.

"The fact that I actually did finish it and the world is still here and I'm still alive is the most gratification."

George Lucas
on completing the sixth and final Star Wars film

REVENGE OF THE SITH proves to be a colossal hit, becoming the highest grossing movie of the year with $848 million in worldwide box office sales. The movie also enjoys great reviews, drawing praise even from critics who may have not connected with the previous prequels. A.O. Scott of *The New York Times* makes the claim, "It's better than [the original] *Star Wars*."

JANUARY

The last of only four pick-up scenes on the final day of shooting consists of Hayden Christensen running across a bluescreen stage, fittingly at Elstree Studios—where it all began in 1976.

The Saga Unfolds

January 4: *Vanity Fair* once again spotlights *Star Wars* through an interview with Lucas and photography of cast and crew by Annie Leibovitz. Setting this commemorative issue apart is a fold-out cover with Lucas alongside actors and characters from all six movies.

Action One Last Time

January 31: Lucas calls "Action" for the last day of Episode III pick-ups at Elstree Studios—inside the same stage used for Aunt Beru's kitchen and several starship cockpits back in 1976. By early afternoon, the crew is packing up and heading out.

FEBRUARY

Tsunami Relief

February 3: Maverix Animation Studio auctions off artwork by the Episode III concept team while MTV Networks auction off tickets to a premiere at Skywalker Ranch to raise funds for survivors of the Indian Ocean tsunami disaster in late 2004.

Broadcast Yourself 🌐🌐🌐

February 15: Youtube.com is founded and begins "broadcasting," forever changing the Internet and the world. Networks, studios, and other content creators struggle with the ramifications of copyright and trademark protection in this new arena, while budding storytellers embrace this powerful new tool.

February 28: LucasArts amps up first-person combat with innovative squad interaction play in the game *Star Wars*: Republic Commando, a release for Xbox and Windows.

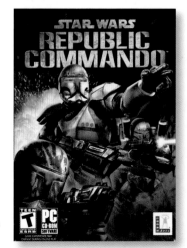

🌐 A 66-YEAR-OLD WOMAN GIVES BIRTH IN ROMANIA 🌐 US GOVERNMENT

MARCH

March 1: Abrams Books publishes *The Cinema of George Lucas* by Marcus Hearn, a lavish hardcover examining Lucas's career from avant-garde film student to head of a creative empire.

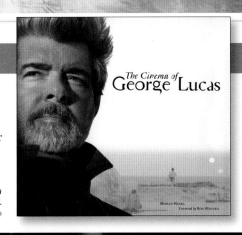

The Cinema of George Lucas contains a foreword by fellow director Ron Howard.

March 8: The Episode III release poster is unveiled online and in theaters.

Drew Struzan has designed the posters for all three Prequel movies.

March 10: The full Episode III release trailer debuts on television during *The OC*. It is followed by an online release and then theatrically, the following day, with the animated feature *Robots*.

The Future at ShoWest

March 17: *Star Wars* wields a powerful presence at the annual motion-picture industry convention in Las Vegas. Hayden Christensen is named the ShoWest 2005 Male Star of Tomorrow, while Lucas is given the Galactic Achievement Award. Anticipating the future of theatrical exhibition, Lucas previews "dimensionalized" 3-D footage of Episode IV in a presentation co-hosted by James Cameron. Lucas voices interest in re-releasing the entire Saga in digital 3-D someday.

Hayden Christensen with his Male Star of Tomorrow award from ShoWest 2005.

A Prelude to *Revenge*

March 21: Season three of the *Star Wars: Clone Wars* micro-series begins airing. The final five installments are longer—12-minute chapters that count down the moments before the debut of Episode III, including the dramatic capture of Chancellor Palpatine by General Grievous.

March 22: The first volume of the *Star Wars: Clone Wars* micro-series—all 20 chapters from seasons one and two—is released on DVD.

For Star Wars: Clone Wars, the Volume One DVD merges the shorts from seasons one and two into one continuous stream.

INTERVENES TO CONTINUE TERRI SCHIAVO'S LIFE SUPPORT

General Grievous doesn't receive a lot of screen time in *Star Wars*: Episode III *Revenge of the Sith*, but multimedia depictions of the Clone Wars often place the villain front and center. This artwork, by Rick Leonardi, was for #1 of the *General Grievous* comics series, which went on sale March 16, 2005. The artwork depicts the general at the head of a Droid Army, though he is quick to take offense if mistaken for a droid himself.

APRIL

Because Grauman's Chinese Theatre did not book *Sith*, Lucasfilm arranges a 501st stormtrooper escort to march fans lined up outside that theater a few blocks east to the ArcLight.

Collecting *Revenge*

April 2: The last Prequel brings about *Star Wars* midnight madness once again, as collectors vie for first dibs on merchandise. Standout toys include Darth Tater, a "mash up" of Darth Vader and Hasbro's Mr. Potato Head, and a Darth Vader mask that transforms anyone's voice into the Sith Lord's stentorian tones. Promotional partners include Pepsi, NASCAR, NBA, Frito-Lay, Kellogg's, Pringles, and Cingular. Of special note for those with a sweet tooth, M&M's introduces—for the first time ever—dark chocolate candies to commemorate Episode III's darker tone.

Main image: Kris Krajewski of the 501st Legion dresses as "Darth Tater" at the American International Toy Fair. Left: The 30.5-cm (12-in) "Darth Tater" Mr. Potato Head. Above: Darth Vader mask with vocal sound effects.

Reading *Revenge*

April 2: Published by Del Rey, *The Art of Revenge of the Sith* and *The Making of Revenge of the Sith* (the latter becoming a *New York Times* bestseller) are hardcover books by J. W. Rinzler. Having shadowed Lucas for all three years of production, the author explores the behind-the-scenes story with unprecedented access. Readers can download a PDF supplement called "The Last Chapter" from StarWars.com, which covers the final phases of postproduction after the book goes to print. The Episode III novelizations—an adult one by Matthew Stover and a juvenile one by Patricia C. Wrede—are bestsellers (all three of Wrede's Prequel junior novelizations are number one *New York Times* bestsellers). Dark Horse prints *Star Wars: Visionaries*, a comics anthology illustrated by the Episode III concept artists. Jude Watson begins a new series for Scholastic, *The Last of the Jedi*, set just after Episode III.

THE MAKING OF STAR WARS REVENGE OF THE SITH

J. W. RINZLER

Celebration III

April 21: Indianapolis welcomes over 34,000 fans for the four-day Celebration III convention. An unseasonable cold snap does not deter fans from camping out overnight for a chance to see Lucas making his first convention appearance since 1987. During an onstage Q&A session, Lucas announces two *Star Wars* television series—a computer-animated Clone Wars series and a live-action series. The hot collectible at the event is an exclusive Darth Vader action figure featuring new lines of dialogue recorded by James Earl Jones.

Some of the more enthusiastic fans at Celebration III arrive dressed as Star Wars characters, perhaps hoping to get hold of the new Darth Vader collectible (right).

MAY

Global Collectible Firsts

Partners around the world create unique *Star Wars* products. Le Gaulois in France delivers the largest ever *Star Wars* entrée promotion. In Japan, there is a specially made R2-D2 Pepsi machine with lights and sounds. The UK's Virgin Airlines releases four *Star Wars*-themed vomit bags, while Zewa in Germany issues the first ever *Star Wars* toilet paper.

The multifunctional R2-D2 is perfectly suited to dispensing drinks.

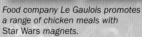

Food company Le Gaulois promotes a range of chicken meals with Star Wars magnets.

Stirring Compositions

May 3: Sony Classical releases John Williams's soundtrack for Episode III. Included is a bonus DVD, *Star Wars: A Musical Journey*, which explores the entire Saga through its music. One of the music videos, *A Hero Falls*, debuts online and on television.

PRINCE CHARLES MARRIES CAMILLA PARKER BOWLES ⊙ SYRIA ENDS

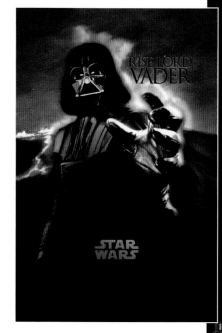

"Rise Lord Vader" is one of six new movie posters created with New Wave Entertainment to promote Episode III.

George Is Wired

May 13: *Wired* magazine interviews Lucas as he looks to the future now that the movie Saga is over. He says, "I've earned the right to fail, which means making what I think are really great movies that no one wants to see."

May 13: *Star Wars*: The Show, a new museum exhibit celebrating the Saga, opens in La Triennale museum, Italy.

May 13: The Official French *Star Wars* Fan Club holds its first ever convention at the Grand Rex movie theater in Paris.

May 13: Good Charlotte performs during MTV's "Total Request Live" Episode III special from Skywalker Ranch.

May 5: LucasArts releases *Star Wars*: Episode III *Revenge of the Sith*—The Video Game for Xbox and PlayStation 2, featuring fight choreography executed by Nick Gillard and Hayden Christensen.

Gamers can pick their side during the events of Episode III by playing as Anakin or Obi-Wan.

May 12: Episode III debuts early in 10 cities across the United States as a fundraising and awareness event for local charities benefiting children and families.

The Saga is Complete

May 16: *Star Wars*: Episode III *Revenge of the Sith* arrives in theaters worldwide. It is the first *Star Wars* movie to warrant a PG-13 rating in the US. The UCI Empire Theater in Leicester Square, England, hosts a *Star Wars* marathon of all six movies, culminating in the premiere of *Revenge of the Sith*, which Lucas and McCallum attend. Domestically, the movie shatters the single day record for a Thursday with $50 million, and ends its opening weekend with $108 million. Within hours of its release, a bootlegged copy of the movie is on the Internet via peer-to-peer networks. Seven people are eventually charged with the theft, which involves a copy of the movie stolen from a postproduction facility in Hollywood.

Episode III's final scene sees Obi-Wan Kenobi on Tatooine, handing baby Luke into the care of moisture farmer Beru Lars and her husband, Owen.

JUNE

Rolling Back the Mask

June 2: *Rolling Stone* magazine interviews Lucas about the cult of Darth Vader. He says, "I had to make Darth Vader scary without the audience ever seeing his face... His character's got to go beyond [his mask]—that's how we get his impersonal way of dealing with things."

Lucas describes the original visualizations of Vader as, "A guy with a cape, a portable iron lung, a mask, a samurai helmet, and a chest piece that had electronics on it."

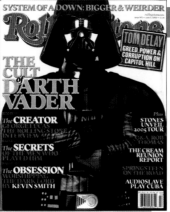

A Lifetime Tribute

June 9: Lucas receives the 33rd annual Lifetime Achievement Award from the American Film Institute, the highest honor the AFI can bestow. At a black-tie gala event at the Kodak Theater in Hollywood, a galaxy of stars—both actors and directors—laud Lucas for his outstanding contributions to the art and technology of cinema. In his acceptance speech, Lucas says, "I've been very fortunate to have had a long career doing what I love to do."

The evening is also memorable for an opening serenade by William Shatner accompanied by dancing stormtroopers.

June 24: MTV2 airs *Video Mods*, a television show that features machinima-style footage of video game characters. The season premiere includes Episode III game characters rocking out on musical instruments.

What's the Story?

June 24: Hyperspace, the Official *Star Wars* Fan Club, offers members an opportunity to establish official *Star Wars* lore. Fans submit stories for perusal by Lucasfilm editors for previously unnamed material. StarWars.com then posts the final back story. These new histories find their way into other products: For example, an unnamed Rodian becomes a Hasbro action-figure with a fan-generated name, Pax Bonkik.

Pax Bonkik's back story explains that he is a Rodian slave who works as a Podracer mechanic for his owner, Mars Guo.

A New Home

June 25: Lucasfilm throws a bash with some 2,000 guests to celebrate the move of the company—and most of its workforce—to the Letterman Digital Arts Center in San Francisco's Presidio park. The staggered move takes place over the coming months, transplanting Lucasfilm, LucasArts, and Industrial Light & Magic to the new campus.

This Time, It's War

June 29: Steven Spielberg's *War of the Worlds* arrives in theaters, featuring many of the talents that made *Star Wars* possible, with visual effects by ILM, supervised by Dennis Muren and Pablo Helman; previsualization supervised by Dan Gregoire; creature design by Ryan Church; and a score by John Williams.

Aliens arrive on Earth in War of the Worlds (above). The poster (right) is nominated by the Internet Movie Awards for Best Blockbuster Poster.

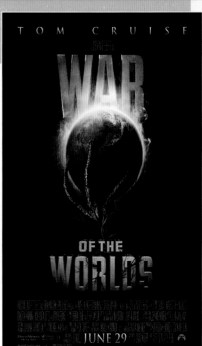

⊕ LIVE-8 CONCERT SERIES BENEFITS THOSE AFFLICTED BY POVERTY

JULY

July 1: Lucasfilm encourages repeat viewings of *Revenge of the Sith* with its "May the Fourth Be With You" promotion, which offers "buy three tickets, get the fourth free."

MAY THE FOURTH BE WITH YOU!

STAR WARS
EPISODE III
REVENGE OF THE SITH

THIS WEEKEND ONLY
BUY 3 TICKETS TO SEE STAR WARS: EPISODE III AND GET THE 4TH TICKET FOR FREE!*
SEE IT AGAIN IN THEATERS EVERYWHERE.

The campaign poster would be released as a StarWarsShop exclusive the following year.

Deep Space Fireworks

July 4: NASA's Deep Impact mission purposely collides an unmanned space probe with 9P/Tempel, a speeding comet 83 million miles from Earth. The collision allows for intimate analysis of the comet's surface and composition. The objective is a well-publicized success for NASA, given the extreme precision it required.

7/7/05

July 7: A coordinated series of suicide attacks, motivated by Britain's involvement in the Iraq War, terrorizes London's public transport system. Four men detonate bombs—three on the London Underground and one on a double-decker bus—killing 56 people and injuring 700.

July 13: A giant planet is discovered in a trinary system that is reminiscent of the binary-star system of Tatooine. The world's unlikely survival challenges accepted planetary formation theories.

July 22: Hayden Christensen enters the Bullrun, an eight-city, 3,000-mile cross-country rally event featuring souped-up race cars and thrill-seeking celebrities.

July 22: Ewan McGregor and Scarlett Johansson star in *The Island*, a sci-fi action movie by Michael Bay with visual effects by ILM (and a plot reminiscent of *THX 1138*).

Beyond *The New Jedi Order*

July 26: Del Rey further explores the Expanded Universe timeline with the *Dark Nest* trilogy by Troy Denning. The three-part paperback saga, *The Joiner King*, *The Unseen Queen*, and *The Swarm War*, unleashes the threat of hive-minded Killiks against the wounded Galactic Alliance, and helps position the character Jacen Solo for the next epic book series to come.

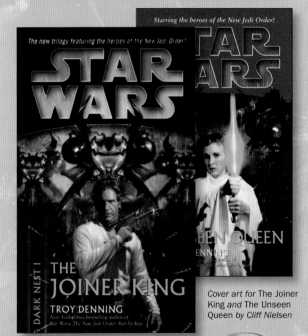

Cover art for The Joiner King and The Unseen Queen by Cliff Nielsen

AUGUST

August 31: Actor Michael Sheard, who played Admiral Ozzel in *The Empire Strikes Back* and Hitler in *Indiana Jones and the Last Crusade*, passes away at the age of 67. His early roles included the terrifying teacher Mr. Bronson in the British children's television series *Grange Hill*.

Michael Sheard as the pompous but doomed Admiral Ozzel in The Empire Strikes Back.

HURRICANE KATRINA HITS NEW ORLEANS: OVER 1,800 DEAD AND $100 BILLION IN DAMAGE

SEPTEMBER

September 9: Lucas begins work on *Star Wars: Frames*, an ambitious ultra high-end book production, consisting of his hand-picked images from the *Star Wars* Saga presented as extra-large glossy pages.

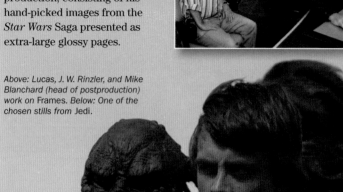

Above: Lucas, J. W. Rinzler, and Mike Blanchard (head of postproduction) work on Frames. Below: One of the chosen stills from Jedi.

September 12: Volume two of the *Star Wars: Clone Wars* micro-series wins Emmy Awards for Outstanding Animated Program and Outstanding Individual Achievement in Animation.

Project Prequel Runway
September 15: The intricately detailed costumes of the Prequel Trilogy go on display at the Fashion Institute of Design & Merchandising (FIDM) in Los Angeles. In conjunction with this exhibition, Trisha Biggar works with LucasBooks, Palace Press, and Abrams to produce *Dressing a Galaxy*, a deluxe hardcover costume retrospective (a Limited Edition of the book includes, among other extras, fabric samples from the cloth used in the films).

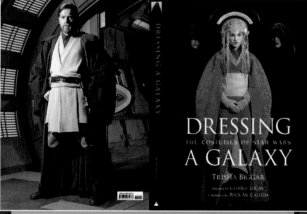

The front and back covers of Dressing a Galaxy showcase the elaborate clothing of Queen Amidala and Obi-Wan Kenobi's iconic Jedi Knight costume.

September 16: Most of Lucasfilm has moved into its new headquarters, the Letterman Digital Arts Center (LDAC). Lucasfilm Animation begins its move into Big Rock Ranch in Marin County, California.

September 26: The American Film Institute (AFI) celebrates 100 years of movie music by naming the top 25 film scores of all time—and John Williams's *Star Wars* music comes in at #1.

OCTOBER

October 1: Abrams Books publishes *Creating the Worlds of Star Wars: 365 Days*, a hardcover book of rare behind-the-scenes photos taken/compiled by visual effects supervisor John Knoll. Many of them are panoramic photos created with Knoll's own computer program.

October 18: Actor John Hollis, known to *Star Wars* fans as Lobot, dies aged 74.

October 23: Actor William Hootkins, who played memorable Rebel pilot Jek Porkins in Episode IV, dies aged 58.

Singapore Ribbon-Cutting
October 27: Lucasfilm officially opens the doors of Lucasfilm Animation Singapore, a digital animation studio designed to produce movies and television programming for global audiences. Its first project is the computer-generated television series *Star Wars: The Clone Wars*. Catherine Winder and Dave Filoni are announced as producer and supervising director, respectively. The Singapore studio will work hand-in-hand with the team at Lucasfilm Animation based in Big Rock Ranch.

October 24: The Hollywood Film Festival's Board of Advisors announce that *Star Wars*: Episode III *Revenge of the Sith* is the winner of 2005's "Hollywood Movie of the Year" Award.

Lucasfilm's 2005 holiday card celebrates the company's move with an illustrated interpretation of its new LDAC headquarters in San Francisco.

🌐 **SECOND MANNED CHINESE SPACECRAFT LAUNCHES** 🌐 **CIVIL UNREST SHAKES PARIS SUBURBS**

OCTOBER

Science Meets Imagination

October 27: After three years in the making, the latest museum tour *Star Wars: Where Science Meets Imagination* opens at the Museum of Science in Boston, Massachusetts. Its two major technological themes are transportation and robotics. National Geographic works with LucasBooks to produce an accompanying tome of the same name, edited by exhibit planner Ed Rodley.

NOVEMBER

November 1: *Revenge of the Sith* is released on DVD. A key bonus is a feature-length documentary, *Within a Minute*, which examines all the work required to produce less than a minute of finished movie. Also in stores is LucasArts' computer game *Star Wars: Battlefront II*.

November 14: ILM is awarded the National Medal of Technology by the White House. ILM is recognized for its "innovations in visual effects technology for the motion picture industry."

The Dark Lens

November 10: Photographer Cédric Delsaux showcases a striking collection, "The Dark Lens," which wins this year's Kodak competition in France. The collection is the first of three series, where *Star Wars* figurines and spaceship models are retouched into urban Paris landscapes. 2010 will see the publication of a book with all three photographic series.

November 22: Del Rey publishes *Star Wars: Dark Lord—The Rise of Darth Vader*, a hardcover novel by James Luceno that captures the moments immediately after Episode III.

November 22: The next generation of gaming arrives as Microsoft is first to the market with the Xbox 360, which supports high-definition games and online connectivity.

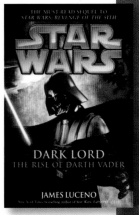

DECEMBER

December 6: Volume two of the *Star Wars: Clone Wars* micro-series arrives on DVD.

December 8: Though it would not win, John Williams's Episode III score is nominated for two Grammy Awards: Best Score Soundtrack Album and Best Instrumental Composition for "Anakin's Betrayal."

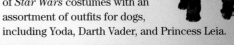

Also in 2005...

Star Wars Goes to the Dogs

Some of the hottest Halloween costumes for 2005 are not even for humans. Rubie's Costume Co. adds to its already popular line of *Star Wars* costumes with an assortment of outfits for dogs, including Yoda, Darth Vader, and Princess Leia.

Imperial Royal Guards survey Paris in artwork by Cédric Delsaux.

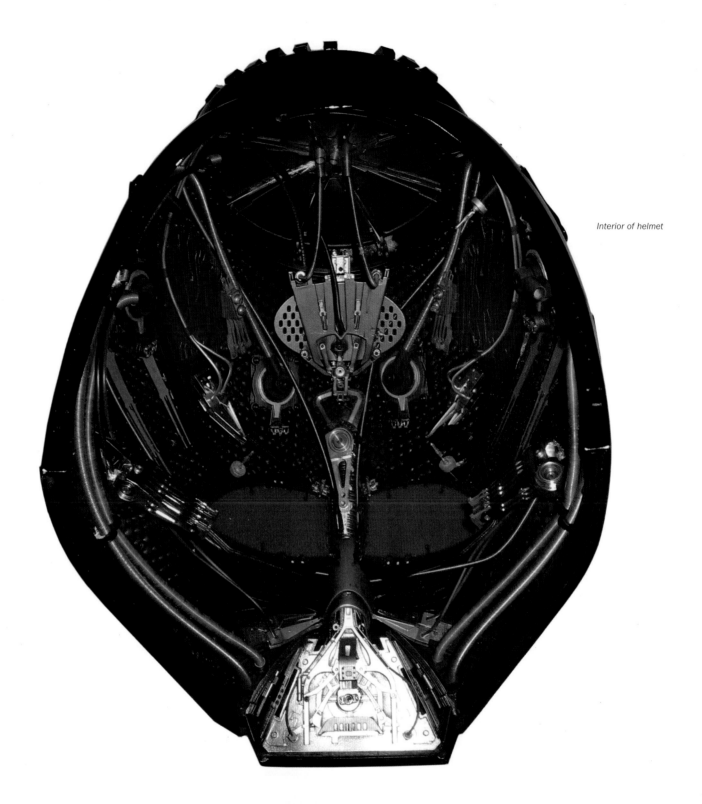

Interior of helmet

Don Bies of the ILM Model Shop creates the never-before-seen inner mask of Darth Vader's helmet. It begins as concept art by Ryan Church. "His direction was that it's supposed to look painful; it goes on easy but it doesn't come off easy," says Bies. "Having that freedom allowed me to start playing around with different materials. I used the readers from computer hard drives in there—which made it look like if you slipped this thing on your face, it would cut into your cheeks."

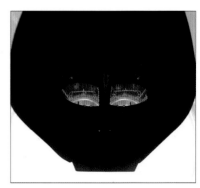

Exterior of helmet

I'M AFRAID SO...

THOUGH THE SAGA is complete, Lucasfilm adopts the mantra "*Star Wars* is Forever," a phrase cribbed from an old Kenner tagline. First up is The Force Unleashed next-generation video game, followed by *The Clone Wars* on television. Contrary to what many presumed, this post-movie era sees extensive hands-on involvement from George Lucas in the future directions of *Star Wars*. He actively participates in the development of three *Star Wars* television series as they get off the ground.

2006-2012

CLONE WARS & BEYOND

2006

THE *STAR WARS* STORYLINE moves beyond the scope of the six movies through Expanded Universe publishing. Del Rey launches a new multi-book epic series, with lessons learned from *The New Jedi Order*. Dark Horse, meanwhile, builds on the extremes of the timeline with two new series: *Knights of the Old Republic* is set thousands of years in the past during the prime of the Jedi, while *Legacy* explores a century after the events of *Return of the Jedi*.

> "It's like having your kids going off to college. They still come back when they need money. They'll be there for the holidays."
>
> **George Lucas**
> *on Star Wars moving from film to television*

MEANWHILE, behind the scenes, a newly reorganized LucasArts concentrates on developing internally a next-generation game for new platforms just arriving on the market. The untitled game has a whispered release date of 2007.

JANUARY

Munich
January 6: Steven Spielberg's *Munich* is released, with visual effects by ILM, supervised by Pablo Helman, and Ben Burtt serving as sound designer and supervising sound editor.

People's Choice
January 10: Episode III wins two People's Choice Awards in the categories of Favorite Movie and Favorite Movie: Drama.

Harrison Ford presents Lucas with the award.

The Old Republic
January 25: Dark Horse Comics publishes *Star Wars: Knights of the Old Republic* #1. Written by John Jackson Miller, the series features artists such as Brian Ching, Dustin Weaver, and Bong Dazo. Set in the same timeframe as the acclaimed video game of the same name, the *KOTOR* comics start with underachieving Padawan Zayne Carrick framed for the murder of his fellow students. The true murderers, a cabal of Jedi Masters with a secret agenda, hunt down the fugitive Padawan. Zayne's only help comes from a down-on-his-luck Snivvian conman named Gryph.

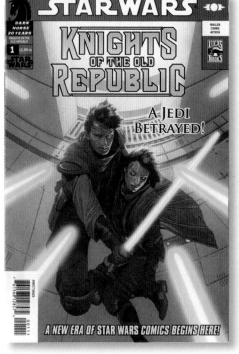

Knights of the Old Republic
cover art by Travis Charest

Oscars
January 31: Episode III represents the last chance for a *Star Wars* movie to add another Academy Award® to the franchise's collection. Despite a campaign by Lucasfilm to have such talents as Ian McDiarmid (Best Supporting Actor), ILM (Best Visual Effects), and Trisha Biggar (Best Costumes) recognized, *Revenge of the Sith* garners only a single nomination: Best Achievement in Makeup (Dave Elsey and Nikki Gooley). Episode III would eventually lose out to *The Chronicles of Narnia: The Lion, The Witch and the Wardrobe*.

NASA'S STARDUST MISSION BRINGS

STAR WARS
OUTBOUND FLIGHT

TIMOTHY ZAHN
New York Times bestselling author of Survivor's Quest

Battlefront Live

January 31: Gamers can expand their *Star Wars: Battlefront II* experience with downloadable content exclusive to the Xbox Live community.

Outbound Flight

January 31: Del Rey publishes *Outbound Flight*, a hardcover novel by Timothy Zahn that picks up a remaining thread from his first *Star Wars* novel 15 years earlier.

Outbound Flight *cover art by Dave Seeley*

FEBRUARY

Anakin (voiced by Mat Lucas) and Obi-Wan (James Arnold Taylor) prepare for battle.

Annie Award

February 4: *Star Wars: Clone Wars* Volume Two wins an Annie award for Best Animated Television Production.

Phil Brown Dies

February 9: Actor Phil Brown, who played Uncle Owen in Episode IV, dies at the age of 89.

Empire at War

February 16: LucasArts releases *Star Wars: Empire at War* for the PC, a real-time strategy game.

STAR WARS
EMPIRE AT WAR

Densely illustrated box art conveys the scope of the conflicts within the game.

An Imperial AT-AT marches across the snowy landscape of Alzoc III.

MARCH

Star of the Year

March 15: At ShoWest in Las Vegas, Natalie Portman is declared Female Star of the Year.

P for Portman

March 17: A bald Natalie Portman stars in *V for Vendetta*, an adaptation of a classic graphic novel directed by James McTeigue, who served as first assistant director on Episode II. Other *Star Wars* veterans on the production include set decorator Peter Walpole and prop master Ty Teiger.

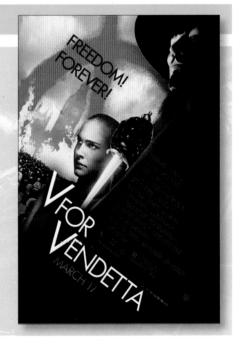

FREEDOM! FOREVER!

V FOR VENDETTA

MARCH 17

Format Wars

March 31: Toshiba releases its first HD-DVD player, a high-definition home video format. Sony's Blu-ray format looms on the horizon, heralding the start of a video format war that some liken to the VHS vs. Beta battle of the previous generation.

The package art for George Lucas's figure is that of the original 1978 stormtrooper figure.

MAY

Saturn Awards

May 2: Episode III wins two Saturn awards from the Academy of Science Fiction, Fantasy, & Horror Films: Best Science Fiction Film and Best Music.

Ultimate Action Figures

Hasbro launches the Ultimate Galactic Hunt, a collection of action figures spanning the entire *Star Wars* Saga. They are packaged on cards reminiscent of the original Kenner run. Proofs of purchase from this series can be redeemed for an exclusive "George Lucas in Stormtrooper Disguise" figure.

Clone Wars on iTunes

May 25: The *Star Wars: Clone Wars* micro-series becomes available for download on iTunes.

Betrayal

May 30: Del Rey begins publishing the *Legacy of the Force* series with the first book, *Betrayal*. Three contributing authors—Aaron Allston, Troy Denning, and Karen Traviss—guide the series as it tracks the fall of Jacen Solo, son of Han and Leia, to the dark side of the Force. Ben Skywalker is now a teenager and figures prominently as a main character alongside Jacen.

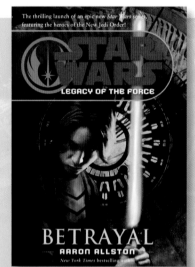

Betrayal cover art by Jason Felix

JUNE

George Lucas and Bernie Loomis, c. 1977

Bernie Loomis

June 2: Bernard (Bernie) Loomis, who was instrumental in bringing *Star Wars* to toys via Kenner action figures in 1978, dies aged 82. He was the president of Kenner Products between 1970 and 1978, and it was he who decided the figures should be 9.5 centimeters (3¾ inches) tall, thereby creating a collectible set with a scale that supported a broad assortment of vehicles and playsets.

Crazy for You

June 3: Hayden Christensen wins Best Villain at the MTV Movie Awards. During the broadcast, Gnarls Barkley performs the smash hit "Crazy" in full *Star Wars* regalia.

Gnarls Barkley performs at the MTV Movie Awards, with vocalist Cee-Lo as Darth Vader and producer/keyboardist Danger Mouse as Obi-Wan Kenobi.

Blu-Ray

June 20: The first Blu-ray titles appear at retail, introducing the new high-definition format to home video enthusiasts.

License of the Year

June 21: *Star Wars* is named the Overall License of the Year by the International Licensing Industry Merchandisers' Association (LIMA). The award recognizes the property that had the most significant impact on the marketplace during 2005. The release of Episode III translated into $3 billion of worldwide retail sales. Almost more impressive is the fact that in 2006, Lucas Licensing generates more money with *Star Wars* products than it did in 2002, the year *Attack of the Clones* came out.

The new generation of Sith Lords— Darth Krayt, Darth Talon, and Darth Nihl—strike a pose on the cover of Dark Horse's Star Wars Legacy #1. Cover art is by Adam Hughes.

Legacy Comic

June 21: Dark Horse Comics publishes *Star Wars Legacy* #1. This new generation of *Star Wars* adventures depicts a resurgent Sith Empire, ruled over by multiple Sith Lords who claim fealty to Darth Krayt. The Jedi are once more diminished, and the last Skywalker, Cade, has refused to take up his heritage and instead lives the life of a pirate. The series is developed by writer John Ostrander and artist Jan Duursema.

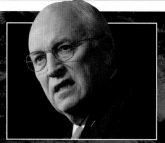

Darth Cheney

June 22: On CNN, Vice President Dick Cheney discusses gathering intelligence during a time of war. He says, "That's not a pleasant business. It's a very serious business. And I suppose, sometimes, people look at my demeanor and say, 'Well, he's the Darth Vader of the administration.'"

JULY

July 1: The first ever *Star Wars* museum exhibition in South Korea opens.

Pirates and Pixels

July 7: *Pirates of the Caribbean: Dead Man's Chest* is released. John Knoll is the visual effects supervisor and ILM's amazing wizardry fools several entertainment press outlets into thinking a computer-generated character—Davey Jones—is some sort of practical makeup effect.

501st Trooper

July 19: Hasbro creates a 501st stormtrooper for the San Diego Comic-Con International exclusive as a nod to the fan organization.

Forces Unleashed

July 21: At Comic-Con, Steve Sansweet debuts explosive previsualization footage for LucasArts' computer game The Force Unleashed.

AUGUST

Kerner Optical

August 20: Kerner Optical, formerly the Model Shop and stage facilities at ILM, opens its doors as a separate, spin-off visual effects company. Though no longer part of Lucasfilm, the Marin County-based Kerner continues to work on movies together with the relocated ILM. The Kerner name is a holdover from the business that had occupied the space that ILM moved into way back in 1978.

A galactic trio appears at a Florida Marlins vs. Washington Nationals game at Dolphin Stadium.

Road Trip

August 22: Lucasfilm sends a trio of costumed *Star Wars* characters— Darth Vader, Chewbacca, and Wicket the Ewok—to 11 cities across the US to drum up publicity for the upcoming Original Trilogy DVD and game releases. Along their journey, the three characters frequently crash local news programs, attend sporting events, and visit children's hospitals.

No Longer a Planet

August 24: Pluto is kicked out of the planet club for not measuring up. The International Astronomical Union sets down conditions for the classification of a planet, and Pluto fails the test and is rebranded as a "dwarf planet." The current count for our solar system is eight planets and five dwarf planets.

SEPTEMBER

Original Trilogy

September 12: The original *Star Wars* trilogy returns to DVD as individual movies outside of a boxed set. Each comes packaged with a bonus theatrical edition of the movie: The 1977 version of *Star Wars* without the "Episode IV" title in the crawl, and the 1980 and 1983 versions of the sequels respectively. Demanding video aficionados are displeased with the picture quality of the bonus originals—they haven't been remastered or enhanced for modern televisions in any way. Meanwhile, LucasArts and Traveler's Tales Games follow up their surprise smash hit of 2005 with LEGO® *Star Wars* II: The Original Trilogy on multiple platforms. The sequel adapts Episodes IV–VI into playable LEGO® environments.

Lucas Donation

September 19: Lucas donates $175 million to his alma mater, the University of Southern California. It is the largest single donation in the school's history.

Visual Dictionary

September 25: With the Saga complete, DK Publishing is able to collect its previous *Star Wars* guides into deluxe editions with new content. *The Complete Star Wars Visual Dictionary* arrives on September 25, *Star Wars: Complete Locations* follows on October 17, and *Complete Cross-Sections* arrives the next year on March 19.

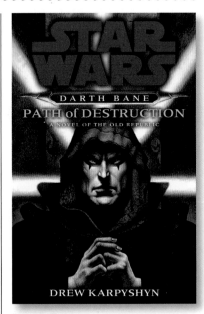

Darth Bane

September 26: Del Rey publishes *Darth Bane: Path of Destruction* by Drew Karpyshyn, a hardcover novel that recounts the origins of the ancient Sith Lord.

Also in 2006...

Live and Learn

Lucas appears on the cover of educational magazine *Live and Learn*. The quote on the cover is taken from his mission statement for The George Lucas Educational Foundation, an organization established to provide the world of learning with modern and innovative technologies.

OCTOBER

Jacen Solo

October 3: Del Rey and LucasBooks allow fans to establish Jacen Solo's Sith name in *Legacy of the Force*. Fans submit suggestions through StarWars.com, and vote for finalists the following year.

October 10: StarWars.com is voted favorite official movie site by over 30,000 readers at Movies.com's annual poll.

Lucas vs. Colbert

October 11: For weeks, TV host Stephen Colbert showcases viral videos created by fans of *The Colbert Report* using footage of the comedian against greenscreen. The resulting "Greenscreen Challenge" comes to a head when the best finalists are presented on television. Coming in second place is an entry with elaborate visual effects and a guest appearance by Jar Jar Binks, courtesy of ILM. Lucas accepts the runner-up title and later engages Colbert in a lightsaber duel.

Lucas proves his lightsaber mastery by soundly defeating Stephen Colbert.

Forces of Corruption

October 24: The follow-up to the Empire at War video game, Forces of Corruption, is released as an expansion, introducing underworld kingpin character Tyber Zann.

NOVEMBER

Star Wars HD

All six *Star Wars* movies are broadcast in high-definition for the first time on Cinemax.

Wishful Drinking

November 7: Carrie Fisher's one-woman show, *Wishful Drinking* debuts in Los Angeles. It is a frank and often hilarious discussion of her career and personal life, including Princess Leia and *Star Wars*.

Console Wars

Two new consoles hit the market. Sony's PlayStation 3—a high-definition machine that doubles as a Blu-ray player—arrives at retail. Meanwhile, Nintendo eschews cutting-edge graphics in favor of ease-of-play with its new Wii, a revolutionary game system that replaces controllers with a new motion-sensing remote-control-like interface.

Also in 2006...

George Lucas Toy

This collector's set by Hasbro features action figures of the four characters played by George Lucas and his family in Episode III. They are Baron Papanoida (George Lucas), Chi Eekway (Katie Lucas), Zett Jukassa (Jett Lucas), and Terr Taneel (Amanda Lucas).

Casino Royale

November 17: *Casino Royale* arrives in theaters. The 21st film in the James Bond series, it features Daniel Craig as Bond and "reboots" the film series with a tougher, more realistic edge.

November 24: Wizards of the Coast expands its *Star Wars* miniature gaming line with starships of varying scales.

DECEMBER

Lethal Alliance

December 5: The *Star Wars*: Lethal Alliance video game arrives on the PlayStation Portable system and later the Nintendo DS.

Sculpting a Galaxy includes such photos as this one of Lorne Peterson putting the finishing touches to a sandcrawler for the Special Edition release of Star Wars.

Model Citizen

November 14: Palace Press publishes *Sculpting a Galaxy*, a densely illustrated hardcover book devoted to the work of the ILM Model Shop, written by veteran model maker Lorne Peterson. A deluxe Limited Edition comes encased in an enormous box that encloses several new models sculpted by Peterson of Luke's landspeeder, an assortment of Death Star surface panels, and part of the *Millennium Falcon*.

ISCOVERY SPACE SHUTTLE COMPLETES ITS MISSION ☢ SADDAM HUSSEIN EXECUTED IN IRAQ ☢

2007

Star Wars *30th anniversary logo*

STAR WARS CONTINUES to make headline news, becoming a part of the annual Rose Parade on January 1. Indeed, the entire year turns into a celebration of the 30th anniversary of *A New Hope*—a milestone brought into the lives of many Americans thanks to the United States Postal Service, which transforms mailboxes into R2-D2 and issues commemorative postage stamps.

> "Today, we're officially declaring it *Star Wars* Day in the City of Los Angeles. We're very excited to host you today."
>
> **Mayor Antonio Villaraigosa**
> *at Celebration IV*

FANS GATHER in Los Angeles and London for two *Star Wars* Celebration events—an international convention being a first for Lucasfilm. The company's message, "*Star Wars* is Forever," resonates during these fan events, especially when Lucasfilm offers a first peek into the future of the franchise—a trailer for the new animated series *Star Wars: The Clone Wars*.

JANUARY

I Love a Parade

January 1: Lucas serves as Grand Marshal of the Tournament of Roses Parade, an annual New Years celebration that has been held in Pasdena, California, since 1890 and is broadcast on television across the US. The two greenest planets in the Saga, Endor and Naboo, are represented by flower-covered floats in keeping with the Parade's eco-friendly theme, Our Good Nature. Filling out Lucas's contingent in the parade are 200 costumed members of the 501st Legion from around the world, marching in Imperial armor and uniforms, and the high-stepping Grambling State University Tiger Marching Band. It's not all *Star Wars*, though. Lucas reveals that the long-delayed fourth *Indiana Jones* movie will begin production this year, reuniting Lucas with Steven Spielberg and Harrison Ford.

This logo (left) adorns signage and pins given to the volunteers who make the Rose Parade an unforgettable Star Wars event.

Helping the troopers keep step is the upbeat tempo of the Grambling State University band, complete with Twi'lek majorettes.

More than 200 costumed fans take part in the march—a grueling task for those in full armor.

Concept art for the eco-friendly Endor float by John Ramirez.

Arise, Lord Caedus

January 23: Having gathered hundreds of suggestions, Del Rey and StarWars.com put Jacen Solo's final Sith name for the *Legacy of the Force* book series to a vote. Of the finalists, Darth Caedus—submitted by Tawnia Poland—eventually wins and is revealed in the pages of *Sacrifice* later in the year.

The Endor forest float during the Rose Parade, complete with Ewoks

The Best Band in the Galaxy,...
GRAMBLING STATE
UNIVERSITY

FEBRUARY

ILM Wins Pirate Treasure

February 26: Visual effects supervisor John Knoll and animation supervisor Hal Hickel bring home to ILM a Visual Effects Academy Award® for *Pirates of the Caribbean: Dead Man's Chest*. It is the facility's first Academy Award® win since 1995's statue for *Forrest Gump*.

MARCH

The Droid You're Looking For

March 15: The US Postal Service decorates 400 mailboxes across the country in the likeness of R2-D2 to celebrate the 30th anniversary of *Star Wars*. Working with Lucasfilm, the post office also issues the first official *Star Wars* postage stamps, with artwork by Drew Struzan. Though unveiled in March, the stamps would not go on sale until May 25, the actual 30th anniversary of *Star Wars*.

Lucas entrusts some vital correspondence to an R2-D2 mailbox.

Anniversary Editions

March 28: Dark Horse begins publishing its *Star Wars* 30th anniversary collection: deluxe reprints of various *Star Wars* comic series bound as hardcovers.

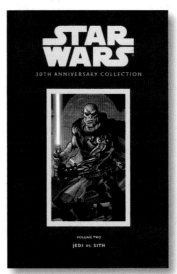

These anniversary collections are deluxe reprints on high-quality paper. The installment Jedi vs. Sith was originally published in 2001.

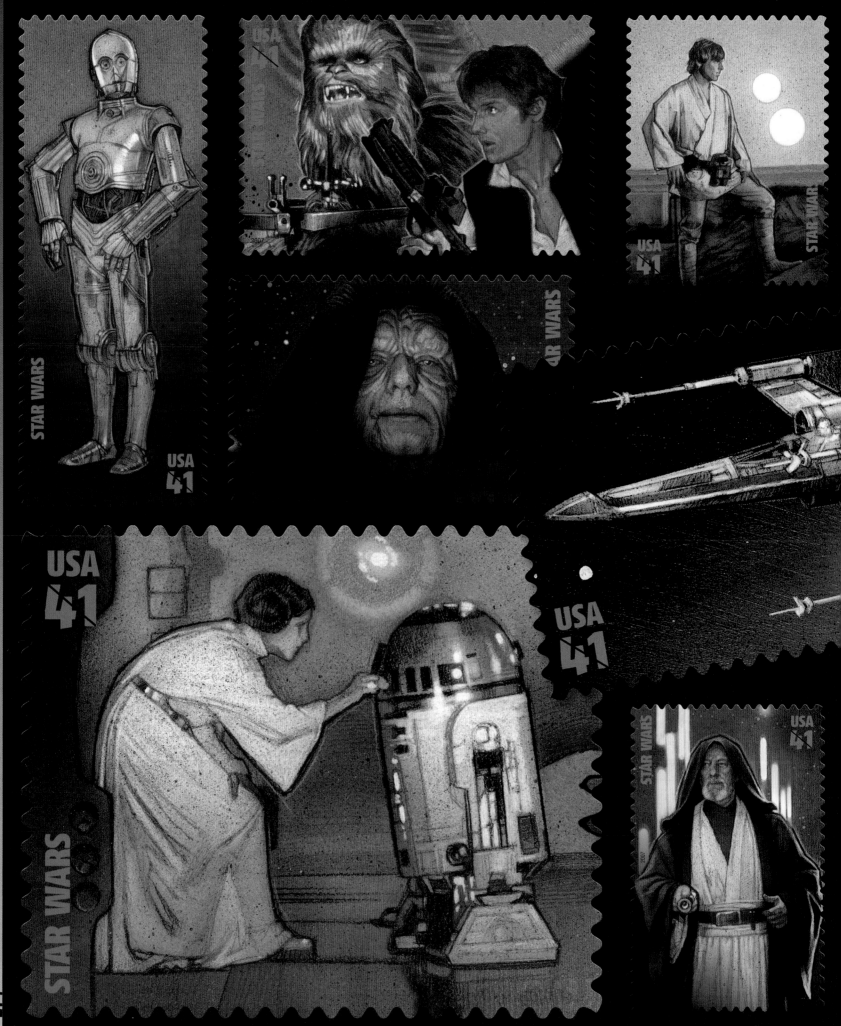

In 2007, the United States Postal Service honors the 30th anniversary of *Star Wars* with the release of fifteen 41-cent commemorative postage stamps. Designed by Drew Struzan, they feature images from all six movies.

The stamps are unveiled at Grauman's Chinese Theatre on March 28. Their first-day-of-issue ceremony takes place at *Star Wars* Celebration IV in Los Angeles on May 25.

The public vote the Yoda stamp their favorite and it is issued as a single stamp later that summer.

APRIL

April 2: *Star Wars* fan and celebrity contestant Joey Fatone gets down alongside R2-D2 in an episode of ABC's *Dancing with the Stars*.

A Cast and Crew Reunion

April 23: The Academy of Motion Pictures Arts and Sciences screens *Star Wars* as part of a series of classic movies that were nominated for, but did not win, Best Picture. Attending the Beverly Hills screening and panel discussion are George Lucas, Gary Kurtz, Ben Burtt, John Dykstra, Carrie Fisher, Mark Hamill, Richard Edlund, Alan Ladd Jr., film editors Paul Hirsch and Richard Chew, composite optical photographer Robert Blalack, art director Leslie Dilley, re-recording mixers Ray West and Don MacDougall, and model shop supervisor Grant McCune.

At Long Last: Behind-the-Scenes

April 24: Del Rey publishes *The Making of Star Wars* by J. W. Rinzler. Oddly enough, the original *Star Wars* is the only movie of the six to have never had a behind-the-scenes book of its production. One was planned 30 years ago by Charles Lippincott, vice president of marketing and merchandise, but the book never came together. However; interviews with more than 50 cast and crew members were conducted during the movie's production. Using this wealth of never-before-published material as a springboard, Rinzler carefully pieces together a complete account of the genesis of *Star Wars*, along with never-seen-before photographs and artwork.

The cover of The Making of Star Wars *captures a moment from the arduous and unprecedented journey undertaken by Lucas to create his mind-blowing film.*

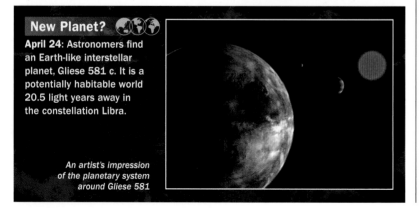

New Planet? 🌍🌍🌍

April 24: Astronomers find an Earth-like interstellar planet, Gliese 581 c. It is a potentially habitable world 20.5 light years away in the constellation Libra.

An artist's impression of the planetary system around Gliese 581

MAY

May 5: Yoshitoku Company of Japan releases a quarter-scale set of Samurai armor patterned on Darth Vader.

Japanese dollmaker Yoshitoku creates the Darth Vader-inspired Gogatsu Ningyo.

May 12: Ewan McGregor and Charles Boorman hit the road again on a second motorcycle tour and documentary, *Long Way Down*, which follows the pair as they travel south from Scotland to South Africa.

Celebration IV

May 24: Celebration IV kicks off in Los Angeles, California. Running through May 28, the fan convention welcomes over 35,000 attendees. While the 30th anniversary of the original movie is a prime focus, the convention also includes a broad range of programming, activities, and highlights. Supervising director Dave Filoni and producer Catherine Winder preview footage from *Star Wars: The Clone Wars*, LucasArts previews *Star Wars*: The Force Unleashed, and Los Angeles Mayor Antonio Villaraigosa proclaims May 25 "*Star Wars* Day" in the city.

The Los Angeles Convention Center is besie[ged] by costumed fans during Celebration[...]

🌐 **SECOND ORANGE REVOLUTION IN THE UKRAINE** 🌐 **33 DIE IN THE VIRGINIA TECH CAMPUS SHOOTING**

May 24: StarWars.com and Eyespot begin *Star Wars Mashups*, a short-lived feature that allows *Star Wars* fans to edit clips from the movies with their own videos or stills.

Star Wars Makes More History

May 28: The History Channel airs *Star Wars: A Legacy Revealed*, a two-hour special that explores the historical, political, and mythological connections of the Saga. Among the luminaries in the program are Tom Brokaw, Stephen Colbert, Newt Gingrich, J.J. Abrams, Peter Jackson, Dr. Camille Paglia, Nancy Pelosi, Joss Whedon, and Dan Rather. The show earns three Emmy nominations: Outstanding Writing for Non-Fiction Programming, Outstanding Directing, and Outstanding Art Direction.

May 29: *Jeopardy!* includes a special *Star Wars* category in recognition of the Saga's 30th anniversary. The clues include video captured at the Lucasfilm Archives.

The Murder of Mara Jade

May 29: The fifth book of the *Legacy of the Force* series, *Sacrifice*, is published by Del Rey. Karen Traviss writes about Jacen Solo, who fully adopts the title of Sith Lord, Darth Caedus. He kills Mara Jade—his aunt—in a shocking move that stuns many fans of the popular character. Ben Skywalker, unaware of his cousin's heinous acts, investigates his mother's death over the coming books.

Sacrifice cover art by Jason Felix and David Stevenson

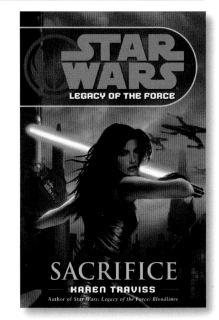

Among the commemorative exclusives are a set of collector medallions.

Collectors snatch up the Hasbro convention exclusive figures—R2-D2 and C-3PO based on the original McQuarrie concept art. Also popular is a series of high-quality collectible medallions available only at the fan-led collecting panels.

Hasbro's convention action figures of C-3PO and R2-D2

These *Star Wars* action figures are based on the original concept drawings by McQuarrie.

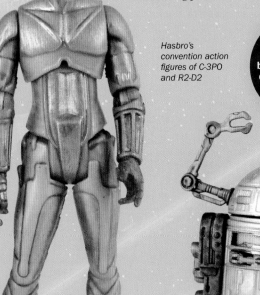

JUNE

June 15: Hasbro releases a Wal-Mart exclusive Father's Day action-figure set of Luke Skywalker and Darth Vader based on their confrontation in *The Empire Strikes Back*.

Nuggets of Parody

June 17: An all *Star Wars* episode of Adult Swim's irreverent *Robot Chicken* airs on Cartoon Network. Created by Seth Green and Matthew Senreich, the show consists of a series of unconnected sketches played out by stop-motion animated toys and figures. It includes a guest voice appearance by Lucas.

Robot Chicken creators Matt Senreich and Seth Green are undeniable Star Wars fans.

Robot Chicken Lucas attends a fan convention.

TER 10 YEARS AS PRIME MINISTER, TONY BLAIR STEPS DOWN AND IS REPLACED BY GORDON BROWN

JULY

Marc Ecko Base

July 2: Artist and entrepreneur Marc Ecko unveils designs for *Star Wars* clothes to be produced by his label for the holiday season. The collection combines classic *Star Wars* iconography with a street-smart style. Among the most popular designs are a sweatshirt that mimics the colors and lines of Boba Fett's armor, and another that does the same for stormtrooper armor.

This stormtrooper hooded sweatshirt, on sale in 2009, epitomizes the 21st century trend of "geek chic."

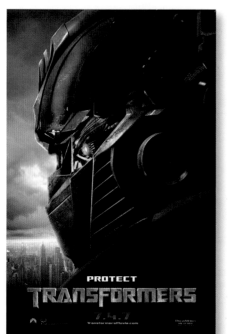

July 3: *Transformers*, directed by Michael Bay, explodes into theaters. Its incredibly complex shape-shifting protagonists are realized digitally by ILM, who are nominated for an Academy Award®.

Release poster for Transformers shows one of ILM's 16 morphing robots.

July 11: *Harry Potter and the Order of the Phoenix*, the fifth film in the series, debuts. ILM is one of the key contributing effects vendors on the production.

The Pink Droid with a Heart of Gold

July 25: In time for Comic-Con International in San Diego, Hasbro releases a commemorative R2-KT action figure. The toy honors Katie Johnson, a brave young *Star Wars* fan who passed away from brain cancer in 2005 at the age of seven. Katie was the daughter of Albin Johnson, founder of the 501st Legion fan group. While facing her ailment, Katie was given a life-sized fan-created astrodroid named R2-KT. In her memory, Hasbro donates $100,000 to the Make-A-Wish Foundations of South Carolina and San Diego.

A full-sized model of R2-KT at Comic-Con

Celebration Europe

July 13: The first ever official *Star Wars* convention outside the Americas begins at the Docklands' ExCel Centre in London through July 15. Organized by Lucasfilm and The Cards Inc. Group, it attracts 30,000 fans. Ian McDiarmid (Palpatine) makes a rare appearance and Warwick Davis (Wicket) is Master of Ceremonies. The commemorative poster and program cover for the event emulate the classic album artwork for The Beatles' *Sgt. Pepper's Lonely Hearts Club Band* in a collage by Randy Martinez.

Martinez creates a full diorama to realize The Beatles album homage. He spends two months assembling over 60 different characters and over 300 plastic flowers.

AUGUST

Topps releases 120 thirtieth anniversary *Star Wars* cards, plus bonus autograph cards by actors and one-of-a-kind artist sketch cards.

August 4: NASA launches the *Phoenix* robotic spacecraft to explore Mars. It is scheduled to arrive the following year.

August 10: *Stardust*, based on a Neil Gaiman novel, arrives in theaters. It features production design by Gavin Bocquet, and fellow *Star Wars* veteran Peter Russell acts as supervising art director.

August 14: A newly restored edition of the Henson-Lucasfilm production, *Labyrinth* is released on DVD, containing an all-new commentary track and bonus material.

Labyrinth remains a noteworthy collaboration between Lucas and Jim Henson with visual effects by ILM.

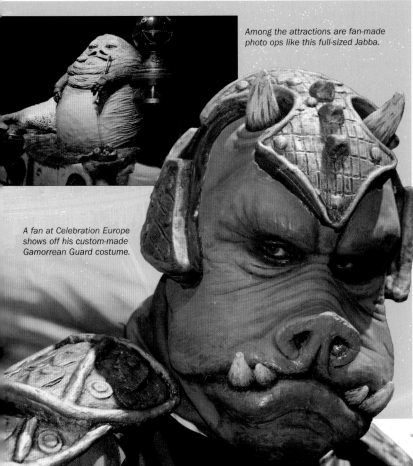

A fan at Celebration Europe shows off his custom-made Gamorrean Guard costume.

Among the attractions are fan-made photo ops like this full-sized Jabba.

SEPTEMBER

September 9: The title of the fourth *Indiana Jones* movie is revealed by one of the film's stars Shia LaBeouf (Mutt Williams) during the MTV Video Music Awards: It will be *Indiana Jones and the Kingdom of the Crystal Skull*.

September 14: Japan launches its most ambitious lunar exploration project to date, SELENE, to study the moon's origins and evolutions and to measure its precise gravitational field.

FOX's promotional poster for Blue Harvest parodies the Star Wars theatrical posters.

Family Force

September 23: The sixth season premiere of the FOX animated comedy *Family Guy* is an hour-long *Star Wars* parody titled *Blue Harvest*. Produced with the cooperation of Lucasfilm, the episode begins with Peter Griffin forced to retell the story of *Star Wars* to amuse his TV-addicted family during a blackout. Peter's version casts *Family Guy* characters in the classic roles: Quagmire as C-3PO, Cleveland as R2-D2, Lois as Leia, Stewie as Darth Vader, Peter as Solo, Brian as Chewbacca, and Chris as Luke. The episode, named after the dummy title used for *Return of the Jedi* (see p.99), would later be released as a special edition DVD and is nominated for an Emmy for Outstanding Animated Program.

OCTOBER

Got It Where It Counts

The LEGO Group introduces its largest *Star Wars* model: The Ultimate Collector's *Millennium Falcon*. It measures 84 centimeters (almost three feet) long and is made from 5,197 pieces. Built to accurate minifigure scale, it includes five figures: Han Solo, Chewbacca, Obi-Wan Kenobi, Luke Skywalker, and Princess Leia Organa.

Battlefront on the Go

October 9: The third entry in the successful *Star Wars: Battlefront* gaming series arrives in stores exclusively for the Sony PlayStation Portable. Its new battles and missions are told through an original story of Renegade Squadron—a team of Rebel special operatives assembled by Han Solo. Their classified exploits take them across the galaxy, while gameplay supports customization options and multiplayer action via wireless Internet connection.

Star Wars in 3-D

October 15: Orchard Books in collaboration with Scholastic Inc. and LucasBooks publishes *Star Wars: A Pop-Up Guide to the Galaxy*, an amazingly engineered work by Matthew Reinhart. The hardcover book includes an AT-AT, a grasping rancor, a crowded Mos Eisley Cantina, and a Darth Vader helmet over a scarred Anakin Skywalker. A small battery even illuminates two lightsabers. It becomes a #1 *New York Times* bestseller and remains on the list for more than 15 weeks. A Limited Edition signed by Reinhart has a sound chip that enables Vader to breathe audibly.

October 16: Del Rey publishes *MAD About Star Wars*

October 16: Del Rey publishes *MAD About Star Wars*, written by *MAD* senior editor Jonathan Bresman (a former Lucasfilm production coordinator). The book brings together 30 years of *Star Wars* parodies by the the usual gang of "Jediots," with a foreword by Lucas.

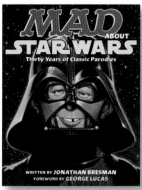

Alfred E. Neuman—MAD magazine's fictional mascot and iconic cover boy—as Darth Vader

Lightsaber Into Space

October 23: A lightsaber prop from *Return of the Jedi* is carried aboard the space shuttle *Discovery* on mission STS-120. Back in August, Lucasfilm handed the prop over to NASA's Space Center Houston in a special ceremony complete with *Star Wars* characters including Chewbacca, Boba Fett, C-3PO, and R2-D2. On the morning of the shuttle's return, November 6, the crew is awakened by the *Star Wars* score. Prior to undertaking his spacewalk, Mission Specialist Scott Parazynski transmits a message to his young son, Luke: "Luke, I'm your father. Use the Force, Luke."

Astronaut Jim Reilly and R2-D2 pose with the lightsaber.

The Pop-Up Guide to the Galaxy contains elaborate paper engineering, such as this featuring Darth Vader.

Young Indy Rides Again

October 23: *The Young Indiana Jones Chronicles* is re-packaged as a trio of deluxe DVD boxed sets titled *The Adventures of Young Indiana Jones*, released by Lucasfilm, CBS Home Entertainment, and Paramount Home Entertainment. The series undergoes restoration and is presented as a total of 22 feature-length movies. Because Lucas envisions *Young Indy* as a gateway to historical education for viewers of all ages, the DVDs include interactive timelines and all-new documentaries produced by a Lucasfilm unit, headed by CBS News veteran David Schneider. The first 12-disc set, subtitled *The Early Years*, includes seven movies and 38 companion documentaries.

The first of three DVD installments of Young Indiana Jones primarily concerns Indy's childhood from 1908 to 1910. In one, young Jones (Corey Carrier) meets T.E. Lawrence, aka Lawrence of Arabia (Joseph Bennett).

A teenage Indy (Sean Patrick Flanery) plans to join the Belgian Army in "Love's Sweet Song."

October 25: Based on more than half-a-million votes, the US Postal Service releases a 41-cent commemorative Yoda stamp, available in panes of 20.

October 27: The Official French *Star Wars* Fan Club hosts Réunion II at the Grand Rex theater in Paris, where all six movies are screened as part of the convention.

Poster advertising for the Réunion II convention in Paris

October 30: Harper Collins publishes *The Star Wars Vault* by Steve Sansweet and Pete Vilmur—a multimedia trove of memorabilia and artifacts from the last 30 years.

NOVEMBER

November 5: A labor strike by the Writer's Guild of America halts film and television production in the US for 14 weeks. Among the contentious issues are royalties from new digital media.

November 6: LucasArts and Traveller's Tales Games release LEGO® *Star Wars*: The Complete Saga, a compilation and enhancement of their previous releases for multiple platforms, including next-generation systems.

November 15: The NPD Group releases data that *Star Wars* is the #2 best-selling boys' toy property of the year—a remarkable achievement for a 30-year-old brand two years after its last feature film.

The Art of *Beowulf*

November 16: Robert Zemeckis releases *Beowulf*, his second performance-capture computer-animated movie, featuring production design by Doug Chiang. Many members of the Prequel Trilogy concept art department helped develop the look of the fantasy epic, including Robert Barnes, John Duncan, Marc Gabbana, Kurt Kaufman, Tony McVey, Dermot Power, and Terryl Whitlatch.

DECEMBER

December 18: The second volume of *The Adventures of Young Indiana Jones* arrives on DVD. The eight-disc set of *The War Years* includes eight movies and 25 new documentaries.

Also in 2007...

As Good as Gold

To celebrate the 30th anniversary of *Star Wars*, gold-colored chrome C-3PO minifigures are inserted at random into LEGO® *Star Wars* sets. Even rarer is a C-3PO minifigure made from solid 14-karat gold.

It is estimated that the chances of finding a gold-colored C-3PO minifigure in your set is 1 in 250.

The Vader Project is first seen at *Star Wars* Celebration IV in Los Angeles toward the end of May 2007 and has since traveled all over the world. For the exhibition, 100 contemporary artists were each given a 1:1 scale replica of Darth Vader's helmet to customize.

2008

THE LAUNCH of *Star Wars: The Clone Wars* marks the debut of a new animation studio, as well as a fresh way of making television. Lucas's vision demands nothing short of a mini-*Star Wars* movie each week. Further complicating production is a late decision to premiere the series with a theatrical release of the pilot episodes reformatted as a feature-length movie.

"I felt there were a lot more *Star Wars* stories left to tell. I was eager to start telling some of them through animation." **George Lucas** *on Star Wars: The Clone War*

THE CLONE WARS quickly finds its footing. It ends the year ranked #1 in the US with all boy demographics across all television and is the top boys' toy license of 2008. The dynamic adventure series secures a new generation of young fans.

JANUARY

Replicas
January 10: New licensee eFX signs on to produce *Star Wars* prop replicas, filling the vacancy left by Master Replicas. Hasbro takes over producing Force FX lightsabers.

Ahsoka
January 29: Lucasfilm unveils new character Ahsoka Tano in anticipation of products being revealed at forthcoming toy industry shows. Fans are caught unaware by the news that Anakin Skywalker had a hitherto unrevealed Padawan apprentice.

Vector
January 30: For the first time, various *Star Wars* titles published by Dark Horse begin a "crossover" event. The year-long Vector storyline begins in the pages of *Knights of the Old Republic*, in the ancient past of the galaxy, and moves through *Dark Times* and *Rebellion*, before finishing off in the far future of *Legacy*. In total, the storyline takes up more than 4,100 years of continuity and is told in 12 issues.

As a Togruta, Ahosoka has lekku (head-tails) and montrals (small hollow horns on the top of the head).

FEBRUARY

Two boys eye Darth Vader warily at the Star Wars exhibition in Brussels, Belgium.

Exhibitions
International museums prepare for the latest traveling *Star Wars* exhibitions. In Brussels, Belgium, *Star Wars: The Exhibition* opens its doors on February 16. São Paulo welcomes *Star Wars* Exposição Brasil on March 5.

Vanity Fair
February 6: *Vanity Fair* devotes unprecedented coverage to a video game in its March issue. It spotlights the digital collaboration between LucasArts and ILM to produce The Force Unleashed.

Concept art for The Force Unleashed by Amy Beth Christenson.

John Alvin

February 6: Renowned movie poster artist John Alvin, responsible for *E.T.*, *The Lion King*, *Young Frankenstein*, and several *Star Wars* commemorative and licensed posters, dies at the age of 59.

Clone Wars Declared

February 12: *The Clone Wars* surprises continue. An announcement notes that the series will arrive on Cartoon Network in the fall as expected—but will be preceded by a theatrical release in August from Warner Bros.

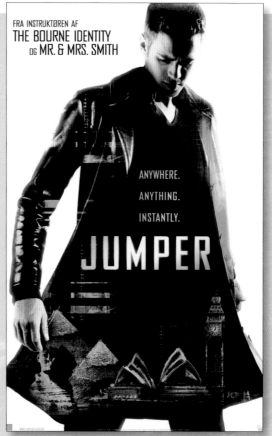

FRA INSTRUKTØREN AF
THE BOURNE IDENTITY
OG MR. & MRS. SMITH

ANYWHERE.
ANYTHING.
INSTANTLY.

JUMPER

Anakin Jumps

February 14: *Jumper*, starring Hayden Christensen (Anakin Skywalker) and Samuel L. Jackson (Mace Windu), arrives in theaters. Christensen's character has the ability to teleport and discovers a hidden war being waged by similarly gifted individuals.

The Danish Jumper theatrical poster depicts some of the worldwide locations David Rice (Christensen) can teleport to at a moment's notice.

MARCH

Tally of the Jedi

March 11: Titan Magazines publishes the 100th issue of *Star Wars Insider*. The centerpiece of the issue is a tally of the 100 most popular characters, vehicles, and items from *Star Wars* as determined by visitor traffic on StarWars.com. The Jedi Order is at the top of the list.

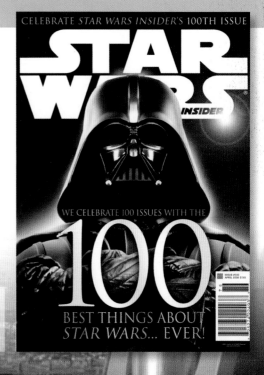

CELEBRATE *STAR WARS INSIDER*'S 100TH ISSUE

STAR WARS
INSIDER

WE CELEBRATE 100 ISSUES WITH THE
100
BEST THINGS ABOUT
STAR WARS... EVER!

The Jedi Order is governed by the High Council: twelve Jedi who sit in the Jedi Temple and make rulings.

APRIL

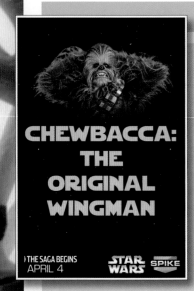

Spike TV

April 4: Spike TV broadcasts all six *Star Wars* movies in HD—a first for basic cable. The network spices up the release with a standout ad campaign, including head-turning outdoor posters. As well as Darth Vader and Chewbacca, they feature Leia ("Gold bikinis never go out of style," below left) and Darth Maul ("You think your tattoo hurt?").

Three of the posters from Spike TV's advertising campaign offer a new take on Star Wars.

John Berkey

April 29: Renowned science-fiction artist John Berkey dies aged 75. Berkey's artwork served as inspiration for the first *Star Wars*, and Lucas picked him as one of the artists to develop *Star Wars* poster concepts. Berkey's illustrations found their way into many ancillary products, including the foldout poster inserted into the soundtrack LP.

Young Indy DVDs

April 29: The third and final volume of *The Adventures of Young Indiana Jones* arrives on DVD. *The Years of Change* includes 10 discs, seven feature length movies, and over 30 related historical documentaries.

Sean Patrick Flanery in full action mode as Indy in "Treasure of the Peacock's Eye."

MAY

Iron Man

May 2: *Iron Man*, directed by Jon Favreau, is quickly declared the first hit movie of the summer. When bidding on the movie, ILM and Skywalker Sound pooled their efforts to produce a convincing demo of their abilities: a scene of Iron Man flying about with fully mixed sound effects. This effort landed them primary roles in the movie's postproduction.

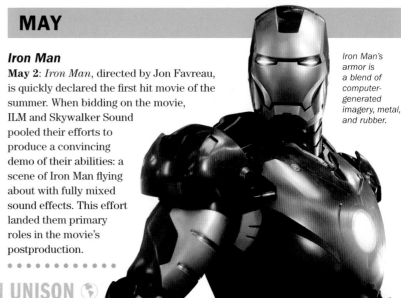

Iron Man's armor is a blend of computer-generated imagery, metal, and rubber.

⊕ **INDIA LAUNCHES A RECORD 10 SATELLITES IN UNISON** ⊕

The poster shows Anakin Skywalker, Obi-Wan Kenobi, Ahsoka Tano, and Yoda.

Clone Wars Trailer

May 8: The trailer for *Star Wars: The Clone Wars* debuts on television on multiple Turner networks across all US time zones. The two-minute preview also arrives in theaters, alongside such features as Warner Bros.' *Speed Racer*. The theatrical poster had been unveiled online two days earlier. Work continues at a feverish pace at Lucasfilm Animation to complete the feature as well as the season-one episodes.

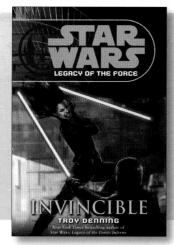

Invincible

May 13: *The Legacy of the Force* novel series concludes with *Invincible* by Troy Denning. Jaina Solo hunts down her Sith-turned brother, Jacen. In a final duel with gut-wrenching consequences, she kills her twin.

Cover art by Jason Felix depicts the decisive lightsaber battle between Jaina and Jacen.

Cause of Death

May 13: George Lucas Books, a new publishing entity within JAK Films that packages and publishes books specific to Lucas's interests, releases its second title: *Cause of Death: A Perfect Little Guide to What Kills Us*. The nonfiction release by Jack Mingo, Erin Barrett, and Lucy Autrey Wilson is published by Pocket Books. (The first George Lucas Books title was *Cinema by the Bay*, a chronicle of filmmaking in North California, published in 2006.)

Indiana Jones IV

May 22: Indy returns to the big screen with a long-gestated fourth film, *Indiana Jones and the Kingdom of the Crystal Skull*. Spielberg once again directs Ford in the title role, with a story by Lucas and a script by Jeff Nathanson and David Koepp. John Williams provides the score. Other returning *Indy* veterans include Ben Burtt, with ILM providing visual effects alongside the model shop of Kerner Optical. The film's release is accompanied by a licensing, publishing, and marketing push unprecedented in *Indy* history.

Fighting fit and adept with the bullwhip, Harrison Ford performs many of his own stunts in the role of Indiana Jones.

Phoenix

May 25: NASA's *Phoenix* probe touches down in the polar region of Mars and begins evaluating the habitability of the red planet.

JUNE

Stan Winston

June 15: Visual effects artist Stan Winston, known for the animatronic dinosaurs in *Jurassic Park* and the robotic endoskeletons in *Terminator*, dies at the age of 62. Stan Winston also developed the Wookiees for *The Star Wars Holiday Special*.

WALL•E

June 27: Once again moviegoers fall in love with a robot "voiced" by Ben Burtt, when Pixar's *WALL•E* arrives in theaters. The movie includes long stretches of screen-time without dialogue, relying instead on a rich visual and aural landscape crafted by Burtt and Skywalker Sound. Unusual for a Pixar movie, *WALL•E* contains live-action segments, realized by ILM and Kerner Optical.

LEGO® Troopers

June 30: Employees of the LEGO Group in the UK assemble clone trooper minifigures in a massive display that raises money and awareness for the National Autistic Society and sets a Guinness World Record.

The display uses 35,310 clone trooper minifigures.

The clone troopers are fronted by a minifigure of Darth Vader himself.

CLONE WARS & BEYOND

The designers at the LEGO Group faced the challenge of capturing the weird and wonderful range of *Star Wars* characters while still working within the requirements of LEGO® minifigures. The result, so far, is an innovative collection of over 240 distinctive LEGO *Star Wars* minifigures.

Star Wars minifigures come in several forms: the classic articulated, detachable, head-torso-legs configuration; undetachable battery-operated variants with light-up lightsabers; creatures with unique head sculpts using flexible rubber rather than traditional ABS plastic; shorter characters depicted with smaller, unarticulated legs; and completely new creations, such as R2-D2 or the gonk droid.

Stormtrooper

Tusken Raider

Luke Skywalker
(Tatooine)

Yoda   Royal Guard

Han Solo
(Carbonite)

Kit Fisto

Zam Wesell

Anakin Skywalker   Buzz Droid

Gamorrean Guard

TIE Pilot

Lando Calrissian

Rebel Hoth
Trooper

Wedge Antilles

Anakin Skywalker
(Boy)

General Grievous

R5-D4

3:1-scale prototypes of new minifigure parts are hand-sculpted out of clay and baked in an oven, like this Mon Calamari Officer. These models are then digitally scanned and the resulting image is used to make the mold for the final plastic pieces.

A-Wing Pilot

Han Solo
(Hoth)

Rebel Fleet Trooper

Anakin Skywalker
(Pilot)

Gonk Droid

Chewbacca

Kashyyyk
Trooper

Jawa

Princess Leia

R2-Q5

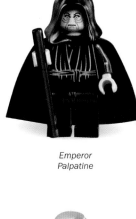

Paploo

Lando Calrissian
(Skiff Guard
Disguise)

Battle Droid

Darth Vader

Cloud City Guard

Han Solo

Obi-Wan Kenobi

Emperor
Palpatine

R2-D2
(Serving Drinks)

C-3PO

Lobot

Captain Antilles

General Madine

Princess Leia
(Cloud City)

Ahsoka Tano

AT-AT Driver

Captain Rex

General Veers

Clone Trooper

EV-9D9

JULY

The Falcon *includes authentic movie sounds: engine boost, cruise mode, fly-by, firing cannons, and more.*

Hasbro *Falcon*

Hasbro releases the ultimate version of the *Millennium Falcon* toy. Nearly 91 centimeters (three feet) long, this newly molded edition of the classic smuggling vessel can now accommodate 18 action figures and includes electronic light-up features and sound.

Force Unleashed Trailer

July 9: A dramatic cinema-style launch trailer for *Star Wars: The Force Unleashed* debuts exclusively on ew.com, the *Entertainment Weekly* website.

Outlander

July 11: The action-packed fantasy film *Outlander* receives limited release. It features concept design by veterans from the *Star Wars* Prequel art team: Robert Barnes, Ryan Church, and Iain McCaig.

The Dark Knight

July 18: Warner Bros. releases *The Dark Knight*. The sequel to *Batman Begins* (2005) reaches $400 million in domestic revenue in an astounding 18 days.

Japan Celebration

July 19–21: The Makuhari-Messe Convention Center in Chiba in Japan, hosts *Star Wars* Celebration Japan, the official fan convention commemorating the 30th anniversary of the Japanese release of *Star Wars*. In attendance are Mark Hamill and Anthony Daniels. The event celebrates the *Star Wars* experience, with many more guests, panels on collecting, and sneak previews of *The Clone Wars* animated movie and series. Event-specific merchandise with a definite Japanese feel include *Star Wars* tea towels, a tiny remote-controlled R2-D2 figure, and a special set of bottle caps blind-packed within plastic eggs.

A stormtrooper patrols the venue on the opening day of Celebration Japan.

Robot Chicken

July 22: The *Robot Chicken: Star Wars Special* is released on DVD with many bonus features.

Kevin Spacey

July 24: Acclaimed actor Kevin Spacey makes a surprise guest appearance at the *Star Wars* Fan Movie Challenge Awards at the San Diego Comic-Con. Aside from being a fan, Spacey is helping to promote *Fanboys*, a long-delayed comedy directed by Kyle Newman that tells the story of a group of *Star Wars* fans going to see Episode I.

A Clone Wars *ammo box exclusive gift.*

Ammo Box

July 25: To promote *Star Wars: The Clone Wars*, Lucasfilm gives away actual ammo boxes, painted to resemble clone troopers, to attendees of their 2008 Comic-Con International party.

Clone Merchandise

July 26: Hasbro launches a salvo of *Star Wars: The Clone Wars* merchandise. The product line adopts a white and blue look that mimics the sleek, clean lines of the clone army. The action figure cards adopt the clone helmet image for their shape, while the toys connected to the live-action movies mimic the style, but with a classic stormtrooper instead.

A Clone Wars *Anakin Skywalker action figure*

Clone Books

July 26: *Star Wars: The Clone Wars* fans can add to their libraries a host of new books directed at young readers from the Penguin Group (including Grosset & Dunlap, Puffin, Ladybird, and DK Publishing). Among the assortment are picture books, activity books, movie novelizations, multi-level readers, and a hardcover reference book.

Star Wars: The Clone Wars literature caters to a wide range of ages.

Soulcalibur

July 29: Yoda, Darth Vader, and the Secret Apprentice from *Star Wars: The Force Unleashed* cross swords with the super-powered heroes and villains from the Soulcalibur franchise in Soulcalibur IV, a Bandai release for the PlayStation 3 and Xbox 360. Because of The Force Unleashed's delayed release, this is the first video game to feature its hero, Starkiller.

SEPTEMBER

The Force Finally Unleashed

September 16: *Star Wars: The Force Unleashed* is released. LucasArts holds a premiere party at a San Francisco Best Buy store, with Lucas making a special appearance alongside actors from the game and executive producer and writer Haden Blackman. Selling 1.5 million units worldwide in under a week, the title becomes the fastest selling *Star Wars* game of all time. The company's first internally developed title for the Xbox 360 and PlayStation 3, it benefited from collaboration with ILM, as well as two revolutionary technologies: Digital Molecular Matter from Pixelux Entertainment and euphoria from NaturalMotion.

AUGUST

Composer Kevin Kiner

Clone Wars Soundtrack

August 12: Sony Classical releases the soundtrack for *The Clone Wars* feature, composed by Kevin Kiner, on CD and iTunes.

The Secret Apprentice Force-zaps a bull rancor in the Felucian swamps.

Mall Tour

September 19: Cartoon Network counts down to the release of *The Clone Wars* TV series with a mall tour that targets eight shopping centers. Activities in the tour include interactive games, photo ops, sneak peek screenings of *Clone Wars* clips, and a lightsaber skill test.

Clone Wars Parties

September 27: More marketing for *The Clone Wars* includes Cartoon Network teaming up with House Party to organize 2,000 in-home viewing parties for thousands of kids across the US. The party kit includes a lightsaber, balloons, masks, tattoos, stickers, and the first two episodes of the series.

Clone Wars Released

August 15: *The Clone Wars* movie, the first animated *Star Wars* feature, arrives in theaters. A prelude to the forthcoming television series, the movie includes several voices supplied by actors from the live-action films, including Samuel L. Jackson and Christopher Lee. Although the movie does excite young fans—the intended target audience—it has trouble connecting with older reviewers.

Christopher Lee returns as the voice of Count Dooku, who masterminds a kidnapping plot.

Clone Captain Rex is a hit with fans young and old.

The Clone Wars movie introduces viewers to Ahsoka Tano, Anakin's Padawan.

ONLINE ⊕ LEHMAN BROTHERS FILES FOR BANKRUPTCY ⊕

OCTOBER

Small Screen Wars

October 3: *Star Wars: The Clone Wars* series debuts on Cartoon Network with a special hour-long premiere at 9 p.m and is the most watched premiere in Cartoon Network History. The series is a ratings hit with the target demographic of young *Star Wars* fans: Audience numbers for kids aged two to 11 are up 125 percent from the same timeslot in 2007. Online, fans can continue the adventure between episodes by playing games at CartoonNetwork. com, while StarWars.com adds exclusive video commentaries, trivia-laden episode guides, and a brand new exclusive web comic. Episodes are also on iTunes.com for users to download and enjoy on the go.

Anakin Skywalker recklessly flies into danger in "Downfall of a Droid."

Yoda inspires the clone troopers under his command in "Ambush."

Kit Fisto faces the roggwart creature in "Lair of Grievous."

Captain Rex and Commander Bly are crack shots in a two-episode storyline set in the grasslands of Maridun.

Hi-Def *Indy*

October 14: *Indiana Jones and the Kingdom of the Crystal Skull* arrives on DVD and Blu-ray, the first new release on the high-definition format from Lucasfilm and Steven Spielberg.

Scream Awards

October 18: Samuel L. Jackson, joined by 50 stormtroopers, presents Lucas with the Comic-Con Icon Award at the annual Scream Awards, honoring the best in fantasy, sci-fi, and comics.

The Old Republic

October 21: LucasArts and BioWare announce the development of The Old Republic, a story-driven massively multiplayer online PC game that is set thousands of years before the Original Trilogy.

NOVEMBER

Mr. President 🌐🌐🌐

November 4: Barack Obama beats John McCain in the presidential election and becomes the 44th American president and the first African-American to reach that office in the nation's history. Lucas describes Obama as a "hero in the making" and attends the historic inauguration in January 2009.

Darth Toaster

November 6: StarWarsShop.com releases an exclusive Darth Vader toaster—one that burns the image of the helmeted Dark Lord onto each slice of toast. It becomes a surprise hit as word of this unlikely kitchen appliance spreads virally across the Internet.

30 Rock

November 6: In an episode of NBC's *30 Rock*, Tina Fey as Liz Lemon dresses up as Princess Leia in order to avoid jury duty.

LucasArts adapts the 3-D models from the animated series for its Clone Wars titles.

Unleashed Expansion

December 4: New downloadable content for *Star Wars*: The Force Unleashed appears on Xbox Live, and a week later on the PlayStation Network. A new single-player level takes gamers into the heart of the abandoned Jedi Temple. A new assortment of costumes and character skins enables players to unleash the Force as Darth Maul, Plo Koon, Jango Fett, Count Dooku, or even C-3PO.

C-3PO is "doomed" no longer when imbued with the unleashed power of the Force.

Jedi Alliance tells an all-new Clone Wars story.

Clone Wars Gaming

November 11: Repeating Lucasfilm's successful formula of coupling home video and video game releases, *The Clone Wars* movie arrives on DVD and Blu-ray, while two new video games hit the shelves. The movie is the first high-definition *Star Wars* home video release ever. On the game front, LucasArts releases *The Clone Wars*: Jedi Alliance, which emphasizes cooperative play for the Nintendo DS. For the popular Nintendo Wii is *The Clone Wars*: Lightsaber Duels, in which players swing a Wiimote (Wii remote) to simulate lightsaber action.

Robot Chicken

November 16: The *Robot Chicken: Star Wars* special gets a sequel, aptly named *Robot Chicken: Star Wars Episode II*, which airs on Adult Swim, on Cartoon Network.

Holiday Special Anniversary

November 17: StarWars.com celebrates the 30th anniversary of the much mocked *Star Wars Holiday Special* with a week of retrospective content, including interviews, collectible spotlights, and a rare animation test.

Complete Encyclopedia

December 9: Del Rey publishes a massive three-volume definitive reference work, *Star Wars: The Complete Encyclopedia*. Over 1,200 pages in length and weighing in at nearly 11 pounds, the book is the largest *Star Wars* reference work published to date. It updates the original '98 *Encyclopedia* with over a decade of new material from books, comics, games, the Prequel Trilogy, and the new *Clone Wars* series. It is researched and written by Steve Sansweet, Pablo Hidalgo, Bob Vitas, Daniel Wallace, Josh Kushins, Mary Franklin, and Chris Cassidy.

DECEMBER

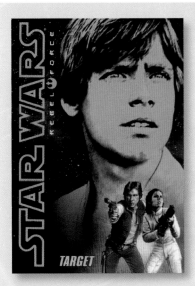

Rebel Force covers feature a mix of photography and original art by Randy Martinez.

Target and Hostage

December 2: Scholastic Inc. starts a new middle-grade fiction series set in the time of the original *Star Wars* trilogy, between Episodes IV and V, with Luke, Han, Leia, Chewbacca, and the droids. Called *Rebel Force* and written by Alex Wheeler, it kicks off with *Target* and *Hostage*.

Chopsticks

December 10: For SIGGRAPH Asia 2008 in Singapore, Lucasfilm Animation issues two different sets of chopsticks.

Loan Wars

December 16: *MAD* magazine spoofs the bailout headlines during the economic crisis with a "Loan Wars" poster parody by Tom Richmond that mimics *The Clone Wars*.

In the spoof poster, Clone Wars characters are replaced with figures from the US administration: Anakin is replaced by Ben Bernanke, Obi-Wan is Henry Paulson, Yoda becomes Barney Frank, and Ahsoka Tano is Nancy Pelosi. George W. Bush and Dick Cheney are droids.

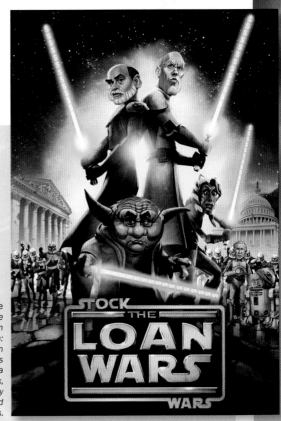

Player Bonus Costume
Father's Robes / Kashyyyk

Star Wars: The Force Unleashed is perhaps the most ambitious *Star Wars* video game ever developed internally at LucasArts. Among the rewards for player success are unlockable costumes that allow for the customization of the main character, the Secret Apprentice. These robes—conceptualized above by artist Chin Ko—belong to Kento Marek, the Secret Apprentice's father, who is destroyed by Darth Vader in the game's introductory level set on Kashyyyk.

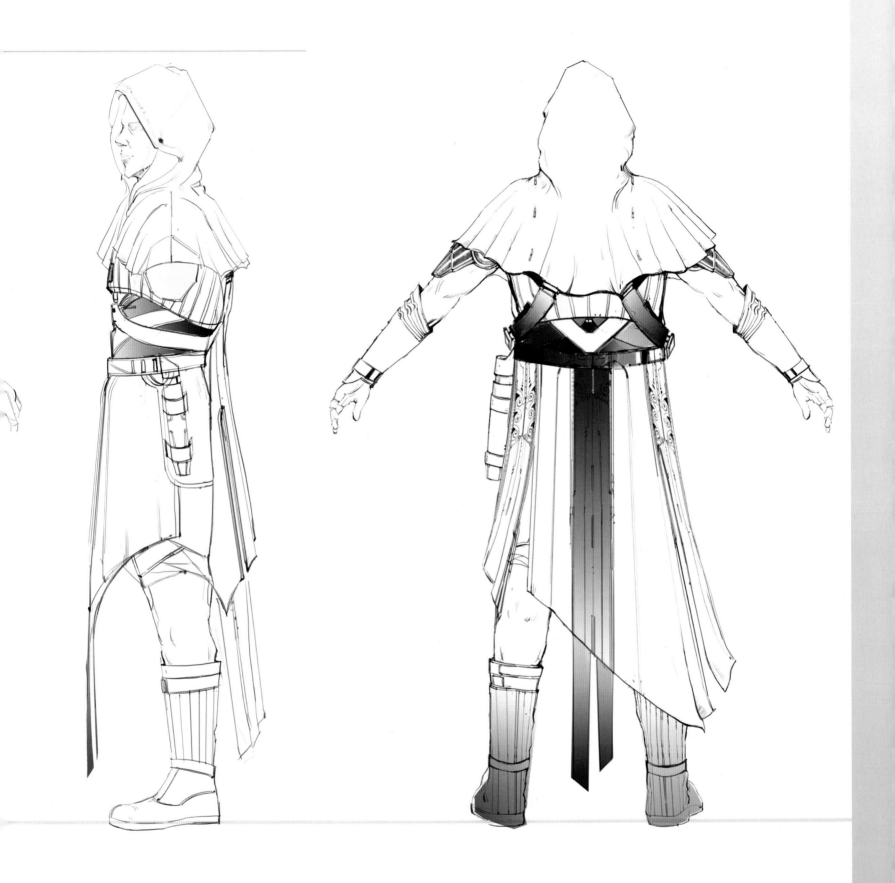

2009

THE INAUGURAL SEASON of *The Clone Wars* hits its stride, growing in technical and narrative complexity. New expansive worlds appear, like the frozen vistas of Orto Plutonia and the sweeping plains of Maridun, complete with native inhabitants. Stories grow more ambitious and are shaded with moral ambiguity.

Chairman Cho faces a Talz on icy Orto Plutonia.

> "Everyone keeps saying how great season one was, and how great it looks, and I keep saying, 'You ain't seen nothing yet.'"
>
> **Cary Silver** Star Wars: The Clone Wars *series producer*

THE NORMALLY CLEAR DELINEATION of Republic versus Separatists is clouded by the addition of "third-party" bounty hunters, epitomized by Cad Bane. The memorable gunslinger would become the poster villain for the launch of the second season, which gains a subtitle: *The Clone Wars: Rise of the Bounty Hunters.*

JANUARY

January 23: *Star Trek* legend George Takei (Sulu) crosses universes to guest star in an episode of *The Clone Wars* as a Neimoidian general, Lok Durd.

Lok Durd sets his evil plans in motion on the peaceful grassland planet of Maridun in the episode "Defenders of Peace."

Lok Durd is a general and a weapons developer for the Confederacy of Independent Systems.

⊕ FLIGHT 1549 LANDS SAFELY IN THE HUDSON RIVER ⊕ POWER-SHARING DEAL IN ZIMBABWE ⊕

FEBRUARY

For the launch of *The Clone Wars* series in Europe, Kellogg's issues *Star Wars*–themed cereals and premiums throughout the continent.

February 4: Lucas Online starts tweeting StarWars.com headlines and content via the popular micro-blogging site, Twitter, and quickly gathers thousands of followers.

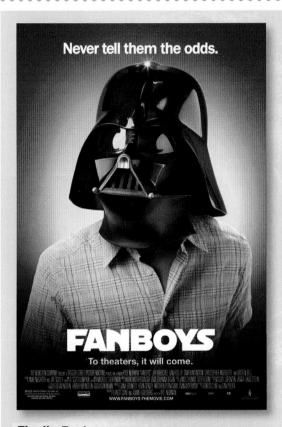

Never tell them the odds.

FANBOYS

To theaters, it will come.

WWW.FANBOYS-THEMOVIE.COM

Finally *Fanboys*

February 6: The much-delayed comedy *Fanboys* arrives in theaters from the Weinstein Company. Directed by Kyle Newman, the movie follows a group of fans who decide to ensure that a friend with a terminal illness sees Episode I by infiltrating Skywalker Ranch in 1998. The seriousness of the cancer plot at first gave producers cold feet, causing a re-edit and rewrite of the material, helmed by a new director. When word of this modification reached *Star Wars* fans, there was an outcry which ultimately led to the heart of the story being restored.

February 7: *Star Wars*: The Force Unleashed wins the Writers Guild award for Best Videogame Writing, recognizing Haden Blackman, Shawn Pitman, John Stafford, and Cameron Suey of LucasArts.

February 7: At New York Comic-Con, Lucasfilm collects "*Star Wars* stories"—video testimonials from fans about their history with *Star Wars*.

February 27: The Guitar Gala in Petaluma, California, features a Yoda-adorned Gibson guitar autographed by Lucas to raise funds for after-school arts programs for at-risk youth.

MARCH

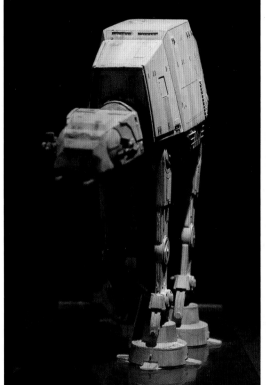

March 6: *Star Wars*: The Exhibition arrives in Santiago. It is the first time an exhibit of Lucasfilm props and artwork has visited Chile.

Costumes, props, models, and maquettes from all six Star Wars *movies are displayed, including an AT-AT walker model (left), and Jabba the Hutt (below).*

Eye on the Heavens

March 7: NASA launches its Kepler space telescope, an orbital observatory designed to discover terrestrial worlds in distant star systems. Kepler analyzes incoming light from these stars to see fluctuations caused by the presence of extrasolar planets.

Enter Cad Bane

March 20: *The Clone Wars* season finale, "Hostage Crisis," airs on Cartoon Network. This episode introduces Cad Bane, a Duros bounty hunter who leads a posse into the Senate building where they demand the release of a prisoner held by the Republic. Bane and this episode were first glimpsed at a Lucasfilm presentation at WonderCon in San Francisco on February 28.

Kilian Plunkett's concept art for Cad Bane explored a number of directions before production settled on a look strongly inspired by Lee Van Cleef's character in The Good, The Bad and The Ugly.

March 13, 2008: Every episode of *Star Wars: The Clone Wars* animated series offers new opportunities for visual design. This sketch by concept designer Jackson Sze shows sketches for the Lawquane family's farmstead in the season two episode "The Deserter." The farm, on the remote planet of Saleucami, is home to Cut Lawquane—a former soldier who is AWOL from the Clone Army—his Twi'lek wife Suu, and their two young children Jek and Shaeeah. The design of the setting evokes the idyllic simplicity of family and farming life on a peaceful planet, far from the troubles of the Clone Wars. Until, that is, the violence comes crashing into their backyard.

Cut's Farm Ep206
Jackson Sze 3.13.08

MARCH

A Fate Unfolds

March 24: Del Rey publishes *Outcast* by Aaron Allston, the first novel in the *Fate of the Jedi* series. Three authors—Allston, Troy Denning, and Christie Golden—will write the nine hardcovers. The series features an odyssey of Force-exploration undertaken by Luke Skywalker and his son, Ben, and the discovery of a lost society of Sith descendents. Meanwhile, an inexplicable mental ailment strikes a generation of younger Jedi Knights, prompting the galactic government to crack down on the Order.

Cover art by Ian Keltie

APRIL

PTI Group Inc's release of licensed *Clone Wars* Easter grass—paper shreds to line baskets—proves that anything can be turned into a *Star Wars* collectible.

Disney theme parks begin selling Jedi Robes in adult and kid sizes. The kid's version includes mouse ears on the hood.

Auction Aid

April 14: *Star Wars* fans in Australia auction items donated by Lucasfilm and others to benefit victims of the devastating bushfires in Victoria state.

Red Tails Takes Flight

April 16: Principal photography begins on *Red Tails*, produced by Rick McCallum with Lucas serving as executive producer. The movie is about the Tuskegee Airmen in World War II and has taken several decades for Lucas to develop. Anthony Hemingway directs the story by Lucas and the script by John Ridley.

April 25: Actress Bea Arthur dies at the age of 86. *Star Wars* fans remember her role as Ackmena, the Cantina bartender in *The Star Wars Holiday Special*.

April 29: Dark Horse Comics publishes a new line of *Star Wars Adventures*, all-ages appropriate digest-sized comics. This time, they are set during the Original Trilogy.

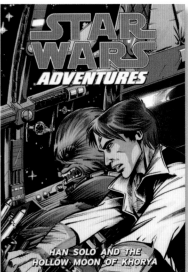

A Story Told in Music

April 10: *Star Wars: In Concert* debuts at the O2 arena in London. The premiere performance is called *Star Wars: A Musical Journey* and features a full orchestra and high-tech stagecraft to retell the story of the Saga. John Williams had selected the music that editors at Lucasfilm then illustrate with key scenes from all six movies played on enormous video screens. Host Anthony Daniels provides the narrative bridges.

The orchestra and choir perform Episode I's powerful "Duel of the Fates" to images of the kinetic lightsaber duel.

MAY

Japanese Machines

Sankyo in Japan releases a new line of *Star Wars* gaming machines for pachinko parlors.

Pachinko machines—a combination of pinball and slot machine—are immensely popular in Japan.

A wealth of promotional materials including flags, posters, face towels, tissues, cell phone charms, pins, and magnets, accompany the launch of the Star Wars pachinko.

In the Details

May 1: To sustain viewership during the summer hiatus, Cartoon Network airs "decoded" versions of *The Clone Wars* in which season one episodes are overlaid with trivia offering background information on characters and storylines.

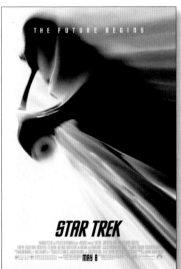

To Boldly Go

May 8: *Star Trek* is reborn as a smash-hit cinematic reboot that recasts the classic roles with new, younger actors. Director J.J. Abrams and writers Roberto Orci and Alex Kurtzman cite *Star Wars* as a huge influence in their approach. ILM delivers the movie's fantastic effects, with Roger Guyett serving as visual effects supervisor. Long-time *Star Trek* fan Ben Burtt works as sound designer and sound editor.

The new iteration of Star Trek earns over $257 million domestically.

Tweets from Space

May 12: Astronaut Mike Massimino launches into orbit aboard the space shuttle *Atlantis*, whose mission is to service the Hubble Space Telescope. Massimino becomes the first person to "tweet" from space, as he updates a Twitter account to keep the Earthbound informed of his progress. Massimino takes a *Young Indiana Jones* DVD with him into space, in acknowledgment of his contribution to one of the historical documentaries found in the set.

Massimino tweets "From orbit: Launch was awesome!! I am feeling great, working hard, & enjoying the magnificent views, the adventure of a lifetime has begun!'"

May 15: Ewan McGregor stars opposite Tom Hanks in *Angels & Demons*, a big-screen adaptation of the Dan Brown novel, directed by Ron Howard.

May 20: *Star Wars* fan and NASA astronaut Scott Parazynski successfully reaches the summit of Mount Everest.

Clone Wars Weekends

May 22: During *Star Wars* Weekends at Disney's Hollywood Studios, *The Clone Wars* takes the form of a stage show, *Behind the Force*, hosted by Ashley Eckstein (Ahsoka Tano). Fellow cast members and supervising director Dave Filoni join Eckstein on stage to discuss working on the show.

May 28: The *Lost Tribe of the Sith* series of downloadable novellas begins with *Precipice*, written by John Jackson Miller, as a tie-in to the *Fate of the Jedi* series.

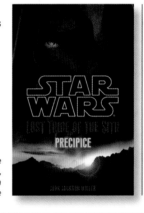

The cryptic cover art of the electronic-only novella, Precipice, the first in a series of three

Pixar's 10 for 10

May 29: Pixar releases *Up* in theaters, its 10th feature, and its first designed for 3-D exhibition. Skywalker Sound once again provides its postproduction sound services. The Lucasfilm Presidio campus is one of the stops in director Pete Docter's tour to discuss the movie.

JUNE

The Old Republic in Motion

June 1: A trailer titled "Deceived" for the forthcoming video game The Old Republic debuts prior to Episode III and becomes an Internet sensation. Game review websites, normally inured to spectacle and notoriously hard to impress, gush about the four-minute computer-animated trailer depicting a Jedi/Sith duel in the heart of the Jedi Temple.

JUNE

June 11: A particularly virulent strain of influenza, H1N1—dubbed "swine flu"—is declared a global pandemic by the World Health Organization.

Death of the King of Pop
June 25: Entertainer Michael Jackson dies of cardiac arrest aged 50. News of his death is reported worldwide via social networking sites. Over a million visitors swamp the Jackson entry on Wikipedia and searches for Jackson on Google nearly cripple the search engine site. His death triggers an outpouring of grief from around the globe.

Michael Jackson's family pays tribute to the pop legend in a memorial service at the Staples Center in Los Angeles.

JULY

July 15: LucasArts releases a special edition of the classic Secret of Monkey Island for download. *Star Wars* titles soon join it, including Republic Commando, Battlefront II, and Starfighter for PC download.

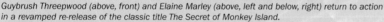

Guybrush Threepwood (above, front) and Elaine Marley (above, left and below, right) return to action in a revamped re-release of the classic title The Secret of Monkey Island.

2005's Republic Commando is re-released.

Also from 2005 comes Battlefront II.

July 21: To help promote the release of *Robot Chicken: Star Wars Episode II* on DVD, the *Robot Chicken* crew undertakes a roller skating tour across the US.

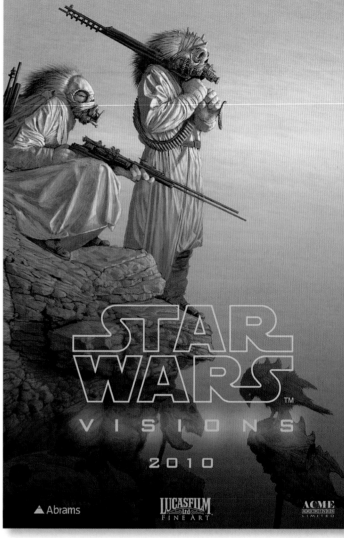

This intriguing interpretation of Tusken Raiders by Ed Binkley is revealed without explanation at the Con.

July 23: At San Diego Comic-Con, a mysterious project—*Star Wars: Visions*—is teased by Acme Archives and Abrams Books as a poster for sale.

Use the Force
July 23: Uncle Milton releases one of the most talked about toys of the year, the *Star Wars* Force Trainer. Incorporating a headset that scans brain waves, it activates a small fan concealed beneath a plastic column that lifts a ping pong ball-sized "training remote." The end result is that mental concentration levitates the remote, emulating Force telekinesis as no toy ever has before.

The Art of The Clone Wars
July 24: Chronicle Books offers *The Art of Star Wars: The Clone Wars* by Frank Parisi and Gary Scheppke for advance sale at Comic-Con. Concept artists Jackson Sze, Russell Chong, Randy Bantog, Thang Lee, and Wayne Lo autograph copies of the Deluxe Edition.

The Spectacular Will Be Televised

July 24: The annual *Star Wars* presentation at Comic-Con International is co-hosted by personalities from G4: Olivia Munn and Kevin Pereira. The two introduce cast members from *The Clone Wars* for a table read of a unique scene penned by Dave Filoni. The presentation is usually seen only by the fans in attendance, but G4 broadcasts it the next day on TV.

Mapping the Galaxy

August 18: Del Rey releases *Star Wars: The Essential Atlas*, a trade paperback by Daniel Wallace and Jason Fry that undertakes the Herculean task of mapping the entire galaxy of the Expanded Universe. The 244-page book is packed with maps and diagrams that not only chart the location of distant planets, but also track the history and Saga's storyline.

The cover of the Atlas shows only Mustafar, though the book inside reveals the whole galaxy.

AUGUST

A Mighty Good Cause

August 1: StarWars.com asks popular artists to customize blank "Mighty Muggs" toys donated by Hasbro, and auctions the eye-catching results online to benefit the Make-A-Wish Foundation. The "Empire Muggs Back" raises over $30,000, with standout entries being a customized George Lucas taking a mini AT-AT for a walk by artist JAKe, Cad Bane and Aurra Sing figures by Dave Filoni, and a wampa and Luke combination by artist Katie Cook.

Katie Cook's wampa has a faux fur coat glued in strips onto a blank Mighty Mugg as well as felt and fleece features.

August 7: Actor Ray Park (Darth Maul) once again plays a deadly, laconic character: the ninja commando Snake Eyes in the movie *G.I. JOE: The Rise of Cobra.*

August 10: Super *Star Wars*, the 1990s Nintendo hit, is made available for download on the Wii virtual console. Its two sequels soon follow.

SEPTEMBER

For the new ride, the StarSpeeder 1000 returns in its first journey since 1986.

Star Tours To Return

September 12: At Disney's first-ever fan convention, D-23, in Anaheim, a trailer for the new Star Tours 3-D ride experience is previewed. Walt Disney Parks and Resorts Chairman Jay Rasulo makes the announcement while accompanied on stage by stormtroopers and, via video, Darth Vader. Commemorative posters are distributed to the lucky fans who get to see the trailer in person.

Yoda poster for Star Tours 2011

September 16: President Barack Obama brandishes a Hasbro lightsaber toy on the White House lawn while playfully fencing with Olympic athletes, in a widely reported photo opportunity.

Barack Obama's antics are to promote Chicago's bid for the 2016 Olympics.

September 22: Carrie Fisher's *Wishful Drinking* one-woman stage show begins previewing at Studio 54 in New York City. The opening date is set for October 4.

OCTOBER

October 1: The worldwide *Star Wars: In Concert* tour begins at the Honda Center in Anaheim. It starts in the US before moving on to other countries in 2010.

Rise of the Bounty Hunters

October 2: The second season of *The Clone Wars* begins on Cartoon Network with two episodes—"Holocron Heist" and "Cargo of Doom"— back-to-back at 8 p.m. Building on the debut of Cad Bane in the first season, Lucasfilm brands this launch as the "Rise of the Bounty Hunters."

The second season launch draws strong ratings from young demographics, and critics remark on the increasing sophistication of the show's visuals and stories. One episode, "Senate Spy," stands apart as a noir-style spy thriller, without a single gunshot, explosion, or lightsaber to be seen.

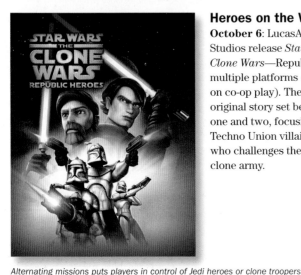

Alternating missions puts players in control of Jedi heroes or clone troopers.

Heroes on the Warfront

October 6: LucasArts and Krome Studios release *Star Wars: The Clone Wars—Republic Heroes* for multiple platforms (with a focus on co-op play). The game tells an original story set between seasons one and two, focusing on a new Techno Union villain, Kul Teska, who challenges the Jedi and their clone army.

Big Book of Bricks

October 10: DK Publishing celebrates 10 years of the perfect match up with *LEGO® Star Wars: The Visual Dictionary*. The photo-packed hardcover by Simon Beecroft is a showcase of every set produced to date, with DK's trademark picture clarity, text, and informative annotations, and a unique Luke Skywalker minifigure.

The exclusive minifigure that comes with the book is "Celebration" Luke from Episode IV.

LEGO® Star Wars: The Visual Dictionary becomes a #1 New York Times bestseller, staying on the list for more than 14 weeks.

Impact on the Surface

October 9: NASA's Lunar Crater Observation and Sensing Satellite (LCROSS) searches the moon for ice water. The multistage spacecraft separates from its Centaur upper module, which slams into the moon at over 90,123 kilometers (5,600 miles) per hour, ejecting 350 tons of debris in a huge plume analyzed by a second module.

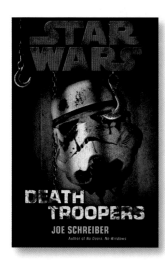

Horror Wars

October 13: Del Rey publishes the hardcover novel *Death Troopers*, by Joe Schreiber. The book has been anticipated and discussed since its cover art was first displayed on StarWars.com in the spring. It is the first all-out adult horror novel in *Star Wars* publishing, mixing the chilling zombie beats of a George Romero film with the space fantasy of George Lucas.

The book cover for Death Troopers, *designed by the artist Indika*

New Planets

October 19: European astronomers find 32 new planets beyond our solar system, ranging from terrestrial worlds five times the size of Earth to gas giants five times larger than Jupiter.

This Weapon Is Your Life

October 26: The Northern Ireland Children's Hospice places on auction for charity a lightsaber prop replica signed by Liam Neeson, Ewan McGregor, Samuel L. Jackson, George Lucas, and stunt coordinator Nick Gillard.

NOVEMBER

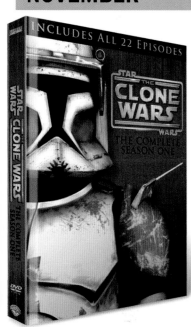

The Complete Season One

November 3: *Star Wars: The Clone Wars: The Complete Season One* is released on DVD and Blu-ray, collecting all 22 episodes in their full aspect ratio and, in the case of seven episodes, as slightly longer-running director's cuts. Both sets are loaded with behind-the-scenes extras and featurettes. The Blu-ray edition features a "Jedi Archive Vault" of concept art, digital model turntables, and work-in-progress animation. Both sets feature unique packaging built around a 64-page booklet of concept art, much of it never seen before.

The Blu-ray set of Star Wars: The Clone Wars: The Complete Season One

Unleashed Revisited

November 3: The hit video game *Star Wars: The Force Unleashed* is re-released as The Ultimate Sith Edition, featuring a new storyline with "what if" levels, depicting what would happen if Darth Vader was killed and the Secret Apprentice were sent to Hoth and Tatooine. It also bundles together the previous downloadable content.

Box art for The Ultimate Sith Edition shows the Secret Apprentice in his assassin's mask.

November 3: LucasArts returns to the battlefront with the game *Star Wars: Battlefront—Elite Squadron*, a portable release for the Sony PSP and Nintendo DS.

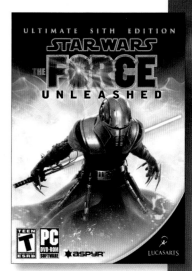

November 6: Ewan McGregor stars in *The Men Who Stare at Goats*, a farcical fictionalization of Jon Ronson's 2004 book exploring the military's application of Jim Channon's "First Earth Battalion" manual. The non-traditional soldiers in the movie are described as "Jedi Warriors."

DECEMBER

Cameron Returns

December 18: James Cameron's sci-fi epic *Avatar* hits theaters. Hollywood earmarks the movie as a game-changer for its expansive vision and use of 3-D. ILM is one of the multiple effects vendors used to make the movie a reality. "Creating a universe is daunting," Lucas says of Cameron to *The New Yorker*. "I'm glad Jim is doing it—there are only a few people in the world who are nuts enough to do it." *Avatar* goes on to break *Titanic*'s box office record, fueling speculation as to whether the time is right for a 3-D release of *Star Wars*.

Family Guy Strikes Back

December 22: The sequel to the *Star Wars Family Guy* special episode, *Blue Harvest*, debuts on DVD and Blu-ray as *Family Guy: Something, Something, Something, Darkside*. The follow up has the Griffin family and friends re-enact *The Empire Strikes Back*, with Carl as Yoda and Mort as Lando Calrissian.

Chris Griffin returns to his role as Luke Skywalker in the second Family Guy episode devoted to Star Wars.

ALLOON ✧ TALLEST BUILDING COMPLETED IN DUBAI ✧ LARGE HADRON COLLIDER RESTARTED ✧

2010

IN ADDITION TO CREATING A BRIGHT future for *Star Wars: The Clone Wars*, Lucasfilm devotes many resources to the 30th anniversary of *The Empire Strikes Back*. In *The Clone Wars* series, new villains enter the stage in the form of armored Mandalorians—space-suited warriors with familiar helmets. Young Boba Fett also makes an appearance, voiced by Episode II actor Daniel Logan, and viewers begin to understand how he becomes the notorious bounty hunter of the classic trilogy.

"We have now three generations of *Star Wars* fans... and some of these kids have never seen any of the films... All they know is *The Clone Wars*."

George Lucas
on The Daily Show, January 5, 2010

MEANWHILE, behind closed doors at the Big Rock campus of Skywalker Ranch, development quietly continues on a second animated *Star Wars* series named *Detours*, inspired by the numerous parodies that have cropped up over the years...

JANUARY

Mandalore Rising

January 25: Lucasfilm screens "The Mandalorian Plot," a forthcoming episode of the *The Clone Wars* TV series, for select fans invited to the company's headquarters in San Francisco. It features a guest role for Jon Favreau (director of *Elf* and *Iron Man*) as the armored villain, Pre Vizsla.

Pre Vizsla possesses the darksaber, which has been passed down through generations of Clan Vizsla.

FEBRUARY

Rebel Mascot
February 24: Students at the University of Mississippi vote to replace their dated team mascot, Colonel Reb. A campaign for Admiral Ackbar to become the new mascot for the team, the Rebels, gains online support over the next few months, but ultimately fizzles out.

MARCH

March 1: Amulet Books publishes *The Strange Case of Origami Yoda* by Tom Angleberger, which becomes a bestseller. The children's book tells the story of Dwight, a misfit kid who draws wisdom from an origami puppet of the Jedi Master. It is followed by *Darth Paper Strikes Back* in 2011, *The Secret of the Fortune Wookiee* in 2012, *The Surprise Attack of Jabba the Puppet* in 2013, *Princess Labelmaker to the Rescue* in 2014, and *Emperor Pickletine Rides the Bus*, also in 2014.

Angleberger received the 2012 Texas Bluebonnet Award for The Strange Case of Origami Yoda.

Angleberger's follow-up book, Darth Paper Strikes Back, provides details on how to make an origami Darth Vader.

Chewbacca is featured in The Secret of the Fortune Wookiee.

APRIL

Make Them Laugh
April 5: Lucasfilm Animation announces that work is underway on a computer-animated *Star Wars* comedy series. It will feature creative involvement from Seth Green and Matthew Senreich, creators of the TV series *Robot Chicken*. Producing the show will be Jennifer Hill, while Todd Grimes will direct.

MAY

May 5: The last year of membership to the official *Star Wars* fan club, Hyperspace, begins. Paid subscription to the club is phased out, "due to changing realities of the evolving fanscape."

Member kits were offered to US subscribers (they could also be bought online), featuring a poster, decal, and membership card.

May 19: A charity screening of *The Empire Strikes Back* at the ArcLight Cinema in Hollywood honors the 30th anniversary of the film, with Harrison Ford, Billy Dee Williams, and Peter Mayhew in attendance.

JUNE

May the Fashion be with You
June 5: Soccer star David Beckham, rapper Snoop Dogg, and musicians Daft Punk are among the celebrities to enter the famous Mos Eisley Cantina to advertise *Star Wars*-inspired sports clothing and footwear by Adidas. The television advert, which debuts online, features new footage of celebrities digitally blended into the original Episode IV footage.

Snoop Dogg with the Star Wars-inspired Adidas footwear range.

DEVASTATING EARTHQUAKES STRIKE HAITI AND CHILE ☉ EUROZONE FINANCIAL CRISIS ESCALATES

JUNE

June 22: Actress Ashley Eckstein (who voices Ahsoka Tano) launches Her Universe, a sci-fi inspired clothing line designed for female fans, featuring *Star Wars* clothing and accessories.

Ashley Eckstein is the voice of the Ahsoka Tano, Anakin Skywalker's eager apprentice in The Clone Wars.

SEPTEMBER

September 15: LucasArts and Sony Online Entertainment launch *Clone Wars Adventures*, a free-to-play, family friendly virtual world featuring weekly updates based on the TV show. Within a week they sign up one million players.

The game is updated with content from aired episodes of the television show; content can also be unlocked through membership.

OCTOBER

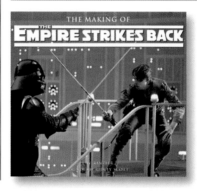

October 12: Del Rey publishes *The Making of The Empire Strikes Back*. Written by J.W. Rinzler, the 372-page tome reveals many previously unreleased details and pictures, and features a foreword by Ridley Scott.

An exclusive unit photograph from the filming of the duel between Luke and Vader makes a fitting cover for The Making of The Empire Strikes Back.

AUGUST

Celebration V

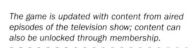

August 11–13: The official Lucasfilm convention arrives in Orlando, Florida, and over 32,000 fans attend. The headline event is an on-stage interview with George Lucas conducted by the host of *The Daily Show* (and long-time *Star Wars* fan) Jon Stewart. As part of Celebration V, fans are allowed nighttime admission into Walt Disney Hollywood Studios to bid farewell to the original Star Tours attraction (which is to be re-imagined in 2011) with one "Last Tour to Endor."

George Lucas and Jon Stewart on stage at Celebration V.

VOLCANO ERUPTION IN ICELAND GROUNDS FLIGHTS ✈ WIKILEAKS RELEASES CONFIDENTIAL US

OCTOBER

October 26: LucasArts releases *Star Wars*: The Force Unleashed II, which resurrects the character Starkiller through cloning and leads the player through a storyline featuring Boba Fett.

Haden Blackman was the executive producer for both editions of the game.

Starkiller is a failed attempt by Darth Vader to create the perfect apprentice.

NOVEMBER

November 28: Irvin Kershner, director of *The Empire Strikes Back* dies, aged 87. "The world has lost a great director and one of the most genuine people I've had the pleasure of knowing," says George Lucas.

DECEMBER

December 7–9: "The Nightsisters Trilogy," a three-part arc from *The Clone Wars* animation series, screens theatrically in 11 cities. The plot reveals the character Savage Opress and hints that Darth Maul may in fact be alive.

Savage Opress is part of the Nightsisters' plot for revenge against Count Dooku.

GOVERNMENT FILES ❂ THE BURJ KHALIFA, TALLEST MAN-MADE STRUCTURE IN THE WORLD, OPENS

Each episode of *The Clone Wars* animated series offers new opportunities for visual design. In this illustration by Matt Gaser, Obi-Wan Kenobi shares a tense moment with Satine, Duchess of Mandalore. Introduced in "The Mandalore Plot," the twelfth episode of season two, Satine shares her name with Ewan McGregor's love interest in the 2001 film *Moulin Rouge*.

2011

WITH THE RELEASE of *Star Wars: The Complete Saga* on Blu-ray, one of the most requested titles for the high-definition home video format finally arrives. Die-hard fans and home theater enthusiasts closely scrutinize information about the release. The unparalleled picture and sound quality, as well as its trove of never-before-seen cut content from the films, are lauded. The latest round of Lucas's tweaks to the movies also ignites the now-traditional cycle of heated online debate.

> "The epic franchise pioneered sound and visual presentation in theaters and is perfectly suited to do it again in the home, with a viewing experience only possible with Blu-ray."
>
> **Mike Dunn,** *president, Twentieth Century Fox Home Entertainment*

BY YEAR'S END, Lucasfilm announces a plan to release the *Star Wars* Saga into theaters for 2012—this time in 3-D. Several studios also look to convert their classic titles to 3-D, buoyed by the phenomenal success of *Avatar*.

JANUARY

January 25: Lucasfilm and Insight Editions release a limited-edition, massive six-volume box set called *Star Wars: Frames*. The leather-bound books encased in a wood-inlaid box contain 1,416 images from the Saga, handpicked by George Lucas.

The Mortis Trilogy

January 28: *The Clone Wars* begins a trilogy that reveals, through deeply symbolic, mythological storytelling, the inner nature of the Force. The brooding storyline features the embodiments of the light side, dark side, and the balance, and guest stars Liam Neeson (Qui-Gon Jinn) and Pernilla August (Shmi Skywalker), who reprise their Episode I roles.

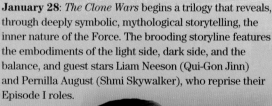

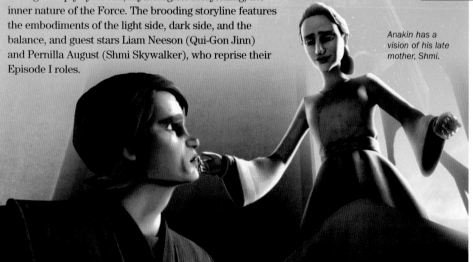

Anakin has a vision of his late mother, Shmi.

FEBRUARY

February 4: During the Super Bowl, Volkswagen® airs a TV spot featuring a young boy dressed in a Darth Vader costume, trying to use the Force on his surroundings. The commercial is acclaimed as the best of the year by *AdWeek*.

MARCH

March 4: Gore Verbinski's *Rango* rides into theaters. The quirky western is ILM's first full-length, animated movie and it receives much critical praise.

Johnny Depp at the premiere of Rango in Los Angeles

LEGO® *Star Wars* III

March 22: LucasArts releases the LEGO *Star Wars* III: *The Clone Wars* video game for PlayStation 3, PlayStation Portable, Xbox 360, Nintendo Wii, Nintendo DS, Nintendo 3DS, and PC and Mac platforms.

March 29: Del Rey Books publishes *The Star Wars Craft Book* by Bonnie Burton, featuring step-by-step instructions for such projects as finger puppets, pet toys, tissue box covers, bird houses, and even a Hanukkah dreidel.

Bonnie Burton also worked as a senior editor for StarWars.com.

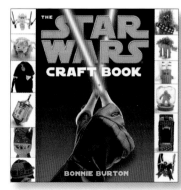

"ARAB SPRING" UPRISINGS BEGIN TO DRASTICALLY RESHAPE POLITICS IN THE MIDDLE EAST

APRIL

Let the Wookiee Guest Star

April 1: Chewbacca guest stars in the season three finale of *Star Wars: The Clone Wars*. Both Chewie and series star Ahsoka Tano are prisoners on a jungle moon, where they are pursued by reptilian hunters. Actor Peter Mayhew visited the animation team to offer his insights on playing Chewbacca.

Prisoners Ahsoka Tano and Chewbacca join forces on a Trandoshan moon.

MAY

May 4: A year after announcing the disbanding of the official fan club, *Star Wars* launches an official presence on the popular social networking site Facebook. By consolidating existing groups and attracting new users, the page quickly amasses four million followers.

All-New Star Tours

May 20: Star Tours: The Adventures Continue officially launches at Walt Disney World Resort in Orlando, Florida, in a daytime gala attended by George Lucas. The simulator ride, featuring all-new 3-D visuals produced by ILM, has been completely redesigned, and is built around custom elements that ensure the ride experience varies upon each visit. Like the original Star Tours, passengers are shuttled aboard a starspeeder, this time piloted by the hapless C-3PO. Destinations in the ride include Tatooine, Naboo, Kashyyyk, Geonosis, Coruscant, and Hoth. The new attraction will also open at Disneyland on June 3, 2011.

JUNE

June 28: Testament to the rapidly changing publishing industry, Del Rey Books makes available its expansive library of older *Star Wars* novels as eBooks. This conversion includes a full catalog of over 100 Del Rey and Bantam titles.

JULY

Chris Evans at the First Avenger premiere in Los Angeles.

July 19: Marvel Studios and Paramount Pictures release *Captain America: The First Avenger*, directed by Joe Johnston. Its throwback style shares the same creative roots as *Star Wars* and *Indiana Jones*, films Johnston worked on.

Atlantis Returns

July 21: With the return of the space shuttle *Atlantis* and the completion of STS-135, its 135th mission, NASA's Space Shuttle Program comes to an end after more than 30 years.

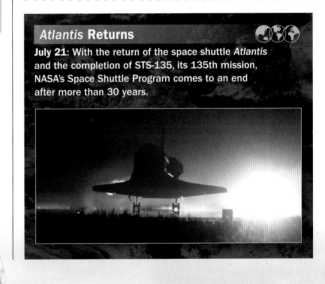

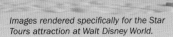

Images rendered specifically for the Star Tours attraction at Walt Disney World.

JULY

The Padawan Menace

July 22: The Cartoon Network airs LEGO *Star Wars: The Padawan Menace*, a 22-minute animated special in the whimsical LEGO *Star Wars* style. Written by Michael Price of *The Simpsons* and directed by David Scott, the fast-paced story follows a group of Jedi younglings on a field trip that goes awry. The special would be released on Blu-ray and DVD on September 16.

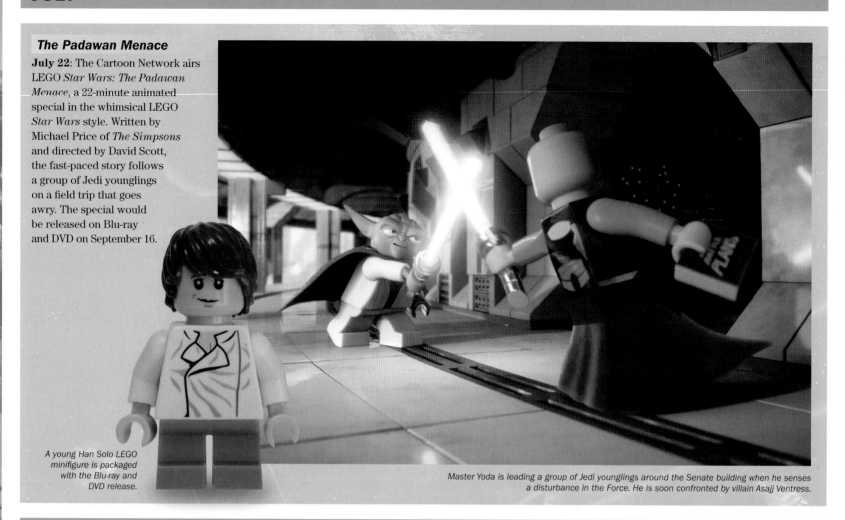

A young Han Solo LEGO minifigure is packaged with the Blu-ray and DVD release.

Master Yoda is leading a group of Jedi younglings around the Senate building when he senses a disturbance in the Force. He is soon confronted by villain Asajj Ventress.

SEPTEMBER

September 4: In anticipation of the *Star Wars Saga* Blu-ray release, World Series champions, the San Francisco Giants, host a *Star Wars* day, which offers an exclusive Brian Wilson-frozen-in-carbonite collectible and a ballpark screening of Episode V.

The Brian Wilson collectible is a parody of Han Solo's ordeal.

September 6: Del Rey Books publishes a 20th anniversary edition of *Heir to the Empire* by Timothy Zahn, full of behind-the-scenes annotations from the author and his editors.

Timothy Zahn also wrote Dark Force Rising and The Last Command.

StarWars.com Revamp

September 13: StarWars.com undergoes an extensive relaunch. Lucasfilm's digital team partners with New York-based agency Big Spaceship to redirect the future of the website. What emerges is a clean and stylish site meant to engage a larger audience with strong visuals and enhanced interaction.

London's Lightsaber

September 14: To commemorate the release of *Star Wars: The Complete Saga* on Blu-ray, Fox Home Entertainment and Lucasfilm transform the landmark BT Tower in the heart of London's West End into an enormous lightsaber.

The BT Tower lights were switched on by actor Anthony Daniels (C-3PO).

EARTHQUAKE AND TSUNAMI DEVASTATE JAPAN ◉ PRINCE WILLIAM MARRIES KATE MIDDLETON ◉

September 16: Epic Ink Books releases *Star Wars: The Blueprints*, written by J.W. Rinzler. The massive tome, limited to 5,000 copies, explores the technical drawings created by the production art departments during the set construction for the *Star Wars* Saga.

Star Wars: The Blueprints measures 15.5 x 18.5 inches (39.4 x 47 cm).

Star Wars on Blu-ray

September 16: *Star Wars: The Complete Saga* arrives on Blu-ray in the US, marking the first time the entire Saga of six movies has been available within a single collection. Each movie benefits immensely from high-definition picture and sound presentation. The release also presents another opportunity for Lucas to add a host of modifications to the movies—some more noticeable than others. Features include an extensive tour of props, costumes, and models from the Lucasfilm Archives, deleted scenes from all six movies, documentaries, and a collection of pop-culture parodies that celebrate *Star Wars*, as gathered from film, television, and the internet.

The release includes eagerly anticipated deleted material from Episode IV.

September 26: After years of delay, the long-rumored and requested sequel *Crimson Empire III* begins publication from Dark Horse Comics.

OCTOBER

Steve Jobs Passes

October 5: Visionary and Apple Chairman Steve Jobs dies after a long battle with pancreatic cancer. "The magic of Steve was that while others simply accepted the status quo, he saw the true potential in everything he touched and never compromised on that vision," says George Lucas.

Darkness in *The Clone Wars*

October 28: *The Clone Wars* tells a dark four-part story that sends the clone troopers to the shadowy planet of Umbara. Series hero Clone Captain Rex is temporarily reassigned to a ruthless Jedi commander, General Krell. Krell's indiscriminate actions lead to the deaths of many soldiers, sparking a mutiny. The second episode of the arc was directed by Walter Murch, a longtime friend and collaborator of George Lucas.

DECEMBER

December 15: After eight years of online community roleplaying, *Star Wars Galaxies* shuts down its servers. Offering some closure to dedicated players of the game, Mon Mothma declares that the Rebel Alliance has triumphed over the Empire in one possible ending.

The Old Republic Launches

December 20: BioWare and LucasArts launch *Star Wars: The Old Republic*, a massively multiplayer online roleplaying game set thousands of years before Episode IV. Slick marketing, feverish anticipation, positive reviews, and previews of the story-driven game lead to a rush of subscriptions upon its launch. Within a month, the game draws over 1.5 million subscribers.

Players can choose to adopt classic Star Wars roles within the game, such as a Jedi or Sith.

2012

GEORGE LUCAS MENTIONED retirement in 2005, but he begins the year in the public eye with two major back-to-back theatrical releases. This year, however, it becomes evident that talk of retirement is more than just talk. Meanwhile, *Star Wars: The Clone Wars* launches its fifth season, with stories well beyond its 100th episode in the works. A second animated series continues development, nearing readiness for an unveiling of the quirkiest, oddest take on *Star Wars* yet.

> "I'm retiring. I'm moving away from the business, from the company, from all this kind of stuff."
>
> **George Lucas**
> in *The New York Times Magazine*, January 22, 2012

IN MARIN COUNTY, planning continues on the development of a new Lucasfilm filmmaking facility. Grady Ranch promises to "one day be a cutting-edge digital media production facility for both movies and television." But a surprising turn of events this year means a change in many, many plans.

JANUARY

January 1: Bob Anderson, fight choreographer, sword master, and lightsaber double for Darth Vader in *The Empire Strikes Back* and *Return of the Jedi*, passes away at age 89.

Plagueis the Wise

January 10: Del Rey releases *Darth Plagueis*, a novel by James Luceno that peels away some of the layers of mystery surrounding Palpatine and his unseen mentor, Sith Lord Plagueis, reputed to have control over life and death. It is a bestseller and praised for interweaving the lore of the prequel era into the narrative.

Red Tails Soars

January 20: 20th Century Fox and Lucasfilm release *Red Tails*, an action-packed adventure film inspired by the true story of the Tuskegee Airmen in World War II, America's first all-black military aviators. Lucas had been trying to get *Red Tails* made for over 20 years, and finally decided to financially back it himself. It is directed by Anthony Hemingway.

Palpatine's Voice

January 26: Actor Ian Abercrombie (left), who voiced Palpatine in the first five seasons of *Star Wars: The Clone Wars*, passes away at age 77. Tim Curry would step in to voice the role for the remainder of the series.

A Not So Elegant Weapon

January 30: David Allen Canterbury of Hayden Island, Oregon, is sentenced to 45 days in jail for attacking three customers with toy lightsabers at a local Toys-R-Us. The melee spilled outside the store, and after a scuffle with police, he was subdued and taken into custody.

Dark Side Burger

January 31: Tied to the Episode I 3-D release, French fast food chain Quick builds a promotion around a limited run of *Star Wars*-themed burgers. Imagery of the Darth Vader burger ("Dark Vador" in French), complete with black buns, garners worldwide internet attention.

The unsettling image of an ebony bun helped this burger go viral across the internet.

FEBRUARY

A Looooong Time Ago…

February 1: Dark Horse Comics begins publication of *Star Wars: Dawn of the Jedi*, a comics series by John Ostrander and Jan Duursema that is set over 25,000 years before the events of the films and purports to chronicle the very origins of the Jedi way.

Dawn of the Jedi tells of an ancient sect of Force-sensitives known as the Je'daii Order.

February 5:
A Volkswagen Super Bowl commercial has a coda that features several faithfully recreated Mos Eisley Cantina patrons debating whether or not this year's ad was better than last year's *Star Wars*-themed one.

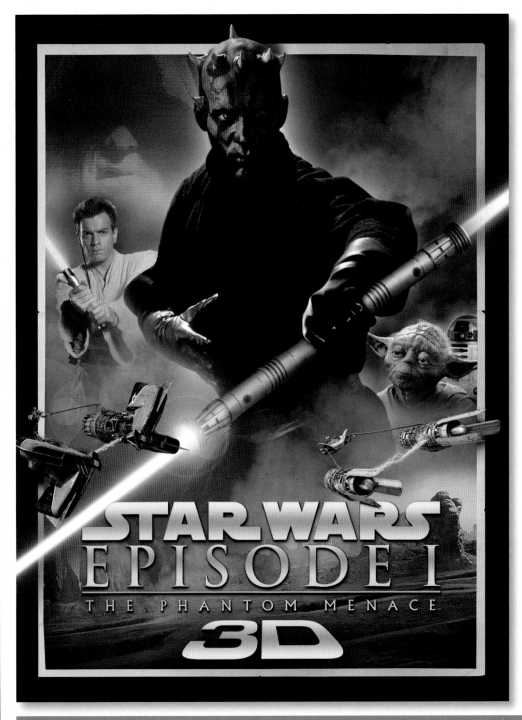

Menace Returns

February 10: *Star Wars:* Episode I *The Phantom Menace* in 3-D opens theatrically. The whole film has been meticulously converted for digital 3-D presentation, with work by PrimeFocus, supervised by ILM. Accompanying the release are worldwide promotional partnerships. New toys and collectibles feature iconic artwork of Darth Maul.

Vanguard Award

February 17: George Lucas receives the prestigious NAACP Vanguard Award recognizing his work in increasing understanding and awareness of social and racial issues through his work.

ILM Rustles Up Animation Oscar

February 26: *Rango*, the first full-length animated feature film created by Industrial Light & Magic receives an Academy Award® for Best Animated Feature Film. Directed by Gore Verbinski, *Rango* features animation and visual effects supervised by John Knoll, Hal Hickel, and Tim Alexander.

ILM developed a new animation method whilst working on Rango. Sequence based lighting allowed the team to edit a whole group of shots that share a similar lighting setup.

MARCH

Loss of a Visionary

March 3: Ralph McQuarrie, the concept artist so essential in defining the look and feel of *Star Wars*, passes away at age 82. Across the industry, artists inspired by McQuarrie's work express their gratitude, including George Lucas: "When words could not convey my ideas, I could always point to one of Ralph's fabulous illustrations and say, 'Do it like this.'"

Fate's End

March 13: The epic *Fate of the Jedi* novel series concludes with the ninth novel, *Apocalypse* by Troy Denning, published by Del Rey Books.

Darth Maul Lives

March 9: *The Clone Wars* season four finale resurrects Darth Maul, revealing that the power of the dark side has somehow kept the bisected Sith Lord alive. Driven insane by a decade of living in wretched depths, Maul (voiced by Sam Witwer) appears as an unsettling half-man, half-mechanical monstrosity.

APRIL

April 3: Microsoft and LucasArts team up to release *Star Wars: Kinect*, a new video game that allows players to control *Star Wars* action without the need for a controller. The special Kinect sensor detects body movement and translates it into game action.

April 3: Del Rey Books examines the battles and military forces of *Star Wars* with *The Essential Guide to Warfare* by Jason Fry with Paul R. Urquhart.

Battle over Grady Ranch

April 10: The ongoing row over Grady Ranch, fueled by Marin County neighbors opposed to George Lucas building a new production facility adjacent to Skywalker Ranch, dramatically concludes as Lucas cancels the project. Lucas announces plans to turn over the land to be developed for low-income housing. Entreaties for Lucas to reconsider are met as too little too late by the frustrated filmmaker. On the positive side, in the coming years, Lucas would propose 224 units of affordable housing to benefit the community.

Father Figure

April 18: Chronicle Books releases *Darth Vader and Son*, written and illustrated by cartoonist Jeffrey Brown. The charming—and bestselling—book imagines Vader as a good, if somewhat beleaguered, father to four-year-old Luke Skywalker in a series of full-page cartoons.

Just like any other father, Vader buys Luke ice cream, teaches him life lessons, and engages in lightsaber battling practice.

Let Me See Your Identity

April 19: *Star Wars* Identities: The Exhibition opens in Montreal, Canada. The exhibition includes artwork and props that define classic characters, while interactive displays allow visitors to examine what factors—history, genetics, culture, peers, and more—define identity.

Created by Canadian advertising agency, Bleublancrouge, the striking posters explore the forces that have shaped each character's identity.

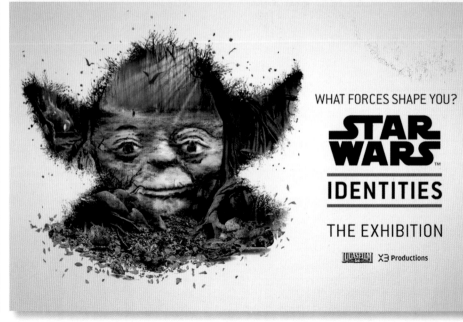

FIRST COMMERCIAL SPACEFLIGHT DOCKS WITH INTERNATIONAL SPACE STATION

Mythos-Making

April 27: Sideshow Toys announces the Mythos line, a collection of high-end polystone statues that, rather than carefully match a moment from a *Star Wars* film, instead extrapolates a previously unseen chapter in an iconic character's life. A striking rendition of Obi-Wan Kenobi as a desert traveler is among the first models revealed.

With flowing robes, tattered by the desert, and a pack holding supplies, machine parts, and weapons, Obi-Wan's statue tells its own story.

MAY

Cinematic Universe

May 4: Marvel's *The Avengers* opens, the culmination of five movies' worth of worldbuilding from Marvel Studios. The blockbuster boasts ILM visual effects, including the most realistic and complex incarnation of a computer-generated Hulk character yet achieved.

marvel.com

© 2016 MARVEL

Inside Coruscant

May 31: At this year's industry E3 show, LucasArts announces *Star Wars* 1313, a next-generation adventure game that spectacularly realizes the environment of 1313, a level deep in the heart of Coruscant that George Lucas had been developing for years for a proposed live-action television series.

JUNE

A New Future for Lucasfilm

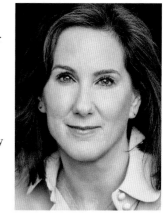

June 1: Acclaimed producer Kathleen Kennedy is named Co-Chair of Lucasfilm, an unmistakable sign that George Lucas is making clear his plans to retire and step down from the company he founded. Lucas's selection of Kennedy, a past collaborator on the *Indiana Jones* films, as well as the producer of many beloved movies such as *E.T.: The Extra Terrestrial*, the *Back to the Future* trilogy, *Jurassic Park*, *The Curious Case of Benjamin Button*, and *Lincoln*, brings with her veteran filmmaking experience. It is a strong indication that Lucasfilm will once again become an active production studio. Over the summer, Kennedy begins assembling the department heads who will serve as the production team essential for new *Star Wars* films, including head of development Kiri Hart, art director Rick Carter, and producers Jason McGatlin, Pippa Anderson, and John Swartz. Though no one says it publicly at the time, this marks the beginning of a new future for the *Star Wars* Saga.

Across the Star

June 5–6: A rare interplanetary conjunction occurs, where the tiny speck of Venus is visible making its trek past the disc of the sun as seen on Earth. The next transit will not occur until 2117, so this mini-eclipse is carefully monitored by scientists, both professional and armchair. Since it was visible from the Pacific coast, optics-experts at Lucasfilm and Industrial Light & Magic made simple pin-hole viewing stations on campus to safely watch and photograph the event.

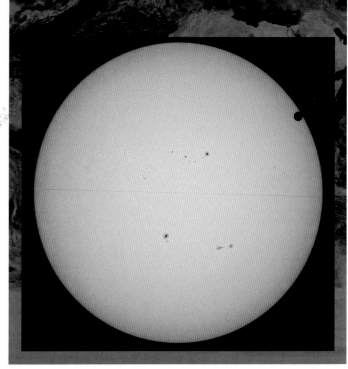

AUTHOR RAY BRADBURY DIES ☉ *GANGNAM STYLE* RELEASED, BECOMING WORLDWIDE HIT

JULY

The Force Runs Strong

July 7: The inaugural Course of the Force run begins. The event, organized by Lucasfilm, Nerdist Industries, Machinima, and Octagon, is modeled after an Olympic torch relay, and is designed to deliver a lightsaber from Skywalker Ranch to San Diego Comic-Con International. Stretches of the three-day run are available for the public to buy (and run in costume), with proceeds going to Make-A-Wish Foundation.

July 11: The latest licensee to develop high-end prop and costumes, Museum Replicas, joins the *Star Wars* stable. This arrangement would last for about a year before this particular category would once again change hands.

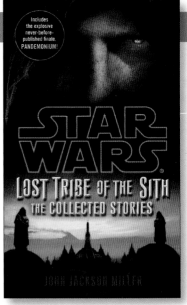

Lost Tribe Finds Print Home

July 24: Bundling their eBook series into a novella, Del Rey Books releases in print *Lost Tribe of the Sith: The Collected Stories* by John Jackson Miller. The series that accompanied and provided back-story to the *Fate of the Jedi* novels also spawns a limited run of comics from Dark Horse Comics.

The Course of the Force relay is led by a 7.5-meter (25-foot) long replica of Jabba's sail barge, which transports hosts Chris Hardwick, Alison Haislip, and Ashley Eckstein.

AUGUST

Red Planet Touchdown

August 5: People around the world are able to watch the NASA control rooms online, live, during the harrowing landing of the *Curiosity* probe onto the surface of Mars. Because of the vast distances involved, the "real-time" feed from the probe lags by 14 minutes, meaning all the maneuvers required during the seven-minute descent from the top of the Martian atmosphere to the surface must be done through carefully planned automated steps. Despite the monumental achievement, no US television network covers the event live—leaving it to the internet to capably capture the moment.

The 14 ingenious dice allow players to determine the success or failure of their actions, including advantages and threats.

X-wing in Hardback

August 7: Aaron Allston revisits the characters he brought to life in his *X-wing* series of books with *X-wing: Mercy Kill*, the final installment in the series. Released by Del Rey, it is the first and only hardback release in the *X-wing* line.

X-wing: Mercy Kill is a side novel to Apocalypse, *the final novel in the* Fate of the Jedi series, *which was released in March.*

RPG Rolls Again

August 18: The *Star Wars* license for tabletop roleplaying games comes to Fantasy Flight Games, who rolls out a Beta version of their forthcoming roleplaying game for the summer convention season. The hefty rule book provides innovative character creation and combat rules that incorporates custom dice for strong story-based gaming experiences.

⊕ CERN ANNOUNCES DISCOVERY OF PARTICLE THAT HAS PROPERTIES SIMILAR TO HIGGS

Celebration VI

August 23–26: Fans once again convene at an official Lucasfilm convention, returning to Orlando, Florida, site of Celebration V. The entire *Star Wars* Saga is the focus of the festivities, with highlights including previews of the fifth season of *The Clone Wars*, special events for players of *Star Wars: The Old Republic* and the only public viewing of the still-in-development animated comedy series, *Star Wars Detours*. George Lucas makes several surprise appearances during the event—he was not listed as an attending guest. Little do attendees—or indeed, organizers—know that a radically different future is in the works for *Star Wars* than what is discussed at the show. No mention of future movies is made, but Lucas takes advantage of Mark Hamill and Carrie Fisher's presence at the convention to arrange a private dinner with them during which he reveals his plans to continue the *Star Wars* Saga with their characters. Also at Celebration, Lucas screens a special assembly of *The Clone Wars* episodes plucked from the series and edited together, branded as "Young Jedi." This is to gauge the viability of a youth-oriented spin-off from the aging *Star Wars: The Clone Wars* show. Though audiences—especially the kids in attendance —enjoy the screening, Lucas ultimately switches track and puts these episodes back in the *Clone Wars* schedule.

SEPTEMBER

September 7: A *Raiders of the Lost Ark* IMAX re-release proves to be a surprise success, necessitating an increase in screenings. The limited event was intended as a promotion to a forthcoming Blu-ray release of the *Indiana Jones* films.

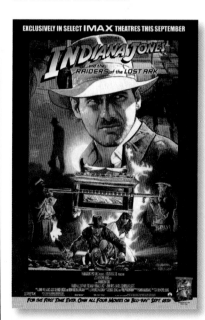

Harrison Ford's first appearance as the snake-hating archeologist, Indiana Jones, proves as popular as ever.

September 18: Indiana Jones rides again, this time in unprecedented high-definition clarity, as the four films of the series are released on Blu-ray from Paramount and Lucasfilm.

September 25: A Craigslist apartment ad surfaces for the house in Benedict Canyon, Los Angeles, where "George Lucas wrote *Star Wars*." A somewhat specious claim, the location does however line up with Lucas's residence during his second year of USC in the 1960s.

September 26: Cartoon Network airs LEGO *Star Wars: The Empire Strikes Out*, an animated comedy TV special featuring the heroes of the Original Trilogy. It would arrive on home video in spring 2013.

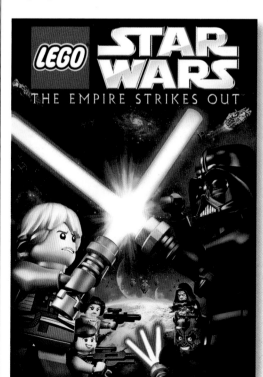

September 29: The fifth season of *Star Wars: The Clone Wars* launches. The series, though acclaimed, struggles with ratings as its original target audience ages out of the show and the series' more intense content—ushered in by a resurrected Darth Maul—serves as a barrier to the youngest viewers. In an effort to bolster ratings, the show is moved to Saturday mornings with mixed results. Moving it out of the prime time slot, dominated by animated adult comedies, does give *The Clone Wars* a shot at long overdue Emmy nominations.

OCTOBER

October 2: Del Rey Books publishes *Star Wars: The Essential Reader's Companion*. The 496-page paperback, written by Pablo Hidalgo, chronicles and summarizes every prose novel and short story of the *Star Wars* Expanded Universe and is filled with new artwork dramatically depicting never-before-visualized scenes.

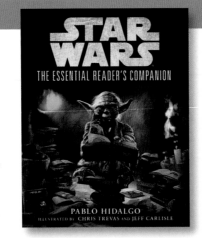

October 3: The Australian fashion brand Black Milk announces a line of eye-catching *Star Wars* apparel, including leggings, dresses, and swimsuits.

When the king of planet Onderon pledges to join the Separatists, Saw Garrera (voiced by Andrew Kishino) and his sister, Steela, form a rebellion.

The Story of Saw Gerrera

October 6: *Star Wars: The Clone Wars* begins airing the four-part Onderon arc, a story involving the Republic backing a local resistance army in a proxy war against the Separatists. Among the young rebels armed and trained is Saw Gerrera, a character who will be essential to the Rebel Alliance that George Lucas has created for the still-in-development live action TV series.

Read You Will

October 6: The inaugural *Star Wars* Reads Day, spearheaded by DK Books, but bringing together all *Star Wars* publishers, involves over 1,200 book store and library events, signings, and costume appearances around the United States. The successful launch causes *Star Wars* Reads Day to become an annual event.

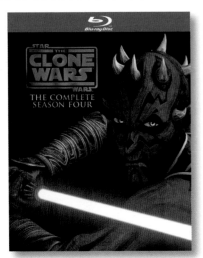

The Angry Bird Gets the Toys

October 11: To tie in with the forthcoming Angry Birds *Star Wars* video game from Rovio, Hasbro unveils their line of toys inspired by the mashup.

To recreate Angry Birds-style play, slingshot-launched toys take aim at larger toys or environments.

October 23: *Star Wars: The Clone Wars* season four arrives on Blu-ray and DVD, featuring a striking portrait of Darth Maul on the cover.

Maul's cover portrait ties in with a year full of Maul-centric advertising.

The Force is with Disney

October 30: In an announcement that stuns fans, the entertainment industry, and Wall Street, the Walt Disney Company begins the process of acquiring Lucasfilm Ltd. from its sole shareholder, George Lucas, for over $4 billion. The culmination of Lucas's long retirement plans, he sells the ownership of his companies and intellectual property to the company he believes most capable of keeping the *Star Wars* legacy alive for years to come. This follows after a long stretch of successful acquisitions under Bob Iger's tenure as Chairman of the Walt Disney Company—including Pixar and Marvel. Countless questions arise as to the nature of the transition and the promise of the future, but the key announcement that gains the most traction is that *Star Wars*: Episode VII, long-declared by Lucas as an impossibility, is now very much in the works.

Disney CEO Bob Iger and George Lucas sign on the dotted line.

☢ SAN FRANCISCO GIANTS SWEEP WORLD SERIES ☢ HURRICANE SANDY HITS THE EAST COAST ☢

NOVEMBER

Lucasfilm's Creative Council
November 5: At Lucasfilm, now president Kathleen Kennedy holds a creative strategy kick-off meeting with key members of the company who will be, in her words, the "Jedi Council." This "council" will help her steer the future of *Star Wars*.

Writing Episode VII
November 9: Academy Award®-winning screenwriter Michael Arndt is announced to be penning the screenplay for Episode VII. He has already been working closely with the newly created Lucasfilm Story Group (convened prior to the Disney acquisition), headed up by Kiri Hart. Arndt is an expert at story structure, and works to expand the seminal ideas left behind by George Lucas into a working screenplay.

Historic Playthings
November 15: The Strong, otherwise known as the National Museum of Play, in Rochester, New York, inducts *Star Wars* action figures into the National Toy Hall of Fame, citing their iconic status, longevity, and innovation. The 8¼-centimeter (3¾-inch) Kenner toys revolutionized the toy industry in many ways.

Birds of Anger
November 8: The phenomenally popular Angry Birds game from Rovio launches a *Star Wars*-themed expansion. Angry Birds *Star Wars* becomes a sub-brand, with apparel, toys, and other collectibles celebrating the whimsical crossover. The game is available on a wide array of mobile platforms.

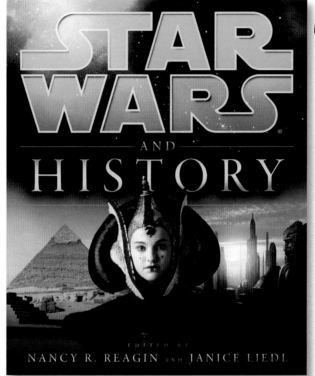

Angry Birds favorites appear as Star Wars characters, such as Red Skywalker and Princess Stella Organa.

Historical Analysis
November 20: John Wiley & Sons publishes *Star Wars and History*, a hardcover non-fiction book. It examines the connections between the *Star Wars* characters and narratives and elements in real-world history.

McCallum's New Future
November 30: As Lucasfilm prepares for a new future of active production without George Lucas, longtime producer Rick McCallum departs the company for other, independent projects. This brings to a close a relationship that had lasted over 20 years, which included *The Young Indiana Jones Chronicles*, *Radioland Murders*, the *Star Wars Trilogy: Special Edition*, the Prequel Trilogy, and *Red Tails*.

DECEMBER

December 11: Rick Carter, Doug Chiang, and David Nakabayashi convene at Lucasfilm headquarters in San Francisco to handpick their "dream team" of concept artists to begin work on Episode VII.

Art director Rick Carter has previously worked on Back to the Future Parts II and III and Avatar.

Fantasy Flight's New Deal
December 21: Fantasy Flight releases *Star Wars: The Card Game*, a two-player collectible card game that pits a light side player against a dark side opponent. Each month sees the addition of new cards, adding more thematic elements and play dynamics. It is the first new *Star Wars* card game to be released in years, and it is enthusiastically embraced by gamers.

A Done Deal
December 21: The purchase of Lucasfilm by the Walt Disney Company is finalized once meeting regulatory approval by the FTC. Based on the closing price of Disney stock at the time of the announcement, the final sale figure for Lucasfilm and its creative components is $4.06 billion. Disney issues George Lucas 37,076,679 shares of Disney stock and a cash payment of $2,208,199.950. Lucas intends to donate most of this money to educational efforts. Thus marks the end of an era where *Star Wars* was an independent production, under the control of George Lucas.

George Lucas has had a long relationship with Disney, including the Star Tours simulator attraction which opened at Disneyland, California, in 1987.

BARACK OBAMA ELECTED TO SECOND TERM ☸ MAYAN CALENDAR ENDS BUT WORLD DOES NOT

WITH THE BACKING OF THE Walt Disney Company, creatives at Lucasfilm are allowed to explore the far-away galaxy once more. An unprecedented spate of activity begins on what will eventually become new feature films in the *Star Wars* Saga. Aside from the new trilogy, George Lucas has left as his legacy starting points for additional "stand-alone" movies. To accommodate such an endeavor, Lucasfilm undergoes a major transformation to once again become a creative production powerhouse.

2013-2016

STAR WARS
A NEW ERA

2013

FOR YEARS, Lucasfilm Ltd. followed a licensing and consumer goods-focused business model. George Lucas would keep his filmmaking endeavors contained at Skywalker Ranch, separate from the business divisions that would turn that film into consumer products. But the new future of *Star Wars* sees an all-consuming emphasis on film and television production—Kathleen Kennedy's motto is that creativity leads. This shift in focus results in some immense changes to the company.

> "We're kick-starting *Star Wars* again with dynamite. It will knock people out, including the people who get to work on it."

Dennis Muren *ILM visual effects supervisor*

JANUARY

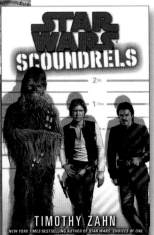

January 1: Del Rey books releases *Scoundrels* in hardback. The novel by Timothy Zahn is the *Star Wars* take on the *Oceans 11* franchise, with Han Solo gathering a band of thieves.

The novel is set before the events of The Empire Strikes Back, and sees Han and Chewbacca teaming up with their old acquaintance and rival, Lando Calrissian.

January 3: Word breaks on *The Huffington Post* that George Lucas and his longtime girlfriend, businesswoman Mellody Hobson, are engaged to be married.

January 5: The 100th episode of *Star Wars: The Clone Wars* airs on Cartoon Network. To commemorate this milestone, Lucasfilm purchases a full-page ad in *Variety*.

Parking Yoda and Indy

January 7: The San Anselmo planning commission in Marin County approves the plans for an 808-square-meter (8,700-square-foot) downtown park on property donated by George Lucas. The park will include bronze statues of Yoda and Indiana Jones atop a 4.5-meter (15-foot) diameter fountain.

Photograph of the completed bronze statues in Imagination Park, San Anselmo.

Art Department Renaissance

January 9: Under the supervision of Rick Carter, the concept art department for *Star Wars*: Episode VII begins to form. Returning to the galaxy as lead production concept artist is Doug Chiang, who had previously served as design director on *The Phantom Menace* and *Attack of the Clones*.

January 9: Dark Horse Comics launches a new *Star Wars* comic series, with the simple label of *Star Wars* #1. Written by Brian Wood with art by Carlos D'Anda, the new series seeks to capture the magic of the Saga as it was when only one movie had graced the screen. The comic sells through its entire print run in 24 hours, with a second printing planned for a February 6 release.

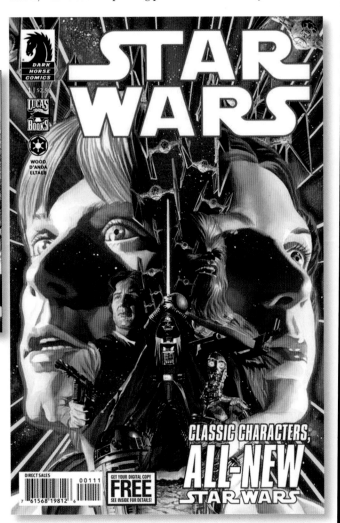

🌐 NORTH KOREA CONDUCTS NUCLEAR TESTS 🌐 A WIDELY RECORDED

Death Star Wars

January 11: 34,435 Americans petition the White House to begin construction of a Death Star, eliciting a humorous reply from the administration. This widely publicized exchange prompts the White House to increase the number of signatures required before official administration response from 25,000 to 100,000.

January 14: The 501st Legion approves a garrison in China.

January 18: The USO screens episodes of *Star Wars: The Clone Wars* at the Marine Corps Air Station Miramar in San Diego, including Q&A sessions with cast and crew.

January 24: Michael Arndt, Lawrence Kasdan, and Simon Kinberg meet with Pablo Hidalgo at a Lucasfilm writers' conference to ask questions about the *Star Wars* universe.

Director Announced

January 24: Word breaks on The Wrap website that J.J. Abrams has been chosen to direct Episode VII. Lucasfilm and Disney confirm this development late on January 25th. The internet eruption is seismic, with Abrams, *Star Wars*, and Episode VII rocketing up to the top of trending Twitter topics.

Back in Black

January 29: In *USA Today*, Hasbro officially unveils their Black Series of action figures, a new format maximizing articulation and accessories. The boxed figures are 15¼ centimeters (six inches) in scale, and the first announced is Luke Skywalker as an X-wing pilot.

FEBRUARY

January 28: Citing a concentration of future projects, Lucasfilm announces it is postponing the forthcoming 3-D releases of Episodes II and III—a mere nine months ahead of release.

February 5: In a call to investors, Walt Disney Chairman Bob Iger confirms speculation that in addition to the forthcoming *Star Wars* trilogy, there will be several spin-off films.

February 6: Make-up legend Stuart Freeborn, responsible for the creation of such characters as Chewbacca, Yoda, and Jabba the Hutt, passes away at age 98 in London.

Stuart Freeborn jokes with actor Peter Mayhew while holding the head of Mayhew's Chewbacca costume.

MARCH

Ahsoka Walks Away

March 2: A moving finale for the fifth season of *Star Wars: The Clone Wars* catches viewers by surprise, as the show's central character, Ahsoka Tano, leaves the Jedi Order. The air of finality is no accident, and fans notice there is no indication of when and if a sixth season will follow. The long lead times of animation mean production did continue beyond this episode, but the complicated business numbers behind the series cloud its future.

March 11: The fate of *The Clone Wars* becomes known as Lucasfilm announces a major shift in focus for its animation division. The series is canceled, though work on the episodes already in production will continue, with a shortened sixth season of so-called "bonus content" to be distributed through yet-to-be-announced means. *Star Wars Detours*, with its irreverent and humorous take on classic *Star Wars* icons, is indefinitely postponed. However, even as these doors close, a new one opens as a new animated series —to become *Star Wars Rebels*— begins early development.

March 12: *Willow* arrives on Blu-ray for the first time.

March 14: The Episode VII art department visits the *Star Wars* archives at Skywalker Ranch to do a deep dive into the visual history of the Saga.

March 14: StarWars.com launches a tournament, using a March Madness-style bracket format to gauge fan favorite characters. Yoda wins this first round of "This is Madness," a competition that would become an annual tradition.

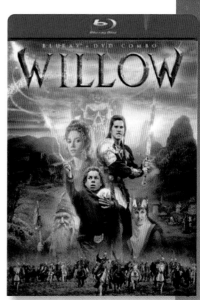

APRIL

LucasArts: Game Over

April 3: Lucasfilm shuts down its game division, LucasArts, resulting in the layoff of more than 100 employees. This means the canceling of two major projects in development—*Star Wars*: First Assault, and the still-embryonic *Star Wars*: 1313. The internet is awash with eulogies for the game developer, some honoring the games of yesteryear while others take critical looks at the recent history of the division. A games group will still continue to function within Lucasfilm, with a core of LucasArts employees remaining. They will continue the brand as the company shifts from an internal development model to a licensing model.

April 4: Film critic, author, and longtime enthusiast of *Star Wars* films, Roger Ebert, passes away.

Like Son, Like Daughter

April 23: Chronicle Books publishes a follow-up to *Darth Vader and Son*, this time focusing on a slightly older Princess Leia. *Vader's Little Princess* is once again written and illustrated by Jeffrey Brown.

MAY

Playing Games

May 6: Lucasfilm and Disney Interactive enter into a 10-year, multi-title exclusive licensing agreement with Electronic Arts (EA) for the creation of new high quality *Star Wars* games spanning multiple genres for console, PC, mobile, and tablets. As part of the agreement, two key EA studios begin work on new console games—DICE on a new incarnation of *Star Wars*: Battlefront, and Visceral studios on a game yet to be announced. BioWare, meanwhile, continues its expansion of *Star Wars*: The Old Republic.

What's in a Domain Name?

May 8: To disguise the registration of domain name StarWarsRebels.com, Lucasfilm purchases a host of gag domain names. With the news of the big EA deal fresh in the minds of the gaming press, breathless articles appear focusing on such fare as Order67.com, BothanSpies.com, and the inexplicable GunganFrontier2, 3, and 4.com.

Storyboards

May 14: Abrams Books publishes *Star Wars Storyboards: The Prequel Trilogy*, edited by J.W. Rinzler.

Concept art depicts the origins of familiar scenes and locations, as well as showcasing many unused ideas.

Back to the UK

May 10: Lucasfilm announces that *Star Wars*: Episode VII will shoot at Pinewood studios. Following the shooting of Episodes II and III primarily in Australia, Brits are pleased that *Star Wars* is coming home.

Pinewood Studios, Buckinghamshire, is Europe's biggest film studio. In 2014, plans for a $300 million (£200 million) expansion were approved.

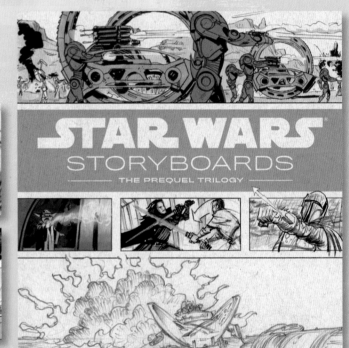

Rebels Revealed

May 20: Lucasfilm announces *Star Wars Rebels*, a new animated series scheduled to premiere in the fall of 2014 on Disney XD. Announced as the show's creative leads are executive producers Dave Filoni, Simon Kinberg, and Greg Weisman. As the first major content to be delivered after George Lucas's retirement, word of the series draws much scrutiny from skeptical fans. On this day at Big Rock Ranch, the very first writers' conference for the series begins. In attendance are Filoni, Kinberg, and Weisman; Athena Portillo and Darci DuBose from Lucasfilm Animation; and Diana Williams, Rayne Roberts, Pablo Hidalgo, and Kiri Hart from the Lucasfilm Story Group.

GARMENT FACTORY COLLAPSE IN BANGLADESH ☩ FATAL BOMBING AT THE BOSTON MARATHON

LEGO X-Wing, Standing By

May 23: The LEGO Group unveils the world's largest LEGO model: a life-size X-wing made of five million LEGO bricks, in Times Square, New York. More than 30 master builders spent over 17,000 hours constructing the 13-meter (43-foot) long craft to celebrate this month's launch of LEGO *Star Wars: The Yoda Chronicles*. After New York, the model moves to the LEGOLAND California resort for the summer.

May 29: LEGO *Star Wars: The Yoda Chronicles* begins airing on Cartoon Network. A series of three animated specials (as well as animated shorts), the comedic series stars Yoda teaching a fresh class of Padawan learners.

Yoda holds a LEGO holocron and watches the exploits of a new character, Jek-14.

JUNE

June 6: Gentle Giant reveals their upcoming San Diego Comic-Con International exclusive. Limited to 500 pieces, "Magnitude" is an Admiral Ackbar mini-bust resplendent in regalia befitting a general in the Napoleonic wars.

"Magnitude" is based on artwork by Steven Daily produced for Acme Archives.

June 15: *The Clone Wars* wins two daytime Emmy awards, with David Tennant (as the voice of droid professor Huyang) winning Outstanding Performer in an Animated Program, and the series itself winning the Outstanding Special Class Animated Program award.

· · · · · · · · · · · · · ·

June 22: George Lucas and Mellody Hobson marry at Skywalker Ranch. In Steven Spielberg's toast to the couple, he jokes that the Force finally has a name: Mellody.

· · · · · · · · · · · · · ·

Left to right: Athena Portillo, Dave Filoni, George Lucas, and Cary Silver accept their Emmy award.

JULY

May the Verse Be With You

July 2: Random House publishes *William Shakespeare's Star Wars*, by Ian Doescher. A retelling of the story of *A New Hope* but done in the Elizabethan style of the Bard, complete with iambic pentameter.

July 9: Del Rey Books releases *Crucible* in hardback. Written by Troy Denning as a follow up to the *Fate of the Jedi* series, it would end up being chronologically the last book featuring Han, Luke, and Leia.

July 9: After the success of the inaugural Course of the Force run in 2012, which enabled more than 1,000 wishes to be granted by Make-A-Wish, the second lightsaber run begins at Skywalker Ranch.

Star Wars Celebration Europe

July 26–28: The first *Star Wars* convention since the Walt Disney acquisition takes place in Essen, Germany. Over 20,000 fans gather to celebrate the past of *Star Wars*, but also to anticipate a very promising future. Host Warwick Davis conducts interviews with Kathleen Kennedy, Carrie Fisher, and Mark Hamill on stage, and reveals first-ever glimpses of the forthcoming *Star Wars Rebels*. Although curiosity about Episode VII is high, it is far too early to reveal anything. Particular highlights of the event are an outdoor 30th anniversary screening of *Return of the Jedi*, and an exclusive screening of *Attack of the Clones* in 3-D.

Star Wars Takes Over the Penguins

July 25: Club Penguin, a popular game and social hub for online youngsters, has its first *Star Wars* Takeover, featuring *Star Wars*-themed downloadables, character costumes, and games.

AUGUST

August 9: George Lucas and Mellody Hobson welcome their daughter, Everest Hobson Lucas, to the world.

August 10: *Star Wars* makes its first appearance at D23 Expo, a Disney convention in Anaheim, California. Lucasfilm holds a *Star Wars* 101 panel to help educate Disney fans on the history of the Saga and the brand.

D23 Expo is an annual convention for Disney fans, which began in 2009.

US SUPREME COURT FINDS FOR GAY MARRIAGE • PRINCE GEORGE BORN TO THE DUKE AND

August 23: British cinematographer Gilbert Taylor, who had worked on *Dr. Strangelove*, *A Hard Day's Night*, and the original *Star Wars* movie, passes away at age 99.

Taylor filmed the aftermath of bombing raids during WWII as a Royal Air Force cameraman.

August 25: J.J. Abrams, Bryan Burk, and Michelle Rejwan of Bad Robot Productions meet with the Lucasfilm *Star Wars* franchise team at Skywalker Ranch to discuss the roll-out of Episode VII to the public.

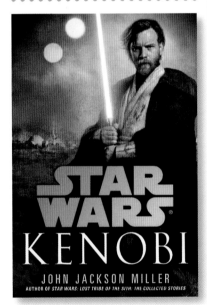

Tales of Old Ben
August 27: Del Rey Books releases *Star Wars: Kenobi* by author John Jackson Miller. The hardback novel takes place in the years between Episodes III and IV, when Kenobi lives as a desert hermit on Tatooine. It follows very much in the mold of an epic western, and is quite well received by readers.

Also in 2013...

Darth's Mall
At the annual *Star Wars* Weekend at Disney World, fans descend upon Darth's Mall—the place to purchase merchandise, including Disney characters dressed in *Star Wars* costumes and stormtroopers printed with fans' own faces.

SEPTEMBER

The Proto-*Star Wars*
September 4: Dark Horse Comics begins publication on *The Star Wars*, an ambitious and unusual work that adapts an earlier draft script of the original film. Historian and author J.W. Rinzler secured the blessing from George Lucas to transform his working concepts into finished imagery, executed by artist Mike Mayhew. The story features such antecedent characters as Annakin and Kane Starkiller, a war general named Vader, and a green-skinned Wookiee-hunter named Han Solo. After running for eight issues through May 2014, the series would be collected in various volumes, including a deluxe hardcover.

September 6: Author Ann C. Crispin, who wrote the *Han Solo Trilogy* in the 1990s, passes away at age 63.

Rancho Record
September 15: Guinness World Records recognizes Rancho Obi-Wan, the massive museum of *Star Wars* items owned by Steve Sansweet, as the "Largest Collection of *Star Wars* Memorabilia" in the world (or, galaxy, for that matter). The 836 square-meter (9,000 square-foot) non-profit museum secures a prominent spread in the next print edition of the records.

September 19: The next installment of the Angry Birds *Star Wars* game is available for download from Rovio. Whereas the first edition focused on the Original Trilogy, volume II is all about the prequels, with the greedy Pork Federation ruffling feathers.

In the Angry Birds Star Wars *world, the heroes are birds and the villains are pigs.*

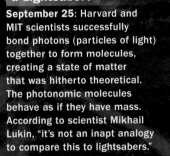

Science Finds a Lightsaber?
September 25: Harvard and MIT scientists successfully bond photons (particles of light) together to form molecules, creating a state of matter that was hitherto theoretical. The photonomic molecules behave as if they have mass. According to scientist Mikhail Lukin, "it's not an inapt analogy to compare this to lightsabers."

Yoda Talks
September 27: The first of several "Yoda Talks" are held at Electronic Arts, with representatives from Lucasfilm speaking to EA employees about what makes *Star Wars* tick. Among the guest speakers at this session are John Knoll and Kim Libreri of ILM to talk shot design and technology, Doug Chiang to talk about art direction, and Kiri Hart and Pablo Hidalgo to discuss the tenets of *Star Wars* storytelling.

Created by Carrie Beck, Dave Filoni, Simon Kinberg, and Kiri Hart, the core idea of *Star Wars Rebels* focuses on a "family" of rebels leading an early charge against the Empire. The heroes were likened to a multi-skilled A-Team-style ensemble in initial exploration. This artwork cements the look and feel of the characters during a very condensed development period. The hulking alien Zeb would undergo further evolution, losing the "scaredy-cat" persona evident in this drawing. The other characters are near their final forms.

OCTOBER

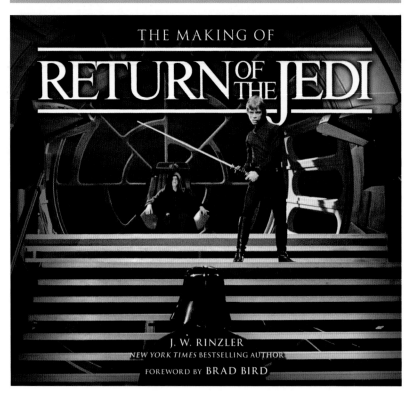

THE MAKING OF

RETURN OF THE JEDI

J. W. RINZLER
NEW YORK TIMES BESTSELLING AUTHOR
FOREWORD BY BRAD BIRD

October 1: Del Rey completes its trilogy of bestselling behind-the-scenes books with *The Making of Return of the Jedi* by J.W. Rinzler.

Blu-ray Trilogies

October 8: The nine-disc, six-movie *Star Wars* Blu-ray sets are rereleased as trilogy sets, making it easier for consumers to select the films they want to add to their high-definition library.

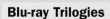

Darth Vader fronts this collection, which includes exclusive audio commentaries for each movie with George Lucas, cast, and crew.

Yoda graces the cover of the Prequel Trilogy collection, which also includes exclusive audio commentaries for each movie.

Nobody Expects the Inquisitor

October 12: At New York Comic Con, Lucasfilm reveals the villain of the forthcoming *Star Wars Rebels* series: the Inquisitor. The mysterious Force-wielding villain is not a Sith exactly, but rather from a sect of dark side-imbued hunters prowling the galaxy for Jedi survivors and Force-sensitives alike. The idea of Inquisitors dates back to the old roleplaying game published by West End Games.

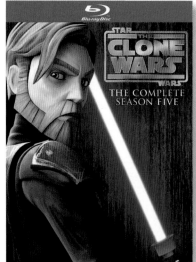

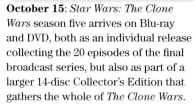

October 15: *Star Wars: The Clone Wars* season five arrives on Blu-ray and DVD, both as an individual release collecting the 20 episodes of the final broadcast series, but also as part of a larger 14-disc Collector's Edition that gathers the whole of *The Clone Wars*.

October 30: Author James Luceno visits Lucasfilm to be briefed on upcoming *Star Wars* content to help him write his next novel focusing on Wilhuff Tarkin.

NOVEMBER

November 7: Disney Mobile, NimbleBit, and Lucasfilm release *Tiny Death Star*, a mobile app that encourages users to build a virtual Death Star while populating it with cute 8-bit iterations of *Star Wars* characters.

Release Date Announced

November 7: Disney and Lucasfilm confirm the release date for Episode VII as December 18, 2015. This was the result of much negotiation between the producers and the studio. The studio wished to see *Star Wars* arrive at the traditional May release, but the needs of the production—and the importance of making Episode VII the best it can be—win out in the end. However, work is already continuing hurriedly to meet this release date.

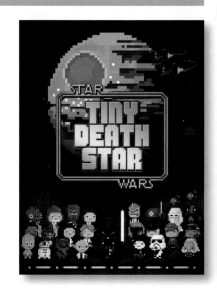

⊛ US ROLLS OUT AFFORDABLE CARE ACT ⊛ US FEDERAL GOVERNMENT SHUTDOWN ⊛

R2-D2 Returns

November 14: The Bad Robot Twitter account tweets a picture of the Pinewood Droid Workshop, confirming R2-D2's expected presence in Episode VII. Also in the photo are J.J. Abrams, Kathleen Kennedy, Oliver Steeples, and Lee Towersey. The latter two are local members of the droid building fan community that so impressed Kennedy during her tour of Celebration Europe that they were hired on to the production.

Next-Gen Gaming

November 15: The console wars heat up again as a new benchmark of high-definition graphics and online interactivity ushers in the next generation of gaming. Sony is to market first, with the release of their PlayStation 4. On November 22, Microsoft releases its Xbox One.

The New Stormtrooper

November 28: After much iteration, the final design for the new stormtrooper for Episode VII is finalized and approved by J.J. Abrams. Chiefly responsible for its look is costume designer Michael Kaplan and costume concept artist Glyn Dillon.

With this photo posted online, fans knew for certain that R2-D2 was to return (was there any doubt?) but also that J.J. Abrams and Kathleen Kennedy had hired fan droid builders to help bring him to life.

The Episode VII stormtrooper leader is angular and severe-looking, with a striking red pauldron.

DECEMBER

December 2: The team behind StarWars.com brings *Star Wars* to the Instagram photo-sharing platform.

The first Star Wars Instagram offering: a Vader selfie

December 10: Representatives from Marvel Comics editorial staff meet with Lucasfilm to plan what will become the future of *Star Wars* comics storytelling.

Laying Out the Story

December 13: After much work, J.J. Abrams pitches the current version of the story of Episode VII at his Bad Robot offices to the film's department heads. This walk-through of the film is accompanied with concept art. Already much of the story is in place, but a first draft script is not yet ready.

December 19: *Star Wars* gets an official presence on the social microblogging platform, Tumblr.

Instead of Princess Leia's secret message, R2-D2 beams a holographic Tumblr stream.

NELSON MANDELA DIES AGED 95 🌐

2014

WHILE *STAR WARS* FANS speculate about the future films, work begins on the next animated TV series. With a smaller budget and a compressed schedule, getting *Star Wars Rebels* into shape requires non-stop work. However, the nine years spent producing the complex *Star Wars: The Clone Wars* proves invaluable. In addition, the involvement of the new Lucasfilm Story Group allows for collaborative workshopping so that when season one emerges, it comes with a well-defined plan.

"To work in the era I grew up with... is... tremendously exciting because... the work of Ralph McQuarrie is open to us in a way that we could never exploit in *Clone Wars*."

Dave Filoni
Executive Producer,
Star Wars Rebels

JANUARY

Make Mine Marvel
January 3: Lucasfilm and Marvel Entertainment announce their partnership in creating new *Star Wars* comics, returning the license that had been held by Dark Horse Comics since 1991 to the publisher that first brought four-color *Star Wars* sequential art to the public. The new titles will begin publishing in 2015.

Revenge of the Myth
January 4: *MythBusters*, the Discovery Channel's long running-science-based reality show hosted by Adam Savage and Jamie Hyneman, recreates several *Star Wars* scenes to gauge their plausibility. The show judges whether or not Luke and Leia could really swing across a chasm with a grappling hook, if Ewoks could actually crush an armored vehicle with logs, and whether it's possible to survive a blizzard inside a gutted tauntaun. The verdict: All three are plausible.

Wish Upon a Star
January 15: The Make-a-Wish Foundation launches a fundraiser where donors of $10 or more to the charity are entered into a contest to meet George Lucas at Skywalker Ranch and then travel to LA to meet Mark Hamill. The winner has this wish come true on February 21.

FEBRUARY

February 2: Authors for a new series of young reader adaptations of the Original Trilogy (due out the following year) meet with editors and Story Group representatives at Skywalker Ranch.

Presidio Distrust
February 3: The Presidio Trust rejects a $700 million proposal by George Lucas for an entirely self-financed museum holding his collection of popular narrative art. The seven-member board concludes that nothing proposed for the 8-acre site on Crissy Field in San Francisco would be suitable.

Rendering of the proposed Lucas Cultural Arts Museum.

The Talent Awakens

February 5: In the lead role of "Kira," *Star Wars: Episode VII* casts relative unknown Daisy Ridley. News of this development would stay under wraps for weeks. The 21 year old lands the starring role following five auditions over the course of seven months.

The Force of Fashion

February 10: At New York Fashion Week, the power of Force turns heads as luxury brand Rodarte sends *Star Wars*-printed dresses down the runway. Founders Laura and Kate Mulleavy describe their fascination with storytelling and cinema, which inspired the dresses.

February 25: *Star Wars*: Episode VII casts little known John Boyega in the code-named role of "Sam," one of the leads, after his ninth audition.

Allston Remembered

February 27: Aaron Allston, author of many *Star Wars* novels in the *X-Wing*, *New Jedi Order*, *Legacy of the Force* and *Fate of the Jedi* series, passes away at age 53. The popular author was also an accomplished game designer during the formative years of the roleplaying game industry.

MARCH

From *Expanse* to Expanded

March 4: Del Rey Books releases *Honor Among Thieves*, a classic trilogy-era novel starring Han Solo. It is written by James S.A. Corey, the pen name shared by authors Daniel Abraham and Ty Franck, scribes of the popular sci-fi series, *The Expanse*.

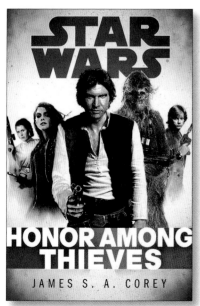

The novel's cover features Han, Leia, Luke, Chewbacca, and rebel spy, Scarlet Hark.

Lost Missions Find Home

March 7: Netflix debuts the entirety of *Star Wars: The Clone Wars* on its online streaming platform, offering the original theatrical movie and all five broadcast seasons in high definition. But the real draw is the "Lost Missions:" 13 episodes from the unaired sixth season. These episodes feature Clone Trooper Fives uncovering the conspiracy of Order 66, Anakin and Padmé's marriage on the rocks, Jar Jar Binks and Mace Windu thwarting a cult, and Yoda undergoing a mystical quest to uncover the secret of Force immortality. Guest starring in this last arc is Mark Hamill as the voice of ancient Sith Lord, Darth Bane.

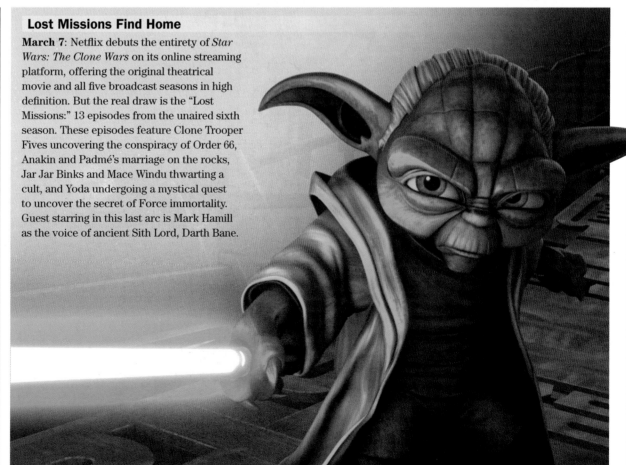

🌐 MALAYSIA AIRLINES FLIGHT 370 DISAPPEARS ☻ OSCAR PISTORIUS TRIAL BEGINS IN SOUTH AFRICA

APRIL

April 2: Although season one remains months away, work begins on season two of *Star Wars Rebels* as the producers, writers, and the Story Group kick off the writers' conference at Lucasfilm.

April 4: Having been based in Paris since February, J.J. Abrams relocates to Pinewood Studios, England, to begin concerted preparations for production of Episode VII.

April 11: As part of their early exploratory work on *Star Wars*: Episode VIII, writer-director Rian Johnson and producer Ram Bergman tour the prop and artwork archive at Skywalker Ranch.

Through the Looking Glass

April 15: Google makes its Google Glass line of internet-connected, data-displaying spectacles available to the public. Designed to take the smartphone experience out of the phone and allow for continued eye-contact while accessing data, reception is decidedly mixed. While early adopters eager for the next wave of technology embrace this step into wearable technology, others balk at the unobtrusive presence of its unblinking built-in camera.

April 24: The working draft of *Star Wars*: Episode VII, as yet untitled but code-named "AVCO," is delivered to Lucasfilm from J.J. Abrams and Lawrence Kasdan.

The Legendary EU

April 25: StarWars.com announces what many fans had suspected since the 2012 bombshell that there'd be new films; that they'd have to unlearn everything they know about the Expanded Universe. Lucasfilm rebrands the vast library of fiction encompassed in the EU as "Legends," meaning that future film, television, and fiction need not be beholden to that storytelling. The core of the existing canon is what George Lucas had deemed his vision of *Star Wars*—the six feature films and *The Clone Wars* series. Under the auspices of the Lucasfilm Story Group, future storytelling will be far more cohesive across different media. The old catalog of Expanded Universe fare remains in print, but now marked with a Legends banner.

First Cast Photo

April 29: Following a cast read-through of the Episode VII screenplay, StarWars.com posts a photo by David James of the assembled cast of the new film, confirming and announcing the new stars and returning legends. Harrison Ford, Mark Hamill, Carrie Fisher, Anthony Daniels, and Peter Mayhew are joined by Daisy Ridley, John Boyega, Adam Driver, Oscar Isaac, Andy Serkis, Domnhall Gleeson, and Max Von Sydow.

MAY

Darth Maul Still Lives (Again)

May 1: In their last year as a *Star Wars* licensee, Dark Horse Comics begins publication of *Darth Maul: Son of Dathomir*, a four-part adaptation of four unproduced scripts from *The Clone Wars*. These episodes would have picked up the story of the captive Darth Maul (as he was left at the end of the fifth season), and revealed his origins as he escapes to seek vengeance. Proving to be as hard-to-kill as ever, Maul survives this story intact.

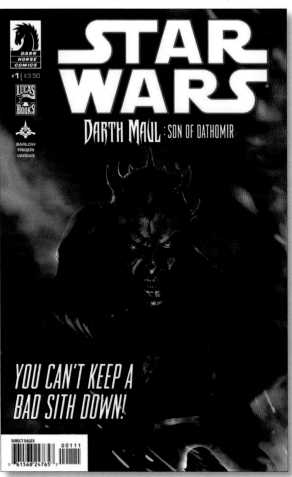

Another Piece of *Yoda Chronicles*

May 4: The next chapter in the LEGO *Star Wars* animated adventure, *The Yoda Chronicles*, airs on Disney XD. "Escape from the Jedi Temple" moves the whimsical series into the classic Rebellion vs. Empire era, and features Luke Skywalker learning to craft holocrons from Yoda and the spirit of Obi-Wan.

The spirit of Obi-Wan and Yoda roast marshmallows outside Yoda's home on Dagobah.

Retro of the Jedi

May 6: *The Goldbergs*, a semi-autobiographical ABC sitcom created by Adam F. Goldberg set in the 1980s, features a *Star Wars*-themed episode ("A Wrestler Named Goldberg") as series lead Adam (Sean Giambrone) and his sister Erica (Hayley Orrontia) stand in line for *Return of the Jedi*.

Adam Goldberg meets many Star Wars fans in line to buy theater tickets, but will any of them keep his place when he goes to the bathroom?

Original Storyboards

May 13: Abrams Books releases *Star Wars Storyboards: The Original Trilogy*, featuring a foreword by Joe Johnston, visual effects art director and storyboard artist from the Original Trilogy (and now accomplished director), and an introduction by fellow art director and artist Nilo Rodis-Jamero.

Abrams Calls Action

May 16: Principal photography on *Star Wars*: Episode VII begins in Abu Dhabi, United Arab Emirates, as J.J. Abrams, John Boyega, Daisy Ridley, and a slew of additional performers, extras, and crew transform the desert environments into the planet Jakku. The production would remain in Abu Dhabi for a week and a half before moving to Pinewood Studios.

May 20: The first completed draft of the *Star Wars*: Episode VII screenplay is finished.

Force for Change

May 21: Lucasfilm and Disney announce the Force for Change, a charity initiative created at J.J. Abrams' personal request. Facilitated by the fundraising company Omaze, Force for Change transforms a $10 donation into a chance to visit the Episode VII set and have a small part in the film. The proceeds go to benefit UNICEF Innovation Labs. These efforts would raise $4.26 million and come August 11, D.C. Barns would be announced as the winner.

J.J. Abrams announces the Force for Change charity initiative from the set of Episode VII.

First Stand-Alone Director

May 23: Director Gareth Edwards is announced as having signed on to helm the first *Star Wars* stand-alone film. The up-and-coming talent has a strong visual style, and a background in visual effects, as exemplified by his first feature film, *Monsters*. His most recent movie, *Godzilla*, was released on May 14.

JUNE

Second Stand-Alone Director

June 4: Josh Trank is announced as director for a *Star Wars* stand-alone, following the completion of his current project, *Fantastic Four*. The strength of his first feature, *Chronicle*, as well as his love of *Star Wars*, lands him the job.

Star Wars Hot Wheels

June 7: *Star Wars Insider* #150 reveals a new partnership between Lucasfilm and Mattel® with a rendering of the first *Star Wars* Hot Wheels car: the Darth Vader Character Car, with an exclusive first edition at this year's San Diego Comic-Con International. This is the start of a collection of 1:64th scale cars that reimagine *Star Wars* characters as Hot Wheels cars.

A Bad Feeling About This

June 11: During the shooting of Episode VII, Harrison Ford is injured on set by a mechanical door, which crushes his leg in the *Millennium Falcon* interior set. Adding injury to injury, J.J. Abrams breaks his back trying to free the pinned Ford. Ford is rushed to hospital, and production scrambles to rejig the schedule to work around Ford's recovery, which early estimates peg at a daunting eight months.

June 13: Shooting resumes on Episode VII without Harrison Ford.

June 18: Lucasfilm Games and Story Group are in Stockholm, Sweden, to brief games studio DICE on the Battle of Jakku, an event that occurs between Episodes VI and VII.

Emmy Finale

June 21: The final season of *Star Wars: The Clone Wars* garners two more Daytime Creative Arts Emmy Awards. Christopher Voy wins an Outstanding Achievement in Animation award for his color and lighting concept designs, while the series again wins Outstanding Special Class Animated Program.

June 23: Though Lucasfilm has yet to announce him as the director of Episode VIII, Rian Johnson's involvement is reported by the *LA Times*.

June 24: Unable to reach an agreement with the Presidio Trust, a frustrated George Lucas abandons San Francisco and chooses Chicago as the home for his museum of popular and narrative art.

JULY

July 1: StarWars.com undergoes another redesign, this time with an eye for the future, with room for growth to cover new feature films and animation.

Film School

July 6: To best communicate his filmmaking influences, Rian Johnson begins screening some of his favorite movies to the Lucasfilm Story Group and art department. Among the films are *Three Outlaw Samurai* (left), *Letters Never Sent*, *Twelve O'Clock High*, *Bridge on the River Kwai*, *Gunga Din*, and *Sahara*.

Rebels Comic-Con Preview

July 24: Lucasfilm holds a screening of the *Star Wars Rebels* premiere episodes at San Diego Comic-Con International, the first public exhibition of completed content. Fan reaction is extremely positive. Attending the screening are Dave Filoni, Simon Kinberg, and cast members Freddie Prinze Jr., Vanessa Marshall, Taylor Gray, Tiya Sircar, and Steve Blum.

Promotional artwork showcases the new style of animation that fans can expect from Rebels.

May the Ferb Be With You

July 26: The Disney Channel animated comedy, *Phineas and Ferb*, does a *Star Wars*-themed episode, which transplants regular characters Phineas, Ferb, Perry the Platypus, Candace, Norm, Heinz Doofenschmirtz, and others into a galaxy far, far away. Having a good grasp of *Star Wars* fandom, the episode stresses it is not canon in its opening crawl. Guest-stars include Simon Pegg as C-3PO, and *MythBusters* hosts Adam Savage and Jamie Hyneman as stormtroopers.

AUGUST

Rebels in Print

August 5: To support the launch of *Star Wars Rebels*, Disney's publishing imprint—as well as several other publishers—launch tie-in books. These include a showcase of concept art, chapter books, young readers, and the start of an original four-part middle grade story, *Servants of the Empire*.

Ezra's Gamble, written by Ryder Windham, is a novel starring Rebels hero, Ezra Bridger, set just before the first episode of the series.

Hera Syndulla thanks Chopper for his good work during a space battle in "Machine in the Ghost."

Rebels Propaganda

August 11: As a lead-in to *Star Wars Rebels*, Disney XD and StarWars.com begin debuting animated shorts that showcase the main characters. The first, "Machine in the Ghost," features Kanan Jarrus (a Jedi in hiding), Hera Syndulla (an idealistic Twi'lek pilot) and Chopper (a cantankerous astromech droid); "Entanglement" introduces Zeb, a tough native of Lasan; "Art Attack" stars Sabine Wren, a Mandalorian saboteur with artistic flare; while "Property of Ezra Bridger" introduces the main character of the series, a 14-year old Force-sensitive street rat.

Ice Bucket Challenge

August 17: J.J. Abrams takes the Ice Bucket Challenge, a viral YouTube sensation where participants nominate others to donate to ALS Association, and then dump a bucket of ice-water on his or her head. On August 21, Gareth Edwards takes the challenge, embellishing his video with a brief swim in the Yoda fountain at Lucasfilm headquarters. On August 24, Mark Hamill and Harrison Ford join the fun as separate participants.

Also in 2014...

Comic-Con Exclusive

Toy company Jakk's Pacific produces a limited run of 500 shadow trooper figures as an exclusive for Comic-Con. The articulated troopers stand at an impressive 31 inches (79 cm) tall.

August 26: Shooting resumes on Episode VII after a three-week hiatus following Harrison Ford's injury. Action continues on the Starkiller Base set—a redress of the First Order Star Destroyer bridge set.

SEPTEMBER

Canonical Novel

September 4: Del Rey Books publishes *A New Dawn*, the first canonical *Star Wars* novel to mesh with the new storytelling in development. Written by John Jackson Miller as a lead-in to the *Star Wars Rebels* animated series, it has the first meeting of two of the main characters —Kanan Jarrus and Hera Syndulla.

September 12: Lucasfilm experts Phil Szostak and Pablo Hidalgo guide production designer Rick Heinrichs through the *Star Wars* archives at Skywalker Ranch in preparation for his work on Episode VIII.

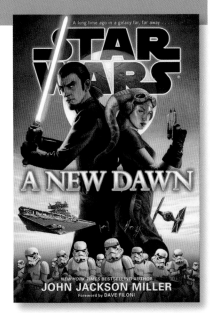

September 15: Beating pessimistic estimations of his recovery time, Harrison Ford returns to the set of Episode VII feeling energized and ready for action.

September 18: On YouTube, Bad Robot shows off the full-sized *Millennium Falcon* exterior set constructed in England for Episode VII.

Unfinished Episode

September 25: StarWars.com posts *Star Wars: The Clone Wars Legacy*, a showcase of four incomplete episodes—fully voiced and edited but incompletely rendered—as a means of getting more canceled *Clone Wars* content to fans. The four episodes focus on a Jedi mission to thwart the transit of a kyber crystal off the planet Utapau.

Anakin battles a MagnaGuard who is trying to retrieve the kyber crystal.

Anakin and Obi-Wan are easily identifiable despite the story reel animation.

OCTOBER

October 2: A day ahead of the series debut, *Star Wars Rebels* is officially green-lit for a second season on Disney XD.

October 3: Original Trilogy producer Robert Watts and production designer Norman Reynolds visit the set of Episode VII, marveling at how faithfully the *Millennium Falcon* has been replicated.

Norman Reynolds, Kathleen Kennedy, Robert Watts, and Lawrence Kasdan pose in front of the iconic ship.

The Rebellion Begins

October 3: *Star Wars Rebels* debuts on Disney XD as an hour-long presentation titled "Spark of Rebellion." The story chronicles how young Ezra Bridger joins a fledgling rebel cell on the Outer Rim grasslands planet of Lothal. Reviews are overwhelmingly positive, praising the snappy pace of the show's action and dialog, and how the look and feel of *Rebels* channels the disarming charm of *A New Hope* in particular, while still serving as fresh entertainment for a new generation of viewers.

Ezra Bridger has never held a lightsaber before.

McQuarrie Back in Print

October 6: Bestselling author Tony DiTerlizzi (*The Spiderwick Chronicles*) adapts the story of the original *Star Wars* trilogy as a children's hardcover picture book illustrated solely with Ralph McQuarrie art. For *Star Wars: The Adventures of Luke Skywalker, Jedi Knight*, many pieces of original McQuarrie art were re-scanned at high resolution, capturing the color and detail better than ever before.

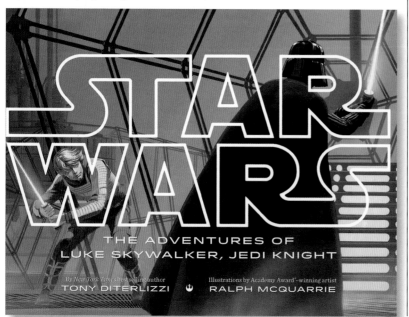

Fan Films Strike Back

October 11: After taking a break in 2012, the *Star Wars* Fan Films competition returns as Lucasfilm opens submissions, with winners to be awarded at *Star Wars* Celebration the following year. Kathleen Kennedy will select the grand prize winner, the Filmmaker Select award. The centerpiece of the new launch is *The Empire Strikes Back Uncut*, an assembled version of Episode V comprising dozens of fan-made segments.

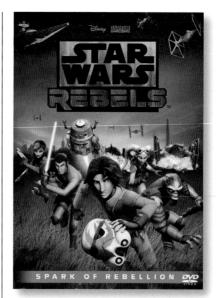

October 14: The broadcast premiere episode of *Star Wars Rebels* comes out on DVD, though a high-definition home video will have to wait.

October 26: "Spark of Rebellion" airs on ABC in prime time, now as a Special Edition featuring a new introduction with James Earl Jones reprising his role as the voice of Darth Vader in a cameo.

Darth Vader assigns the Inquisitor the task of destroying all the remaining Jedi.

October 28: Gaming website GOG.com offers LucasArts classic games for download, including X-Wing, TIE Fighter, and Knights of the Old Republic, configured for play on current-generation computers.

Costumes Chronicled

October 28: Chronicle Books releases *Star Wars Costumes: The Original Trilogy*, a lavish hardcover book brimming with rare photography and insightful information on the costumes of Episodes IV, V, and VI. Written by Brandon Alinger, with introductions by John Mollo, Nilo Rodis-Jamero, and Aggie Rogers, the book becomes the final word on Original Trilogy garb.

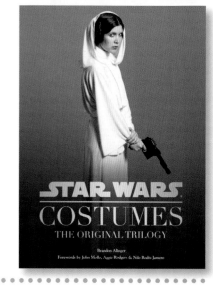

EBOLA CASE FOUND IN THE UNITED STATES ✪ *ROSETTA* SPACECRAFT LANDS ON A COMET ✪

NOVEMBER

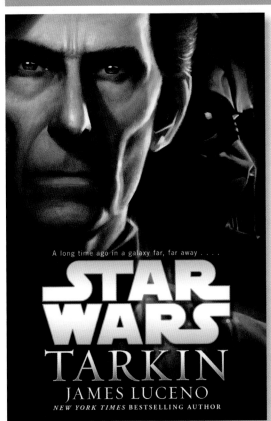

The Title Awakens

November 6: Lucasfilm officially announces the title of *Star Wars*: Episode VII as *The Force Awakens*. The title sparks discussion, speculation, and countless iterations of the "was it sleeping?" joke online. Also noteworthy is the studio's move away from the Episode numbering, mirroring the simple title treatments of the Original Trilogy. Lucasfilm clarifies to skittish fans that yes, the Episode number will indeed be part of the opening crawl.

November 4: Del Rey Books releases *Tarkin*, a novel by James Luceno, who crafts a historic tale of the Imperial official's emergence. Tarkin is set to appear in animated form toward the end of *Rebels* season one.

November 6: The final day of first unit photography on Episode VII ends with fireworks over Pinewood Studios.

Lost Missions Release

November 11: The final season of *Star Wars: The Clone Wars* arrives on DVD and Blu-ray, the first time the animated series is available as a Disney release. In addition to the 13 episodes that debuted on Netflix, bonus material includes the proxy-animation Utapau arc released on StarWars.com.

There has been an Awakening

November 28: The world stops in its tracks to make time for the very first publicly unveiled footage of *The Force Awakens* in 30 select theaters as well as online. The 88-second teaser trailer consists solely of seven scenes, with a sinister voice-over (later revealed to be Andy Serkis). Mystery pervades the trailer which mixes the old and the new—John Boyega as a stormtrooper in the desert, an instantly-popular rolling droid, new stormtrooper designs aboard a carrier transport, Daisy Ridley riding some sort of speeder, Oscar Isaac in the cockpit of an X-wing fighter, and a mysterious villain with a three-pronged lightsaber. By the time the trailer ends with an acrobatic shot of the *Millennium Falcon*, audiences are hungry for more. The trailer draws over 100 million views in its first week online.

DECEMBER

December 11: An *Entertainment Weekly* exclusive places images of the new trailer into classic *Star Wars* Topps trading card frames and reveals new character names: Kylo Ren, Finn, BB-8, Rey, and Poe Dameron.

Kylo Ren ignites his Lightsaber!

The cast brought their own personalities to the iconic roles. Merchant's C-3PO benefited from a sarcastic edge, while Simmons voiced an even more menacing version of Vader.

Reitman Strikes Back

December 18: Director Jason Reitman leads an all-star cast through a live reading of *The Empire Strikes Back* at a sold-out, one night only event at the Ace Hotel Theater in Los Angeles. This version of Episode V stars Aaron Paul as Luke, Ellen Page as Han, Jessica Alba as Leia, J.K. Simmons as Vader, Kevin Pollack as Yoda, Stephen Merchant as C-3PO, Dennis Haysbert as Lando, Rainn Wilson as Chewbacca, and as a surprise addition: Mark Hamill as both Obi-Wan and the Emperor.

2015

THE DAY MANY FANS thought would never come arrives in record-shattering force in 2015: the big screen debut of a live-action *Star Wars* sequel, the movie George Lucas once said would never happen. At the start of 2015, though, the film had a long way to go before it was completed. By April, when each day of *Star Wars* Celebration dominated the news, the true scale of the worldwide appetite for Episode VII was fully realized. *Star Wars* was back, reawakened, and bigger than ever before.

"Spending the last two years in the world of lightsabers and TIE fighters has been absolutely a dream come true."

J.J. Abrams
accepting his VES award

JANUARY

Forceful Cameo

January 5: In *Star Wars Rebels* episode "Path of the Jedi," Kanan and Ezra explore an ancient Jedi temple on the planet Lothal. Ezra is able to make contact with the disembodied voice of Yoda, performed by Frank Oz. The episode is written by Charles Murray and directed by Dave Filoni.

Ezra is guided through the Jedi Temple by mysterious lights.

Truly on the path to becoming a Jedi, Ezra is thrilled when his visions materialize into a kyber crystal, for use in a lightsaber.

January 7: Actor and martial artist Khan Bonfils, who played Saesee Tiin in Episode I, and had roles in *Batman Begins* and *Skyfall*, dies at age 42.

Marvelous Debut

January 14: Marvel begins publishing its flagship *Star Wars* comics title, written by Jason Aaron and illustrated by John Cassaday. The initial arc, "Skywalker Strikes," takes place between the events of Episode IV and V—territory well-worn by the now "Legend"-ary stories of the Expanded Universe. Under the direction of the Lucasfilm Story Group, these new stories fit within the canon of the films. These new adventures of Luke, Han, and Leia are an instant bestseller, with estimates of just under a million copies sold in January, nine times the amount of the next biggest seller in the comics field.

Issue #1 follows the rebels as they infiltrate an important Imperial weapons factory.

The Course Awakens

January 15: Disneyland holds its first annual *Star Wars* Half-Marathon, organized by Lucasfilm and runDisney. The three-day health and fitness event includes 5k, 10k, and half-marathon events, taking runners through the Disneyland resort and surrounding Anaheim. A series of kids races are specially designed for kids aged 12 months to 8 years old. Race finishers receive exclusive medals designed for the event.

TERRORISTS STRIKE AT *CHARLIE HEBDO* OFFICES IN PARIS ⊕ MEASLES OUTBREAK IN

Smooth-Talking Smuggler

January 19: Another *Rebels* cameo sees that suave and cunning gambler, Lando Calrissian, guest starring in the episode "Idiot's Array." Billy Dee Williams returns to the iconic role, playing a younger Calrissian who, while prospecting on Lothal, hoodwinks the rebels into helping him transport living contraband in a madcap episode, written by Kevin Hopps and directed by Steward Lee.

Having won Chopper in a game of sabacc, Calrissian will only return the droid if the rebels work for him.

A Lucas Fairy Tale

January 23: After nearly a decade in production, the Lucasfilm animated feature film *Strange Magic* debuts theatrically, distributed under the Touchstone label from Disney. Despite a stellar cast (Alan Cumming, Evan Rachel Wood, Elijah Kelley, and Kristin Chenoweth), classic songs, stunning visuals from ILM, and lively direction by Gary Rydstrom, the film is lost in the January marketplace and pelted by critics, though it fares better with audiences in its prompt home video and television releases.

FEBRUARY

February 4: The VES (Visual Effects Society) gives J.J. Abrams its Visionary Award for his past work, though his current work on *Star Wars* is very much the talk of the night.

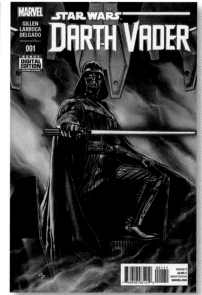

The Vader Comic

February 11: Marvel launches a second flagship *Star Wars* series, *Star Wars: Darth Vader*, written by Kieron Gillen and illustrated by Salvador Larroca.

The Science Continues

February 12: NASA unveils a poster for its International Space Station Expedition 45 mission slated for launch in September. It features international astronauts Scott Kelly, Mikhail Kornienko, Kjell Lindgren, Sergei Volkov, Oleg Kononenko, and Kimiya Yui dressed in Jedi robes and wielding lightsabers.

Leonard Nimoy Remembered

February 27: Actor and director Leonard Nimoy, known for his role as Spock in *Star Trek*, passes away at age 83. In a tweet just five days ealier, he passed along parting words to his fans: "A life is like a garden. Perfect moments can be had, but not preserved, except in memory. LLAP." The last is an acronym for one of Spock's most well-known phrases, "Live long and prosper."

MARCH

She's Back!

March 2: The first season of *Star Wars Rebels* comes to a dramatic close as "Fire Across the Galaxy" airs. The final three episodes of the season build to a moment where the rebels infiltrate Grand Moff Tarkin's Star Destroyer to rescue Kanan Jarrus. As the rebels breathe a sigh of relief, they are welcomed into a larger rebellion by an adult Ahsoka Tano, the animated character who walked off *The Clone Wars* two years (to the day!) earlier. The finale episode was written by Simon Kinberg and directed by Dave Filoni.

Ford is famous for his stunt-heavy movie roles, including the Indiana Jones series.

Never Tell him the Odds

March 5: An accident suffered by Harrison Ford again makes headlines worldwide as the actor, a seasoned aviator, guides a malfunctioning World War II-era ST3KR trainer plane into a controlled crash at a golf course near Santa Monica Airport. Ford suffers critical injuries, and is hospitalized for a month before making a full recovery.

Rogue One, Standing By

March 12: The title of the first *Star Wars* stand-alone movie is revealed to be *Rogue One*, with Chris Weitz joining Gary Whitta as screenwriter. Also confirmed via a posting on StarWars.com is Felicity Jones as the film's lead. Although early speculation among fans and media is that the movie will focus on fighter pilots, it soon becomes apparent that it's a more grounded military tale than that. Additionally, the release date for *Star Wars*: Episode VIII is announced as May 26, 2017.

APRIL

Download the Saga

April 10: Catching up with the media consumption times, Lucasfilm releases the six movies of the *Star Wars* Saga for digital-only HD release. Platforms like Amazon Instant Video, iTunes, Xbox video, PlayStation video, M-GO, Vudu, the Nook store, Cineplex Store, and Disney Movies Anywhere become the source for streaming and downloading. Bundled with the release are a number of newly created behind-the-scenes documentaries.

April 17: Electronic Arts, DICE, and Lucasfilm debut *Star Wars: Battlefront* to the Celebration audience, showcasing the incredible fidelity the much anticipated next generation game will deliver to players later in the year.

April 18: *Star Wars Rebels* takes the spotlight on this day of Celebration, with cast and crew on the main stage discussing what's to come. A new trailer features Darth Vader (voiced by James Earl Jones) in action and heralds the return of Captain Rex, once again voiced Dee Bradley Baker. Rex, who ages twice as fast due to his clone heritage, may be grayer, but he is still a fighter. Audiences are also treated to the first ever screening of the two-part season two opener, "Siege on Lothal."

Formerly a clone trooper, Captain Rex is set to join the rebels in their battle against the Empire.

Celebration Anaheim

April 16–19: Foregoing the Roman numeral title that would have proclaimed this the seventh U.S. event of its kind, *Star Wars* Celebration Anaheim welcomes over 60,000 fans eager for a peek at what's to come. *The Force Awakens* draws the most attention—with the can't-miss event being the April 16th panel with J.J. Abrams and Kathleen Kennedy. A snaking queue of fans waits overnight to attend, with Abrams and Kennedy treating them to free pizza deliveries. On stage, the writer-director and producer are joined by stars Daisy Ridley, John Boyega, Oscar Isaac, Mark Hamill, Carrie Fisher, Anthony Daniels, Peter Mayhew, and—stealing the scene—a mesmerizingly functional BB-8 droid. The star-packed panel debuts a new teaser for *The Force Awakens* that ends with the first on-screen look of Han Solo and Chewbacca from the film. Celebration Anaheim is the first Celebration to be live streamed on StarWars.com.

The sentiment "we're home" is echoed many times over during Celebration Anaheim.

Warwick Davis joins C-3PO, R2-D2, and some stormtroopers outside the convention center.

April 19: What lies beyond *The Force Awakens* is the topic of discussion as director Gareth Edwards takes the stage at Celebration Anaheim to discuss *Rogue One* (identified at this panel as a "*Star Wars* Anthology" film). Though no footage exists yet, Edwards treats the fans to a newly created ILM teaser that shows the Death Star looming over a verdant world.

April 29: StarWars.com posts another series of "lost" stories from *The Clone Wars*. This is a proxy, work-in-progress version of the four-part "Bad Batch" storyline that was first publicly screened at Celebration Anaheim in April.

Mace Windu, Obi-Wan Kenobi, and their clone troopers battle against swarms of battle droids.

MAY

May 1: Lucasfilm announces that Josh Trank, previously identified as a director of a future *Star Wars* stand-alone, has departed the project.

May 17: The tradition continues as *Vanity Fair* releases a *Star Wars* cover story, featuring in-depth interviews and photography of *The Force Awakens* cast and set by Annie Leibovitz.

JUNE

The Passing of a Legend

June 11: Actor Christopher Lee, who counted among his credits literally hundreds of movies, passes away in London at age 93. With a career spanning more than 70 years, Lee was known by many for his macabre roles in Hammer Films, as the titular Bond villain in *The Man with the Golden Gun*, and to a whole new generation of filmgoers as Saruman in *The Lord of the Rings* series and Count Dooku in *Star Wars*: Episode II and Episode III.

Virtual Horizons

June 12: A new division within Lucasfilm—ILMxLAB—is announced as an experimental development group drawing on talents from ILM, the Lucasfilm Story Group, and Skywalker Sound. ILMxLAB will be the exclusive creators of new immersive story experiences for *Star Wars*, taking advantage of technological innovations for use in the burgeoning virtual and augmented reality media space.

Rebels Summer Return

June 20: Disney XD airs the hour-long season two premiere of *Star Wars Rebels*, a combined two-parter called "The Siege of Lothal." Originally previewed at Celebration Anaheim, the premiere shows the effects of the continued successes of the rebel group, as the Empire cracks down on Lothal with the arrival of the Dark Lord of the Sith himself, Darth Vader. James Earl Jones provides the voice of the classic character, and this season debut puts into motion the inevitable collision course between Ahsoka Tano and Vader. "Siege of Lothal" is written by Henry Gilroy with directing duties split between Bosco Ng and Brad Rau for each half.

JULY

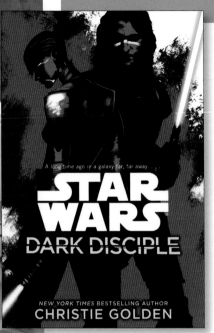

Ventress and Vos

July 7: Del Rey releases the novel *Dark Disciple*, which focuses on an unlikely romance between bounty hunter Asajj Ventress and Jedi Quinlan Vos. Based on eight unproduced *Clone Wars* scripts, the novel is written by Christie Golden with a foreword by Katie Lucas, George Lucas's daughter, who is *The Clone Wars* writer most associated with the development of Ventress's character.

Han Solo Story

July 7: Directors Christopher Miller and Phil Lord, fresh from their success with *The LEGO Movie*, are announced as directors for a Han Solo stand-alone movie, set early during Solo's career as a lawbender. The screenplay will be written by Lawrence and Jon Kasdan, with a release date set for May 25, 2018.

It's an App!

July 8: StarWars.com launches an official app for iOS and Android devices. This portal to online *Star Wars* entertainment includes a selfie function that puts users into Jedi robes or rebel pilot uniforms, animated GIFs, *Star Wars* emojis, sound effects, and much more.

Surprise *Star Wars* Concert

July 10: After a packed *The Force Awakens* panel at San Diego Comic-Con International, J.J. Abrams treats the audience to a surprise. In addition to celebrated *Star Wars* panelists, Abrams leads over 6,000 fans to a secret *Star Wars* concert by the San Diego Symphony at nearby Embarcadero Marina.

Pluto Flyby

July 14: NASA's unmanned *New Horizons* spacecraft makes its closest approach to distant Pluto, coming to within 470,000 km (290,000 miles) of the planetoid.

July 23: A splinter unit for *Rogue One* captures some footage of Felicity Jones, Diego Luna, and Adam Tudyk on location in Jordan.

July 23: At the Ani-Com and Games convention in Hong Kong, Hot Toys reveals its enormous sixth-scale *Millennium Falcon*, compatible with their articulated 12-inch figure line. The 5.5-meter (18-foot)-long model dominates a head-turning diorama at the event.

AUGUST

Cameras Roll on *Rogue*

August 3: The first day of *Rogue One* principal photography begins. Gareth Edwards directs Felicity Jones, Diego Luna, and Adam Tudyk on a specially constructed outdoor set in Bovingdon, near Hertfordshire in England.

August 11: Lucasfilm and HP announce the Art Awakens program, encouraging amateur artists to create their own *The Force Awakens*-inspired artwork. The winners will display at a professional art exhibit later in the year.

August 15: Colin Trevorrow is announced as the director of *Star Wars*: Episode IX, the final installment in this new trilogy. It is set for release in 2019.

Star Wars Land Unveiled

August 15: At the Annual D23 EXPO in Anaheim, Walt Disney Chairman and CEO Bob Iger announces that *Star Wars*-themed lands will be coming to Disneyland in Anaheim and Disney's Hollywood Studios at Walt Disney World Resort in Orlando. The ambitious expansions of over 14 acres each will create a new world in the *Star Wars* canon to visit and explore. The development of these lands and the experiences within are the result of close collaboration between the artists and story teams at Lucasfilm and Disney Imagineering.

Bob Iger reveals concept art that shows the enormous scale of the proposed Star Wars-themed lands.

August 15: Also at the D23 EXPO, George Lucas is named a Disney Legend for his significant contributions to the Disney legacy.

Phasma Burn on Facebook

August 28: Commenting on an image of Captain Phasma, a user on the *Star Wars* Facebook page posts, "Not to be sexist but it's really hard to tell that's female armor for me." The Lucasfilm administrator responds, "It's armor. On a woman. It doesn't have to look feminine." The exchange goes viral around the internet.

Star Wars Meets Disney Infinity

August 30: The Disney Infinity video game introduces *Star Wars* characters in its 3.0 incarnation. The collectible figures—from the *Star Wars* movies, *The Clone Wars*, and *Rebels*—have their characters and abilities imported into the game where they can interact with Marvel, Disney, and Pixar characters.

SEPTEMBER

September 1: The first season of *Star Wars Rebels* arrives on Blu-ray and DVD.

September 2: LEGO unveils the first of its *The Force Awakens* sets, which include Poe's X-Wing Fighter, Rey's Speeder, Kylo Ren's Command Shuttle, and the *Millennium Falcon*. Fans are thrilled to learn these will be available on Force Friday— September 4th.

Force Friday

September 4: The first *Star Wars* retail products hit shelves today, dubbed Force Friday by Lucasfilm. Fans can snatch up a host of new *Star Wars* publishing, branded as the "Journey to *The Force Awakens*," including Chuck Wendig's adult novel *Aftermath*. Hasbro and LEGO release new *The Force Awakens* toys, and the must-have product is the Sphero BB-8 app-enabled droid. The *Star Wars* YouTube channel hosts a worldwide product unboxing live stream.

Sphero's BB-8 can transform any video into a hologram.

Shattered Empire

September 9: Marvel Comics' contribution to the "Journey to *The Force Awakens*" begins with *Star Wars: Shattered Empire*, a mini-series written by Greg Rucka and illustrated by Marco Checchetto, Angel Unzueta, and Emilio Laiso. Set immediately after *Return of the Jedi*, the four-issue series features new characters Shara Bey and Kes Dameron, revealed to be the parents of Poe Dameron, Oscar Isaac's character in *The Force Awakens*.

Mobile Uprising

September 10: Lucasfilm and Kabam launch *Star Wars*: Uprising, a story-driven roleplaying mobile game for iOS and Android. The story is set after the events of *Return of the Jedi*, and focuses on an Imperial warlord, Adelhard, who refuses to acknowledge the death of the Emperor.

September 15: A splinter unit shoots Mark Hamill and Daisy Ridley at Skellig Michael island for a sequence in *Star Wars*: Episode VIII.

Start the Engine, Jock!

September 22: Downtown Disney at the Walt Disney World Resort undergoes a revamping as Disney Springs, featuring an aviation-themed drinking hole called Jock Lindsey's Hangar Bar—said to belong to Indiana Jones's trusty pilot seen rescuing him from the jungle in *Raiders of the Lost Ark*.

Trilogy for a New Generation

September 22: Disney Press publishes a set of Original Trilogy adaptations for young readers, with a fresh, dynamic take on the Saga. Alexandra Bracken adapts Episode IV as *The Princess, the Scoundrel, and the Farm Boy*, Adam Gidwitz adapts Episode V as *So You Want to be a Jedi?*, and Tom Angleberger adapts Episode VI as *Beware the Power of the Dark Side!*

September 23: The *Star Wars* Facebook page posts a 360-degree video created by ILMxLAB that depicts a ride through the Jakku desert atop Rey's speeder.

The release of Disney Infinity 3.0 in August 2015 saw *Star Wars* become a part of Disney's popular video game. When placed onto the game base, the collectible figures are imported into the game, each with unique powers and abilities. Ahsoka Tano can use her double lightsabers to defeat multiple enemies, while Ezra Bridger's Force abilities can be unlocked the more he is played. Characters can explore *Star Wars* Play Sets or enter the Toy Box mode, where they can create new stories and adventures with Marvel, Disney, and Pixar characters.

Rey

Poe Dameron

Kylo Ren

Finn

Princess Leia Organa

Darth Vader

Chewbacca

Han Solo

Luke Skywalker

Boba Fett

Ezra Bridger

Kanan Jarrus

Zeb Orrelios

Sabine Wren

Yoda

Ahsoka Tano

Anakin Skywalker

Obi-Wan Kenobi

Darth Maul

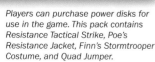

Players can purchase power disks for use in the game. This pack contains Resistance Tactical Strike, Poe's Resistance Jacket, Finn's Stormtrooper Costume, and Quad Jumper.

Can heroes Poe Dameron and Finn defeat the sinister Kylo Ren?

Han, Leia, and Chewie race against Boba Fett in Toy Box 3.0! Will Boba win as he rides General Grievous's wheelbike around the Great Pit of Carkoon?

Play as Zeb, Obi-Wan Kenobi, and Sabine in Toy Box 3.0!

OCTOBER

Enter The Jedi Slayer

October 8: Actress Sarah Michelle Gellar, famous in fan communities for her role as Buffy the Vampire Slayer, joins *Rebels* co-stars Taylor Gray, Ashley Eckstein, and series executive producer Dave Filoni on a panel previewing the second season of *Star Wars Rebels* at New York Comic Con. Gellar joins her husband Freddie Prinze, Jr. as a cast member on the show, playing the recurring role of the Seventh Sister Inquisitor, a Force-imbued, Jedi-hunting villain.

Rebels Season Two Continues

October 14: The second season of *Star Wars Rebels* continues to air weekly following a break after its summer launch of the "Siege of Lothal" opener. In "The Lost Commanders" (written by Matt Michnovetz and directed by Dave Filoni and Sergio Paez), the *Rebels* crew recruits the help of some Clone Wars veterans, including an aged but still capable Captain Rex.

A concealed figure, hinted to be Rey, is shown exploring a huge spaceship.

A menacing shot of Kylo Ren reveals how much he has been influenced by Vader.

The Trailer Awakens

October 20: A brand new trailer for *Star Wars: The Force Awakens* debuts during Monday Night Football on ABC and is promptly posted online. Accompanying its launch, online vendors begin selling tickets for theatrical screenings, and the online servers for such robust outlets as Fandango and MovieTickets.com are overwhelmed. According to Fandango, *The Force Awakens* sells eight times as many online tickets than its next highest record-holder, *The Hunger Games*.

Finn and Poe Dameron share a moment at a busy Resistance base.

October 21: *Back to the Future* fans commemorate this day, for it is the future that Marty McFly travels to in *Back to the Future Part II*, released in 1989.

NOVEMBER

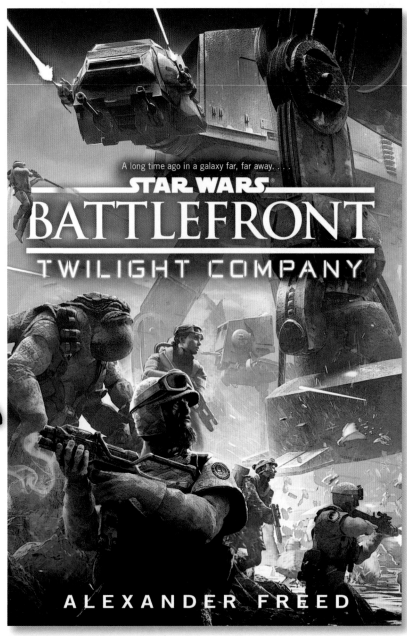

Battlefront Book

November 3: In anticipation of the launch of the new *Star Wars*: Battlefront video game, Del Rey Books publishes *Star Wars Battlefront: Twilight Company*, a novel by Alexander Freed. The book takes the point of view of hard-bitten rebel soldiers in their ongoing war against the Empire during the events of Original Trilogy.

One Last Wish

November 5: Daniel Fleetwood, a terminally ill *Star Wars* fan whose dying wish was to see the new movie, entreaties Lucasfilm and Disney for a glimpse of *The Force Awakens*. J.J. Abrams accommodates this request by arranging a private screening. Fleetwood would die of spindle cell sarcoma, a rare form of cancer, five days later.

November 10: As new and relapsed fans are clamoring for their *Star Wars* fix prior to the new movies, Lucasfilm re-releases the Blu-ray discs of the six existing movies in commemorative steelbook cases.

⊕ MICROSOFT LAUNCHES WINDOWS 10 ⊕ ISIS CLAIMS RESPONSIBILITY FOR CRASHING

'Tis the Season

November 16: In anticipation of the new film, Disneyland in Anaheim and the Walt Disney World Resort in Orlando launch the Season of the Force event. This includes the creation of Launch Bay—a locale that houses a collection of *Star Wars* props, merchandise, character meet-and-greets, and a video showcasing the new teams adding to the Saga. Another attraction, *Path of the Jedi*, serves as a mega-trailer detailing the story of Episodes I through VI in anticipation of *The Force Awakens*.

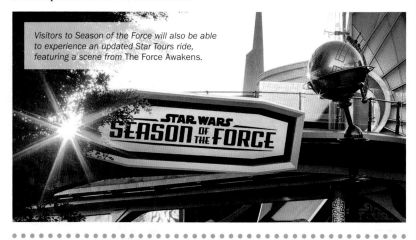

Visitors to Season of the Force will also be able to experience an updated Star Tours ride, featuring a scene from The Force Awakens.

Back to the Battlefront

November 17: DICE, EA, and Lucasfilm launch the eagerly anticipated *Star Wars: Battlefront* for Xbox One, PlayStation 4, and Windows PC platforms. The game uses DICE's robust Frostbite graphics engine to create real-time visuals of unprecedented fidelity. Gameplay focuses on multiplayer combat arenas, with upward of 60 players fighting as Imperials or rebels on vivid recreations of Hoth, Tatooine, Endor, or Sullust.

November 22: The American Music Awards pays tribute to John Williams with the group Pentatonix starting off a capella before transitioning to a full orchestral presentation of classic *Star Wars* themes.

November 23: Google gets in on the *Star Wars: The Force Awakens* excitement with a host of interactive features and Easter eggs across their platforms. Search results are rendered in the opening crawl style, YouTube play-bars are swapped out with lightsabers, and the Google Maps app offers GPS guidance complete with X-wing or TIE fighter avatars.

DECEMBER

Step Inside Jakku Spy

December 2: ILMxLAB, in conjunction with Google and Verizon, releases Jakku Spy, a virtual reality experience that can be enjoyed using the Google cardboard viewer. Users who place their smartphone into a Cardboard viewer (either branded or not) can witness *Star Wars* moments set on the planet Jakku and accompanied by BB-8. The visuals are new scenes created by ILM.

Awakens at Last

December 15–18: *The Force Awakens* and its box office performance dominates this week of news. The Hollywood premiere kicks off on Monday night, the 15th, with a giant tent taking over Hollywood Boulevard to house the red carpet and after-party, and *The Force Awakens* playing in three adjacent theaters. J.J. Abrams, concerned about preserving the secrets of the story, did not screen the film early for critics, but word of mouth is instantly strong. On the eve of its public debut, *The Force Awakens* has already racked up more than $100 million in pre-sales domestically. When the film debuts on December 18th in 2-D, 3-D, and 3-D IMAX formats across 4,134 screens in North America, it smashes all records, with opening day totals north of $120 million. Its weekend total is $247.9 million—a total of $528.9 million worldwide. Even the most unreasonable expectations of box office performance are being smashed, as the movie crosses the $1 billion mark worldwide on December 27th. Beyond its financial success, the movie is a critical hit. Rotten Tomatoes, the online review aggregator, certifies it "fresh," with reviews above 90% positive. It seems the entire world is once again swept up in *Star Wars* excitement.

December 19: *Rogue One* principal photography wraps.

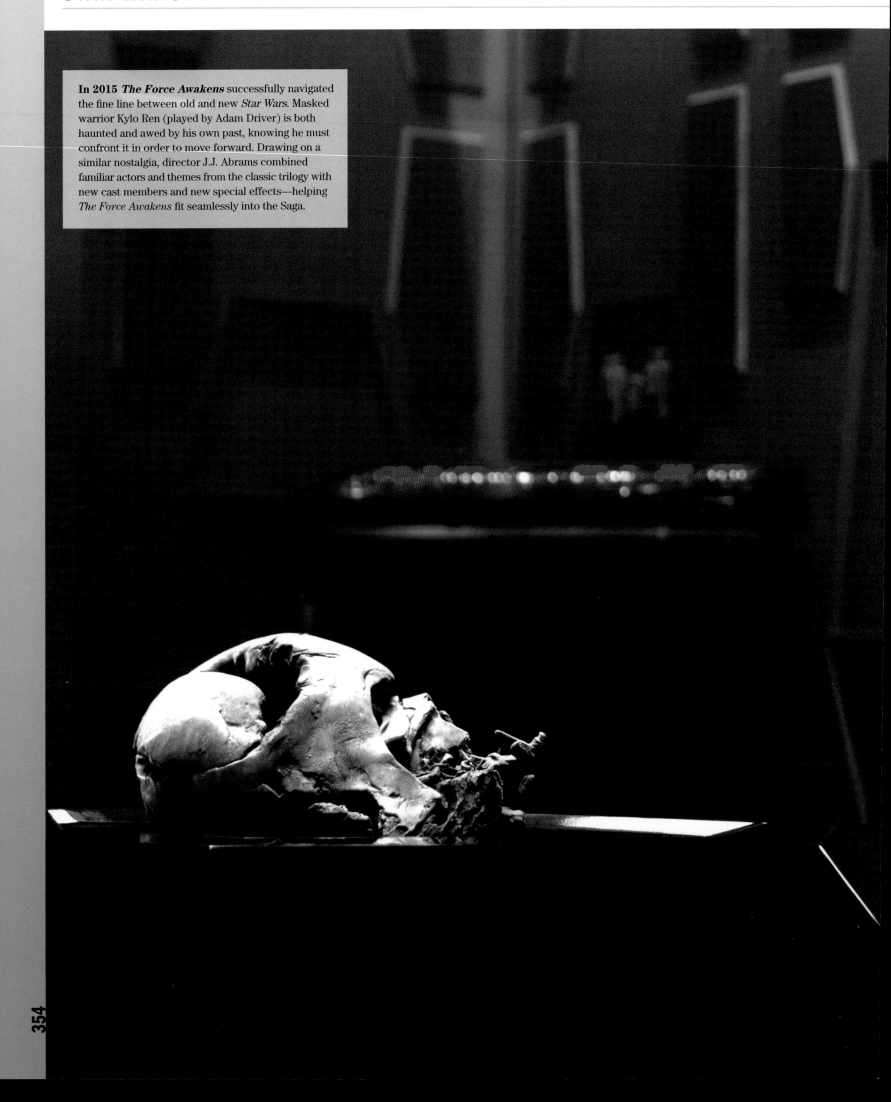

In 2015 **The Force Awakens** successfully navigated the fine line between old and new *Star Wars*. Masked warrior Kylo Ren (played by Adam Driver) is both haunted and awed by his own past, knowing he must confront it in order to move forward. Drawing on a similar nostalgia, director J.J. Abrams combined familiar actors and themes from the classic trilogy with new cast members and new special effects—helping *The Force Awakens* fit seamlessly into the Saga.

2016

THE FACE OF *STAR WARS* has changed with the worldwide success of *The Force Awakens*. New characters like Rey, Finn, Poe, and Kylo Ren are instantly embraced as classics by fans old and new. The emergence of Rey as a female lead in a *Star Wars* movie draws praise and attention. Merchandise cannot keep up with the demand for Rey, and manufacturers and retailers who had previously thought of *Star Wars* primarily as a "boy thing" are challenged to diversify their product lines.

> "Filming of *Star Wars*: Episode VIII, the next chapter of the legendary Saga, has just commenced..."
>
> **Bob Iger**
> Walt Disney Chairman and CEO

AS THE WORLD BASKS in the glow of *The Force Awakens*, Lucasfilm continues active development on a host of feature film and television work that charts the future of the Saga well into the next decade. The future of the Force is bright indeed.

WINTER

Representing Rey
January 3: The hashtag #WheresRey explodes in popularity when writer Carrie Goldman tweets an image of her daughter's letter to Hasbro, asking the toy company how they could have left Rey out of a *Star Wars* Monopoly set. Hasbro announces the Monopoly set will be amended to include Rey.

Best-Selling Novelization
January 5: *The Force Awakens* novelization, written by Alan Dean Foster, debuts at #1 on the *New York Times* bestseller list when it arrives in hardcover. Unlike previous novelizations, this one did not come out months before the film's release. It came out first as an eBook on the day the movie debuted.

January 6: *The Force Awakens* overtakes *Avatar*'s $760.5 million box office record as the highest-grossing film in US history in only 20 days of release.

January 6: Marvel publishes the first issue of an *Obi-Wan & Anakin* mini-series, taking place between the events of Episodes II and III. It is written by Charles Soule and illustrated by Marco Checchetto.

January 16: Adam Driver hosts *Saturday Night Live* on NBC, and stars as Kylo Ren in a hilarious sendup of the reality TV show, *Undercover Boss*.

January 20: The release date for *Star Wars*: Episode VIII is officially pushed back to December 15, 2017.

February 14: At the BAFTA awards, *Star Wars: The Force Awakens* wins for Best Special Visual Effects, while John Boyega is awarded the EE Rising Star Award.

The Next Journey Begins

February 15: Principal photography begins on *Star Wars: Episode VIII* on Stage B at Pinewood Studios. StarWars.com confirms that returning cast members Mark Hamill, Carrie Fisher, Adam Driver, Daisy Ridley, John Boyega, Oscar Isaac, Lupita Nyong'o, Domhnall Gleeson, Anthony Daniels, Gwendoline Christie, and Andy Serkis will be joined by new cast members Benicio Del Toro, Laura Dern, and Kelly Marie Tran.

Droids Take the Stage

February 28: At the 88th Academy Awards, *The Force Awakens* is nominated for Best Visual Effects, Best Editing, Best Sound Editing, Best Sound Mixing, and Best Musical Score—John Williams's 50th nomination. While it ultimately didn't win, a highlight of the evening sees R2-D2, C-3PO, and BB-8 live on stage to celebrate John Williams.

Indy: Back in the Saddle

March 15: In a surprise announcement from Lucasfilm and Disney, Steven Spielberg and Harrison Ford pick the date of July 19, 2019 for the big screen return of Indiana Jones in his fifth feature film installment.

March 30: The *Star Wars Rebels* season two finale airs as a double-length episode, "Twilight of the Apprentice." It makes good on the season's promise of Ahsoka crossing lightsaber blades with Darth Vader.

In Rebels, Ahsoka is a more assured character, strong enough to take on her former mentor, Darth Vader.

SPRING

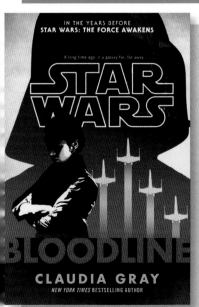

A Novel of the New Republic

Del Rey Books publishes *Bloodline* by Claudia Gray. Set seven years before the events of *The Force Awakens*, the book focuses on Leia Organa's last days as a New Republic senator, as her investigations into strange activities prior to the rise of the First Order expose her to political scandal. The novel continues the slow revelations of major events that happened in the 30-year gap between Episodes VI and VII.

As the daughter of Darth Vader, Leia faces many prejudices.

Aftermath Continues

The second book in Chuck Wendig's *Aftermath* trilogy, *Life Debt*, is released in hardcover by Del Rey Books. This novel focuses on Han Solo and Chewbacca's mission to help liberate the Wookiee homeworld of Kashyyyk after the Battle of Endor.

SUMMER

Building New Adventures

Disney XD launches its second *Star Wars* animated series with the debut of LEGO *Star Wars: The Freemaker Adventures*. The adventure comedy series focuses on a new family of characters—the Freemakers—and how their salvage operation turns into a quest for a mythical Force artifact that draws the attention of the Empire. The new half-hour animated series is a production of Wil Film, the LEGO Group, and Lucasfilm, and developed for television by Bill Motz and Bob Roth.

July 15–17: *Star Wars* Celebration Europe returns to London's ExCel Exhibition Centre, with fans from across the world ready to gather and revel in the past, present, and tantalizing future of *Star Wars*.

FALL

Rebels Strikes Again

The third season of *Star Wars Rebels* debuts on Disney XD. Following the shocking finale of the second season, the third season jumps ahead in time, aging the characters into more mature forms, and bringing the storyline chronologically closer to the events of *Rogue One* and *A New Hope*.

Rogue One: A Star Wars Story

The big-screen debut of the first ever *Star Wars* stand-alone film brings a fresh, new vision to the galaxy. Gareth Edward's distinct visual style, marked by raw, kinetic camerawork tells the grounded military tale of the Rebel Alliance's first victory and the theft of the Death Star plans, as described in the opening crawl of *A New Hope*. The film stars Felicity Jones, Diego Luna, Donnie Yen, Mads Mikkelsen, Forest Whitaker, Ben Mendelsohn, Adam Tudyk, Jiang Wen, and Riz Ahmed.

Index

PICTURE CREDITS

Hoth Rebel Troopers in Episode V

ACKNOWLEDGMENTS

We owe the biggest thanks to the man who started the whole thing—George Lucas. By bringing *Star Wars* into our lives, he not only changed the world of movies, but he also gave many young imaginations a whole new galaxy of possibilities.

Dorling Kindersley would also like to thank Frances Vargo, Tina Mills, and Stacey Leong, for their tireless picture research—without their efforts this project would not have been possible; Frank Parisi, J.W. Rinzler, Troy Alders, Leland Chee, and Stacy Cheregotis at Lucas Licensing; Tony Rowe from LucasArts; Steve Sansweet in Lucasfilm's marketing department; Ryder Windham, Pablo Hidalgo, and Daniel Wallace for their vast *Star Wars* knowledge and for writing this epic book; Gus Lopez and Duncan Jenkins for their *Star Wars* merchandise knowledge and for supplying photographs of the collectibles throughout the book; Evan Reynolds for scanning and supplying the original *Star Wars* newspaper strips; Pete Vilmur for his *Star Wars* expertise; Jonathan Wilkins from *Star Wars Insider* magazine; Robert Jan for supplying some great *Star Wars* artifacts and images; Dean Plantamura and Albin Johnson from the 501st Legion (www501st.com); Emma Pritchard and Rebecca Bridge for their editorial help; Martin Copeland in the DK Picture Library; Matthew Knight at Penguin; Randi Sørensen at the LEGO Group; Heather Scott for her early editorial work on the book; Katie Cook, Cédric Delsaux, Alexander Ivanov, Ralph McQuarrie, Randy Martinez, Anne Neumann, and Michael Wiese for supplying images.

Pablo Hidalgo: I would like to thank Paul Ens, Nicole Love, David West Reynolds, Francis Lalumiere, Aaron Meyers, Marc Hedlund, Bill Gannon, Steve Sansweet, Tina Mills, Kathryn Ramos, Randy Martinez, Denise Vasquez, Pete Vilmur, Bonnie Burton, Marni Taradash, Doug Chiang, Robert Barnes, Rob Coleman, Dave Filoni, Jo Donaldson, Cindy Young Russell, Carol Moen Wing, and Robyn Stanley.

Daniel Wallace: I would like to thank my co-writers Ryder Windham and Pablo Hidalgo; contributor and collectibles expert Gus Lopez; Lucasfilm's J. W. Rinzler; and Dorling Kindersley's Lucy Dowling, Elizabeth Dowsett, and Ron Stobbart and his design team.

Ryder Windham: I would like to thank my brother Corey for letting me have his *Star Wars* comics, my mother and stepfather, Karla and Tom Moran, for not throwing away my *Starlog* magazines, and everyone at Dorling Kindersley who worked so hard to make this book a reality.

Lucasfilm would like to thank the team at Dorling Kindersley; Jo Donaldson, Robyn Stanley, and Carol Moen Wing in the Lucasfilm Research Library; Tony Rowe and Hez Chorba at LucasArts; Pete Vilmur and Bonnie Burton at StarWars.com; Chris Holm for the legal legwork; Stacy Cheregotis and Chris Gollaher in Product Development; Kelly H. Smith at Industrial Light & Magic; Lynne Hale and Steve Sansweet for the key assists from PR and marketing; Matthew Azeveda in Image Archives; Robert Gianino at Lucasfilm Animation; Sean McLain at Acme Archives; Jonathan Wilkins at *Star Wars Insider*; and Ralph McQuarrie.

C-3PO, R2-D2, Mark Hamill, and Alec Guinness are filmed with the landspeeder for Episode IV.